AF412187

# Russian Trade Unions and Industrial Relations in Transition

# Russian Trade Unions and Industrial Relations in Transition

Sarah Ashwin

and

Simon Clarke

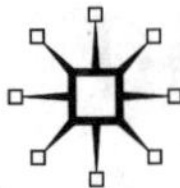



First published 2003 by
PALGRAVE MACMILLAN
Houndmills, Basingstoke, Hampshire RG21 6XS and
175 Fifth Avenue, New York, N.Y. 10010
Companies and representatives throughout the world

PALGRAVE MACMILLAN is the global academic imprint of the Palgrave Macmillan division of St. Martin's Press, LLC and of Palgrave Macmillan Ltd. Macmillan® is a registered trademark in the United States, United Kingdom and other countries. Palgrave is a registered trademark in the European Union and other countries.

ISBN 0–333–73518–8

This book is printed on paper suitable for recycling and made from fully managed and sustained forest sources.

A catalogue record for this book is available from the British Library.

Library of Congress Cataloging-in-Publication Data
Russian trade unions and industrial relations in transition / Sarah Ashwin and Simon Clarke.
    p. cm.
  Includes bibliographical references and index.
  ISBN 0–333–73518–8 (cloth)
   1. Labor unions—Russia (Federation) 2. Industrial relations—Russia (Federation) 3. Labor movement—Russia (Federation) 4. Working class–
–Russia (Federation) 5. Privatization—Russia (Federation) 6. Russia (Federation)—Economic policy—1991– I. Clarke, Simon, 1946– II. Ashwin, Sarah.

  HD6735.15 .R88 2003
  331.88'0947—dc21

                              2002068332

10  9  8  7  6  5  4  3  2  1
12  11  10  09  08  07  06  05  04  03

Printed and bound in Great Britain by
Antony Rowe Ltd, Chippenham and Eastbourne

# Contents

# List of Figures and Tables

# Acronyms and Abbreviations

| | |
|---|---|
| AFL-CIO | American Federation of Labor – Congress of Industrial Organizations |
| AMROS | Association of Industrialists of the Mining-Metallurgical Complex of Russia |
| ASTI | Social-Labour Information Agency |
| CIS | Commonwealth of Independent States |
| CLMS | Centre for Labour Market Studies |
| CPSU | Communist Party of the Soviet Union |
| ERP | Unity for Progress |
| ESN | Unified Social Tax |
| ETS | Unified Tariff Scale |
| EU | European Union |
| FNPR | Federation of Independent Trade Unions of Russia |
| FPAD | Federation of Air Traffic Controllers' Trade Unions |
| FTUI | Free Trade Union Institute |
| FZK | Factory Committee |
| GMPR | Mining-Metallurgical Trade Union of Russia |
| ICEM | International Federation of Chemical, Energy and Mining Workers' Unions |
| ICFTU | International Confederation of Free Trade Unions |
| ILO | International Labour Organisation |
| IMF | International Monetary Fund |
| ISITO | Institute for Comparative Labour Relations Research |
| ITS | International Trade Secretariat |
| IUF | International Union of Food and Allied Workers |
| KGB | State Security Committee |
| KSORR | Co-ordinating Council of Employers' Associations of Russia |
| KPRF | Communist Party of the Russian Federation |
| KTR | Confederation of Labour of Russia |
| KTS | Labour Disputes Commission |
| MFP | Moscow Federation of Trade Unions |
| MRP | Marxist Workers' Party |
| MVD | Interior Ministry |
| NEP | New Economic Policy |
| NPG | Independent Miners' Union |
| OFT | United Workers Front |

| | |
|---|---|
| OVR | Fatherland – All Russia |
| PARRRSR | Trade Union of Aviation Employees in Radar, Radio-Navigation and Communications |
| PLS | Trade Union of Flying Staff |
| PRIASGA | Trade Union of Civil Aviation Engineering Employees |
| RKRP | Russian Communist Workers' Party |
| RLFS | Russian Labour Flexibility Survey |
| ROPP | Russian United Industrial Party |
| RSPP | Russian Union of Industrialists and Entrepreneurs |
| RTK | Russian Tripartite Commission |
| STK | Labour Collective Council |
| VKP | General Confederation of Trade Unions |
| VKT | All-Russian Confederation of Labour |
| VTsIOM | All-Russian Centre for Public Opinion Research |
| VTsSPS | All-Union (All-Russian) Central Council of Trade Unions |
| WFTU | World Federation of Trade Unions |

| | |
|---|---|
| *Gorkom* | City Committee |
| *Goskomtrud* | State Committee for Labour |
| *Ispolkom* | Executive Committee |
| *Narkomtrud* | People's Commissariat for Labour |
| *Obkom* | Regional Branch Trade Union Committee |
| *Oblsovprof* | Regional Trade Union Council |
| *Raikom* | District Committee |
| *Rostrudinspektsiya* | Russian Labour Inspectorate |

# 1

# Introduction

Many people expected that, following the collapse of the Soviet Union, the official Russian trade unions would disappear along with the system of which they were an integral part. The future, for many commentators, lay with the new trade unions which had arisen on the back of the wave of strikes which had played an important role in the collapse of the soviet system. As key supporters of Yeltsin, the new trade unions also hoped to flourish in the new Russia. While the traditional unions were deeply compromised by their subordination to the Party, their integration into the state apparatus and their close collaboration with management in the workplace, the new unions appeared to be the movement of the future. They were identified with the 'democratic' opposition to Party rule, associated themselves with the new politics of privatisation and the 'transition to a market economy', excluded management from union membership and organised militant collective action against employers. While the traditional unions organised on a branch basis, suppressing differences of occupational interest as they sought to represent the interests of all those employed in a particular branch of the economy, the new unions organised on a professional basis and exploited the bargaining power of key occupations. But the traditional trade unions proved far more resilient than their critics had anticipated. By the end of the century the new trade unions represented at the very most five per cent of trade union members, in a very limited number of occupations, and had largely come to terms with the continued dominance of the traditional unions.

The presumption that the future lay with the new unions has meant that there has been very little research on, or publication about, the former official trade unions. In this book we hope somewhat to redress the balance by reporting the results of our research on Russian trade unions at the end of the twentieth century. Both authors have been researching and working with both the alternative and the traditional Russian trade unions since the beginning of the 1990s (our own earlier work in the field, initially in collaboration with Peter Fairbrother, can be found in Ashwin, 1991; Ashwin, 1994; Ashwin, 1995; Ashwin, 1999; Borisov and Clarke, 1994; Borisov, Fairbrother and Clarke, 1994; Clarke, 1992b; Clarke, 1993; Clarke, 1994; Clarke, 1996a; Clarke, 1996b; Clarke, 1998; Clarke, 2001; Clarke, 2002; Clarke and Borisov, 1996; Clarke and Fairbrother, 1994; Clarke, Fairbrother and Borisov, 1994; Clarke et al., 1993). From 1998 we have been involved in a collaborative research project involving eight regional associates of the Institute for Comparative Labour Relations Research (ISITO) in Moscow, Kemerovo, Samara, St Petersburg, Syktyvkar, Perm', Ekaterinburg and Ul'yanovsk, which has focused particularly on trade unionism at the regional level. The research teams have been monitoring the activity of regional trade union organisations (the regional federation and three branch organisations in each region) over a period of three years, interviewing officers, attending conferences and meetings, observing the work of the apparatus, shadowing particular officers, interviewing workers and enterprise trade union presidents, conducting archival and documentary research and regularly updating their research reports.[1] In addition, as part of this project, we have conducted case studies in more than 50 enterprises in which conflicts have arisen in the course of the research and conducted two surveys, one of presidents of primary trade union organisations and the other, with the financial support of the Free Trade Union Institute, an annual survey of the employees of nine enterprises in three regions (Saratov, Sverdlovsk and Western Siberia). Overall, the research covers regional organisations of the education, health, coal-mining, mining-metallurgical, chemical, construction and timber trade unions.

At the Federal level we have monitored the activity of the Federation of Independent Trade Unions of Russia (FNPR) and trade unions in four contrasting branches (health workers, chemical workers, the mining-metallurgical union and the coal miners), using the same research methods. The research teams have also monitored the local and trade union press and constructed databases in which the information is categorised. Finally, we have monitored the monthly ASTI bulletin of reports on the activity of the labour movement across Russia and the national and regional trade union websites. In the course of the research we have all regularly exchanged comments by email, have held meetings of representatives of all groups every three months to discuss findings and elaborate hypotheses, and conducted a conference every year involving all the participants in the research presenting their own analytical papers, many of which they have then prepared for publication. In addition to journal publication, a first collection of articles based on the project has been published (Borisov and Clarke, 2001). Project reports and analytical papers can be found on the project website at www.warwick.ac.uk/russia/trade. In writing the book we have drawn heavily on the reports and fieldnotes of our Russian colleagues.

The aim of this book is to provide as comprehensive an overview of the development of trade unions and industrial relations in post-soviet Russia as is possible in a relatively short space and in a form that will be accessible to non-

---

[1]    The project was financed by the British Economic and Social Research Council and by INTAS. The Russian side of the project was directed by Vadim Borisov, Director of ISITO and concurrently ICFTU Representative for the CIS countries. We are very grateful to our colleagues, especially to Vadim, and to all the Russian trade unionists who collaborated with the research, none of whom bears any responsibility for the errors and omissions or the judgements in this book. We would also like to thank those Western colleagues with whom we have shared this research field over the past ten years, particularly Peter Fairbrother, David Mandel, Rick Simon, Jochen Tholen and Frank Hoffer. Researching Russian trade unions can be a depressing occupation unless one works with colleagues who are also friends and comrades. Some sections of the book are based on a report prepared by the authors for the ILO Task Force on Industrial Relations in 1996. We are grateful to the ILO for permission to use this material.

specialists. One limitation that should immediately be noted is that we have paid little attention to the alternative trade unions, which we would justify by their marginal relevance to contemporary industrial relations and trade union development in Russia. Alternative trade unions are strongest in coal-mining and transport, organising underground miners, pilots and air traffic controllers, with small but active unions of locomotive drivers and dockers, these unions belonging to the two main alternative union federations, the All-Russian Confederation of Labour (VKT) and the Confederation of Labour of Russia (KTR). There are a lot of small independent unions, particularly in health, education and municipal transport, which have replaced (or sometimes developed out of) branches of the traditional unions, many of which are affiliated to Sotsprof. The main significance of the alternative unions, beyond their own limited sphere, is to act as a spur to the traditional trade unions. As the President of FNPR conceded in an interview: 'In general the existence of the alternative trade unions is even helpful. Competition does not allow us to stagnate' (*Vesti FNPR*, 1–2, 1999, p. 60).

In Chapter 2 we briefly outline the character of trade unions and industrial relations in the soviet system and chart the changes brought about in the period of perestroika. Trade unions first emerged in Russia in parallel with the growth of revolutionary politics, but at the time of the revolution the trade union apparatus was dominated by the Mensheviks, while the Bolsheviks had the majority in the factory councils. The Bolsheviks did not take long after the revolution to assert their control of the trade unions, but the issue of the independence of the trade unions or their subordination to the Party-state simmered for several years. Lenin finally laid down the principles on which the soviet trade unions would be constructed, but it was not until after the death of Stalin that the trade unions came to play a significant role in soviet society as nominally independent bodies which, nevertheless, performed predominantly state functions under the direction and control of the Party. While the nominal priority of the trade unions was to encourage the improvement of labour discipline and the growth of productivity, in practice their primary role was to administer the social and welfare apparatus of the Party-state. In the workplace they functioned primarily as the social welfare department of the enterprise administration, distributing a wide range of benefits to the 'labour collective', and this was the principal significance of the trade unions for their members. The reforms of perestroika presented a serious challenge to the structure and functions of the trade unions as new institutions arose to threaten their representative claims and as democratisation and economic liberalisation threatened their hierarchical structure. The trade unions responded to this challenge by democratising and decentralising their own structures, but were hard-pressed to give substance to these changes in their form.

In Chapter 3 we look at the role of the trade unions in the political sphere in post-soviet Russia. The integration of the soviet trade unions into the Party-state meant that they were very vulnerable in the wake of the collapse of the soviet system and could not avoid becoming embroiled in the political conflicts that marked the first decade of Russian independence. The first priority of the trade unions was to ward off the threats to their existence, but they could not hope to survive as trade unions if they did not also seek to defend the interests of their members in the face of the catastrophic decline of the Russian economy that had begun in the last years of perestroika, but that accelerated rapidly under Yeltin's shock therapy. The trade unions had generally functioned as a conservative force in the period of perestroika, although the Russian unions had supported Yeltsin in his confrontation with Gorbachev, and they aligned themselves increasingly with the opposition to Yeltsin's reform programme in his first two years of office, culminating in their support for parliament in its final confrontation with Yeltsin in October 1993. In retaliation, Yeltsin stripped the trade unions of some of their key state functions and threatened them with dissolution, precipitating the replacement of the founding president of FNPR, Igor' Klochkov, by the President of the Moscow Federation of Trade Unions, Mikhail Shmakov. Under Shmakov, FNPR took a much more conciliatory line, committing itself unequivocally to the strategy of 'social partnership' and support for democratic institutions, based on a respect for the law and the constitution. Under Shmakov's leadership, trade union 'days of action' were transformed into ritual displays of opposition to government policy to allow the members to let off steam, but which had only a very minor role in FNPR's political strategy.

The government was by no means as committed to social partnership as was FNPR, routinely ignoring the trade unions and violating the terms of the tripartite General Agreement, so FNPR increasingly focused its attention on lobbying the legislature for the passage of favourable legislation and on bureaucratic collaboration with government bodies in the development and implementation of social and labour policy. This commitment to the legislative process underlay FNPR's participation in electoral politics with the aim, firstly, of increasing the weight of the trade union lobby in parliament and, secondly, of participating in the establishment of a centre-left opposition as a potential 'party of power'. This strategy resulted in humiliation in the 1995 Duma election and little more success in the election of 1999. With the election of Putin, FNPR hoped that the prospects for meaningful social partnership would be improved, but their hopes were soon dashed when the government took advantage of its new-found control of the Duma to push through a Unified Social Tax, without consultation with the trade unions, which threatened to undermine the financing of much of the trade unions' social welfare activity, and a revised Labour Code, which threatened severely to limit the security of employment and the rights of trade unions to participation in management. During 2001, Shmakov's leadership came under challenge from the Communist Party and the presidential administration.

In Chapter 4 we look in more detail at the structure of the post-soviet trade unions. The unions continue to be constituted on the branch-territorial principles which marked them in the soviet period, but the hierarchical subordination which was a feature of 'democratic centralism' has been replaced by associative organisation according to the principles of confederation. This means that higher bodies have lost their powers to direct lower trade union bodies, so that each level of the trade union organisation sets its own priorities and has to find its own space. The loss of responsibility for social insurance and health and safety and the fall in income from dues has led to a dramatic decline in the size of the trade union apparatus and the resources available to the trade unions to fulfil their functions, with an ageing staff and limited prospects to attract young people to a trade union career.

In Chapter 5 we review the legislative framework of post-soviet trade unionism and industrial relations. Labour relations in the soviet period were subject to the most detailed legal and administrative regulation. The Soviet Labour Code prescribed in detail working hours and working conditions, the benefits and guarantees for specific categories of workers and gave extensive regulatory powers to the trade unions, including the requirement that the trade union should approve dismissals and redundancy and had the right to sanction management. The trade unions resisted attempts radically to revise the Labour Code, and successfully lobbied for the introduction of favourable legislation on trade unions, collective agreements and the regulation of labour disputes. However, the retention of favourable labour legislation was not so much a sign of the strength of the trade unions as of the weakness of their workplace organisation, which could not be relied on to defend the interests of union members on the basis of their own collective organisation.

While the trade unions have relied heavily on the legal regulation of labour relations, their overall strategy has been articulated within the framework of the ideology and practice of 'social partnership'. In Chapter 6 we examine the origins and character of social partnership in Russia, looking in some detail at the role of tripartite institutions at federal, branch and regional levels. We show that social partnership in Russia has essentially been bipartite, because of the weakness and lack of representativity of employers' associations, and that it has brought few benefits to unions or their members. On the one hand, federal and regional government bodies have been willing to make few concessions to the trade unions within the framework of social partnership. On the other hand, the trade unions have had no effective sanctions to ensure that they are consulted by government or that agreements entered into are fulfilled. Although the aspiration of the trade unions is for social partnership to be a partnership between equals, in practice it reproduces the traditional dependence of the trade unions on the state and management and the unions' participation is dependent on their continued performance of state and management functions.

In Chapter 7 we outline the functions of the Russian trade unions. At the federal level, the trade unions have declared their priority to be the defence of the labour and social rights of their members in the 'transition to a market economy', which they seek to achieve through the minute regulation of labour relations on the basis of laws and agreements, which have to be given substance by enterprise trade union organisations, but at the enterprise level the trade unions are dependent on management and continue to give priority to their social and welfare role. This leads to considerable tension between the priorities of higher and workplace trade union organisations in the exercise of trade union functions and the allocation of trade union funds, the point of intersection of the two being the regional trade union organisations which are charged with realising the priorities of the federal organisation, but have to respond to the demands of their affiliated primary organisations, on whom they depend for the bulk of their income.

In Chapter 8 we look at trade unions and industrial relations in the workplace. The content of labour legislation and the limited achievements of social partnership are of little value if they are not enforced. FNPR and its branch and regional organisations have become increasingly aware that the defence of the rights and interests of their members depends on primary trade union organisations establishing their independence of management and giving priority to the negotiation of effective collective agreements and to the monitoring of the enforcement of labour legislation and collective and other agreements. However, trade unions and industrial relations in the enterprise have still changed very little since the soviet period. Paradoxically, despite growing discontent, the stability of workplace labour relations has in some respects been reinforced by the economic crisis to which enterprises have been subject.

The collapse of investment has removed one of the principal levers of internal change in the direction of capitalist forms of labour regulation, while the success or failure of an enterprise depends more on its legacy from the past and on the formal and informal support of federal and regional state bodies than on the scale and character of its internal restructuring. The lobbying of regional and federal government gives some substance to the claims of management and enterprise trade union leaders to a common interest of employers and employees and to the reproduction of the traditional structure and functions of the enterprise trade union organisation as a subordinate branch of the management of the enterprise, responsible for the social welfare of enterprise employees.

In the concluding chapter we review the evidence to provide an assessment of the achievements and failures of the trade unions in post-soviet Russia and to locate the development of Russian trade unionism in a comparative perspective. The greatest achievement of the trade unions has been to secure their institutional survival. On the other hand, the survival of an institution is of dubious benefit if survival has been achieved at the cost of its effective functioning: even the trade unions admit that they have had only a limited ability to defend their members in the 'transition to a market economy'. Trade union membership has halved while around a quarter of all jobs have been destroyed; average real wages have been cut by half, with well over a third of all workers earning less than the subsistence minimum and millions of workers being paid nothing at all for months on end; inequality has increased from Scandinavian to Latin American proportions; the social and welfare infrastructure has been devastated and getting housed has become an unrealisable dream for virtually all young people.

The FNPR leadership attributes the limited achievements of the trade unions to the ineffectiveness and dependence on management of their workplace organisations and to the failure of their regional organisations to take effective steps to transform trade unionism in the workplace. Our analysis leads us to concur with this diagnosis, but at the same time we cannot absolve the trade union leadership of blame. The commitment of the trade unions to 'social partnership' and to respect for the established constitutional and legal order has played a very important role in consolidating democratic institutions in Russia. Moreover, the trade unions have not simply accommodated themselves to the imperfect democracy forged in the Yeltsin era, but have been powerful campaigners for democratic accountability and the establishment of the rule of law. However, the failure to develop the active participation of the trade union membership in the defence of their own interests has partly been a result of the trade unions' commitment to defending the interests of their members within the framework of social partnership and legislative regulation. Social partnership defines an institutional framework for the bureaucratic regulation of labour relations on the basis of a commitment of the trade unions to the amelioration of social conflict which has led the trade unions to attempt to suppress rather than to encourage the collective mobilisation of their own members. Legislative regulation leads to the individualisation of labour conflicts and their resolution through long-drawn-out judicial procedures rather than on the basis of the collective organisation and mobilisation of the trade union membership. These commitments have undermined the otherwise laudable attempt of the trade unions to foster and realise an ideology of economic and social democracy.

It is important not to judge the success and failure of the Russian trade unions against some abstract yardstick. Trade unions around the world are only imperfect defenders of their members' interests, constrained by the powers of capital and the state that they confront and compromised by their collaboration with employers and the state in institutions of conciliation. In every trade union movement the members complain about the bureaucratism of the leadership, while the leaders complain about the passivity of their members. We conclude our assessment of trade unionism in Russia by reviewing the unions' achievements in comparative perspective. The trade unions retain many of the structures and functions of their soviet past, but to what extent does post-soviet trade unionism mark a distinctive model of trade unionism, or to what extent is it converging on one or more of the models characteristic of countries in which capitalism has been long established?

# 2

# Trade Unions and Industrial Relations in the Soviet System

## The formation of the soviet trade unions

The birth of trade unionism in Russia was inextricably bound up with the rise of the revolutionary movement. The first explosion of trade union organisation was associated with the strike wave in Russia's emerging industrial centres that accompanied the 1905 revolution. Strike committees linked up to form inter-factory and district associations out of which city-wide trade union organisations emerged in the main industrial cities. The institutional consolidation of trade union organisations culminated in the First All-Russian Conference, held in Moscow in October 1905, which established the Central Bureau of Trade Unions. However, this initial burst of trade union development was reversed by subsequent repression so that the trade unions were almost extinguished.

The resurgence of the revolutionary movement in 1917 was associated with the rapid growth of factory committees (*Fabrichno-zavodskie Komitety* – FZK), which were legally recognised as representatives of workers in April 1917 and which were to play the leading role in the revolution. However, trade union organisation again developed in parallel with the factory committees, with the re-establishment of Central Trade Union Bureaux to co-ordinate trade union activity in the main cities. Through 1917 the role of the trade unions and factory committees was the subject of continuing and heated debate, but in practice it was the factory committees which made the running, with the trade unions lagging behind. The Third All-Russian Conference in Petrograd on 21–8 June 1917 decided on the branch principle of trade union organisation, with each trade union representing all the employees of a particular branch of the economy rather than particular professions, and established the All-Russian Central Council of Trade Unions (VTsSPS). The Conference was dominated by the Mensheviks, who argued that the trade unions should continue primarily to defend the interests of their members and who wished to incorporate the factory committees, dominated by the Bolsheviks, into the trade unions. The Bolsheviks, who had not at this stage worked out a consistent position, proposed a more active role for the trade unions after the revolution in taking command of the organisation of the economy. This dispute simmered through the autumn, as the Bolsheviks strengthened their position at the expense of the Mensheviks, and dominated debate within the trade unions after the Revolution.

The central issue facing the trade unions after the Revolution was whether they should continue to be independent organisations defending the interests of their members, as the Mensheviks argued, whether they should become agencies of workers' control based on the factory committees, as the syndicalists argued, or whether they should become instruments of the workers' state, as Lenin stressed.

The power base of the Bolsheviks in the Revolution had been the factory committees and the soviets, while the more conservative trade unions had been dominated by the Mensheviks. However, with the victory of the Revolution the priorities of the Bolshevik leadership changed radically as it had to find ways of consolidating and extending its power over society, a task in which it saw that the trade unions could play a leading role. As early as December 1917 the trade unions were given responsibility for administering the system of social insurance, in the absence of any alternative administrative structure which could be given the task.[1] Moreover, the centralised structures of the trade unions provided an ideal framework within which to impose some order on the factory committees.

The First All-Russian Congress of Trade Unions in January 1918, held two days after the Constituent Assembly had been disbanded for refusing to pass a Bolshevik-proposed Declaration of the Rights of Exploited People, was boycotted by the main Menshevik-led unions but the Bolsheviks, who had engaged in three days of heated discussion before the Congress, by no means presented a united front.[2] Although Lenin and the Bolshevik leadership stressed the need to subordinate the trade unions to the organisation of the economic life of the country and identified their mission as being 'to play a role in the organisation of the state' (cited Sorenson, 1969, p. 28), several Bolshevik trade union leaders, most notably David Ryazanov, spoke out in support of the continued independence of the trade unions. Nevertheless, the Leninist view prevailed in the resolution passed by the Congress: 'The centre of gravity of the work of the trade unions at the present moment must be transferred to the sphere of organisational-economic work. The trade unions as class organisations of the proletariat, built on the production principle, must take on themselves the important work of the organisation of production and reconstruction of appropriate productive forces of the country. The most energetic participation in all central bodies regulating production, the organisation of workers' control, the registration and redistribution of the labour force, the organisation of exchange between the town and the country, participation in the demobilisation of industry, the fight against sabotage, the conduct of universal labour conscription and so on – that is the task of the day. Particular attention should be paid to the initiation of the centralisation of strong unions of agricultural workers' (Gritsenko, Kadeikina and Makukhina, 1999, p. 84). It was also

[1]   Social insurance was transferred to the People's Commissariat for Labour (*Narkomtrud*) in 1922 (Madison, 1979).
[2]   The rapid growth of the trade unions is indicated by the fact that half the delegates were under 30 and two-thirds had less than a year's experience of trade union work (Gritsenko, Kadeikina and Makukhina, 1999, p. 81).

resolved to unite the FZK with the unions and to turn them into primary trade union organisations in the enterprises, a decision endorsed by the FZK conference later in January, which was implemented over the following two months, the FZK central committee being disbanded at the beginning of May (Gritsenko, Kadeikina and Makukhina, 1999, p. 86).

The devolution of state functions onto the trade unions gathered pace as the new regime grappled with the threat of economic collapse and sought to consolidate its hold on power and mobilise the population against the counter-revolutionary and interventionist military forces. In April 1918 VTsSPS assumed the role of encouraging the growth of productivity by establishing norms and piece-rates and enforcing labour discipline. Over the summer the trade unions were given responsibility for establishing detachments to be sent into the countryside to procure food, a task they set about with enthusiasm and which became a major focus of their activity. The trade unions participated in setting up soup kitchens to feed the impoverished and were made responsible for setting up labour exchanges, three-quarters of which in the middle of 1918 were managed by the unions, although in October they were formally taken over by *Narkomtrud*, most of whose officials were nominated by the trade unions.

In the summer of 1918 the trade unions were mandated to participate in the nationalisation of the means of production and transport decreed in June, while a July decree effectively gave *Narkomtrud* and the trade unions the right to establish wages and the conditions of employment determined by collective agreements. Nationalisation meant that the trade unions were now the intermediaries between the state, as the employer, and the workers, which brought the debate about the role of the trade unions to the fore. The Mensheviks continued to press for the independence of the trade unions, but they were weakened by intimidation and mass arrests. Nevertheless, while the Bolshevik political leadership demanded that the trade unions assume state functions, and some pressed for the full incorporation of the trade unions into the state apparatus, a significant number of Bolshevik trade union leaders stood out for the independence of the trade unions because they feared that the assumption of state functions would undermine the authority of the trade unions in the eyes of their own members.

The issue came to a head at the Second All-Russian Congress of Trade Unions in January 1919, which was firmly under Bolshevik control, the resolutions of the congress being amended and confirmed in advance by the Party Central Committee. The Second Congress affirmed the role of the trade unions in securing economic reconstruction, increasing productivity and improving labour discipline, endorsed the branch principle of trade union organisation and adopted the principle of rigid hierarchical subordination of lower to higher bodies. Lenin spoke on the central issue of the tasks of the trade unions, stressing the inevitability of the statisation of the trade unions – 'they have to be fused with state bodies' (Lenin, [1919], p. 329) – in order for them to take part in the work of soviet power, including the functions of workers' control, but he also warned, against the syndicalists, that the unions' role was restricted because of the lack of knowledge and experience among the masses. He concluded that the main function of the unions was to become bodies for the practical training of the broadest mass of workers in the business of management.

The final resolution of the Second Congress stressed that at the present stage of their development it would be premature to convert the unions into state organs or for them arbitrarily to usurp the functions of the state (Sorenson, 1969, p. 35). However, the Civil War produced new pressures and saw the state functions of the trade unions further augmented as they came to play a leading part in the recruitment, organisation and training of the Red Army and, with an end to the fighting, military detachments were transformed into 'labour armies' and drafted to fill labour shortages rather than being demobilised. This activity provided a model for the role of the trade unions in the 'militarisation of labour' proclaimed by Grigorii Zinoviev, former President of VTsSPS, who had coined the phrase 'trade unions are a school of communism' in September 1919, in a speech in which he proposed the trade unions' principal task to be to extract the country from economic crisis by strengthening administrative authority, 'to work in military order, that is to the highest precision, attentiveness, responsibility and speed'. Trotsky, the principal exponent of the militarisation of labour, also proposed that the trade unions should be closely involved in a strict bureaucracy 'not as a mass organisation but as an apparatus in the system of military-communist economic management' (Gritsenko, Kadeikina and Makukhina, 1999, p. 113).

At the Third Trade Union Congress in April 1920, overwhelmingly dominated by the Bolsheviks, Trotsky called for the militarisation of the trade unions. This would involve the compulsory mobilisation of labour, repression of those who defied the state, a labour army and political departments in the key trade unions. In accordance with the decisions of the Congress, trade unions further developed their role in the organisation of production and local trade union organisations began to organise *subbotniks* (unpaid Saturday work), compulsory overtime and extended working days and to develop training programmes.

The growing statisation of the trade unions hardly enhanced their authority in the eyes of their members, and this was reflected in the unease with which the union leadership viewed their subordination to the Party and incorporation into the state apparatus. The issue again came to a head in heated debates over the winter of 1920–1, with Mikhail Tomsky, President of VTsSPS, defending the independence of the trade unions and Trotsky and Bukharin demanding their complete subordination to the state. At the same time, the newly formed Workers' Opposition pressed the syndicalist position that the trade unions should be an instrument for the workers' control of production. The issue was resolved at the Tenth Party Congress in March 1921, when Lenin aligned himself with Tomsky to press a compromise between the Workers' Opposition and Trotsky and his allies. Lenin's proposal emphasised the role of the trade unions in encouraging the growth of labour productivity and enforcing labour discipline, but favoured persuasion over compulsion and rejected the militarisation of labour and the rapid statisation of the trade unions, allowing the trade unions to retain their independence from the state, even though they would retain their state functions, a position which won an overwhelming majority.[1] The independence of the trade unions from the state by no means implied that the unions would not remain subject to Party control. Members of the Central Council were appointed by the Central Committee of the Party and under War Communism, when wages were paid mostly in kind so that membership dues were not paid, the trade unions depended almost entirely on state funding channelled from the centre. The dominance of the centre over its constituent organisations was sealed by a resolution at the Fourth All-Russian Congress of Trade Unions in May 1921.

With the move from War Communism to the New Economic Policy (NEP) unemployment increased sharply and the ideas of the militarisation of labour became outdated and unnecessary, while there was a clear need for the trade unions to protect the interests of workers as many of the institutions of a capitalist market economy were restored. These changes gave added weight to Lenin's centrist position which formed the basis for his prescription for 'The Role and Functions of Trade Unions Under the New Economic Policy', which was adopted as policy by the Politburo on 12 January 1922 and was published five days later in *Pravda* (Carr, 1952, p. 326). The arguments he developed in some respects referred specifically to the NEP period in which the market and private trading were restored, small-scale private enterprise was permitted, and 'large-scale' (factory) production was re-organised on commercial lines, so that the trade unions were required to check the re-emergence of capitalist forms of exploitation. But Lenin's view of the proper relationship between workers, trade unions and the Soviet state was not only applicable to this period since managers of state enterprises and organisations were as likely as capitalists to pursue their own interests at the expense of the interests of the socialist state directed by the leading elements of the working class. With small modifications, therefore, Lenin's position formed the theoretical justification of the role of trade unions in the Soviet state thereafter.

The commercialisation of production in the NEP period would, according to Lenin, 'inevitably give the masses the impression that there is an antagonism of interest between the management of the different enterprises and the workers employed in them' (Lenin, [1922], p. 760) and in this situation the job of the trade unions was to defend workers' interests against management and to try to ensure that their living standards were raised. To this end the trade unions were permitted to 'constantly correct the blunders and excesses of the business organisations resulting from the bureaucratic distortions of the state apparatus' (p. 761), which would in turn further the cause of socialism because 'the ultimate object of every action taken by the working class can only be to fortify the proletarian state and the proletarian class state

---

[1]   For more details on this debate see Carr, 1952, pp. 222–7.

power' (p. 762). This last sentiment gets to the crux of the Leninist position on soviet trade unions: under socialism, or the transition to socialism, the interests of the working class are identified with and defined by the (socialist) state, so the role of unions is reduced to one of 'mediators' (p. 762), trying to avert the disputes arising from 'distortions' through a 'foresighted policy' (p. 763).

In the post-revolutionary context, one of the main problems of trade unionism from a Leninist perspective was its assumed sectionalism.[1] Lenin saw the interests of the working class as a whole as distinct from the sum of the interests of particular groups of workers. Spontaneous development would, he feared, only lead to the flourishing of sectional trade unionism, which had been exploited by the Mensheviks. It was the Communist Party alone, representing the most advanced elements of the working class, which comprehended where the objective interests of the whole working class lay so that it was control of the Communist Party 'which alone will be capable of withstanding the inevitable petty-bourgeois vacillations... and the inevitable traditions and relapses of narrow-craft unionism or craft prejudices among the proletariat' (Lenin, [1921], p. 684). Disputes over union priorities at all levels were to be settled by the 'higher authority' of the Communist Party (Lenin, [1922], p. 767), to which the trade unions were to be strictly subordinate.

Lenin was quite clear about the fact that trade unions should be under the control of the Party. Trade union groups should be run by 'responsible comrades', though not necessarily Party members (p. 766),[2] who should be close to the workers and able to 'stoop to their level', but at the same time able to resist the temptation to 'pander to the prejudices and backwardness of the masses' (p. 767). Thus, in place of the self-organisation and representation of workers, the 'responsible comrades' were to 'judge the mood, the real aspirations, needs and thoughts of the masses' (p. 766). Lenin recognised that one of the greatest dangers facing the Communist Party was 'divorcement from the masses' – a grave risk considering that the self-appointed vanguard of the working class had no reliable institutional mechanisms for maintaining links with the class in whose name they exercised their dictatorship – and the trade unions were supposed to avert this danger by becoming, in Lenin's famous phrase, 'the transmission belt from the Communist Party to the masses' (p. 766).

While the trade unions might perform a useful role in checking the excesses and distortions which might arise from the abuse of bureaucratic power and position, the 'real' interest of the working class lay in increasing the output of manufactured goods

---

[1]   In the pre-revolutionary context, the main problem had been the 'bourgeois economism' of the trade unions, which led them to concentrate on improving immediate conditions rather than on revolutionary struggle.

[2]   The Eleventh Party Congress in 1922 decided that only Party members of several years standing could be elected to leading posts in the trade unions. As E.H. Carr remarks with reference to this decision, 'The fate of the trade unions was an excellent illustration of the way in which the NEP, by conceding a measure of economic freedom, provoked a strengthening of direct political control by the party over individuals or organs which might be tempted to abuse this conditional freedom' (Carr, 1952 p. 327).

by 'enormous dimensions' (p. 763). The trade unions were therefore charged with enlisting 'the working class and the masses of working people generally for all branches of the work of building up the state economy' (p. 765). They should explain to workers that this was in their interest, while fighting to improve labour discipline. In addition to this, the trade unions were to act as 'schools of communism' (p. 764), training the future managers of soviet industry and providing a channel for the advancement of workers.

## After Lenin: the fate of the unions

It was one thing for Lenin to lay out the basic guidelines for trade union activity in the new society, but it was quite another to put these guidelines into practice. The threat to the Party posed by trade union independence had been neutralised, but the trade unions could not be relied on to commit themselves positively to their new role as agents of the Party-state. With the introduction of NEP the trade unions moved into the background. State bodies took over the functions of social insurance, health and safety, the regulation of overtime and grievance procedures which had been assigned to the trade unions, and state funding of the unions was withdrawn. Although union membership recovered from an initial decline, the unions were accorded little role in the late 1920s and were subjected to increasingly strict Party supervision as the union leadership was replaced by Party cadres (Ruble, 1981, pp. 12–13). The President of VTsSPS, Mikhail Tomsky, was purged in 1929 as the trade unions were brought firmly under Stalin's control.

The productivist orientation of the trade unions was reiterated in the famous slogan of the early period of Stalinist industrialisation which instructed union officials to 'turn their faces towards production' (Ruble, 1981, p. 13), meaning that they were to direct their attentions to the overriding task of plan fulfilment. Rigorous subordination of the trade unions to the Party was required to prevent the socialist project being subverted through unions' pursuit of either their own or sectional interests, or through union collusion with management. Unions were thus deprived of any independence that they had retained during the NEP period: those who opposed the new policy were dismissed as 'right deviationists' and many trade union leaders were shot in the Great Purge.

In the Stalin era the unions' chief concerns became those of 'socialist emulation' through the organisation of socialist competition, production conferences and so on. From 1929–34 the central union agencies even attempted to use collective agreements as an instrument for increasing productivity (Ruble, 1981, p. 17), but this attempt proved ineffective. Collective agreements were abolished in 1934 and were not formally reintroduced until 1947.

The ending of the unions' role in collective bargaining was linked to a wider change in the role of the trade unions as they were transformed into quasi-state agencies through their growing involvement in the gradually developing apparatus of state paternalism which was administered through the workplace. In 1933 the People's Commissariat of Labour was abolished and its functions taken over by the trade unions, including the duties of the state inspectorate for labour, monitoring health and safety and the implementation of the terms of the Labour Code, as well as assuming responsibility for the distribution of state welfare benefits.[1] Given the tightly circumscribed representational role of unions and their limited effectiveness in the struggle for increased productivity, social administration quickly became their most important practical function within the enterprise. It filled the days of union officers and defined their position as part of the enterprise administration: effectively the unions functioned as enterprise social welfare departments under the dual supervision of enterprise management and Party bodies. The fact that the unions were to give priority to the interests of management rather than workers in the execution of their welfare work was established early on. In 1938 factory trade union and management officials were required to consider attendance and production records in the distribution of welfare benefits (Ruble, 1981, p. 24). Although this requirement was annulled in 1951, in practice the control of welfare benefits gave the unions a good deal of discretionary power over workers and they were expected to use it: there were, for example, 18 different categories of disability allowance, which could be granted or not according to criteria such as length of service, work record and the role played by alcohol in the disability (ibid., p. 88).

The trade unions were given a major role in the mobilisation of the labour force during the war, and after the war saw their status gradually increase as they took on more functions. In 1948 Stalin undertook a major reorganisation of the trade unions, their structure now strictly paralleling that of the Party so that they could be kept more firmly under Party control.

The shift from coercion to encouragement as a means of promoting industrial growth which characterised the Khrushchev era obviously had implications for the role of the unions. Their role was enhanced by a resolution of the Central Committee of the Communist Party in December 1957. This demanded increased worker involvement in production administration and recognised the need to improve the education, safety and welfare of soviet workers. The resolution also stated that the collective agreement was the juridical foundation for all trade union activity at the enterprise level. Nevertheless, promoting production remained the unions' primary formal obligation, and their relationship with the Communist Party was not altered by the resolution (Ruble, 1981, pp. 33–4). The 'central task' of the unions, defined in the Preamble to their constitution, was unambiguous and unchanged from that defined by Lenin: 'to mobilise the masses for the attainment of our principal economic goal – the creation of the material and technical basis of communism, for the further

---

[1]    These included sickness and invalidity benefits, maternity benefits and childcare allowances for low-income families, but not unemployment benefit which was abolished in October 1930. These benefits, though distributed by the unions, were financed through a state tax of 4.4–14 per cent against each ministry's and enterprise's pay roll.

strengthening of the Soviet Union's economic and defence power, for ensuring a steady rise in the people's material and cultural standards' (Godson, 1981, p. 113).

These duties were enshrined in the typical collective agreement, which included not only the administration's responsibility to realise the 'social development plan' of the enterprise, but also the trade union's responsibility to ensure that the workers realised the enterprise's production plan. The centrality of the production plan to the collective agreement is exemplified by the fact that collective agreements were not signed in the 'non-productive sphere', such as public administration, health and education.

There was no place within the collective agreement for negotiation over the terms and conditions of employment, which are central to any collective agreement in a capitalist country. Under the soviet system wage rates were determined centrally and embodied in a universal tariff scale which defined the rate for every job in terms of a coefficient applied to the minimum wage, with various other coefficients applied to allow for harmful working conditions, geographical location and so on. These wage rates were in principal the universally operative rates, it being illegal to pay above scale, although, as will be seen, in practice there was room for some informal adjustment at enterprise level. In principle wage rates could be changed by revision of the scale, but wage reforms were extremely complex and provoked considerable conflict, so scale revisions took place at most every ten years or so.

The central determination of wage rates left little role for trade unions in the determination of wages. In principle the VTsSPS was consulted by the State Committee on Labour, *Goskomtrud*, in matters relating to labour, but since wage rates were so rarely changed this had little significance. The minimum wage was determined primarily on the basis of macroeconomic consideration of the consumer balance, the sum of wages having to correspond to the sum of consumption goods available. At shop floor level there was considerable scope for manipulation of pay, usually with a view to rewarding loyal and committed workers or to securing scarce categories of labour, through the allocation of piece-work, inflation of grades and the payment of various bonuses, but this was an individual matter, a lever of management, arranged informally between the foreman or shop chief and the individual workers, and could not be a matter for the trade union. From 1966 the enterprise could make payments from its material stimulation fund, but these amounted to less than five per cent of manual workers' wages. Following Gorbachev's 1986 wage reform, enterprises enjoyed more freedom in the allocation of their wages fund, although within quite strict limits. These limits were eased through 1990 and 1991, allowing enterprises to pay higher than the tariff-scale wages within the limits of their wages fund, but it was only from October 1991 that enterprises suddenly had the freedom to determine their own pay rates and scales.

## The structure and functions of soviet trade unions

Soviet trade unions, as the 'transmission belts' between the Party and the masses, were deeply embedded in the structures of the Party-state. The organisational structure of the trade unions mirrored that of the Party-state, the majority of their functions were Party-state functions and their authority derived from the Party-state.

The trade unions were organised on the branch principle, corresponding to the ministerial structure of the administrative-command system, representing all employees from top ministerial officials through directors of enterprises and organisations to cleaners. A branch of the economy is generally broader than a single industry, so some branch unions might cover several industries. The Mining-Metallurgical Union, for example, covered workers in 22 industrial sub-branches. Reorganisation of the ministerial system was generally followed by a corresponding reorganisation of the branch trade unions,[1] and the transfer of an enterprise from one ministry to another would be accompanied by the transfer of its union organisation to the appropriate branch union. Membership of the unions was automatic, so that union density was around 99 per cent. The trade unions were formed into a strictly hierarchical monolithic structure governed by the principle of 'democratic centralism', according to which decisions taken through the procedures of soviet democracy were binding on the organisation and were rigidly imposed on all levels of the organisation from the centre. Trade union officers at all levels were elected according to the *nomenklatura* principle, with candidates for office selected by higher trade union and Party bodies before their names were submitted for approval by those whom they were to represent. The trade union organisation was subject to close Party supervision at all levels. Trade union office was considered to be the 'graveyard of Party cadres' rather than a step on the ladder to a glittering career, but trade union leaders were well paid and enjoyed many of the privileges of the *nomenklatura*.

In 1931 the trade unions adopted the organisational principle of the Party, that a member was anybody who participated actively in the life of a primary organisation and personally paid his or her membership dues. Every month the workplace trade union organiser collected the membership dues, one per cent of the salary, from each member, reminding the member that he or she was indeed a member of the trade union and formally confirming that membership with a mark on the membership card. In 1984 the trade unions moved to a check-off system, with union dues being paid automatically by the enterprise, and the ritual confirmation of membership (and trade union membership cards) fell into disuse (Ilyin, 2001). Every subdivision of an enterprise had its trade union organiser and trade union committee, a group of people who performed their trade union functions on a voluntary basis, though they

---

[1] Khrushchev made an abortive attempt to re-organise the unions along territorial lines as part of his plan to reform the economy on the basis of regional economic councils (*sovnarkhozy*). After the attempt to unseat him in June 1957, however, Khrushchev was disinclined to force this measure on the resistant trade unions and the branch union structure remained.

obviously enjoyed privileged access to the goods and benefits that were distributed by the trade union. The trade union organisation of the enterprise was directed by the trade union committee, the president of which was a full-time officer in all but the smallest enterprises or organisations.

Trade union primary groups were subordinated to the regional committee of the relevant branch trade union, which were in turn subordinated both to the regional trade union committee and to the central committee of the branch union. Finally, the regional and central committees were subordinated to the All-Union Central Council of Trade Unions (VTsSPS). In all the Republics, apart from Russia, there was an intervening Republican-level of trade union organisation.

After the death of Stalin, the trade unions played an increasing role in the soviet planning apparatus, with responsibility for planning the 'human element' in the struggle for production. The trade unions participated in the elaboration and implementation of Party social and labour policy, through the close collaboration between VTsSPS and *Goskomtrud* and on the basis of the trade unions' 'right of legislative initiative', which gave them responsibility for formulating the social and labour legislation that they were expected to monitor and enforce. VTsSPS and the branch trade unions participated in the elaboration of manpower plans in collaboration with their ministerial counterparts, identifying problems of recruitment and retention, the needs for training and retraining in the branch, systems of certification and accreditation, health and safety regulations, the elaboration of scientific norms and corresponding wage scales, all of which were incorporated into the central Plan and embodied in administrative regulations. In the late soviet period, the trade unions lobbied for increases in wages and social spending, and for correspondingly greater priority to be given to the production of consumer goods and the social infrastructure, in order to provide more meaningful incentives to encourage the labour force to greater productive efforts. The branch and regional trade union organisations collaborated with their corresponding ministries and regional bodies in lobbying for the allocation of more human and material resources to enable them to achieve their plan targets.

Although the trade union was an integral part of the Party-state apparatus, it was nominally the representative of the interests of the workers and it was in their name that it signed collective agreements and lobbied in higher state and party bodies. The traditional western arguments about soviet trade unions focused on the issue of whether the trade unions in reality had the 'dual function' defined by Lenin of imposing the policies of the Party from above at the same time as defending workers' interests (Ruble, 1981) or whether they were simply part of the repressive apparatus (Conquest, 1967, Schapiro and Godson, 1981), their defensive claims being purely rhetorical. There is no doubt that the trade unions were under the close supervision of the Party at all levels, and were not able to play an independent role in the defence of workers' interests without the endorsement of the relevant Party bodies, so in this sense the trade unions were an integral part of the Party-state. Moreover, as will be seen, there was also a strong tendency for the trade unions to collaborate with enterprise management, since they were heavily dependent on management for the goods and services they controlled, while in terms of the career structure, union officers were part of enterprise management, so they were in no position to oppose enterprise management on behalf of the workers, unless authorised or encouraged to do so by the relevant Party bodies.

So did the trade unions play any role in defending workers' interests? There was obviously no question of the trade union encouraging or facilitating the collective representation of the workers' interests, which would pose a threat to the Party's political monopoly and was thus not allowed. As has been seen, the 'collective agreement' was a document of purely formal significance since wages were set from above. The 'labour collective' was a rhetorical figure which expressed the common interests of the enterprise as a whole, managers as well as workers, not the self-conscious representation of the collective labourer (Ashwin, 1999, pp. 9–17). The important point to understand about the unions' defensive role was that they were not mandated to act by or on behalf of workers, but by the Party. The rights and interests of workers were not to be defined by the workers themselves, but were minutely prescribed in laws and regulations. The trade union was supposed to ensure that these were enforced, but the law was not an abstract codification of rights but an expression of the social and labour policies of the Party, so the implementation of the law was a matter of political judgement. The law could not stand in the way of achieving the priority aims of the Party, in particular, of achieving the legally binding plan targets assigned to the enterprise.

The trade unions were supposed to act as the 'eyes and ears' of the Party, monitoring the performance of enterprise management to ensure that the director did not attempt to achieve plan targets through the over-exploitation of the labour force, with the risk of undermining the health of the workers, provoking social tension and, in the worst of cases, overt conflict. In this capacity, the trade union might make representations on behalf of the workers, for example regarding working conditions or the quality of food in the canteen, and the unions could defend *individual* workers in order to keep discontent within the labour collective in bounds.[1] The union was, for example, obliged to give its agreement to any dismissals of workers proposed by management. McAulay estimates that in Leningrad in the period of her study (1957–65), the unions agreed to half of all management requests for dismissal. The reason

---

[1]   There were several channels of individual complaint available to workers, however. In addition to the enterprise trade union, an individual worker had the option of approaching management, the enterprise Party committee or the enterprise *yuriskonsul't* (legal advisor). *Yuriskonsul'ty* were often able to provide meaningful assistance to enterprise employees, both over personal matters such as divorce and alimony, and work-related issues such as overtime pay and vacation entitlements (Shelley, 1981), while the Party could also provide highly effective help when it saw fit (Ashwin, 1999, pp. 59–60). Indeed, in many enterprises such channels were no doubt more effective than that provided by the trade union.

generally given for refusing assent was that the worker should be given another chance, rather than because there was no legal basis for dismissal (McAulay, 1969, p. 123). Such defence, however, took place within the parameters set by the Party. Thus the unions did, to a limited extent, defend workers' interests, but only as these were defined from above by the Party and codified in law and not as expressed by workers from below.[1] Moreover, the trade union was a rather toothless watchdog over the legal rights of workers and could normally only assert itself when it had the backing of the Party within the enterprise. This would usually occur in the context of conflict within the enterprise administration, or of a Party campaign organised from above (Clarke et al., 1993, p. 112). Thus, the trade union, rather than representing the collective interests of the workers, was the junior partner in the *troika* of enterprise director, Party secretary and trade union president which ran the enterprise.

The primary role that the trade unions were charged with performing was, as has been mentioned, that of stimulating production. Here, again, the unions were supposed to control the behaviour of management on behalf of the Party. Specifically, they were required to break up the collusive relations which developed between workers and managers over plan fulfilment that were a barrier to the development of productivity and the improvement of the living and working conditions of the working class as a whole. The 'production pact' between soviet workers and managers (Clarke et al., 1993, p. 99) was an expression of the fact that, while individual workers and line managers had opposing interests in the everyday struggle to meet the plan, they had a common interest in maximising supplies, minimising plan targets and keeping plan overfulfilment within limits, which would permit the earning of bonuses without risking an excessive ratcheting of the plan. Unlike a capitalist enterprise, where such collusion between workers and line managers is kept in check by financial constraints imposed from above, within a soviet enterprise this commonality of interest in thwarting the system ran all the way from the bottom to the top. The soviet enthusiasm for the crudest version of Taylorism is a reflection of this contradiction at the heart of the system: one way of trying to check such collusion was the systematic application of the 'scientific organisation of labour', the ideal being for scientifically determined technical norms to be applied to every task in every workplace in the country. Such a mechanistic approach to the organisation of labour could not possibly work, for obvious and well-known reasons, so the scientific

[1]   In the case of dismissals, for example, the trade unions' attitude was governed not by a commitment to defend workers, but by the interests of the labour collective as a whole, as represented by the Party. From the Party perspective, reasons for keeping a worker included the labour shortage, and the potential social disruption that could come from removing undisciplined workers from the care and control of the labour collective and throwing them 'on to the street'. On the other hand, McAulay claims that if the worker was having a bad influence on others (mainly by persuading them to drink), or worked in a young collective, the trade union was very unlikely to defend him (or her): production was the Party's number one priority.

organisation of labour had to be supplemented by more direct intervention, that intervention being primarily the responsibility of the trade union. Stakhanovism, counter-plans, socialist competition, production conferences, unpaid working Saturdays, campaigns to encourage invention and innovation, the award of honours and awards were all the responsibility of the trade union, which was supposed constantly to exhort the workers to greater efforts, but such activities had little impact. On the one hand, they were regarded with scepticism or derision by the majority of workers – production conferences, which had been reintroduced in the 1950s, were dominated by engineers and specialists rather than ordinary workers (Ruble, 1981, Chapter Five). On the other hand, management resisted any attempts by the trade union to interfere in the management of production, which were likely to prove disruptive and to undermine the authority of production managers.

The trade unions were very unsuccessful in their attempts to carry out their thankless task of encouraging the growth of production, which acquired an increasingly ritualistic quality as the trade unions concentrated instead on the more fulfilling work of administering the social and welfare facilities of the enterprise, such as sanatoria, kindergartens, sporting and holiday facilities, and distributing housing, material assistance, holiday vouchers and other insurance and social welfare benefits to their members. The scale and extent of this provision reflects the fact that the enterprise was the basic unit of soviet society which provided not only employment, but also housing, medical care, and sporting, cultural and leisure facilities for its workers, and the trade union committee was supposed to be responsible for all these questions. These benefits were financed by the enterprise, directly or through its social insurance contributions, further sealing the dependence of the trade union on management, but their provision was much the most important role of the unions for their members, absorbed the bulk of union resources and took up the overwhelming part of the time of union officers.

The benefits provided by the union to its members varied considerably between enterprises, regions and branches of production, with the most generous benefits being provided by large enterprises in the priority branches of production and in the large cities. The inequality of provision is a clear indicator of the subordination of such provision to the priorities of production rather than to the needs of the workers. The distribution of benefits within the enterprise was similarly closely bound up with the role of the union in stimulating higher productivity and improving labour discipline: the trade unions' involvement in issues of service and leisure provision was a source of patronage and control, with allocation being tied to length of service and disciplinary record, rather than an extended frontier in collective representation.

Social and welfare provision was as much to do with the moral and spiritual as the physical health of workers and their families and as much to do with surveillance and control as liberation from the burdens of work. Trade union volunteers would visit the sick not only to provide comfort and encourage a rapid recovery, but also to ensure a rapid return to work and to weed-out malingerers. Kindergartens not only enabled both parents to work full-time, but also ensured the proper moulding of a socialist personality in the most impressionable years. Children would be sent to trade-union-run camps during the school holidays not just to give them a good time and some healthy fresh air and exercise, but also to educate them in the socialist spirit, rather than letting them hang around the streets. Similarly for their parents, a vacation at an enterprise resort gave them a well-earned rest, but it was also another celebration of the collective: the priority of the collective is exemplified by the fact that it was often very difficult for husband and wife to go on vacation together. The organisation of sporting and cultural events, the distribution of new year presents and the celebration of state and professional holidays were similarly means of 'raising the cultural level' of the labour force and affirming the identity of the collective. Many trade union workers still view their social and welfare activity in such traditional moral terms, not just as handing out a few miserly benefits but as elevating the moral and spiritual tone of society as a whole.

While trade union members valued the benefits they received from the trade union, such provision did not increase the prestige of the trade union in the eyes of its members since it was always marked by its qualitative and quantitative inadequacy. The role of the trade union was to ration the distribution of scarce resources, and it was always suspected, not unjustly, of favouring not only exemplary workers and those in most need, but also senior managers, trade union officers and their friends and relatives.

Overall, what is striking is the trade unions' ineffectiveness in performing their allotted role in the soviet system. The trade unions had little weight in leading Party bodies so had only a very limited ability to affect the policies of the Party-state, providing specialist advice rather than influencing policy on behalf of their members. They were not very effective champions of the Party's social and labour policy in the workplace since they lacked strength to challenge management on a consistent basis, while they had a similar limited efficacy in their role as promoters of production. Again, the unions did not have the requisite power to challenge the established industrial culture of enterprises: they were too weak in relation to management and the Party and lacked the active support of the bulk of their membership. Rather, they collaborated with the Party and enterprise administration to ensure that the prevailing form of relations within the enterprise was not challenged. The enterprise unions were therefore at the same time constrained by their formally prescribed role and unable properly to fulfil it.

## The regulation of the employment relationship

The employment relationship in the soviet system was nominally regulated by the dense network of law, administrative regulations and collective agreements, the latter of which both had the force of law, which the trade unions were charged with monitoring and enforcing. But, as we have seen, the enforcement of the law was a matter of Party policy priorities so that the trade unions could not act as its independent executors but only on behalf of, or with the approval of, the relevant Party body.

The principal law governing labour and employment relations was not the Labour Code but the Plan. The Plan determined the wage and employment levels, the funds available for social and welfare benefits and to pay bonuses, to pay for re-equipment and investment in health and safety, training and retraining. The Plan not only had the force of law, but was reinforced by the penalties imposed for failure and the bonuses that were paid for overfulfilment. As against the sanctions and incentives associated with fulfilment of the Plan, the Labour Code could usually be flouted with impunity so that it at best provided a normative framework for the regulation of the employment relation.

Labour relations in the workplace were primarily regulated through informal bargaining at all levels, in which legal regulation was subordinate to the over-riding priority of achieving plan targets. The trade unions were almost entirely excluded from participation in the informal bargaining over the allocation of work, wages, bonuses and the imposition of disciplinary sanctions which went on at shop level, although in more general terms they colluded with management, overlooking violations of labour legislation and using their distribution of social and welfare benefits as a means of encouraging loyalty, diligence and discipline in the 'labour collective' and improving the 'culture of labour'.

The actual conduct of production in the soviet system was left largely to the responsibility and initiative of the direct production workers. This was not, however, an indication of a control of production wrested from management but of an abdication of responsibility on the part of management for the rational organisation of production as a result of the constraints and limitations of the soviet system. Soviet workers did not question management's right to manage: rather they questioned management's competence and complained at management's failure to manage.

Management retained formal control of production through the payment system, which was based until the end of the 1970s on individual piece-rates, supposedly established scientifically, which tied pay to results. The piece-rate system suffered from the familiar weaknesses, exacerbated in the soviet context by shortages of supply and inadequate maintenance which meant that workers suffered from a very uneven rhythm of production and faced frequent down-time through no fault of their own, leading to endemic conflict between workers and line managers over pay.

While workers had a high degree of control over the immediate process of production and conflict between workers and their managers was endemic, the limits of worker solidarity did not normally extend beyond the immediate work group, since the principal levers of production management were based on fomenting and exploiting divisions within and between work groups. Workers depended for their earnings on the allocation of work by their line managers and on the fulfilment of plan targets by those on whom they depended for supplies. Workers assigned to the most reliable machines and assured a steady supply of parts and materials could overfulfil their norms and earn healthy bonuses, while the less fortunate had to struggle to make their targets. Those who worked shifts depended on those who worked the previous shift to leave their machines in good order with an adequate reserve of parts and raw materials. Managers were able to exploit the dependence of the workers by encouraging competition between work groups, rewarded with the allocation of work which provided earning opportunities, supplemented by the discretionary payment of bonuses diverted from various funds, the imposition of fines and the distribution of non-monetary benefits, which were the principal levers of production management. A good manager was one who was 'firm but fair', who would manage the shop or department in such a way that it fulfilled or overfulfilled its production targets and the rewards were allocated among the workers on the basis of their initiative and hard work, personal loyalty and commitment, which had made it possible to achieve the plan.

The success or failure of a production manager did not only depend on his or her ability to manipulate social relations on the shop floor, but also on his or her ability to ensure that the external conditions of production were maintained. While the workers were responsible for direct production, the shop and section chiefs and even the foremen would scurry around the enterprise and go on business trips to suppliers, doing deals to maintain the supply of essential parts and raw materials and to ensure that the plant and equipment was adequately maintained, repaired and replaced. Just as the line manager exploited competition between individual workers and primary work groups to secure the manageability of the shop, so senior managers exploited competition between their shop and division chiefs to ensure that each section contributed to the achievement of the plan of the enterprise as a whole.

While the deficiencies of soviet production were systemic, their immediate manifestations appeared to depend on the personal qualities of individual managers. Conflict was therefore highly personalised. If a shop or department was not able to make its production targets, levels of overt conflict would increase as workers failed to earn their bonuses, the manageability of the department would decline and the situation would deteriorate further, blame for the situation being attached to the responsible manager. In such circumstances senior management and the workers had a common interest in removing the apparent source of failure, and this common interest might be expressed through the trade union: the workers might appeal to senior management directly or through the trade union representative and the trade union might intervene, usually with the support of senior management and the Party, and demand the removal of the guilty manager.[1] In the rare event of the conflict reaching the stage of a work stoppage, the legitimacy of the workers' grievances

---

[1]   According to Krest'yaninov, 1995, p. 59, on the eve of perestroika there were more than 10 000 cases of managers being disciplined or dismissed on the initiative of the trade union each year.

would usually be recognised, but they would be admonished for the methods chosen to express their grievances and the instigators severely punished, but the responsible manager and trade union leader would also be removed from their posts. Thus conflict did not throw the system into question, but was addressed by an appeal to higher authorities, the 'good Tsar', and was resolved by assigning personal responsibility for failure.

The result of the soviet system of production management was that industrial relations were centred on informal personal relations at every level of the enterprise. Access to earnings opportunities and other monetary and non-monetary benefits depended on line managers having good personal relations within the management hierarchy and on the workers cultivating good relations with their line managers, in competition with other managers and workers who would be excluded from such opportunities. It was similarly the line managers who controlled the hiring, retraining, promotion and regrading of the workers as further instruments through which to manage and upgrade the labour collective, while the personnel department of the enterprise did little more than keep the employment records and prepare the regular reports on the comings and goings and on the socio-demographic characteristics of the workforce. Labour relations in the soviet enterprise, far from being regulated by the formally established system of grading, qualifications, scientific norms and rates of pay, were in practice regulated by the informal relations through which managers divided and ruled the labour collective (Alasheev, 1995).

The wage system was only one of the means by which control of the labour force was maintained, and the limited monetisation of the system and low levels of income differentials meant that it was one of the least effective. Despite repeated attempts from above to increase pay differentials as a means of increasing incentives, such differentials remained relatively modest and had much more of a symbolic than a real significance. This was because the labour force was divided and hierarchically structured not so much through the use of economic levers as through the establishment of a status hierarchy, in which pay levels were a sign of status rather than a means of acquiring it, just as it was status rather than money that was the prime means of acquiring a wide range of goods and services (Kozina and Borisov, 1996).

While management's monetary levers were weak, the fact that the economy was largely non-monetary meant that management had direct control over the distribution of a wide range of resources, from housing, garden plots and vacations through social, medical and welfare facilities and, from the 1970s, the distribution of consumer goods, all of which were allocated through the trade union in close association, at shop level, with line management. Workers secured access to such privileges on the basis of long and loyal service, and the threat of withdrawal of such privileges was a very effective means of maintaining such loyalty. The so-called *kadrovyi* workers were those who had demonstrated their commitment over ten years or more of loyal service and who enjoyed access to the full range of benefits. These were the people often referred to as the 'backbone' of the labour collective on whom the manageability of production and the fulfilment of the plan depended.

While the loyalty of the core workers could be secured with the sticks and carrots provided by the system of distribution, and the promise of access to this system could maintain the loyalty of less-experienced skilled workers, these methods were not so effective at controlling those outside the system or on the lowest ranks of the hierarchy, particularly the young and the unskilled who were required in large numbers by the soviet enterprise. It was these people in particular who had to be motivated and controlled primarily through monetary incentives, and this, in combination with the growing shortages of unskilled labour, is the principal reason for the relatively low pay differentials between different grades of worker, indeed for the fact that unskilled workers could sometimes earn more than skilled. Nevertheless, although they may have earned more, such unskilled workers did not have access to the things that money could not buy.

This system of work organisation and production management developed out of the conditions of rapid industrialisation in the 1930s, but soon acquired its own logic as it became deeply embedded within the framework of the administrative-command system of production and distribution, subverting the 'scientific organisation of production'. Stalin, Khrushchev and Gorbachev all sought to rationalise the payment system through wage reforms, all of which failed when confronted with the realities of the soviet system of production management. Attempts in post-soviet Russia to develop more rational payment systems at an enterprise level have foundered on the same barriers, being thwarted as they are subverted by line management which has to retain its informal levers of control in conditions of irregular production rhythms (Vedeneeva, 1995). As the most recent past has shown, the soviet system of work organisation and production management has a resilience which has enabled it to persist despite the disintegration of the system of which it was a part. And the trade unions, as institutions which had adapted fully to this form of work organisation, have played an important role in securing its reproduction.


## Trade unions and the labour collective under perestroika

We have noted that the primary formal responsibility of the trade union was not to defend the workers against the managers, nor even to reinforce the authority of the managers over the workers, but to challenge the collusion between workers and managers which held back the growth of production. The consistent failure of such trade union efforts is exemplified in the stream of reforms from the 1960s, all of which sought to find some more effective way of breaking worker-management collusion on the shop-floor, in many cases drawing on Western experience: from the 1960s more attention was played to the 'role of the human factor in production', and sociology departments, staffed with sociologists and psychologists, were attached to large enterprises, researching labour motivation and advising on personnel selection, often in close liaison with the 'first department' (KGB officers), an approach strongly reminiscent of Henry Ford's use of 'sociology' in his plants in the 1930s.

Partly as a result of the findings of sociologists and psychologists, the late 1970s saw a growing interest in worker participation as a means of stimulating their work effort, culminating in the introduction of the 'brigade system'. These initiatives were supplemented under Gorbachev with an enthusiasm for the decentralisation of the administrative command system and, eventually, the 'transition to a market economy', all of which would supposedly give workers and managers a more direct and immediate interest in the results of their work. These reforms had an important impact on the trade unions, which found their responsibility for production being assigned to other, competing, institutions which threatened their own representative claims.

The decision to generalise the brigade system was officially adopted in 1979, and the system already (at least formally) covered almost three-quarters of all workers by 1985. The 'brigade system', in its pure form, sought to integrate the informal organisation of the labour process into the formal structure of management by identifying the informal leaders as the brigadiers of self-managing work groups. The logical corollary of the development of workers' self-management at brigade level as a means of harnessing workers' initiative and imagination to the production effort was its extension to the enterprise level. The amended 1977 Soviet Constitution re-established the constitutional rights of labour collectives, which had been abolished in the 1920s, without giving the collective any legal-political form. The introduction of labour collective councils (STK) with wide-ranging powers had already been raised in discussion of the brigade system as a part of a broader reform perspective, which included greater autonomy of the enterprise (Moses, 1987). In the early 1980s it became a centre-piece of the reform strategy. Underlying the reform was an unstated, but clearly implicit, assumption that the trade unions had signally failed in their duty of harnessing the productive energies of the working class, and that they were structurally incapable of doing so. The relation between the trade union committee and the STK, which would take over many of the unions' powers, was never spelt out, but the unions clearly feared being marginalised. For this reason 'trade union officials probably objected to the proposed new labour collective as a threat to their institutional authority' (Moses, 1987, p. 207, c.f. Teague, 1986; Slider, 1985). The 1983 Law on Labour Collectives, which implemented the new clause in the 1977 Constitution, established the STK as an advisory body with very limited powers.

Alongside the introduction of the STK, the late Brezhnev regime codified the role of the trade union in the enterprise with the 1984 Law on Collective Agreements (which remained in force until 1992). The new law codified existing practice rather than introducing any radical innovations, but the collective agreement would assume an increasing significance with the development of self-management since the latter would provide for more discretion in managerial decision-making. The new law ensured that such discretion did not exceed the bounds of party policy by prescribing the format of the collective agreement in detail, so that there was little scope for discretion in negotiating the agreement. Inscribed within this law were all the customary assumptions regarding the role of trade unions under communism. The model agreement began with a formal undertaking of the labour collective to fulfil the plan and their socialist obligations, so that 'planning targets for the enterprise become part of each worker's individual responsibility' (Butler, 1988, p. 226). The employees similarly committed themselves to engagement in socialist competition and the development of a communist attitude to labour, to take the initiative in making inventions and introducing technological innovations. This was followed by provisions regarding pay, which implemented the centrally determined tariff scales and norms, and the right (and duty) of workers to participate in production conferences, where they were supposed to put forward suggestions for increasing productivity and improving conditions. The typical agreement specified the extent of training and re-training to be provided, and resolved to improve labour discipline. The only real scope for modification of the standard terms of the collective agreement lay in the final section which dealt with health, housing, social and welfare provision, spelling out the details of the enterprise's social development plan, which could include the provision of facilities out of the enterprise's own funds, and this was usually the only section in the formulation of which the trade union played any role.[1] The leading commentator on Soviet law concludes:

> The collective contract has been moulded into a device representing ideally a harmony of planning, administrative, management, and labour interests; its object is to enlist workers' support in giving effect to planning and to sublimate areas of conflict in the larger interests of a presumed community of labour-management concerns (Butler, 1988, p. 227).

The collective agreement had the form of a 'social contract' between management and the labour collective. However, it would be a mistake to take the form for the substance. If it was a contract, it was pretty one-sided. On the one hand, the collective agreement was drawn up by management, with the trade union functioning as a branch of enterprise management, within strictly defined parameters in which the labour collective had a minimal input and no bargaining power. On the other hand, most of the obligations specified were imposed on the trade union, on behalf of the labour collective, and the trade union thereby assumed a legal obligation to work for its fulfilment. Rather than a social contract, the collective agreement expressed the

---

[1]   The draft of this section of the agreement would usually be prepared by the trade union in collaboration with the relevant managers, and it would be circulated through the enterprise to gather suggestions from the shop floor, before the agreement as a whole was submitted to a meeting of the labour collective for approval. This section could go into such minute detail as a promise to repair the toilets or to repaint a cloakroom, a promise which might be carried over from year to year.

obligation of the labour collective to subordinate itself to the achievement of the economic and social objectives of the Party-state.[1]

When Gorbachev came to power it was not long before he identified himself with the movement for self-management, but Gorbachev's reforms further undermined the role of the trade union in the enterprise. The Law on State Enterprise (Association) of July 1987 simultaneously defined the enterprise as self-financing, established the principle of managerial election right up to the level of director, and strengthened the elected Council of the Labour Collective, which had the power to 'decide all production and social questions', although it simultaneously reaffirmed the traditional principle of one-man management. The extensive patronage network of unions and management, and the persistence of the state repressive apparatus within the enterprise, meant that the STK remained firmly under management control (Krotov, 1990).

There was considerable ambiguity about the relationship between the STK and the trade union committee, both of which were supposed to represent the labour collective as a whole and both of which had responsibility for 'production and social questions'. In practice the division of responsibilities appears to have been achieved on an *ad hoc* basis, with the STK taking over responsibility for production questions, while the trade union concentrated on its welfare and distribution functions. One enterprise director interviewed in 1991 saw the distinction thus: 'the trade union is the representative of the labour collective only within the limits of its responsibility for the implementation of the collective agreement. Other issues can be handled by the STK'. Some trade union leaders welcomed the opportunity to shed some of their managerial functions, while others resented the erosion of their position, particularly when the director sought to use the STK to weaken further the union's authority.

The principle of managerial election provoked widespread opposition from management and within the Communist Party and, following the emergence of independent workers' organisations on the basis of the strike wave of 1989, a new law in 1990 downgraded the STK to an optional institution, whose only function was to arbitrate over the implementation of the collective agreement.[2] The new law also enhanced managerial power by increasing enterprise independence and abolishing election for all posts above brigade leader.

---

[1]   The conceptualisation of the relationship between workers and the Soviet state as a 'social contract', at least from the Brezhnev period, was popular among western analysts (Cook, 1993; Hauslohner, 1987). The fact that the abrogation of the supposed 'social contract' under Yeltsin did not lead to a significant radicalisation of the working class casts considerable doubt on such an interpretation (for a more detailed criticism of this approach see Ashwin, 1999, pp. 3–5).

[2]   Following the collapse of the soviet system there were occasional suggestions from government circles that the STK should be resurrected, specifically as a means of by-passing the trade union. The trade unions managed to thwart a government attempt to introduce a new law on the labour collective in December 1997, but it was brought back by the Communists and was due for a second reading in November 2001.

In the end, more significant than the development of the STK in determining the changing role of the trade unions under perestroika was the increase in industrial conflict that was most dramatically expressed in the strike waves of 1989 and 1991 based on the coal-mining regions. The strikes erupted spontaneously, leading to the formation of strike committees which by-passed the trade union structures. The strikes were often harnessed by management and local authorities to press their own demands for resources on central state bodies, sometimes through the STK in the name of the labour collective, setting a precedent for the use of 'directors' strikes' as a lobbying tactic in the 1990s, but the trade unions were at best marginalised and at worst opposed their own striking members (Clarke, Fairbrother and Borisov, 1995). The strikes brought home to the Party-state authorities the detachment of the trade unions from their members, the trade unions often being made the scapegoat for having failed to articulate workers' legitimate demands through the appropriate channels, and were followed by a large-scale renewal of the trade union apparatus.

## The reform of the trade unions under perestroika

The decentralisation of the systems of economic management and increasing independence of the enterprise under perestroika was associated with radical changes in the structure of the trade unions. At the start of perestroika, in 1985, the trade unions organised virtually the entire adult population of the Soviet Union, including pensioners and students in technical schools and colleges, in 31 enormous branch unions (the largest being the trade union of the Agro-industrial complex, which had 37.4 million members) in 713 000 primary groups, 10 per cent of which had full-time officers. The trade unions employed 7500 health and safety inspectors, but a further 4.6 million union members served as voluntary inspectors or participated in trade union health and safety commissions at the workplace. The unions had an income from membership dues of 3.8 billion roubles, 67.1 per cent of which was allocated to the primary organisations, but this was dwarfed by the 51.9 billion roubles of expenditure from the state social insurance fund administered by the trade unions. The trade unions owned property valued at nine billion roubles, including about 1000 sanatoria, more than 900 tourist centres, 23 000 clubs and cultural centres, 19 000 libraries, around 100 000 pioneer camps and 25 000 sports centres, and they occupied large and prestigious buildings in Moscow and in the centre of every regional capital. The trade union newspaper, *Trud*, had a daily circulation of 20 million, and the unions published 10 mass-circulation journals as well as hundreds of books and pamphlets. The trade unions had a rigidly hierarchical centralised and bureaucratic structure, whose staff had increased by 2.5 times since 1970, in which the apparatus dominated elected union bodies at all levels (Gritsenko, Kadeikina and Makukhina, 1999, pp. 297–9, 305–6).

As an integral part of the ruling apparatus, performing a variety of Party-state functions, the position of the trade unions was undermined by the processes of perestroika and glasnost' and their very existence was threatened by the collapse of the soviet system. A number of factors seriously weakened the trade unions in the period of perestroika. First, as noted in the last section, the trade unions were by-passed by Gorbachev's thwarted attempts to introduce industrial democracy to the soviet workplace, which in 1987 established the Labour Collective Council (STK) rather than the trade union as the representative body of the labour force in its interaction with management. Second, at the XIXth Party Conference in June 1988 Gorbachev proclaimed a clear division of labour between the Party, soviets and executive bodies, with the Party assuming its role as political vanguard with priority being given to ideological work. This removal of the Party from interference in economic life threatened to remove the most important prop supporting the authority of the trade unions. Third, the botched wage reforms introduced by Gorbachev, followed by the growing dislocation of the economy, provoked increasing unrest among workers and sporadic strikes from 1987, culminating in the great strike wave of July 1989 which swept across the coal-mining regions and in which the trade unions found themselves opposing their own members. Fourth, the dismantling of centralised control and the 'transition to a market economy' transferred the locus of wage and employment decision-making to the enterprise, presenting new challenges to trade union primary organisations which they were not well-equipped to meet. In the growing conflicts within the leadership over the course of reform the trade unions generally aligned themselves with the conservative opposition, but the divisions soon penetrated the trade union movement itself.

The All-Union Central Council of Trade Unions (VTsSPS) asserted its 'independence' from Party and state as early as 1987, distancing itself from the project of perestroika, pressing for the continued expansion of the social sphere and for an increased priority to be given to consumption goods industries. At the XIXth Party Conference in 1988 the VTsSPS President, S.A. Shalaev, in the name of freeing the political system from administrative-command management methods, condemned 'party bodies which have begun to understand the transmission belt from the party to the masses as the strict coupling of a gear in a gearbox' (cited Gritsenko, Kadeikina and Makukhina, 1999, p. 314). The VTsSPS increasingly stood out against government plans to introduce market reforms, insisting on very substantial social guarantees, high levels of unemployment pay and so on, as preconditions for any agreement to new legislation. For example, in August 1990 VTsSPS responded to the radical Abalkin plan for a transition to a market economy with an extensive package of demands for the protection of workers (*Soviet Labour Review*, 4, 8, December 1990). This rearguard action was extremely ineffective, and simply meant that the unions lost what little impact on policy they may once have enjoyed.

VTsSPS came under growing pressure to decentralise and democratise its structure in response to the changes of perestroika and glasnost'. The second half of the 1980s saw a steady increase in the role of collective agreements, particularly following the 1987 Law on State Enterprise, which considerably increased the scope for discretion of enterprise management in determining wages and employment and therefore required that more initiative and responsibility be shown by trade union primary groups. The urgency of encouraging more grass roots initiative in the trade unions was increased by the challenge posed to their authority by the new Labour Collective Councils and by the growing unrest among workers which was expressed outside trade union channels. The IInd and IIIrd Plenums of VTsSPS in December 1987 and August 1988 recommended the democratisation of trade union primary groups through regular reporting to union meetings and the direct election of officers and delegates and removed many of the regulations which limited the independence and initiative of primary trade union groups. In September 1989, following the miners' strikes in the summer, the Plenum decided to grant much greater independence to primary groups, endorsed the principle of delegation as the basis for the election of higher trade union bodies and increased the accountability of the apparatus to elected bodies. The Plenum also adopted a new statement defining the tasks of the trade unions which put their role of social protection unambiguously in first place, emphasising this by freeing trade union committees from their responsibility to participate directly in economic management. However, even the unions' official history acknowledges that changes on the ground were few and far between as officials continued in their habitual ways (Gritsenko, Kadeikina and Makukhina, 1999, pp. 316–20).

These structural reforms culminated in the reconstitution of VTsSPS as a new General Confederation of Trades Unions (VKP) in October 1990, which was formed as a federation of independent trade unions in which the branch and republican union organisations had a greater degree of autonomy. The formation of VKP marked the formal separation of the trade unions from Party and state bodies, a separation which was confirmed by the USSR Law on Trade Unions of 10 December 1990. VKP declared that the unions should be the government's 'constructive opponents', opposing the government's plans for privatisation. At the same time, it was decided to establish a Republican trade union organisation in Russia, the only Union Republic which had hitherto not had its own organisation.

In the 1989 miners' strike, the unions had sat at the negotiating table alongside the government, opposite the representatives of workers in the mining regions. In response to the 1991 miners' strikes, VKP co-ordinated its activity closely with Pavlov's Soviet government, opposing the strikers and stressing the need for a new system of collective bargaining within a corporatist tripartite framework, reaching an agreement with the government in April which included a no-strike pledge. However, the agreement was not worth the paper it was written on, because the VKP was disintegrating along with the system of which it was a part, as trade union bodies at every level asserted their independence from higher levels.

The Founding Congress of the Federation of Independent Trade Unions of Russia was held in two stages. In March 1990 an Organisation Committee was established to co-ordinate the formation of Russian committees by the various branch unions and to organise the second stage of the Congress in September, at which the constitution was approved, governing bodies elected and a programme defining FNPR's tactical objectives was adopted. FNPR was established according to the federal principle as a voluntary association of trade unions 'independent of state and economic bodies, political and social organisations, not accountable to them and not under their control'. Although FNPR rejected democratic centralism in favour of voluntarism, FNPR member organisations still had an obligation to carry out the democratically arrived at decisions of elected bodies, although there were no means of enforcing such compliance. At its foundation in September 1990, FNPR claimed to have 54 million members affiliated through 19 branch and 75 regional organisations, covering 72 per cent of the Russian labour force. Igor' Klochkov, a Deputy President and formerly Secretary of VTsSPS, was elected President of FNPR.

Relations between FNPR and VKP were never easy, not least because of a conflict over the allocation of trade union property between the two bodies, but they rapidly deteriorated when FNPR allied itself with Yeltsin in his struggle with Gorbachev on the basis of a common interest in undermining the central Soviet powers and establishing Republican sovereignty. While VKP backed Gorbachev in resisting the miners, FNPR threatened a general strike if Gorbachev did not back down, and later, on the initiative of Klochkov,[1] supported Yeltsin in the Russian Presidential elections. While VKP had signed a no-strike agreement with the Soviet government, FNPR called a one-hour strike on 26 April 1991, with support from Democratic Russia, to protest against higher prices and worsening living conditions, and claimed that 50 million workers had responded, although very few enterprises actually struck, and it is most likely that at best the 'representatives' of 50 million workers had attended meetings. The August 1991 putsch accentuated the division between VKP and FNPR, with FNPR denouncing VKP's failure to distance itself from the plotters, although the FNPR had also sat on its hands at the time. Following the collapse of the Soviet Union at the end of 1991 VKP retained substantial assets, which gave it the leverage which enabled it to sustain itself as the international trade union federation for the newly independent states of the former Soviet Union. In 2001, VKP was still headed by its founding president, Vladimir Shcherbakov.

## Post-soviet trade unions in search of a role

Mikhail Gorbachev's attempts to reform the soviet system had culminated in the collapse of the Party-state and the disintegration of the Soviet Union, destroying the ideology which had rationalised the activity of the trade unions and removing the prop which had underpinned their authority. The trade unions had been marginalised

---

[1] Before his appointment as Secretary of VTsSPS in 1986 Klochkov had been Second Secretary (for ideology) of the Moscow Regional Committee of the CPSU, in which post he had come into contact with Yeltsin when the latter served as First Secretary of the Moscow City Party Committee.

in the programme of perestroika and by-passed by the upsurge of unrest which culminated in the strike waves of 1989 and 1991. The decentralisation of the planning system, the 'transition to a market economy' and mass privatisation demanded that the unions adopt a new role for which they were unprepared, of defending the interests of their members in the face of a government and employers who had abrogated their former responsibility for their well-being.

It is therefore no surprise that the trade unions approached the challenges of perestroika and of the transition to a market economy on the basis of their existing form. The first priority of the trade union apparatus was to retain intact the power, privileges and property of the trade unions, which meant that they had to find a new basis for their authority. While they might proclaim themselves the representatives of the interests of their members, the absence of commitment on the part of their members and the lack of any experience of collective organisation meant that such a claim was a very fragile basis on which to seek to retain their position. The strategy which came naturally to the leadership of the trade unions, and which was most realistic in the situation in which they found themselves, was to seek to survive as organisations by reconstituting and consolidating their relationship with those in power. This was not simply a matter of subordinating themselves to the new authorities, but much more of finding a new role for themselves by reconstituting their traditional functions on new foundations. The trade unions have therefore been not passive victims but active participants in the constitution of the structures of post-soviet power.

The destruction of the Party-state not only removed the external support for the authority of the trade unions, but also removed the support for their hierarchical internal structures. The abandonment of democratic centralism led to a radical decentralisation of the trade unions, which were reconstituted according to a federative structure in which each level of the organisation acted as an independent agent. This meant that the evolution of the trade unions in the wake of the collapse of the soviet system has not been a coherent and integrated process, but one in which each part of the organisation has tried to find its own way. At the federal level, the reconstituted Russian trade unions have sought an accommodation with the organs of Federal government, the Presidency and the Legislature. At the regional level, meanwhile, the trade unions have sought a role by reconstituting and consolidating their relations with the regional and municipal authorities. At the level of the enterprise, by contrast, the trade union organisation has sought to retain and build on its relations with enterprise management, securing its position by fulfilling its traditional social and welfare functions, institutionalising and developing its role in personnel management and even restoring some of its functions of encouraging the development of production, fostering the 'culture of labour' and strengthening labour discipline.

The relative independence of the trade union at the federal, regional and enterprise levels has meant that the trade union has developed different practices and priorities at each of these levels, and this has in turn led to a certain amount of tension within what is known as the 'trade union vertical' (hierarchy) as the different levels make conflicting demands of each other as each level seeks to subordinate the others to the pursuit of its own interests. Moreover, while the trade unions are dependent on the relevant authorities at each level, trade union officers at every level are only too aware of the need for the trade unions to become more independent in order to assert their institutional interests and the interests of their members. However, each sees the key to establishing their independence as lying not in their own hands, but in the hands of the other levels, bemoaning the dependence of the others without taking responsibility for their own situation. Thus, the FNPR leadership sees the dependence of the regional trade union organisations on the regional administration and of enterprise trade unions on the enterprise directors as the main barrier to their being able to assert their own independence as representative of their members, 'the working class', or even 'the Russian people'. At the other end of the scale, enterprise trade union presidents bemoan the dependence of the regional and national organisations on government which prevents them giving enterprise trade unions the support that they need to be able to defend their members and their families.

In the following chapters we will look in more detail at this contradictory process of regeneration and reformation of the Russian trade unions in order to identify the possibilities of and barriers to trade union renewal in Russia.

# 3

# Trade Unions and Politics in Post-Soviet Russia

In this chapter we will look at the transformation of the soviet trade unions under the impact of democratisation and radical economic reform by focusing on the activities of the unions at the Federal level, and in particular at their involvement in politics.

The collapse of the soviet system threatened the very existence of the trade unions that had been such an integral part of that system. The trade unions were very vulnerable to the fate that had befallen the Communist Party, of dissolution of their organisation and nationalisation of their property. This immediately implied that they had to be very cautious in their opposition to the proposals for radical reform that were emerging from the Yeltsin camp. On the other hand, particularly after the imposition of 'shock therapy' in January 1992, unrest amongst union members was reflected in pressure from below for FNPR to constitute itself as an effective opposition to the course of the government's reform programme. FNPR sought to reconcile the conflicting pressures to which it was subject by committing itself strategically to the development of 'social partnership'. 'Social partnership', which we will look at in detail in Chapter 6, offered the trade unions much more than an opportunistic device to enable them to survive the immediate crisis. It also provided a framework within which they could hope to preserve or reconstitute their traditional functions within a radically changed environment.

'Social partnership' requires the participation of the other social partners, employers and the government, which were two arms of the state until the onset of mass privatisation in the middle of 1992. The Federal government had an interest in establishing a framework within which it could negotiate social peace and use trade union endorsement to corroborate its claims to represent the interests of the mass of the working population, but the weakness of the trade unions meant that they had no levers to pressure the government to modify the course of reform. The trade unions sought to increase their bargaining power by holding pickets, demonstrations and days of action and calling or endorsing warning or full-scale strikes, but such attempted displays of strength more often than not backfired by attracting very limited support. The trade unions' political restraint has been reinforced by their vulnerability in a situation in which they depend for their existence on rights and privileges which are embodied in legislation and administrative practices which the state has given and the state can just as easily take away.

This weakness is exemplified by the involvement of FNPR in politics at the Federal level. During the first two years of Russia's existence as an independent state,

FNPR moved from an initial position of 'loyal opposition' to identification with the 'defenders of the White House' in the confrontation between Yeltsin and parliament in October 1993, with potentially disastrous consequences when the government froze the FNPR bank accounts and cut off the telephones, banned the check-off of union dues, took away the unions' responsibility for social insurance and health and safety and threatened to confiscate their property. Only the rapid replacement of the founding President of FNPR by the more conciliatory leader of the Moscow trade unions, Mikhail Shmakov, enabled FNPR to survive the crisis and, much chastened, commit itself to achieve its aims through participation in the institutions of social partnership and lobbying in legislative bodies.

After the disastrous experiences of 1991–3, the FNPR leadership has been wary of organising collective actions and has generally only done so under pressure from the activists. There have been two reasons for FNPR's caution in this respect. First, the risk that such actions will be considered as a provocation by the government, with the consequent risk of retribution, a risk which is exacerbated to the extent that FNPR demonstrations present directly political demands and attract the participation of radical opposition parties and movements. FNPR has accordingly gone to great lengths to insist that its collective actions are in pursuit of purely economic demands and to prevent other forces from associating themselves with FNPR demonstrations, even going to the lengths of changing the time and place of meetings at the last minute. Second, the risk that such demonstrations will not attract a substantial turnout and so will demonstrate not the strength but the weakness of FNPR.

For these reasons, FNPR has put much more faith in legislative activity than in popular mobilisation as the means to advance its institutional interests and the interests of its members. Until Yeltsin's new Russian Constitution of 1993 the trade unions had the right of legislative initiative, which meant that they could submit bills and amendments directly to the legislature. The trade unions had had 100 seats reserved for them in the Congress of People's Deputies of the USSR elected in 1989, but had enjoyed no such privilege in the election to the Russian Congress of People's Deputies in 1990. Nevertheless, FNPR had managed to organise a trade union fraction that backed up its right of legislative initiative. Under the new constitution, following the 1993 election, it was essential that FNPR should establish a lobby in the Duma in support of its legislative proposals. FNPR was successful in assembling a fraction of deputies sympathetic to the cause of the trade unions through which it was able to participate actively in legislative processes and eventually to secure the passage of a number of favourable laws, while amending and blocking other laws which were counter to its interests.

Although FNPR's Constitution defines it as an apolitical organisation, it has never been able to resist involving itself in politics in the attempt to achieve its aims. On the one hand, it has sought to support its lobbying by securing the election of trade union representatives to legislative bodies. On the other hand, it has dreamed of providing the nucleus of a centre-left political movement that can aspire to political power.

Between 1992 and 1995 it sought to pursue these twin objectives through an alliance with Arkadii Vol'skii's Union of Industrialists and Entrepreneurs, an organisation of the old industrial *nomenklatura*, around a programme for the regeneration of domestic industry on the basis of protectionism and state investment. However, Vol'skii's organisation performed very poorly in the 1993 Duma election, in which FNPR did not participate, and the alliance between the two was humiliated in the 1995 Duma election. In the run-up to the 1999 Duma election FNPR established a very close relationship with the Mayor of Moscow, Yurii Luzhkov, whose movement *Otechestvo* was expected to dominate the parliamentary and subsequent presidential elections, particularly when Luzhkov linked up with sacked Premier Primakov. But the dreams of a dominant centre-left coalition were dashed by the poor showing of *Otechestvo* in the Duma election and the withdrawal of Luzhkov and Primakov from the Presidential race, leaving FNPR with little choice but to back the winner by endorsing Vladimir Putin's candidacy for the Presidential election.

## Trade unions and politics in the Yeltsin era

### The challenge of Yeltsin's reforms

Following Yeltsin's counter-coup in August 1991, FNPR found itself in a very difficult situation. On the one hand, it faced pressure from many of its constituent branch and regional organisations to take a firm stand against the more radical reformist policies of the Yeltsin government. On the other hand, it was only too aware how vulnerable was its situation. Already in July 1991, when Yeltsin had banned political organisations from the workplace, there had been an immediate fear that the FNPR trade unions would also fall under this decree. Gorbachev set a further dangerous precedent when he nationalised the property of the Communist Party in August 1991. Yeltsin's suspension of the Communist Party, which he was to ban outright in November 1991, renewed fears that an attack on the trade unions would follow. The new alternative trade unions, which had played a major role in supporting Yeltsin's rise to power and had good connections in his entourage, were clamouring for the abolition of the former soviet trade unions and the nationalisation of their property and it was made known in September 1991 that a draft decree to this effect sat on Yeltsin's desk, awaiting only his signature.

The threat of dissolution had receded somewhat by the autumn of 1991, not least because the government had realised that it was impractical to dissolve the trade unions since it would be impossible to establish overnight state agencies to handle the wide range of social and welfare functions that the unions fulfilled. Nevertheless, over the following years the government repeatedly made FNPR aware that it retained its privileges (and its property) on sufferance and that it would be tolerated only to the extent that its opposition was kept within bounds.

Caught between the pressures from above and from below, FNPR oscillated between passivity and rhetorical opposition to the government. The immediate response of FNPR to Yeltsin's reform programme was to try to establish its credentials as representative of the interests of its members, who constituted the vast majority of the population, and to mobilise them in its support. The FNPR leader, Klochkov, called 'unity of action' days for Oct 21–6 1991, despite Yeltsin's appeal to the trade unions to enter into negotiations with the government over its reform plans. However, FNPR's attempted display of strength back-fired when its demonstrations attracted a derisory turn-out and a warning strike called for November was cancelled, supposedly on the grounds that Yeltsin had accepted FNPR's main demands. The demonstrations also proved counter-productive in identifying the FNPR with the 'red-brown' communist-patriotic opposition.

In January 1992, just as the government launched the economy into hyperinflation by freeing prices, the FNPR Plenum adopted a four-month moratorium on strikes on the grounds that they were pointless and paralysed economic activity. Rather than risk being drawn into a dangerous confrontation with the government, FNPR sought to reconcile the conflicting pressures to which it was subject within the framework of 'social partnership', participating in the Russian Tripartite Commission (RTK) and negotiating an annual General Agreement, which we will discuss in Chapter 6.

The liberalisation of prices in January 1992, which provoked hyperinflation unmatched by wage increases and, in the middle of the year, the first wave of non-payment of wages, presented FNPR with its first challenge. Despite FNPR's moratorium on strikes called in January 1992, spontaneous strikes, subsequently supported by the trade unions, erupted, particularly in coal-mining, health and education, all of which depended on government funding, the strikes being settled by the government through the RTK and direct negotiation with promises of pay rises and cash to pay for them.

FNPR was coming under increasing pressure to act more effectively in support of those hardest hit by hyperinflation, but it was divided internally over its attitude to the reforms. Some branch unions, particularly the metallurgists, were strongly in favour of the transition to a market economy, which they anticipated would markedly improve the position of their branch and their members, while others, particularly the budget-sector unions, such as health and education, and the military-industrial complex were in the front ranks of the victims of reforms and demanded government action (and money). FNPR tried to paper over the cracks by insisting that it supported the general direction of reform, but differed over its details. However, the difference over the details amounted to a comprehensive programme of opposition to the Yeltsin programme, embodied in FNPR's Declaration on Socio-Economic Policy issued in March 1992, which aimed at averting the collapse of production and living standards and included a proposed minimum wage of 1000 roubles a month. Following a visit by Klochkov to Japan, FNPR launched its 'Spring Campaign', 'Days of Unity of Action of Russian Trade Unions', with the slogan 'Market Prices – Market Wages'.

Klochkov threatened to demand the resignation of the government, but the action was not a success because it again did not get mass support. Although FNPR continued to make veiled threats through its frequent references to the dangers of rising social tension, its criticism was largely rhetorical because it knew that it could not risk a confrontation with the government.

Having made no headway with its half-hearted (and internally divisive) attempt at popular mobilisation, FNPR threw in its lot with the 'industrial *nomenklatura*', becoming actively involved in the formation of a centre-left 'loyal opposition' around Arkadii Vol'skii's Union of Industrialists and Entrepreneurs, joining with Vol'skii to create the 'Assembly of Social Partnership' in July 1992 (the initiative came from FNPR, which could not join Vol'skii's centrist party 'Civic Union' because it was constitutionally barred from engaging in political activity), and jointly publishing a newspaper, *Rabochaya tribuna*. Although Vol'skii's organisation was nominally an employers' body, the leaders of FNPR and VKP played a dominant role: FNPR and VKP officials filled one-fifth of the seats at the November 1993 plenum of Vol'skii's Union.

FNPR was spurred into action again in September 1992, when Yeltsin signed a decree nationalising the FNPR social insurance fund, an action which was not referred to the moribund Tripartite Commission. In response, the FNPR General Council announced a series of new actions in the run-up to the December Congress of People's Deputies, but these demonstrations continued to attract a derisory turnout, largely confined to apparatchiks, pensioners and peasants, many of whom were bussed in for the purpose. However, as Yeltsin's confrontation with the Congress loomed, he did not want a confrontation with FNPR and, at the end of September, following negotiations between Klochkov and Gaidar, the decree was annulled, although the administration of the social security funds was modified so that they remained nominally the property of the state, although still administered by the trade unions, which simply implied, at least in principle, that the unions would have to account to the government for the use of these funds.

The replacement of Gaidar by Chernomyrdin as Prime Minister in December 1992 was at first acclaimed as a victory for the coalition between FNPR and the industrial lobby and boded well for relations between the government and FNPR. *Rabochaya tribuna* reported that Chernomyrdin and Klochkov had met and agreed that 'intelligently organised and fairly paid labor plus tough discipline at all levels – there is the formula for resolving Russia's current problems' (*Rabochaya tribuna*, 5.2.93, p. 1 cited Connor, 1996, p. 108). However, Chernomyrdin did not live up to expectations and there was no significant change in the course of the government as Yeltsin moved into his confrontation with the Supreme Soviet, headed by Khasbulatov.

In parallel with its rhetorical declarations and occasional demonstrations, FNPR had been actively lobbying its interests in the Supreme Soviet of Russia, which was moving into increasingly sharp opposition to Yeltsin. In addition to a trade union fraction which, according to FNPR, could count on the support of 89 deputies, FNPR had been cultivating connections with non-party political allies, to avoid being accused of engaging in politics, among opposition fractions in the Supreme Soviet and the apparatus of Khasbulatov.

## FNPR in the confrontation between Yeltsin and Parliament

In the confrontation between Yeltsin and the Congress of People's Deputies in March 1993 FNPR stood on the side, calling for simultaneous elections of parliament and president in the near future. In the middle of the year there were new waves of protest in the regions as the budget squeeze led to delays in the payment of public sector wages. In the summer the coal miners and workers in defence plants were particularly active, while in September the teachers and scientists took action. FNPR repeatedly warned of growing unrest, unavoidable consequences if the government did not change course, and so on. The government issued an appeal to trade union organisations and labour collectives over the head of FNPR, charging that branch trade union leaders were increasingly making political demands and calling for mass collective action, work stoppages and even civil disobedience instead of engaging in constructive dialogue within the established framework of social partnership. FNPR replied on 26 August with its own appeal in which it declared its readiness 'to struggle for the interests of labouring people with all the methods available to trade unions' (Gritsenko, Kadeikina and Makukhina, 1999, p. 363).

FNPR planned an autumn campaign of meetings and warning strikes building up through September to a general strike at the beginning of October, but no dates had been fixed and the campaign was cut short by Yeltsin's suspension of parliament on 21 September, which was accompanied by dire warnings to FNPR to stay out of politics. The FNPR Executive Committee responded to Yeltsin's challenge the following day, declaring that,

> The trade unions do not aspire to political power, but they cannot accept the trampling on constitutional rights and freedoms, because it inevitably entails a series of violations of the socio-economic rights of working people. The unconstitutional limitation of the activity of one of the branches of power leads to the strengthening of the other and opens the way to a regime of personal power. This can be called nothing other than a *coup d'état* (Gritsenko, Kadeikina and Makukhina, 1999, p. 364).

FNPR called for workers to use all available means, including strikes, to protest the anti-constitutional actions and again called for simultaneous presidential and parliamentary elections. Klochkov, meanwhile, called on the Moscow regional organisation to strike and to join the defenders of the White House (Connor, 1996, 130). However, the Moscow Federation of Trade Unions (MFP) opposed Klochkov's radical stand, warning trade unionists 'not to be drawn into bloodshed while all means of defending the constitutional order have not been employed' (Buketov, 1995, cited Simon, 2000, p. 131).

The government was equally sharp and rather more effective in its response to FNPR. On 23 September First Deputy Prime Minister and chair of the Russian Tripartite Commission (RTK), Vladimir Shumeiko, invited the alternative unions to an extraordinary meeting of the RTK, which was boycotted by FNPR, at which he announced that he had just signed a decree banning the check-off of union dues (Connor, 1996, p. 130–1). On 28 September 1993 Yeltsin's Decree 1503 limited the rights of the trade unions to administer the state social insurance system, transferring control of the Social Insurance Fund to the state to administer 'with the participation of the trade unions',[1] which the trade unions immediately denounced as a violation of the government's declared aspiration to create social partnership and construct a democratic and legal state. The trade unions also lost their responsibility for health and safety, having already lost their right of legislative initiative under Yeltsin's new 1993 constitution. There were calls from Yeltsin's supporters for the liquidation of FNPR. On 28 September FNPR held an emergency meeting of regional and branch leaders (already in Moscow for the VKP Congress) to consider a strike, at which Klochkov backed off, declaring that local union organisations were not ready for a mass strike, and the meeting called for the sides to find a rational compromise and achieve a peaceful solution to their conflicts. Nevertheless, the FNPR leadership made preparations to continue to work underground if necessary (*Segodnya* 28.9.93, p. 2 cited Simon, 2000, p. 131).

### FNPR's change of line

After the fall of the White House the FNPR Executive denounced extremist violence and called for calm, order and legality to allow the people to express their will in free elections. The meeting decided to call an extraordinary congress for 28 October. This provided the opportunity for the opposition within FNPR to unseat Klochkov, who resigned on 11 October and was replaced by the Moscow Federation leader, Mikhail Shmakov, who was formally elected on 28 October at the IInd (Extraordinary) Congress (it was reported that Klochkov's resignation had been demanded by Shumeiko, Connor, 1996, p. 132). The Congress was attended by 253 delegates from 37 branch trade unions and 247 delegates from 77 regional associations, claiming to represent 60 million members. Shumeiko, who gave a very conciliatory speech, even on the issue of social insurance, also attended the Congress. Shumeiko proposed the unification of the unions into one centre, which was considered by the Congress, but got nowhere, also being rejected by the alternative unions.

---

[1]  The trade unions were given seven seats on the 26-person governing body of the social insurance fund. In early 1994 a scandal arose when it was revealed that the Social Insurance Fund had been transferred to the FNPR's bank, and the chairman of the fund, Yurii Shatorenko, was appointed as chairman of the bank in place of former FNPR boss Klochkov.

Considerable attention was paid to organisational questions, and the FNPR Constitution was amended, stressing that FNPR acts on the basis of the 'principles of freedom, independence, democracy and self-management, observance of complete independence, equality of the rights and duties of member organisations according to the conventional norms of international law'. Shmakov emphasised the need to move beyond the question of survival to address the strategy for the development of the unions in new economic conditions, arguing that open pressure on power structures without considering economic realities undermined the mechanisms of social partnership from within. He also stressed the need to take account of different branch and regional interests in formulating demands and the need to maintain political neutrality. The Congress considered a draft programme document, 'Freedom, Justice, Solidarity', based on the MFP programme, that was eventually adopted in April 1994.

Shmakov's speech to the Congress expressed the dissatisfaction with Klochkov's leadership that had been mounting steadily as the differential impact of reforms led to a growing divergence of views among the branch unions. Dissatisfaction with the position of the FNPR leadership had already emerged at a meeting of the FNPR Presidium on 5 April 1992 at which a number of unions (including the shipbuilders, seafarers, coal-miners, engineering workers, metallurgists and agricultural workers, as well as the Moscow Federation) criticised the leadership's authoritarian and unconstitutional methods, demanding that the question of confidence in the leadership should be put to the next FNPR Plenum. The Moscow Federation, miners and metallurgists walked out of the Presidium meeting in protest at the leadership's draft resolution proposing that the government transfer all social insurance funds and trade union property from the jurisdiction of branch and regional unions to that of FNPR. The FNPR strike call in October 1992 had brought these divisions to a head, with the metallurgists withdrawing from the Federation on 15 October as a result, although most regional committees of the union remained affiliated to the FNPR regional organisations.[1] Shmakov's ousting of Klochkov represented a move away from the legacy of authoritarianism towards a much greater sensitivity to the divergence of interests among the branch unions. It also represented a move away from the confrontational politics that had ended with the storming of the White House towards an emphasis on the 'social partnership' that had been developed by Shmakov with the Moscow City government, a turn which was reinforced by the results of the

---

[1]  The metallurgists had only voted narrowly to affiliate to the FNPR in the first place, and had been courted by Burbulis ever since the autumn of 1991. There was an element of conflict of personal ambition in the withdrawal of the metallurgists, and there was also the question of control of social insurance funds. The decision of GMPR to leave was taken by its plenum. GMPR leader Misnik denounced FNPR for its effective rejection of a market economy, of which GMPR largely approved, and its desire to return to the administrative-command system. He denounced the control of FNPR by the apparatus and Executive and its unwillingness to negotiate and compromise with the government. He promised to take his share of social insurance funds.

December 1993 Duma election.[1] At the same time, the election result raised the question of the political affiliation of FNPR. While the centrist Civic Union had been thrashed, the Communist Party and the Agrarians, with whom the private sympathies of many trade union leaders still lay, had put up a strong showing. In the elections eight out of 54 trade union candidates were successful, and Klochkov was elected on the list of the Agrarian Union.

After the election, there was a fear within the presidential apparatus that FNPR would use its considerable funds and organisational resources to support the resurgent Communists. In December 1993 Yeltsin signed a decree authorising an audit of the assets of 'social organisations' and the presidential apparatus again let it be known in February 1994 that a decree appropriating the unions' assets had been drawn up and only awaited Yeltsin's signature.[2] On 10 March 1994 Yeltsin launched his 'Memorandum of Civic Accord' at a meeting to which all the significant trade union leaders were invited, calling on all social partners to commit themselves to the peaceful resolution of their differences, including a commitment on the part of trade unions to refrain from calling or endorsing strikes not immediately related to wages, working conditions and the preservation of jobs,[3] the main political purpose of Yeltsin's initiative being to draw a line between the centre and the left-right 'extremes'. FNPR welcomed the initiative, hoping to be able to extract more than paper concessions from their assent to the memorandum, which they signed on 28 April, although reserving the right to strike in the event of the non-fulfilment of agreements as a result of the failings of the authorities, and the Accord was signed by 31 of FNPR's 42 constituent branch unions.

### Trade unions during the first Duma (1994–6)

Although FNPR's favoured party had been trounced in the election for the first Duma, the new Duma included strong representation of parties opposed to the government's reform programme. Faced with continuing intransigence on the part of the government, FNPR placed increasing emphasis on lobbying the legislature to secure the passage or amendment of legislation in the interests of its member

---

[1]   The Moscow Federation under Shmakov had tended to take a syndicalist position, flirting with both the radical left and the 'patriotic' right. Initially its relations with Luzhkov, then Deputy Mayor of Moscow, were combative, but after some time Luzhkov came to see that he could use the trade unions to his advantage. Although MFP pioneered social partnership with the Moscow City government, it had criticised FNPR for participating in the RTK (Teague, 1994).

[2]   When the audit eventually took place the unions were able to show that their assets had been financed overwhelmingly from union funds (rather than from social insurance funds) and on that basis secured their title.

[3]   All parties also pledged to refrain from campaigning for early federal elections. The government promised to reduce inflation, to accelerate the restructuring of the economy, to take steps to eliminate budget debt for wages, to conduct an active social policy aimed at stabilising and increasing the living standards of the population and carry out various other socio-economic measures.

organisations and their members, with its demonstrations performing a symbolic role, allowing the activists to let off steam and providing some indicator of the depth of social tension and opposition to the government. By contrast to the 'days of action' organised under Klochkov's leadership, which were increasingly confrontational, those under Shmakov were much more restrained. While many regional organisations put forward political demands, the official slogans of the days of action focused on specific economic demands, particularly the timely payment of wages, increasing the minimum wage and reducing unemployment, which were for FNPR the key points in its negotiations with the government.

Following the December 1993 election, FNPR had to build new alliances in order to have an impact in the State Duma, where budgetary decisions had a major impact on many trade unionists and reform of the labour and trade union legislation held out both threats and opportunities. The unions even had some hopes that the social insurance funds might be restored to them by legislative action. FNPR established a new department for interaction with parliament and social movements, responsible primarily for lobbying in the Duma, through which FNPR managed to organise an informal trade union lobby, comprising 40 deputies recommended by FNPR member organisations, and to achieve observer status. FNPR also established co-operation agreements with three parties: *Nash Dom Rossii*, the Communist Party and *Yabloko*. This was backed up by the lobbying of deputies in their constituencies organised by FNPR's regional organisations. All of this enabled FNPR to play an active role in discussion of draft legislation and, through the trade union lobby, to table its own proposals.

FNPR's participation in the Tripartite Commission and its lobbying in the Duma were supported by its regular days of action. FNPR held a peaceful May Day demonstration in 1994 around the theme of reconstruction and reconciliation as part of the new strategy of 'passive protest', which included the symbolic picketing of government buildings by representative delegations, but no longer the attempt to organise mass demonstrations. As part of the May Day activity, FNPR claimed to have collected 2.5 million signatures in support of its demands from 37 regions (FNPR, 1996, p. 93). However, new waves of strikes broke out in the coalfields in the first half of the year, on 2 June regional engineering centres held a picket in Moscow and on 9 June defence industry workers held a day of action. FNPR's passivity again met with some internal opposition. A meeting of leaders of its affiliated organisations at the beginning of September 1994 called for mass demonstrations on 27 October, demanding an increase in the minimum wage, measures against inflation, a halt to the rise in unemployment (which had increased rapidly in the first half of 1994) and the timely payment of wages. Shmakov insisted that these were purely economic demands called 'only to correct the government's course' (ITAR-TASS 26.10.94 cited Simon, 2000, p. 134), but many of the local demonstrations were dominated by political slogans demanding the resignation of the government and early presidential elections (these demands were adopted in 23 regions, Gritsenko, Kadeikina and

Makukhina, 1999, p. 353). The meetings were somewhat better attended than those called two years before, although not by anything like the eight million in 73 regions claimed by FNPR.[1] At a meeting of the FNPR General Council on 22 December 1994 Mikhail Shmakov threatened to withdraw FNPR's signature from the Memorandum of Civic Accord and launch mass acts of protests if their negotiations with the government did not produce results, but Shmakov was suspected of playing to the gallery. The FNPR Executive called for a demonstration to protest falling living standards on 12 April 1995, FNPR calling for a 'change in the course of the reforms', and this too was well attended, FNPR claiming that there had been two million people on the streets, with a further ten million participating in meetings. Again, many regions demanded the resignation of the government and early presidential elections, but the leadership of FNPR was much more concerned with its parliamentary lobbying and with the manoeuvring in the run-up to the December 1995 Duma election. The May Day demonstrations were also much larger than in previous years, the union ranks being swelled by the KPRF and other left and 'national-patriotic' organisations. A further Day of Action was called for 30 November 1995, immediately before the Duma election.

The demonstrations allowed FNPR to demonstrate to the government that it was a significant force for social peace in being able to channel such criticism into harmless protest, but they were never part of a concerted FNPR campaign of opposition. On 1 June 1994 Shmakov had declared to the General Council,

> Today it is clear that a decisive, open confrontation with the regime would throw our trade unions into the backwaters of public life, would deprive them of all of the constitutional means of defending the interests of the toilers, and would be a real threat to the existence of the Federation and of FNPR unions as a whole (quoted in Mandel, 1995).

FNPR's lobbying of the Duma involved slow and patient work behind the scenes that was eventually crowned with some success, most notably in the passage of a raft of trade union and labour legislation in 1995–6 which not only consolidated most of the trade union and labour rights inherited from the Soviet Union, but also heavily favoured FNPR, as a national trade union federation, over the more fragmented alternative trade unions. FNPR also claimed credit for securing nine increases in the derisory minimum wage between 1993 and 1995 and for securing the repeal of the 'excess wages tax' which penalised enterprises which paid relatively high wages. It also secured the passage of laws on the subsistence minimum and on the payment of compensation for the delayed payment of wages, but these were vetoed by Yeltsin.

---

[1]   FNPR relies on reports from its regional organisations, which have a strong interest in exaggerating the degree of activism in their region since this is an important indicator of the strength of the regional organisation.

## The unions in the 1995 election

The question of the political affiliation of the trade unions came to the fore again in the run-up to the 1995 Duma elections, although many trade unionists could still see little point in participation in the electoral process, expecting to achieve their aims through corporatist structures and the beneficence of the state. However, Shmakov presented electoral participation as a much more productive avenue than mass protests, which he regarded as being subordinate to the electoral campaign, declaring that it would be irresponsible to exacerbate the current social crisis (Simon, 2000, p. 139). In December 1994 the FNPR Executive established a committee to negotiate with parties and movements regarding participation in the election. FNPR recommended member organisations to start work selecting candidates and organising election campaigns in single-mandate constituencies and on 17 February 1995 set up the pre-election organisation *Profsoyuzy Rossii* (Trade Unions of Russia) to provide a framework for its political activity. In the middle of March Shmakov appealed to various left and centre parties and movements to start discussions about collaboration to form a centre-left block in the elections, but the appeal met with no response. In May it was reported that FNPR was to form an electoral block with the Russian United Industrial Party (ROPP, a new Vol'skii front) and the Union of Realists, but this anticipated the discussion to take place at a trade union conference on the question of trade union participation in the elections.

At its conference on 1 June FNPR adopted its basic election platform and established *Profsoyuzy Rossii – na vybory!* (Trade Unions of Russia – to the elections!), registered on 24 June, which received declarations of support from 35 trade unions, of which 25 were FNPR affiliates, and 55 regional organisations. The platform recognised the need for reform and economic modernisation, but stressed the need for a new direction of government policy putting the interests of working people and domestic producers first and defining the social guarantees which FNPR deputies would press on the government, including the right to work, the right to a fair wage, the right to holidays, to free education, the right to a pension and health care, the right to housing and so on. The programme included a section on economic democracy which saw collective agreements as the form of workers' participation in the determination of wages and working conditions, participation in the management of production and in the formation of state socio-economic policy through their trade unions; control of investment, prices, imports and exports; preservation of a strong social sector of the economy with an increased role for trade unions in their management, and equality of all forms of property. The programme stressed its support for democratic political rights and freedoms. In order to get the country out of the crisis, the programme recommended such mechanisms of state regulation as changes in tax policy, protectionism, regulation of prices on raw materials, energy, subsistence goods, monopoly products, restrictions on the income of monopolised branches and strict control of the use of state property.

There was lively debate in the meeting about whom to support. The compromise decision was to continue discussion to try to form a centre-left block, but also to free the hands of local organisations to allow them to form a block with those political forces supported by the workers in their regions. The conference rejected an alliance with KPRF, unless it became a centre-left party. Negotiations with the government-supported Ivan Rybkin block broke down because the latter would not endorse the FNPR programme or give FNPR enough places on its list. Despite the preference expressed at the June conference for FNPR to go into the elections with an independent list, on 5 September, at the second stage of the conference, FNPR again sealed its alliance with Arkadii Vol'skii's Union of Industrialists and Entrepreneurs in the elections (the Union of Realists ended up joining Rybkin) by establishing the social-political organisation *Profsoyuzy i promyshleniki Rossii – Soyuz truda* (Trade Unions and Industrialists of Russia – Union of Labour) headed by Shmakov, Vol'skii and the President of VKP, Vladimir Shcherbakov, which went into the election under the slogan 'Wages – Employment – Legality'.

There was a lot of opposition within FNPR to renewing the alliance with Vol'skii, but Andrei Isaev, Ideology Secretary of FNPR, explained that such an alliance was possible because the fundamental cleavage was between the government and industry, not between workers and employers. However, the fragmentation of the unions and the sectional lobbying character of Russian politics (Buketov and Nikul'nikov, 1996, p. 6) was expressed in the fact that a number of branch and regional unions followed their own independent course in the elections. On the one hand, the metallurgists, who had left FNPR, formed an alliance with *Yabloko* through which a number of union officials, headed by the President of the union, Boris Misnik, were assigned positions on the party list.[1] On the other hand, the Unions of Trade Workers and Educational Workers aligned themselves with Women of Russia and others with the Agrarians, while several individual trade union candidates were backed by the Communists and three branch unions set up their own political organisations to endorse and campaign for any candidates who would declare themselves in support of the union's programme.

The motor industry trade union was a co-founder of the Russian Motorists' Party, the transport workers formed the All-Russian Transport Workers' Social-Political Movement and the coalminers' union, Rosugleprof, established the social-political association Miners of Russia. The former two organisations included both trade unions and employers' organisations. Miners of Russia was initially established by the trade union on its own, but later tried unsuccessfully to secure campaign finance by including the quasi-ministerial management body, Rosugol', and the coal

---

[1]   Under the electoral system introduced in 1993 each elector in each constituency votes for one individual and one party. The Duma comprises 225 members elected directly from single-mandate constituencies and a further 225 elected from federal and regional party lists according to the proportion of the vote received by each party that gets over the five per cent threshold across the whole of the Russian Federation.

associations as collective members. Miners of Russia commissioned ISITO to conduct surveys in one mining and one non-mining region to establish the attitude of the electors to miners' candidates. On the basis of the results of the survey it was decided not to put forward an all-Russian party list, but to encourage regional committees to put forward candidates in the coal-mining regions and to endorse all candidates who declared their support for the miners' minimal programme. In the event Rostov was the only region that was sufficiently active to put forward its own candidate, Vladimir Katal'nikov being elected for the Shakhti single-mandate constituency.

Overall, the results of the 1995 Duma election were a disappointment for the trade unions. *Soyuz truda* secured only 1.59 per cent of the party list vote, well below the threshold required to secure Duma representation (and less than was polled by Viktor Anpilov's revanchist *Komunisty – Trudovaya Rossiya – za Sovetskii Soyuz*), with its highest vote being in the impoverished Ivanovo oblast, a stronghold of Vol'skii's organisation, where it received 9.8 per cent of the poll. A total of only nine trade unionists were elected to the Duma, including Katal'nikov, Misnik and two other metallurgists on the *Yabloko* list, four on the Communist Party list and one endorsed by *Soyuz truda* from a Krasnodar constituency. *Soyuz truda* was effectively dissolved. Shmakov drew five lessons from the election campaign: 1) that there had been insufficient solidarity between the unions; 2) that many people on elected trade union bodies could not manage an election campaign properly; 3) that it had suffered from bad information provision; 4) a lack of a political strategy; and 5) financial difficulties (Gritsenko, Kadeikina and Makukhina, 1999, pp. 370–1).

Underlying the lack of commitment of trade union organisations to FNPR's electoral strategy lay the fact that the 'industrial lobby' had lost any coherence that it might once have had. Privatisation had intensified the fragmentation of interests so that in place of a single industrial lobby, enterprise directors looked to their own efforts or to more narrowly branch or regionally based organisations in lobbying for their interests. Although social partnership had made slow progress at the federal level, with successive governments showing little sympathy for the trade unions and the annual General Agreement offering no more than vague promises and empty declarations of intent, at branch, regional and enterprise level the institutions of social partnership had put down much more solid roots and the trade unions had established their own allegiances, which did not necessarily coincide with those of the FNPR leadership. Social partnership had integrated the trade unions into the emerging political system, but at the cost of their political subordination and of reproducing divisions of branch and regional interest within their own ranks. The result was that branch and regional trade union organisations subordinated themselves to diverse sectional and regional interests and there was no concerted trade union campaign.

**Lobbying the second Duma (1996–9)**

The political activity of the trade unions during the 1996–9 parliament was oriented to the development of the institutions of social partnership at all levels and the articulation of a constructive opposition to the course of economic reform. The quiet lobbying and bureaucratic dialogue with the government was accompanied by FNPR's regular days of action, which had by now acquired a ritual quality. Although the 'days of action' were progressively better organised, many regions and branch unions did not give them more than token support and the FNPR leadership did not put much faith in such actions as a means of achieving its aim of overcoming the intransigence of the government. It claimed that the massive turnouts at its demonstrations had forced the government to address the problem of the non-payment of wages and benefits, and in 1998 had even forced the dismissal of Chernomyrdin as Prime Minister for failing to deal with the issue, but at best the demonstrations brought home to the government the electoral risks involved in not resolving the problem, and FNPR recognised that the demonstrations had little impact on the government's willingness to make substantive concessions to the trade unions. Moreover, the FNPR leadership was always afraid that its demonstrations would compromise its democratic credentials and its attempt to establish a centrist political niche by providing a vehicle for left and 'national patriotic' forces.

Yeltsin emphasised the importance of social partnership in his address to the Federation Council in March 1997, adding that 'it is difficult to overvalue the trade unions' role in the future regulation of such a relationship' (cited Hoffer, 1997, n. 115, p. 55), but the FNPR leadership came increasingly to see the futility of attempts to pressure the government to change the course of its reforms and to take account of the interests of the mass of the population and focused its attention instead on the Duma, in which the opposition again had a clear majority, and on regional governors and legislatures. When a journalist suggested that the trade unions should adopt more effective forms of work than things like the Tripartite Commission, Shmakov replied

> Of course. But one should not forget that the miserable expenditure items of the budget are adopted by the State Duma. With them it is possible to lobby not for branch or territorial interests, but to fill with money the articles [of the budget] which are protected by the laws on science, education and so on. I think that we should not only gesture to the government, the Duma must share responsibility with it. I have already given the example of the minimum wage – who postponed adopting a law which is so urgent for the workers?... The Duma says time and again that everything is bad here, but every year it adopts the budget! The parliamentarians claim that on Okhotnii Ryad [where the Duma is located] they express the will of the electors, and call on the trade unions to bring down the government! Where is the logic in that? Why does the Duma not use its legal right to do it itself? (*Vesti FNPR*, 3–4, 1998, pp. 27, 33).

In accordance with these changing priorities, the character of FNPR's demonstrations changed. While May Day continued to be celebrated in the traditional way with mass demonstrations, days of action focused more on token pickets of executive and legislative buildings and the holding of meetings which would transmit messages and appeals to the appropriate authorities, although FNPR could not prevent its more radical regional organisations from organising more militant actions or even participating in the actions called by the Communist Party and other left organisations.

An All-Russian protest action under the slogan 'For work, wages and social guarantees' was organised in two stages, the first demonstrations being held on 5 November 1996, and the second being called for 27 March 1997, with a series of demands relating to the payment of debts for wages and benefits with compensation; the working out by the government of a series of anti-crisis measures to secure the growth of production and the preservation and creation of jobs;[1] the realisation of a socially orientated economy and the unconditional realisation of the rights of labour. According to FNPR, 15 million people turned out on 5 November 1996, with strikes in 41 regions, picketing of local government buildings in 37 regions and demonstrations and meetings in 59 regions, while it claimed that on 27 March 1997 over 20 million people participated in meetings and demonstrations and 5.1 million in strikes in 16 204 enterprises, 70 per cent of which were schools, although the Interior Ministry estimated that 1.8 million were involved in public demonstrations and Goskomstat reported only 2658 strikes. The March Day of Action was a landmark in being supported not only by FNPR but also by the two alternative trade union federations, the All-Russian Confederation of Labour (VKT) and the Confederation of Labour of Russia (KTR), and by the International Confederation of Free Trade Unions (ICFTU), which announced an international campaign of solidarity with Russian workers over the non-payment of wages, in collaboration with the ILO, which culminated in an international conference in Moscow in November 1997. The demands put forward were also endorsed by a resolution of the Duma, which Shmakov addressed on 11 April.

A further Day of Action 'in defence of the constitutional rights of workers' was called for 3 February 1998 in conjunction with the Duma hearings on the legal protection of the labour rights of employees. In the course of this action, FNPR reported that there had been work stoppages in seven regions, picketing of government buildings in 11 regions, demonstrations in two regions, meetings of the tripartite commission in eight regions, and meetings of labour collectives, trade union activists, meetings with government representatives and deputies in 43 regions. Primary organisations were mandated to hold union meetings during February and

---

[1]   As in the past, FNPR's demands revealed its own weakness: while it could express the grievances of its members it was unable to formulate any alternative programme, demanding instead that the government should do so.

March to discuss furthur collective action. The failure of the government to meet its commitment under the General Agreement to ensure the payment of wage debts was the pretext for more a militant All-Russian Action on 9 April 1998 'For the full payment of wages', at which FNPR claimed the participation of 14 million people, with more than two million striking at 12 000 enterprises and organisations with unpaid wages, 39 regions demanding the resignation of the President. In July the FNPR Executive decided to make preparations for a General Strike in October, but in August the General Council, endorsing the demands of FNPR member organisations for Yeltsin to resign, called for a further day of action on 7 October, under the slogan 'No to the pernicious economic reforms', in which FNPR claimed 25 million people participated, of whom 12 million participated in strikes and work stoppages.

Although little progress was made by the government in resolving the problem of the non-payment of wages, and real wages fell sharply in the burst of inflation following the August 1998 financial crisis, FNPR was very cautious about organising further mass protests for fear of playing into the hands of the Communist Party and other left opposition groupings. Although FNPR supported the All-Russian action of the teachers' union in January 1999, in March, Shmakov, as co-ordinator of the trade union side of the Tripartite Commission, and the co-ordinator of the employers' side issued a joint statement condemning the 'campaign of psychological pressure on the government', insisting that the present government should be given 'the opportunity to work normally and to be judged not by its political complexion but by the real results of its activity' (*Vesti FNPR*, 3–4, 1999, p. 18). In place of the traditional Spring Day of Action, the FNPR General Council called for enterprises and regional organisations to hold meetings of trade union activists, to which they should invite representatives of the employers and local authorities, to consider the future course of trade union action and report back, although local organisations were also permitted to organise local collective actions appropriate to their situation. Member organisations reported that five million people had participated in 100 000 such meetings. The traditional May Day demonstration was kept low-key, FNPR claiming the participation of only 2.8 million people.

Reviewing the results of the May Day actions, the FNPR Executive condemned the passivity of many of its regional and primary organisations, which had made little or no effort to organise the meetings and demonstrations proposed by FNPR's General Council. Two-thirds of labour collectives had not organised meetings, nine regional federations had only held festive and sporting events on May Day, four had only participated in demonstrations organised by political parties or the regional administration and a dozen more had organised poorly attended meetings and demonstrations. Eight regional organisations were charged with having failed to organise May Day demonstrations for several years, their passivity being exploited by 'various political parties and movements' which organised such measures in their place (*Vesti FNPR*, 5–6, 1999, pp. 1–12).

FNPR's lobbying in the Duma was co-ordinated with its negotiations with the government in the Tripartite Commission, where legislative proposals and draft laws were discussed in detail, and in the General Agreement, which included government commitments to introduce various items of legislation and ratify a number of ILO Conventions. Where the government was resistant, FNPR could introduce legislation on its own initiative on the basis of the trade union block in the Duma. It also lobbied in the Duma to block government proposals, claiming to have succeeded in securing the rejection by the Duma of a Law on Labour Collectives, which would have eroded trade union representative rights, in December 1997 and preventing two attempts of the government in 1998 to reduce the dues paid by employers to the off-budget social funds. FNPR was successful in securing amendments to the new Law on the Russian Tripartite Commission, signed by the President in May 1999 and in securing the rejection by the Duma of a draft Law on Employers' Associations, which had ignored FNPR's proposals. FNPR secured the rejection of a government draft law on the social insurance fund in April 1999 in favour of its favoured alternative, which was signed in July. FNPR also succeeded in getting a set of amendments to the Labour Code through both houses of parliament, but Yeltsin vetoed these. FNPR's proposals were also taken into account in a new basic law on health and safety, signed in July 1999 and in the 1999 Law on Employment, which included an increase in the rate of unemployment benefit, but among the last acts of the second Duma were the rejection of a law on the minimum wage and deferral of consideration of an increase in the budget sector wage scale, which had been strongly supported by FNPR.

Much of FNPR's lobbying concerned issues of general economic policy, such as taxation, tariff and investment policy, in which it collaborated with the industrial lobby in seeking to increase government support for domestic producers, though on the issue of taxation FNPR was opposed to shifting the burden from the taxation of enterprises to income and value-added taxes. FNPR could also count on qualified support from employers in its lobbying for the introduction of laws on social partnership and on employers' associations and even on minimum social guarantees. Even the most pressing issue of the non-payment of wages was regarded by FNPR, though not by the alternative unions, as the responsibility primarily of the government rather than the employers, and was addressed by lobbying the government and the legislature. As FNPR President Shmakov noted in an interview,

> We understand that the majority of enterprises are pauperised not through the fault of their leaders, but as a result of the economic conditions pressing on them. Addressing demands to the directors and entrepreneurs at the same time forces them to move, to insist on the adoption of laws that will permit the recovery of production. Everyone must shift for himself (*Vesti FNPR*, 3–4, 1998, pp. 23–4).

A central issue with regard to the non-payment of wages was that of the relative priority accorded to the payment of wages and taxes by cash-strapped employers. The issue became acute in 1996, since the government had borrowed heavily in the pre-election period (short-term and at very high interest) to pay off wages, and the trade unions and Duma deputies feared, with good cause, that after the election the government would step up tax collection at the expense of wages. Under the existing tax legislation, taxes had a claim on enterprise's balances prior to wages, and the tax inspectorate even had the right to sequester enterprise funds allocated to the payment of wages. In July 1996 the State Duma amended Article 855 of the Civil Code to instruct enterprises and banks to give priority to the payment of wages (and payments to pension, social security and employment funds, which by law have to be paid at the same time as wages) over payment of taxes. Yeltsin signed the amendment, which had been promoted by FNPR and included in the 1996 General Agreement, into law on 12 August.

The result of the change in the law was predictable: tax payments slumped in August and the rate of growth of private sector wage arrears slowed, arrears actually falling in November. Prime Minister Chernomyrdin blamed the slump on the change in the law, proposing that the government and Duma should review it. A memo of 30 October from Finance Minister Livshits to Chernomyrdin said that

> The main reason for the disruption of tax revenue collection for the federal budget... was the fact that commercial banks began invoking Article 855 of the Civil Code, which amended the order of making payments, and assigned taxes and other payments to the budget to the fourth category (*Moscow Tribune*, 16.11.96).

At precisely this time the government was coming under increasing pressure from the IMF over its poor tax collection record and the IMF suspended payment of its loan. The government's response was for the Finance Ministry, Tax Service and Central Bank to issue a joint instruction to banks which simply ordered them to disregard Article 855 of the Civil Code and continue to give tax payments priority over wage payments. In October, the outraged Duma adopted a resolution challenging the legality of the government's order and condemning the government's refusal to withdraw it. The IMF refused to discuss the question of whether it endorsed the government's violation of the law in order to meet the IMF's targets for the payment of taxes (*Moscow Tribune*, 16.11.96). The government claimed that in the case of a conflict between tax law and the Civil Code it was the former which had priority, but at a hearing in December 1996 of a case brought by workers of the giant Noril'sk metallurgical complex, one of the largest debtors to the Federal budget, the Supreme Court endorsed Article 855 and declared the government's instruction illegal (*Segodnya*, 21.12.96). Nevertheless, the banks were completely dependent on the government for their viability and so the banks continued to violate the law, under government direction, and to give precedence to tax payments. Just in case the banks had any doubts about their loyalties, the government through 1997 warned repeatedly of the need to cut the number of banks and curtail their privileges. Finally, in

December 1997, the Constitutional Court ruled that the amendment to Article 855 was unconstitutional, primarily on the grounds that giving payment of wages priority over payment of taxes favoured non-state over budget-sector employees whose wages depended on the receipt of tax revenues.

The issue of the competing claims of taxes and wages was not only one of the legal priority but also of the unequal sanctions imposed on employers for violation of the payment of one or the other. Thus, while the tax police had the power to sequester enterprise balances and could impose severe fines for the late payment of taxes, employers faced no such penalties for the late payment of wages. In collaboration with the employers, FNPR appealed to the government in January 1997 to exempt enterprises which were owed money from the budget from fines for the late payment of taxes, which secured some concessions in the government's proposals for the restructuring of budget debts issued in March. FNPR also achieved the amendment of Article 145-1 of the Criminal Code, signed by Yeltsin on 15 March 1999, which increased the criminal sanctions on employers who deliberately withheld wages or diverted wage funds to other uses.

Although FNPR claimed considerable success in its lobbying efforts in the Duma, some of its successes were blocked or reversed by the government, and it was unable to have any significant impact on the key issue of the budget, the Duma regularly passing the budget proposed by the government with few significant alterations, although lobbying their branch interests by representatives of particular branch unions had some success. In its review of its participation in legislative activity at the end of 1998, FNPR implicitly acknowledged that its lobbying had been excessively bureaucratic. It recognised that the Department for Interaction with Parliament had not always secured a sufficient degree of interaction with specialists of FNPR and its member organisations and had not made full use of the scientific and educational resources at its disposal, recommending that FNPR regional organisations should work more actively with their Duma deputies and members of the Federation Council (*Vesti FNPR*, 1–2, 1999, pp. 47–51).

### The 1999 Duma election

If FNPR could induce the 25 million people it claimed participated in its demonstrations to vote for FNPR-endorsed candidates, its prospects for the 1999 Duma election should have been much more favourable than the result of the 1995 election might have indicated. Although many trade union leaders still felt that trade unions should keep out of politics, the experience of lobbying the Duma over such issues as trade union and labour legislation and the distribution of budget funds over the period 1995–9 persuaded a growing number of trade union leaders of the importance of participating in the electoral process to secure their trade union aims.

From this point of view, the political affiliation of a deputy was unimportant. What mattered was that he or she would support trade union interests, and in particular the interests of the trade union of the appropriate sponsoring branch or region. However, the problem was how to get trade union-endorsed candidates into the State Duma. As one regional branch union leader put it, 'the trade union is not a real political force, we can't do what they did in Poland'. Thus, it seemed that collaboration with other blocs on some basis or another was inevitable.

*Soyuz truda* (Union of Labour) was reconstituted at a two-part conference whose first stage took place in May 1998. This time FNPR had cut its ties with the industrial lobby and came forward as the sole founder of the organisation, of which Andrei Isaev, Ideology Secretary of FNPR, was elected President. Nevertheless, the FNPR leadership remained committed to a centrist course based on a strategy of corporatist social partnership. Shmakov had a long-established relationship with the mayor of Moscow and presidential aspirant, Yurii Luzhkov, who held up his relationship with the Moscow Federation of Trade Unions as a model of social partnership for Russia, a view endorsed by FNPR (*O 'Soyuze truda'*, Moscow: Profizdat, 1999).

Luzhkov, whom a resolution of the conference declared to be one of the leaders around whom all progressive forces in Russia could unite, attended the second stage of the founding conference of *Soyuz truda* in October 1998. In return, Luzhkov invited *Soyuz truda* to participate as a founder member of his own political vehicle, *Otechestvo* (Fatherland), whose founding conference was held in December 1998 in the trade unions' historic Hall of Columns and was attended by 96 delegates of the national and regional organisations of *Soyuz truda*. Isaev, with two other FNPR representatives, became a member of the political committee of *Otechestvo*. Nineteen trade union representatives were eventually included in the *Otechestvo* party lists for the election and a further eight were nominated by OVR in single-mandate constituencies. At a meeting of the Executive Committee of FNPR in August 1999 Shmakov acclaimed the role of Isaev in *Otechestvo*: 'Luzhkov and Primakov are the public face of *Otechestvo*, but its real policy in many respects is determined by Isaev'.

The affiliation of *Soyuz truda* was important for *Otechestvo* in providing the potential base for a nation-wide organisation; the trade unions were not vote-winners and they did not have money, but they did have organisation that extended across the whole of Russia. However, it was quite another thing to translate the endorsement of *Otechestvo* by the national FNPR leadership into active support on the part of the branch and regional trade union organisations. The idea of setting up *Soyuz truda* as the political wing of the trade union movement, independently of the employers and any other political forces, was widely supported in the trade union movement, but by no means all the branch and regional trade union leaders shared Shmakov's enthusiasm for collaboration with Luzhkov, who was regarded outside Moscow with considerable suspicion by trade unionists as much as by regional leaders. However, rather than openly debating the decision to join *Otechestvo*, most of the dissident branch and regional trade union organisations simply ignored the decision.

In April 1999, the Federal Council of *Soyuz truda* berated those regional organisations which had only gone through the motions of establishing regional branches for their lack of executive discipline, scorned their complaints of a lack of information, money and personnel and noted that in some cases there had been direct agitation against the creation of *Soyuz truda*, while some of its regional branches had distanced themselves from the regional organisations of *Otechestvo* or even affiliated to other political movements (*Vesti FNPR*, 3–4, 1999, pp. 48–9). The situation was not improved by the merger of *Otechestvo* with an association of powerful regional governors, *Vsya Rossiya* (All-Russia), to form *Otechestvo-Vsya Rossiya* (OVR) and the recruitment of former Prime Minister Primakov, who had disappointed the hopes of FNPR when in office, to share the leadership with Luzhkov, an alliance which only intensified the government-sponsored media campaign against OVR.

The problem with unifying the trade unions behind OVR was not only distrust of Primakov and regional suspicions of Luzhkov, but more importantly was the fact that, as in 1995, branch and regional trade union organisations were embedded in their own structures of social partnership and were not willing to compromise their position for the sake of solidarity with the FNPR leadership, so that branch and regional union organisations only supported *Otechestvo* when it suited their own political interests (Clarke, 2001).

For many branch trade union leaders the lesson of the 1990s was that the trade unions should not ally themselves with any other political blocs or parties since any such political affiliation was bound to be divisive and because the trade unions had to work with whoever held power. This was a view that was particularly strong among the budget-sector unions, the teachers and health service workers, who stood to lose the most from identification with the political opposition, whether at regional or federal level. Moreover, many union leaders believed that the experience of the past decade was that the political agitation of the trade unions had achieved next to nothing. Everything that the trade unions had achieved had been through compromise within the developing institutions of social partnership and through lobbying in parliament and in regional assemblies.

On the other hand, other trade union leaders had come to recognise the value of parliamentary representation, as had been demonstrated by those unions which had secured representation in 1995, the metallurgists, the coal-miners and the agro-industrial workers, which were also the only branch unions to participate actively in the 1999 Duma election campaign.[1] The giant Agro-Industrial Workers' Union had always been closely associated with the Communist Party (KPRF) and in 1999 its president was elected to the Duma from the Federal list of the KPRF, while local union officials were unsuccessful in two single-mandate constituencies. The metallurgists were not able to agree on supporting any bloc, despite having secured three Duma seats through their collaboration with *Yabloko* in 1995, and instead

---

[1]   These are also industries that are geographically concentrated, so that the unions have a large number of members in particular constituencies.

backed five candidates in single-mandate constituencies, only one of whom was successful.[1]

Miners of Russia, the political wing of the coal miners' union, had agreed to endorse OVR in the coal-mining regions in exchange for financial support for the union's candidates in single-mandate constituencies, but the deal was rejected by the union's presidium, ostensibly on the grounds that the trade union embraced a wide range of political viewpoints and so should not endorse a particular bloc but should support trade union candidates in single-mandate constituencies, but in some coal-mining regions relations with *Otechestvo* were already strained. In practice the support of the trade union amounted to little and counted for little. Thus, for example, the union was not even sufficiently organised to collect the signatures required for the nomination of Sergei Neverov, the Kuzbass miners' leader, the signatures being collected by the regional coal company, which also financed Neverov's successful campaign, but it was the support of the regional governor, not that of the trade union and employers, that won him the seat.

Apart from the agro-industrial workers' agreement with the KPRF, the electoral activity of the branch unions was conducted at the regional level and the success or failure of their candidates was determined by local considerations. However, at the local level the trade unions were usually already embedded in relations of social partnership with their own regional administration, and consideration of their regional interests took precedence over their commitment to FNPR. Thus, regional trade union organisations tended to support OVR only where that was the local 'party of power' or where support for OVR promised to pay dividends at the regional level. As in 1995, in many regions the trade union organisation did next to nothing in the Duma election campaign, and in many more it actively supported other parties.

FNPR lacked the discipline and organisation to establish a united electoral strategy in which the trade unions could play their part in building a new power bloc. This loss of trade union discipline was not just a result of the abandonment of democratic centralism but more fundamentally was a result of the fragmentation of trade union interests that is a product of their integration into the branch and regional structures of social partnership, which meant that trade unions were more identified with and influenced by regional and branch interests than by concerns for trade union unity or the interests of the trade union movement, let alone the working class, as a whole. Their commitment to the strategy of social partnership also reinforced the dependence of the trade unions on the existing power structures, which severely constrained their political options.

The inability to establish a unified trade union position in the elections was also a result of the fact that FNPR did not establish such a position on the basis of common trade union interests articulated within *Soyuz truda*, but on a pragmatic, not to say

---

[1]    The three incumbents were all defeated in single-mandate constituencies. Two were also included on the *Yabloko* list, but were not elected by this route either.

opportunistic, political basis. The strategy of supporting *Otechestvo* was not simply a tactical misjudgement, but was rather a strategic blunder, adopted by the Moscow leadership of FNPR without serious discussion in the Executive or in the General Council of the union. Luzhkov's model of social partnership was specific to Moscow, where the city had enormous revenues and a relatively prosperous economy, which could not be generalised and which had probably had its day even in Moscow. The suspicion that *Otechestvo* was merely a vehicle for Luzhkov's political ambition was reinforced by the fact that, even when it sealed its alliance with Primakov, it had no clear economic or political programme. However, because the FNPR leadership's commitment to *Otechestvo* was not binding on its constituent organisations the doubts of regional and branch union leaders were not properly aired and resolved. As noted above, those who did not like the decision simply ignored it or, at best, paid it lip service.

Twenty-one candidates from FNPR-associated trade unions (including GMPR, which reaffiliated to FNPR nationally in February 2000) were defeated in single-mandate constituencies, usually with a derisory vote, indicating that a trade union affiliation on its own had no appeal to voters, at least in Federal elections. The only successful independent trade union candidates in single-mandate constituencies were the coal miners' leaders Neverov in Kuzbass and Katal'nikov in Rostov and the local metallurgists' leader, Lev Yarkin, in Lipetsk. In addition to these candidates, a further four associated with the trade unions but nominated by political parties were also successful: Vera Lekareva, candidate of the Union of Right Forces in Samara, two incumbent deputies backed by the KPRF and the managing director of a trade union hotel complex, elected in Moscow on the OVR ticket.

The hopes that many trade union representatives would vault in to the Duma on the OVR list were destroyed by the collapse of OVR in the later stages of the campaign. In the end only four trade unionists, including Isaev, were elected to the Duma on the OVR list, three were elected on the KPRF lists and one, Cheremushkin from Samara, on the *Yedinstvo* list. In total the trade union movement had seventeen deputies in the new Duma: two from the alternative unions, one from GMPR and fourteen associated with the FNPR unions, of whom five were backed by KPRF, five by OVR, one each by *Yedinstvo* and the Union of Right Forces, the remaining five having been elected as independents. Although this was an increase in trade union representation as compared to the eight trade union deputies elected in 1995, it did not indicate an increase in the political appeal of the trade unions. On the one hand, parties and blocs were not clamouring for trade union support, so that the trade unions secured substantially fewer places on the party lists than they had in the 1995 election. On the other hand, the pattern of voting for trade union candidates in single-mandate constituencies strongly suggested that the electors were voting for them not as trade unionists, but on the basis of their endorsement by regional and/or branch leaders.

The four trade union candidates who stood successfully as independents comprised two coal-miners (Neverov and Katal'nikov in Novokuznetsk and Shakhti), one metallurgist (Lyakin in Lipetsk) and the alternative trade unionist Ivanov in Togliatti, perhaps the exception who proves the rule. There is no evidence that voters were any more willing to support a trade unionist than an enterprise director to represent their interests in Moscow: in the oil and gas regions, for example, senior managers were elected to the Duma, with the trade unions not even putting up candidates.

## The 2000 Presidential election and FNPR under Putin

FNPR President Shmakov had referred to the Duma election campaign as the 'prelude to the Presidential election', expecting a contest in which FNPR would be backing Luzhkov or Primakov as figurehead of the new 'party of power', but the election, followed by Yeltsin's resignation, had unexpectedly resulted in a consolidation of the existing 'party of power' and left FNPR with the task of rebuilding its position in the new Duma and redefining its stance in relation to the forthcoming Presidential election.

At a meeting attended by fifteen deputies on 20 January, 2000 it was decided to establish an inter-fractional group of trade union deputies, *Solidarnost'*, in the new Duma, headed by Isaev, who managed to secure the important position of Deputy Chair of the Duma Committee on Labour, Social Policy and Veterans' Affairs. In January Shmakov had a long meeting with Putin, with whom FNPR had established what it saw as good partnerly relations during his time as Prime Minister, Putin having expressed his desire to listen to the trade unions.

On 14 February the Federal Council of *Soyuz truda* declared its support for Putin's candidacy, a lead followed unconditionally over the next two days by the Executive and General Council of FNPR, following Putin's address to the latter in which he declared that 'the trade unions should have a worthy place in society' and appealed for the collaboration of the trade unions with the state in monitoring working conditions, promising government support for this, although he also warned the trade unions that 'to demand what cannot be fulfilled is to inflame social tension' (*Vesti FNPR*, 1–2, 2000, pp. 1–6, 38–9). However, there was some strong opposition in the General Council to FNPR making a hasty decision, particularly from those who favoured other candidates. Aleksandr Davydov, President of the Agro-Industrial Workers' Union and Communist Party Duma Deputy, declared that it was naïve to endorse anybody before the candidates had even issued their programmes and the FNPR risked making a laughing-stock of itself after having already burned its fingers over Luzhkov. Yurii Shcheglov, President of the Yaroslavl' trade union federation, noted

I would warn members of the General Council against the haste with which we are now approaching this decision... If the President will carry out our decisions, decisions that we support, we will support him... The Yaroslavl' trade unions will not vote for this resolution, I can tell you in advance that we will not carry out your instructions... We declared on the Vasil'evskii Slope that Luzhkov is our President. In Yaroslavl' I am still untangling what you have done here.

There was no need for Shcheglov's outburst – as in the Duma elections, the commitment of the General Council was not binding, and branch and regional trade union leaders made their own decisions whom to support.[1]

FNPR refused to support a proposal of the health workers' union to picket the White House on 14 March and decided that the May Day demonstrations in 2000 would be 'quiet and festive' on the grounds that a new government was being formed and that FNPR had hopes that it would address the central issue of economic regeneration. FNPR claimed that 2.5 million people participated in demonstrations and meetings in more than 1000 cities and towns (*Vesti FNPR*, 5–6, 2000, pp. 1–7). The trade unions were disabused of their belief that the people had elected 'their' president soon after the election, however, when the government introduced a Unified Social Tax, which had been vigorously opposed by all the trade unions (apart from Sotsprof) and was in clear violation of the 2000 General Agreement, introduced its draft of a new Labour Code into the Duma without any consultation with the unions and nominated former tax minister, Aleksandr Pochinok, who had a reputation as a hard man, as Minister of Labour. Finally, in his speech to the Federal Assembly on 9 July, Putin paid special attention to the claims of the trade unions, insisting that there was no longer any call for the trade unions to perform state functions in the distribution of social benefits. The role of the trade unions should be confined to defending the rights of hired labour by studying the market, organising legal training and determining the priorities for retraining the unemployed. Meanwhile, the situation in the Duma, which had appeared promising immediately after the election, progressively deteriorated as the government, through the traditional methods of bribery and cajoling, assembled a majority in the Duma for the first time. This made it even more important to make the best possible use of the trade union fraction in the Duma and to lobby individual Duma members in the regions.

The IIIrd Congress of *Soyuz truda* assembled in Moscow on 17 September 2000 to review its position in the new political situation, in which the government was attempting to consolidate the Party system by excluding small parties from electoral participation and representation. The leader of *Soyuz truda*, Andrei Isaev, judged this a potentially favourable development since *Soyuz truda* was well placed to fill the centre-left niche in the political spectrum. Isaev defended *Soyuz truda*'s participation in *Otechestvo*, but recognised that the alliance with *Vsya Rossiya*, which collapsed immediately after the Duma election, had been a mistake. The priority in the new situation was to build up *Otechestvo* as the core of a centre-left 'loyal opposition' to

[1]   Thus, for example, the President of the miners' union was one of Putin's trustees, but the Kuzbass miners supported Tuleev. Another of Putin's trustees, Yevgenii Makarov of the Saint Petersburg Federation, emphasised that he was supporting Putin in a purely personal capacity.

Putin's governments, supporting Putin's project of stamping out corruption and building a strong law-governed state, while opposing any tendencies of the government to restrict social and labour rights and to pursue neo-liberal policies. However, Isaev warned that there were also pressures on *Otechestvo* to align itself with the centre-right presidential party, *Yedinstvo*, which came to fruition soon after, the two parties eventually merging, which put the *Otechestvo* trade union deputies in a difficult position and left the *Solidarnost'* Duma faction of trade union deputies relatively isolated. Nevertheless, the primary focus of the political activity of *Soyuz truda* was identified as its parliamentary lobbying in federal and regional legislatures, to which end it was proposed to build more active links between trade union representatives in legislatures at all levels.

### The campaign against the Unified Social Tax and the Labour Code

The initial experience of FNPR in lobbying the new Duma was quite positive. A law increasing the minimum wage in three steps, to 300 roubles ($10) a month in July 2001, barely enough to keep up with inflation, was adopted by the Duma in April and signed by Putin on 20 June 2000, while progress was made with legislation to increase budget sector wages and to compensate workers for delays in the payment of their wages. FNPR also continued its close collaboration with various ministries, particularly the Ministry of Labour, and the Social Funds to realise the terms of the 2000–1 General Agreement, and made progress in its collaboration with the Labour Inspectorate and other federal agencies to extend the role of the trade unions in monitoring the implementation of health and safety legislation. However, the biggest challenges to FNPR's lobbying efforts came with the government's introduction of a Unified Social Tax and the proposed amendment of the Labour Code. FNPR's campaigns over these issues are indicative of its priorities and campaigning methods in the Putin era. These government proposals were important to FNPR not only because they threatened the social and labour rights of their members, but also because they threatened the rights and income of FNPR and its constituent union organisations.

The government introduced the proposal for a Unified Social Tax (ESN) in the second part of the Tax Code, which it submitted to the State Duma without prior discussion with the trade unions. The Unified Social Tax would replace the separate contributions made by employers to the various off-budget funds (the pension fund, the employment fund, the social insurance fund and the medical insurance fund) at a reduced overall rate, a reform which successive governments had been trying to push through since 1994. The government insisted that the total revenue raised would be increased by the extended coverage of the tax and that the allocation of resources to the various funds would not be affected by the reform. FNPR campaigned against the Unified Social Tax on the grounds that the consolidation of the off-budget funds into the general budget would allow the government to divert resources from the former into other items of government spending, while the benefits currently provided by the funds would no longer be in accordance with workers' contributions, according to the insurance principle, but would now be at the discretion of the government. Not the least serious concern of FNPR was that the new system would reduce the role of the trade unions in the allocation of funds. FNPR President Mikhail Shmakov met Putin, at Shmakov's request, to discuss the issue in April 2000.

On 16 May a meeting of branch trade union presidents decided unanimously to oppose the introduction of the ESN, not only on the grounds that the new system would load an unsupportable financial burden onto the shoulders of the employed population and that the proposals had been introduced without any discussion with the trade unions, but also, and perhaps as much to the point, that it would undermine the established system of financing the activity of the trade unions (in particular, the role of the social insurance fund in financing the social welfare benefits distributed through the trade unions). FNPR decided to launch a campaign against the ESN by referring the issue to the Federal and Regional Tripartite Commissions, lobbying the federal and regional legislatures, sending protest telegrams to federal and regional executives, picketing legislative and administrative buildings in Moscow and in the regions and writing to Duma deputies and regional governors asking them to vote against the proposal in the Duma and the Federation Council. There was a long and inconclusive discussion of the ESN at a meeting of the Tripartite Commission on 26 May 2000 (from which the press was excluded, against virulent protest from the trade union side), followed by protest actions in the regions, with 22 000 people picketing government buildings in 48 regional capitals on 31 May and a picket of the White House on 7 June, attended by about 800 people. On 2 June the trade union and employer representatives on the Tripartite Commission issued a joint statement condemning the consolidation of the Employment Fund into the ESN. The Duma deferred consideration of the proposal for two days, according to FNPR under the influence of its picket, but passed the second reading of the Bill on 9 June, despite Shmakov's appeal to the Duma to introduce the new system in two or three regions on an experimental basis, with the agreement of the trade unions, before deciding whether to proceed. The government made some minor concessions in the drafting of the Bill, but on the central principle it was unmoveable.

The FNPR Executive promised to continue the campaign against the new tax, hoping to overturn it at its third and final reading in the Duma, appealing for compromise, with the threat of three months of mass demonstrations, but this was rather a hollow threat since, although some regional Federations had organised some forms of protest, mostly confined to writing letters and lobbying deputies, with the occasional picket or demonstration, it was reported to the FNPR Executive on 12 July that 30 of them had done absolutely nothing. The Duma was picketed again for the third hearing of the Bill on 19 July, which went through narrowly. FNPR did not give up the battle, because the vote in favour was not enough to overturn a negative vote of the Federation Council, to which FNPR directed its final lobbying efforts, and the repeal of the tax was one of the demands put forward in the course of the 2001 May

Day demonstrations, in which FNPR reported the participation of 2.5 million people in 71 regional centres, including a record turnout of more than 40 000 in St Petersburg. Although FNPR declared the May Day demonstration better organised than in previous years, there were still some regional centres in which no action had been organised (*Vesti FNPR*, 5–6, 2001, pp. 3–6).

The campaign against the introduction of the Unified Social Tax coincided with the campaign over the revision of the Labour Code. While the question of the Unified Social Tax appeared a technical issue, remote from the interests and knowledge of most trade union members, the reform of the Labour Code threatened to affect each and every one of them. Yeltsin had issued a decree in October 1991 urging the speedy reform of the Labour Code and successive governments had declared the reform of the Labour Code a priority. A draft produced early in 1994 provoked almost universal opposition by proposing to remove virtually all the defensive rights of trade unions, giving managers the freedom to alter the terms and conditions of employment, to transfer and lay-off workers and to assign overtime without the consent of worker or union, while the sanctions on employers for violations of labour law or collective agreements would have been removed. Further government drafts proposed even more draconian revision of the rights of workers and trade unions but made no progress in the face of a hostile Duma, despite growing pressure from the World Bank and International Monetary Fund which saw the reform, and particularly the removal of restrictions on the deployment and dismissal of workers, as an essential part of the establishment of a competitive market economy.[1] Meanwhile, a law drawn up in collaboration with the trade unions, revising the Labour Code to strengthen the protection of workers and, particularly, to introduce stiff penalties for employers who failed to pay wages on time, passed its first reading in the Duma in December 1995 and was eventually adopted in July 1999, only to be vetoed by Yeltsin in November. The election of a more compliant Duma in December 1999 made it possible for the government to act.

Three variants of a new Labour Code had been submitted to the previous Duma, including a government variant which proposed a radical deregulation of the labour market, with the replacement of collective agreements by individual fixed-term contracts and a dramatic reduction of trade union rights, and a variant proposed by Teimuraz Avaliani, a member of the Duma from the Russian Communist Workers'

---

[1]   The introduction of a new Labour Code to the Duma by December 1997 was a condition of the $800 million Social Protection Adjustment Loan approved by the World Bank on 25 June 1997. The following year, the IMF attached the disbursement of the next tranche of its loan to the same condition, but it would be wrong to see the reform of the Labour Code as being dictated by the international financial institutions (Isaev, 1999). The IMF was requested to include the condition by the neo-liberals in the Russian government to strengthen their hand against resistance to reform in the Ministry of Labour (Mikhail Dmitriev, then Deputy Minister of Labour responsible for the revision of the Labour Code, personal communication, June 1998).

Party (RKRP), which strengthened the protective elements of the existing Labour Code. A further 'deputies' variant', proposed by a working group of eight deputies from various parties and backed by the trade unions, was introduced into the new Duma in May 2000. FNPR and all of the alternative unions were opposed to the government's draft of the Labour Code, but they had rather different concerns. Although the government's draft Labour Code extended the grounds for dismissal, weakened the legal limitation of the working day and allowed for the more extensive use of fixed-term contracts, the trade unions were also concerned about the changes which threatened their own rights and privileges, especially the removal of the requirement of trade union approval for a wide range of management decisions, replaced only by a right to consultation, and the removal of the requirement that the employer provide the trade union with premises and facilities. While FNPR wanted a new Labour Code to consolidate its established position, the alternative trade unions were concerned that it should endorse trade union pluralism, which would enable them to secure recognition and bargaining rights against the established trade union.

The alternative trade union associations Sotsprof, once the most ardent supporter of neo-liberal reform, and the left-Communist Zashchita formed an unlikely alliance to campaign against the revised Labour Code, with Sotsprof eventually supporting the Avaliani draft, which had been adopted in the new Duma by Oleg Shein (a Duma Deputy and co-President of Zashchita).[1] The two organisations jointly organised a series of demonstrations against the Labour Code, including co-ordinated actions on 17 May 2000 in which they claimed the participation of 300000 workers, and 1 December 2000, when the organisers reported that there had been more than 30 events, in addition to a picket of the State Duma by 150 people, and 90 telegrams and faxes had been sent to the Duma (*ASTI*, 48, 2000). Meanwhile FNPR and the two leading alternative trade union federations, VKT and KTR, maintained a united support for the 'deputies' variant' in opposition to the government draft.

On 22 November the FNPR Executive met to discuss tactics. On the grounds that the decision was now in the hands of the Duma, assessing the chances of the 'deputies' variant' defeating the government variant as no more than 50–50, and in the light of their experience of the campaign against the Unified Social Tax,[2] the Executive decided that the priority was to organise workplace trade union meetings to

[1]   The four co-presidents of Zashchita were provided by the Russian Communist Workers' Party (RKRP), the Communist Party of the Russian Federation (KPRF), the United Workers' Front (OFT) and the Marxist Workers' Party (MRP). Zashchita, which is strongest in Shein's home region of Astrakhan, claims to have around 300 primary groups in 45 regions.

[2]   In his address to the Executive, Shmakov laid much of the blame for the failure of the campaign against the Unified Social Tax on the temporising of many of the leaders of member organisations. 'They betrayed a misunderstanding of the possible consequences of the introduction of the social tax, expressing doubts about the need to support the proposals of the Federation and the expediency of participation in protest actions. About 30 territorial trade union associations refused to organise collective actions or to work with the deputies, thus sharply reducing the effectiveness of all our efforts' (Tyurina, 2001).

explain the issue to the members and to try to influence individual Duma deputies while they were back in their constituencies by bombarding them with appeals during the week of 4 to 12 December. Opinion in the Executive was divided as to whether FNPR should take to the streets with its demands. If they failed to organise demonstrations they risked being outflanked by the alternative trade unions, with many FNPR members and some of its regional organisations participating in their demonstrations. Some regional leaders were ready to organise demonstrations, but others asked what was the point of picketing the regional legislature or administration when nothing depended on them.

Concluding the discussion, Shmakov doubted that meetings would have any impact on the Duma deputies who would decide the issue, and, if the demonstrations fell flat, they would be counter-productive, but those who wanted to organise demonstrations should be able to do so. Delegates were asked to discuss the issue with their colleagues and report back, as a result of which it was decided to organise demonstrations for the week of 14 to 19 December under the slogan 'For the deputies' variant of the Labour Code. No to the government's variant'. Member organisations were mandated that by 10 December every Duma deputy should receive at least 100 letters appealing for his or her vote at the Duma hearing scheduled for 21 December. According to FNPR, more than 12 million people took part in more than 100 000 meetings to discuss the draft Labour Code, mass actions took place in 63 regions during the week, with half a million participants, 90 000 letters and appeals were sent, signed by 8 million people, with an average of 200 letters being sent to each Duma deputy, and regional organisations met personally with 284 deputies, 223 of whom promised to support the deputies' variant, which was officially supported by about 60 per cent of regional legislatures and half the regional governors and, at Federal level, by *Otechestvo*, the KPRF, the Agrarians and Regions of Russia (Report to the FNPR General Council, 28 February 2001).

The Duma hearing of the Labour Code scheduled for 21 December was postponed at the last minute following a letter from Prime Minister Kas'yanov on 15 December proposing postponement to allow a conciliation commission to draw up a compromise variant of the Labour Code (and, of course, to allow the government time to marshal its forces in the Duma more effectively). The government claimed that its draft of the Labour Code protected the rights of workers and, in the words of Yevgenii Gontmakher, head of the Department of Social Development in the government apparatus, 'the trade unions will agree to everything, apart from changes in their role in the enterprises', a charge which FNPR vehemently denied, Andrei Isaev insisting that until there was an effective system of labour courts there was no substitute for the rights of the trade unions enshrined in the Labour Code (Tyurina, 2001). After consultations, a conciliation commission established by the Duma started work on 15 March, including representatives from the employer and trade union sides of the Tripartite Commission.

In the middle of May the government declared that the new Labour Code was ready to be laid before the Duma on 19 June (the changes are discussed below, pp. 111–114). FNPR President Mikhail Shmakov told journalists that the new version of the Labour Code strengthened the position of FNPR, but this, of course, was at the expense of the alternative unions, whose reaction was predictable, so that any semblance of unity in opposition to the government's plans collapsed. Sotsprof called for demonstrations in favour of the Avaliani-Shein Labour Code for 19 June. VKT objected to the cessation of discussion and its largest affiliate, the Independent Miners' Union, decided to picket the White House from 19 June until 20 July in favour of continued conciliation (VKT later sought to postpone the action to avoid being identified with the supporters of the Avaliani-Shein version or with Sotsprof, with whose leader, Sergei Khramov, the VKT leaders had very bad personal relations). On 28 May, KTR denounced the new Labour Code, withdrew from participation in the conciliation commission, endorsed the Avaliani-Shein draft and recommended its member organisations to participate in the demonstration in support of the latter called by Sotsprof for 19 June.

On 5 June, FNPR invited the leaders of all the Russian trade unions, including those not part of FNPR, to participate in a round table to discuss the Labour Code. The discussion was heated. FNPR and most of the VKT unions were in favour of continuing negotiations with a view to reaching an agreed compromise variant, but Oleg Shein, supported by Sotsprof and most of the KTR unions, rejected such a conciliatory position in favour of outright opposition. The following day, at a meeting of alternative unions called by Sotsprof, the latter's decision to demonstrate in favour of the Avaliani-Shein version of the Labour Code on 19 June was endorsed. The Moscow government denied permission for a picket of the White House or State Duma on 19 June, but Khramov and about 50 other people tried to picket the Duma and Khramov was arrested and held by the police for an hour. The following day, 40 members of NPG picketed the White House against a hasty vote on the Labour Code and in support of continued discussion. However, there were few reports of other protest actions around the country (there was a small picket in Yekaterinburg).

Despite the hopes of FNPR and VKT, there was no scope for further conciliation and the revised draft was sent to the Duma on 19 June for a first reading on 5 July 2001. At a press conference the previous day, FNPR endorsed the draft, Isaev commenting that 'it is that balance, which, on the one hand, will permit the progressive development of the real economy and, on the other hand, will protect the interests of the workers' and Shmakov noting that 'the agreed variant has integrated the best points of the seven draft laws'.

The deputies entering the Duma for the vote on the Labour Code on 5 July were greeted by two pickets. One militant picket of more than 1000 people was mounted against the agreed variant by the alternative trade unions and supported by the 'national patriotic' and left Communist parties. The other, smaller, peaceful picket was mounted in support of the agreed variant organised on behalf of FNPR by the

Moscow Federation of Trade Unions. The agreed variant was passed by 288 votes to 133, while the Avaliani-Shein draft was rejected with 189 votes in its support. The Deputy President of the Moscow Federation, Oleg Neterebskii, was reported as saying that 'the rights of the trade unions in the new Labour Code will be even greater than they are in the Law on Trade Unions' (*Rosbalt*, 10.07.01). FNPR welcomed the agreed variant, Andrei Isaev noting that 'all the proposals of the trade unions had been incorporated into the agreed variant' (*Rosbalt*, 10.07.01), although FNPR called for member organisations to submit proposed amendments to the Code before it returned to the Duma in December. Meanwhile the alternative trade unions continued their campaign of demonstrations against the agreed variant of the Labour Code. The trade unions submitted literally thousands of proposed amendments to the draft labour Code, but the agreed variant, with only minor further concessions to the trade unions, passed its second and third readings in the Duma on 21 December by 289 to 131 votes, passed the Federation Council on 26 December and was signed in to law by President Putin on 30 December 2001, to come into effect on 1 February 2002.

FNPR regarded the campaign against the government's draft of the Labour Code as having demonstrated the merits of its conciliatory approach. While the new Labour Code was by no means perfect, FNPR felt that trade union pressure and willingness to compromise had been effective in blocking the government's variant and achieving an acceptable compromise, despite the right-wing majority in the Duma, while if FNPR had adopted the uncompromising opposition of the Communist Party and alternative trade unions, they would have allowed the government's variant to sweep through (Shershukov, 2001).

**FNPR under threat**

Under Shmakov's leadership, FNPR had committed itself fully to the democratic process and to achieving its ends by constitutional means. While many criticised FNPR for its conciliatory position in relation to the government, Shmakov rejected such accusations, insisting that negotiated agreement was the only way for trade unions to achieve their aims and the Tripartite Commission 'the most effective way of resolving social problems through agreement', with the 'small proviso' that the agreements are adhered to. Failure of the government to respect the Agreement could lead to the outbreak of strikes, in which case FNPR could not stand aside, but this would be worse for everybody, strikes being a 'destructive weapon' (*FNPR Vesti*, 3–4, 1998, p. 28). Even if the achievements of the trade unions' pursuing such a strategy have been limited in the face of an intransigent government, it cannot be denied that Shmakov's FNPR has made a substantial contribution to the consolidation of democratic institutions in Russia, which is, of course, not at all the same thing as democracy. Nevertheless, in the interview just cited, Shmakov also warned that 'today there are renewed attempts to turn the trade unions into transmission belts, and every party wants to draw us in' (ibid., p. 31), an ominously prescient remark.

While FNPR had welcomed Putin's project of constructing a strong law-governed state, it had not envisaged the extent to which Putin's vision derived from his KGB background, of a state that penetrated every recess of society. From this perspective, however conciliatory FNPR might be, its existence as an independent force represented a challenge to order and good government. Putin had made clear his view of the limited role that FNPR could legitimately play, which was not one to which FNPR was content to confine itself.

During 2001 there were growing rumours that there would be an attempt to replace Shmakov at the IVth Congress of FNPR at the end of November. Shmakov was not short of enemies within FNPR. Those associated with the Communist Party resented Shmakov's attempt to draw a sharp line between FNPR and the Communist opposition, while Shmakov's decision to affiliate to the International Confederation of Free Trade Unions (ICFTU) was the last straw for his enemies in VKP, only compounded by Shmakov's leading role in the ICFTU and ILO campaign of support for the Belarusian trade unions in their struggle against Belarusian President Lukashenko. Aleksandr Davydov, Communist Party Duma Deputy and President of the Agro-Industrial Workers' Union, who cast the only vote against the entry of FNPR into the ICFTU, published an open letter to Shmakov in *Sel'skaya Zhizn'* on 5 June, amounting to a tirade against ICFTU and alleging that Shmakov had only dragged FNPR into the ICFTU in order to get himself a place as an ICFTU nominee on the Administrative Council of the ILO. On 19 September Davydov published an article in *Trud*, declaring his intention to oppose Shmakov at the Congress. The Agro-Industrial Workers' Union accounted for almost a third of FNPR's claimed membership, but it was only assigned eight delegates to the Congress because it only paid FNPR dues for 200 thousand members.

The candidate supported by the Communists to replace Shmakov was Anatolii Chekis, who had been President of the Kemerovo Federation of FNPR Trade Unions from 1990 until his election to the Duma on the Communist Party list in 1999. Vladimir Makavchik, chairman of the Shipbuilders' Trade Union, who had been one of the initiators of a review of FNPR's property, openly declared at the plenary session of his trade union (25 April 2001):

Mr Shmakov and I do not… see eye to eye. I will do everything in my power to make sure this gentleman leaves the premises of the FNPR building… There is Chekis… and we will support his candidacy for the post of chairman of FNPR.

FNPR's support for the new Labour Code hardened the opposition to Shmakov within FNPR, since many branch and regional leaders, particularly those linked to the Communist Party, shared the doubts of FNPR's critics about the new Labour Code, though few voiced their doubts openly. It also weakened FNPR's collaboration with KTR and VKT, which had been growing since they campaigned jointly over the non-payment of wages in 1997. Meanwhile, Sotsprof, long the most vehement antagonist of FNPR, called on its members to convince FNPR colleagues to engage in the preparations for the FNPR Congress in order to support the candidacy of Chekis and invited Chekis to discuss with them the means of removing the 'artificially forced tensions between Sotsprof and FNPR'.

There were reports that the moves to replace Shmakov by Chekis were backed by Boris Berezovskii, the tycoon who had fallen from presidential favour following Yeltsin's departure.[1] He was said to want to use a militant trade union centre, to be formed either by taking over or splitting FNPR, as a battering ram in his feud with Putin. But at the same time, there were reliable rumours that the presidential administration had ambitions to bring FNPR under its control.

The biggest threat to the FNPR leadership was presented not by the Communists but by proposals, reliably reported to emanate from the presidential administration, to establish a new trade union federation for the company trade union organisations of Russia's largest corporations. The immediate impact of such a federation was faced by the oil and gas, chemical and mining-metallurgical trade unions, which risked losing their most prosperous member organisations and largest financial contributors, but other branch unions would also be affected since these corporations had been diversifying into all areas of the economy. The alternative trade union federation, VKT, was also under threat from the new association since it was heavily dependent on the trade union of Noril'sk Nikel', which provided the majority of its funding. The trade union leaders of the companies met to discuss the possibility of creating such an association in May and June 2001, but in June it was rumoured that FNPR had been persuaded to endorse the revised Labour Code in exchange for the withdrawal of the proposal. However, the Association of Trade Union Organisations of Workers of Pan-National and Transnational Enterprises held its Founding Congress on 2 August in Moscow, the founders being the company unions of Lukoil, Yukos, Apatit and Electrosila, with reports that the Association would also be joined by Noril'sk Nikel' and by the railroad workers' union, which had attended the Congress as guests. Konstantin Krylov, a former FNPR Secretary and head of the legal department, who had been sacked in 1999, was elected as a Vice-President of the Association. The

---

[1]   A document leaked to Pravda in March (www.trud.org\buluzhnik.doc) outlined a plan, code-named '*buluzhnik*' (cobblestone) to transform FNPR into the nucleus of an effective populist liberal-democratic opposition. The main barrier to the oppositional capacity of FNPR was identified as 'the conservatism of the leadership in relation to the *status quo*' and its 'servile relation to the authorities'. Dissatisfaction with the FNPR leadership provided the opportunity either to replace Shmakov at the Congress or to split FNPR into three parts, representing budget-sector unions, basic branches (electricity, transport and so on) and other industrial branches. The document proposed in the first instance a whispering campaign against the FNPR leadership and support for all potential opponents of Shmakov, identifying Shcherbakov, Chekis and Makavchik, with Chekis being seen as the most promising (and controllable) candidate. The subsequent development of events closely matched this plan, but such a development was predictable in any case and there was no further evidence of the hand of Berezovskii.

relevant branch unions were not admitted to the conference, the preparations for which were made in secret, and no FNPR officials were invited.[1]

The members of the new Association did not declare any intention to withdraw immediately from FNPR or their branch trade unions, but it was rumoured that they would do so if 'their' candidate failed to replace Shmakov at the Congress in November. Just who would be 'their' candidate remained to be seen, although Vladimir Shcherbakov, President of VKP (which had long had close KGB connections), was among the guests at the Founding Congress. The initiative, and Shcherbakov's participation in particular, was denounced by FNPR, VKT and KTR on 10 September in a joint appeal to the international trade union movement. The hopes of the leaders of the new Association that they would achieve some international recognition were dashed when ICFTU and ICEM both sent strong protest letters to Putin, condemning the involvement of government and the employers in the formation of the Association and referring to the relevant ILO Conventions. In reaction to these letters, on 1 October the leaders of the new Association were summoned to a meeting with the presidential administration and informed that the presidential administration regarded any attempt to replace Shmakov as being unrealistic. Nevertheless, Shcherbakov undertook what was clearly a pre-election campaign, with the backing of the leaders of the Transnational Association, but was unable to find any eligible body to forward his nomination and withdrew his candidacy the week before the Congress. In the event, Putin, in an endorsement of Shmakov, attended the Congress and Chekis turned out to be his only opponent, securing only 80 votes to Shmakov's 659, with 13 abstentions. Nevertheless, the opposition to Shmakov in the run-up to the Congress reflected not only personal and political ambitions but real tensions within the trade union movement between divergent branch and sectoral interests that the FNPR leadership had not adequately addressed.

## Conclusion

FNPR narrowly avoided liquidation in 1991 and again in the wake of Yeltsin's confrontation with parliament in 1993. With the election of Shmakov as President, FNPR committed itself to pursuing its ends through constitutional channels on the basis of peaceful negotiation with the government within the framework of 'social partnership' and lobbying the State Duma, its days of action designed more to provide a ritual display than to put effective pressure on the government. The

---

[1]   The railroad workers, with two and a quarter million members, had only affiliated to FNPR at Federal level in May 2001, having hitherto worked with FNPR under a co-operation agreement, although all of their regional organisations had been affiliated to the FNPR regional federations. It was reported that they had been invited on the initiative of the notorious Nikolai Aksenenko, Railways Minister and former Deputy Prime Minister of Russia.

intransigence of successive governments under Yeltsin convinced the FNPR leadership to seek to use political means to secure its trade union ends, supporting the failed attempts of Vol'skii and Luzhkov to establish themselves as leaders of a centre-left movement which could challenge for state power. However, FNPR lacked the unity and discipline to mobilise its member organisations in support of its political ambitions and was unable to have any significant influence on the voting behaviour of its members. Although FNPR managed to create a trade union fraction in the Duma elected in December 1999, it was weakened as a political force once the government had secured control of the Duma. Nevertheless, in Putin's Russia even the semblance of an independent social movement is regarded as a threat and through 2001 the presidential apparatus sponsored initiatives to undermine FNPR and replace Shmakov as its President.

FNPR has long recognised that its political weakness rests on the failure of primary trade union organisations to secure the loyalty and commitment of the membership by effectively defending the interests of the workers in a steadily deteriorating economic situation. FNPR has made the activation and increased independence of primary trade union organisations a key priority, above all by extending and improving the use of collective agreements. However, the reform of the trade unions in 1990 involved a rejection of 'democratic centralism', so that trade union bodies at all levels became federative organs based on the equal participation of all affiliates, the democratic election of representatives and the sovereignty of representative bodies over the apparatus. The destruction of the 'trade union vertical' means that FNPR can do no more than make recommendations to lower-level bodies. Primary trade union organisations determine their own priorities and practices, while the task of supporting and encouraging their reform falls to trade union organisations at the regional level.

The political weakness of FNPR does not only lie in its inability to secure the active support of its membership, but also in its failure to secure the unity and concerted action of its member organisations, which pursue their own regional and branch interests without much consideration or concern for the interests of the trade union movement as a whole. This fragmentation of the trade union movement has been reinforced by its participation in the branch and regional structures of 'social partnership', which leads branch and regional trade union organisations to seek a common interest with employers and state bodies on the basis of their branch and regional affiliation. At the same time, the continued predominance of bureaucratic forms of trade-union decision-making meant that differences within the trade union movement were never aired and few attempts were made to forge a common ground through democratic debate. Under both Klochkov and Shmakov these differences simmered but were always ready to explode when the spark was lit. In October 1993 they were exploited by the presidential administration to secure the removal of Klochkov. In 2001 they were again exploited by the presidential administration in the attempt to remove Shmakov.

# 4

# The Structure of Russian Trade Unions

The collapse of the soviet system barely dented the branch and territorial principles on which the Russian trade unions are constructed (Figure 4.1). As we have seen, the decentralisation of state structures was associated with a decentralisation of trade union structures, while the abandonment of democratic centralism led to a reversal of the lines of accountability, with a federative structure replacing hierarchical subordination to the centre.

Primary organisations are affiliated to their regional branch committees (obkoms) and the obkoms are affiliated to the regional federation and to their central committees. The branch obkoms have a dual affiliation to FNPR, since the General Council of FNPR comprises delegates from both the central committees of the branch trade unions and from the regional trade union federations. In some cases, for example if there is no regional committee for their branch trade union or, occasionally, if they have fallen out with their own regional organisation, a primary organisation may affiliate directly to the Federation. Some large organisations that are directly subordinate to the federal government may affiliate directly to the Central Committee of the branch union. In some branches, particularly health and education, there has been a tendency to form an intermediate level of district (*raikom*) or city (*gorkom*) organisation to which primary organisations are affiliated. This is associated with the decentralisation of the administration of public services to the municipal level, so that the *raikomy* and *gorkomy* can negotiate directly with the city and district authorities, and with the proliferation of a large number of small union branches. In some cases links are missing as, for example, in the case of the metallurgists' union (GMPR) between 1992 and 2000, when the Central Committee was not affiliated to FNPR but in most regions the obkom affiliated to the regional Federation, or some of the Moscow City unions, such as the health workers' union, which withdrew its affiliation to the Central Committee of the branch union, with which it collaborates on a contractual basis. Finally, as a reflection of Putin's establishment of seven Federal Districts to oversee the administration of the regions, FNPR has established parallel structures at the level of the Federal District in order to develop partnership relations with Putin's plenipotentiaries. By the end of 2001, co-operation agreements had been signed in the Central and Volga Federal Districts.

Figure 4.1: The Structure of Russian Trade Union Organisation

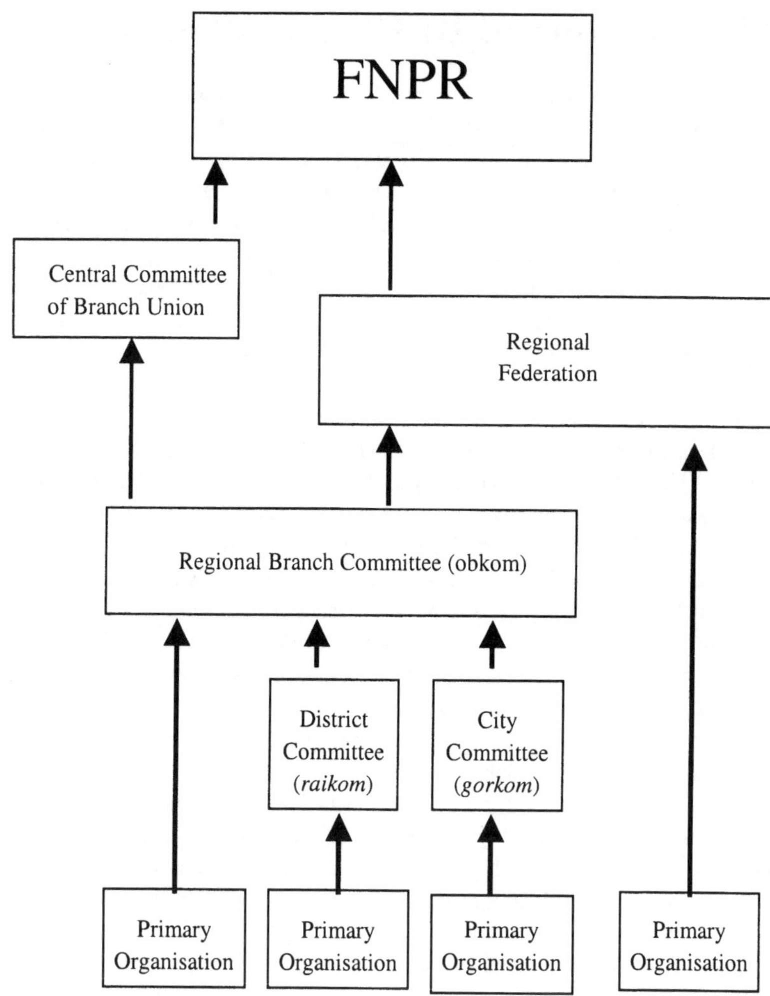


According to the report presented to the IVth Congress in November 2001, FNPR claimed to have more than 38 million members in more than 300 000 primary organisations grouped into 43 affiliated branch trade unions, plus a further five with which it collaborated on a contractual basis, and 78 regional organisations (FNPR, 2001b). There are sectoral trade union associations that provide a framework for the collaboration of trade unions in cognate branches and define constituencies for election to the FNPR Executive. These associations cover trade unions in the basic branches of industry and construction, the non-productive sphere, military industries, the transport industry, the engineering industry, non-state forms of ownership and fishing, river and sea transport. Similar associations of regional trade union organisations have been reconstituted to correspond to the Federal Districts, covering the Greater Volga region, Central Russia, the Urals, Siberia, the Far East, the Caucasus and the North West.

## International Relations of the Russia trade unions

The soviet trade unions were the leading organisation in the World Federation of Trade Unions (WFTU), established after the Second World War as the principal international organisation of the world trade unions, from which the non-communist western unions withdrew in 1949 to establish the International Confederation of Free Trade Unions (ICFTU). After 1949 WFTU became an instrument of soviet foreign policy, although bilateral contacts between soviet and western trade unions still took place. The Soviet Union rejoined the ILO in 1954, ratifying a significant number of ILO Conventions and participating actively in its bodies. The international department of VTsSPS was one of its largest departments, with around 100 staff in the late seventies (Godson, 1977, pp. 28–9, cited Ruble, 1981, p. 131).

Following the collapse of the Soviet Union, VKP suspended its membership of WFTU and in April 1992 left the organisation altogether, to reconstitute itself as the international trade union centre for the former soviet trade unions. FNPR was only ever indirectly affiliated to WFTU, through its affiliation to VKP, although some of the branch unions retained membership of WFTU's Trade Union Internationals (TUIs), and the Russian Agro-Industrial Workers' Union remained a WFTU affiliate even after the withdrawal of VKP, its President continuing to serve as a Deputy President of WFTU.

Following a visit to Russia at the beginning of 1992, the ICFTU decided at its 15th World Congress to support the 'free trade union movement' in the former Soviet Union and appointed a representative in Moscow, who collaborated with both FNPR and the alternative trade unions. However, there were divisions between the national centres affiliated to ICFTU as to the strategy to be adopted in Russia. While many of the Western European trade union centres already had well-established bilateral links with the FNPR trade unions, the AFL-CIO and the non-communist trade union federations of Southern Europe were strongly opposed to supporting the development of the former Communist trade unions. The AFL-CIO, in particular, provided very considerable support to the alternative trade unions through its Free Trade Union Institute (FTUI), with massive funding provided by the National Endowment for Democracy and the US State Department (Cook, 1997, Chapter Five), but refused to have any contact with the FNPR unions until its line changed in 1997, when a FNPR delegation was invited to attend the AFL-CIO Congress. A number of FNPR branch trade unions and alternative trade union organisations were admitted to membership of International Trade Secretariats (ITS), several of which appointed Moscow representatives. By the end of the nineties 15 of FNPR's 42 branch unions were affiliated to various ITS, comprising almost a quarter of the total membership of the latter.

Collaboration with ICFTU intensified in the second half of the nineties, following FNPR's participation in the 1996 ICFTU Congress. In 1997 the ICFTU and ILO supported an international campaign against the non-payment of wages in Russia. This campaign was noteworthy for the collaboration between FNPR and the alternative trade union federations, VKT and KTR, and as the first occasion on which FTUI collaborated with FNPR. The softening of opposition to collaboration with FNPR, particularly on the part of the AFL-CIO, was the prelude to the affiliation of FNPR, together with VKT and KTR, to the ICFTU, which was accepted in November 2000. FNPR retained its affiliation to VKP even after affiliating to ICFTU, but relations between the two organisations had never been good. At the IIIrd Congress of VKP, in September 1997, Mikhail Shmakov insisted that VKP should only be a co-ordinating body for the various national centres rather than any kind of inter-state body with its own policies and programmes (*Vesti FNPR*, 9–10, 1997, pp. 81–6). In September 2001, FNPR publicly denounced VKP President Shcherbakov's collaboration in the formation of the new Association of Trade Union Organisations of Workers of Pan-National and Transnational Enterprises (see p. 70 above).

The developing contacts of FNPR with the international trade union movement and its more active participation in the ILO enabled the FNPR leadership not only to learn the language of international trade unionism, but also to learn much about the realities of trade union practice. The principal substantive component of the international co-operation of FNPR has been an extensive programme of advice, training and bilateral exchanges that has been provided by ILO, ICFTU and its affiliates, including substantial programmes funded by the European Union and the Friedrich Ebert Foundation.

## FNPR

The sovereign body of FNPR is the Congress, which has to be held at least every four years. Delegates to the Congress are elected from its member organisations which are represented in proportion to their affiliated membership. The Congress considers reports, debates resolutions and elects the President of FNPR and the Revision Commission, which is responsible for overseeing the proper use of trade union resources between congresses. The first three Congresses were dominated by the trade union apparatus, but for the Fourth Congress in November 2001 FNPR introduced quotas for the selection of the 800 delegates, so that each delegation should include at least 30 per cent women, 30 per cent of delegates should be under

35 and 30 per cent should be from primary trade union organisations, although member organisations found it very difficult to meet the quota for young delegates.

Between Congresses the decision-making body is the General Council, which normally meets quarterly, and elects the FNPR Deputy Presidents. The General Council has 168 members, comprising the FNPR leadership, the President of each affiliated organisation, regardless of its size, and one elected delegate from each branch trade union (some of whom are presidents of primary organisations). This ensures more or less equal representation of regional and branch trade union representatives on the General Council, although many of the second representatives of the branch unions are from their regional organisations. Despite their equal representation, many of the branch trade unions feel that their interests are neglected, although the branch trade unions, being based in Moscow, most in the FNPR building, have much more extensive informal interaction with each other and with the FNPR apparatus than do the regional leaders.

The executive body of FNPR is the Executive Committee, comprising the FNPR leadership and equal representation of branch and regional trade union organisations, elected from the associations of branch and regional union organisations (pp. 74–5 above). The Executive Committee meets around six times a year and has a number of Permanent Commissions to deal with particular issues, including a Commission on the Social Equality of Women, established in 2000 when the issue was declared a priority of FNPR, which also put the topic on the agenda of the Russian Tripartite Commission. In September 2001 the FNPR General Council adopted its Conception of the Gender Policy of FNPR.

The trade union apparatus comprises 129 staff (including both officers and office staff) consisting of the President, six Deputies, 11 Secretaries and a permanent staff organised into 12 functional departments: General (12 staff); Organisational (11); Legal (13); Socio-Economic Relations and Defence of Economic Rights of Workers (13); Labour Inspectorate (5); Relations with Parliament and Social Movements (8); Problems of Social Guarantees (8); Information-Analytical Centre (6); International Relations (7); Finance (6); Administration (14, including personnel and accounts); and the Revision Commission (5).

FNPR is nominally a federal organisation, accountable to its affiliates, without any of the sanctions that VTsSPS could impose on trade union organisations that failed to follow the directives of the centre. However, the FNPR leadership has come to see the abandonment of democratic centralism as threatening the integrity and unity of the trade union movement as the branch and regional trade unions went their own way and ignored the decisions of FNPR, most conspicuously in relation to reporting and the remission of dues, but also in the organisation of days of action and participation in election campaigns. In an attempt to strengthen the discipline of the trade union movement, FNPR introduced a series of amendments to the Constitution at its IIIrd Congress in 1996. Member organisations are now obliged not only to observe the Constitution; support the activity of the Federation and actively participate in the realisation of its aims and tasks; and show solidarity in defence of the rights and interests of member organisations; but also to implement decisions taken by elected FNPR bodies on questions which fall within their jurisdiction; to submit regular financial accounts relating to payments to the Federation; inform FNPR about their participation in federal and local elections; show solidarity and participate actively in collective trade union actions organised by FNPR; and provide financial and other support to mass media outlets established by FNPR. Further amendments to the constitution to 'strengthen organisational and financial discipline' were introduced at the IVth Congress in November 2001. However, FNPR still has no effective sanctions to force its member organisations into line.

The aspiration to restore what is known as 'the trade union vertical' has not been connected with any conspicuous aspiration to democratise decision-making in the union, which continues to be dominated, as in the past, by its apparatus. Thus, critics have charged that there has been no accountability or transparency regarding the management and disposal of trade union assets and decisions are taken without going through the procedures laid down by the constitution as, for example, in the case of the decisions regarding participation in the 1995 and 1999 elections, where the decisions were formally taken not by FNPR but by *Soyuz truda*. The affiliated branch and regional trade union organisations rarely challenge the decisions of the apparatus, but continue to ignore or pay no more than lip-service to those decisions which do not suit them, as was shown in the Duma elections.

## The branch unions

Like FNPR, the sovereign body of the branch unions is their Congress, held every four or five years according to the Constitution,[1] which elects the President of the union and the Revision Commission, while the ruling body between conferences is the Central Committee (TsK), which in turn elects a Presidium or Executive Committee. Most of the branch union head offices are located in the FNPR building and they have much smaller apparatuses. The health workers' union, for example, services a membership of some three million in more than 22 000 primary organisations grouped into 77 regional organisations with a staff of 25 working in four departments (organisational; economic and wages; legal and social protection; international). The Mining-Metallurgical Union services a membership of 1.3 million in 835 primary organisations, with 30 regional organisations and 52 enterprises affiliated directly to the Central Committee, with a staff of 33 working in eight departments (organisational; health and safety and environment; socio-economic; juridical; information-publishing centre; international; financial; administration). The Chemical Workers' Union services a membership of almost 1.5 million members

---

[1]   Following a resolution of the IIIrd Congress, FNPR has sought to co-ordinate the electoral cycle of its branch and regional organisations and reduce it to two years.

with a staff of 15, including the President and two deputies, organised in seven departments (organisational; economic; legal; health and safety; defence of social rights; international; finance and administration).

Differences of branch interest which were suppressed in the soviet period by the rigidly hierarchical character of the trade unions and centralised control of the economy have become a potential source of disunity. During 1992 the differential impact of the reform process introduced growing political tensions between the different branch unions within the trade union movement. While workers in budget organisations found their pay lagging far behind as public authorities lacked the tax revenue to meet their salaries, the pay of workers in other branches of industry lagged behind inflation as a result of the inability of employers to pay, which many blamed on the crushing burden of taxation. Meanwhile, other groups of workers found their relative economic situation improving in the new conditions of the market economy, with the strategically crucial power workers and those working in the export sectors of gas and oil, mineral extraction and metallurgy enjoying large real pay increases in 1992, which more than made up for the fall in their wages in the last year of the Soviet Union. FNPR based its political strategy during 1992–3 largely on the plight of the workers in budget organisations and the military-industrial complex, to the relative neglect of the interests of workers in other branches of production. As a result, the metallurgists left in 1992 and many other branch unions distanced themselves from FNPR, each pursuing its own course.

Klochkov's failure to take sufficient account of the interests of the branch unions was one factor that eroded his authority and led to his downfall (although it was his attempt to centralise control of trade union property, rather than his policy platform, that provoked the sharpest response). Shmakov insisted that he would be more sensitive to the interests of the branch unions, with FNPR performing a servicing role for the branch unions and campaigning only on the most general issues, such as unemployment and the late payment of wages. In practice, however, the General Council and the Executive do not provide fora in which FNPR tries to work out a common programme that can reconcile differences of branch interest. As with other decisions of FNPR, those branch unions that do not like elements of the programme tend to keep quiet in meetings, grumble in the corridors and ignore them in practice.

The sectoral associations of branch unions provide fora for the consideration of their common branch interests, the Association of Trade Unions of Basic Industrial Branches and the Association of Trade Unions of the Non-Productive Sphere being the most active in this respect. The existence of these Associations is sometimes seen as an indication of the danger that FNPR might disintegrate into distinct sectoral federations for the budget sector, basic industry, the military-industrial complex and the agro-industrial complex. However, for the moment they provide no more than a framework for the discussion of common problems and do not in themselves present any threat to the unity of FNPR, although there is no doubt a potential for the exploitation of such differences of interest (see above p. 70). FNPR has been encouraging the merger of trade unions in related branches in order to strengthen their regional organisations, and particularly the branch unions in the face of the new giant corporations. The most significant proposed merger has been that between the oil and gas and chemical workers' unions but progress has been slow.

Differences of political affiliation have been superimposed on differences of branch interest. While most branch unions have distanced themselves from politics or made opportunistic alliances, GMPR collaborated with the liberal *Yabloko* block, while at the other end of the spectrum the Agro-Industrial Workers' Union has been closely identified with the Communist Party. In the 1995 and 1999 Duma elections this fragmentation was manifested in the affiliation of different branch unions with different parties and electoral blocks.

The branch unions seek to serve the trade union interests of their members primarily by representing the interests of the branch. They do this by maintaining their traditional relations with ministerial or quasi-ministerial structures to collaborate in the consideration of a wide range of branch-specific issues such as training, certification and health and safety and to press their branch interests in Moscow. In the case of public services, such as health and education, or heavily subsidised sectors, such as coal-mining, agriculture and the military-industrial complex, this has sometimes meant the branch unions collaborating with the appropriate ministries to press the interests of the branch in the struggle between ministries over the formation of government policy and, above all, for the allocation of budget funds. The coal miners' union, for example, worked closely with the quasi-state body established to manage the coal industry (Ugol' Rossii, later reconstituted as Rosugol') and the Coal Committee of the Ministry of Fuel and Power. National strikes were covertly co-ordinated with Rosugol' in the first half of the nineties and did not take place without their approval. When that approval was withdrawn as Rosugol' was brought under firmer control, national strikes ceased (Borisov, 2001). The health workers' union and the education union have similarly worked closely with their relevant ministries, the Minister of Health even attending meetings of the plenum of the health workers' union.

Mass privatisation transferred the ownership of great swathes of the economy into private hands, but even private industry was heavily dependent on government policy, if not on direct government funding, in relation to taxation; the setting of prices and tariffs; money, credit and investment policies; licensing and other forms of regulation and the remnants of the old ministries retained responsibility for policy in relation to their industries. The branch unions continued to lobby these ministries and state committees on behalf of their branch interests, and continued to sign branch tariff agreements with them, even when the industry was no longer in state hands.

The branch principle of trade union organisation has come under pressure from two directions. On the one hand, from the aspirations of particular professional groupings to improve their relative position within the branch. The branch principle of organisation was appropriate in the conditions of the administrative-command economy, where trade union structures mirrored management structures at all levels, but was ill-adapted to articulating and expressing the diverse interests of a membership spread across a wide range of occupations and industries. This was a major reason for the rise of the new alternative unions, the most successful of which organised strategically important workers, such as underground miners, pilots, air traffic controllers, dockers and road and rail transport drivers, who had a strong bargaining position which the branch unions did not and could not exploit. On the other hand, the formation of holding companies which control enterprises across a number of branches and regions has undermined the territorial-branch principle of trade union organisation which underlies the practice of 'social partnership', as the companies do not fall unambiguously within the jurisdiction of any of the branch or regional agreements. This has led to the formation of a new generation of company unions in such organisations as Gazprom, Lukoil and Noril'sk Nikel', some of which came together to establish a new trade union federation in 2001 (see above, p. 70).

## Regional trade union organisations

In the soviet period the regional trade union council (*oblsovprof*) was a bureaucratic link in the vertical chain of Party-state power, subordinate to VTsSPS and under the supervision of the Regional Party Committee. The *oblsovprof* supervised the regional committees of the branch trade unions (obkoms), which were in turn responsible for monitoring and supporting the primary organisations in their branch. The division of labour between *oblsovprof* and obkom was not always clear-cut, but between them the regional organisations were responsible for organising socialist competition; monitoring the performance of trade union primary groups; approving the nomination of primary group presidents; providing regular training in accordance with Party priorities; providing specialist advice to primary groups, particularly in relation to health and safety; administering the waiting list for municipally allocated housing; organising celebrations on public holidays and, above all, administering social and welfare facilities financed from local authority and social insurance, as well as trade union, funds and allocating access to such facilities for redistribution by primary groups. The high point of the trade union year was the 'sanitary campaign' to prepare the children's holiday camps for the summer season. As a part of the structure of Party-state power, the *oblsovprof* participated in the policy process at regional level and supported the lobbying of the Regional Party Committee in Moscow.

With the formation of FNPR in 1990, regional trade union bodies were transformed from hierarchical into federal organisations, the regional trade union councils of VTsSPS being reconstituted and in most cases renamed as regional Federations of Trade Unions. Although this reconstitution was the result of a directive from above, in some regions it also responded to pressures for independence from below. For example, in December 1989 in the Komi Republic, the territorial organisations of the coal-mining regions of Inta and Vorkuta and the geologists' union had decided to leave the *oblsovprof* in reaction to its equivocal support for the miners' strikes in July, but they attended the founding conference of the Komi Federation of Trade Unions in January 1990 and decided to join the new federation.

The decentralisation of trade union organisation under perestroika gave the regional trade union organisations more independence and, as at the Federal level, the collapse of the Party-state left the regional trade union organisations to find themselves a new role. However, in most regions there was more continuity of state power than at the federal level, making the transition smoother as the trade unions built on established formal and informal connections with the regional authorities.

Each regional organisation has developed its own constitution, though most are modelled on the constitution of FNPR and the structure of the regional organisations is fairly uniform. The sovereign body of the regional trade union organisations is the conference, but these are only held every five years and usually do little more than hear formal speeches and reports and elect the slate of candidates put forward by the apparatus for the Presidency and the Revision Commission. As the person responsible for organising the conference of the Komi Federation cynically commented:

> How are the conferences conducted? Well, all the old people are immediately re-elected. They will have gone around all the districts, they will choose their people as delegates – their re-election is guaranteed. The pensioners will be gathered. Why spoil their relations? The chairmen of the branch committees are glad that nobody bothers them and they cannot interfere in the business of the Federation and silently vote for the re-election of the president.

The ruling body between conferences is the Council, which comprises delegates elected on the basis of the equal representation of all member organisations and which meets at least twice a year. The executive body is the Presidium, which meets at least quarterly, though in practice usually meets more often. The Presidium establishes Commissions of its members which prepare documents for Council and Presidium meetings and which carry out other tasks as necessary. Commissions usually meet immediately after Council meetings, and the responsible departments of the apparatus do the actual work.

Problems of communication with widely dispersed small organisations have been one of the factors lying behind the formation of sub-regional trade union organisations, but a more significant factor has been the decentralisation of regional administration, so that it is now municipal authorities which are responsible for running and financing public services and for setting rents, charges for local transport and many communal service charges. At the beginning of 2001 FNPR had 8089 city and district trade union organisations and a further 1233 city and district trade union co-ordinating committees. Sub-regional organisation is especially important for public-sector unions, the health and education workers and municipal employees, and provides a new focus for social partnership in negotiating the disposition of the local budget, charges for public services and the terms and conditions of employment of municipal employees.

Sub-regional organisations are usually constituted by the presidents of the primary organisations in the city or district, but rarely have a full-time president or any permanent staff, typically being serviced by the trade union organisation of the largest enterprise in the district, which supplies the president. The problem of resourcing sub-regional organisations is partly a manifestation of the struggle over the distribution of trade union dues. Because the regional organisation does not want to surrender any of its meagre resources, the funding of sub-regional organisations depends on the willingness of primary organisations to pay. The viability of a sub-regional organisation also depends heavily on the willingness of somebody to take on the work of co-ordination for little or no additional pay.

The formation of sub-regional federative organisations has generally been on the initiative of the regional federation, sometimes with the encouragement and support of the regional administration. However, the branch obkoms have generally been at best unenthusiastic about such a development because they are afraid that it will take over their own role of servicing primary organisations, with a consequent diversion of funds as primary organisations prefer to pay to their local co-ordinating committee than to their branch obkom.

There is very little lay participation in any of the regional trade union governing bodies, and in practice the apparatus and the full-time elected officers dominate the union today, as they did in the soviet period. The participation of most presidents of trade union primary organisations is limited to their attendance at semi-annual meetings of their regional branch committee and attendance at the conferences of the regional branch and FNPR organisations. Only the full-time presidents of the largest primary organisations have a reasonable chance of being selected as delegates to the national Congresses of FNPR and the branch trade union.

Despite the radical decentralisation of authority at the end of the 1980s, decisions of collegial bodies of most regional trade union organisations are, according to the constitution, binding on member organisations, but there are no effective sanctions to enforce fulfilment of resolutions and in practice member organisations can simply ignore resolutions that they do not like. The collapse of democratic centralism also means that ineffective trade union leaders cannot easily be removed from office by higher bodies,[1] leading to some traditionally soviet approaches to the 'personnel

---

[1]   The Mining-Metallurgical Union, at its Congress in February 2000, adopted constitutional amendments which allow higher bodies to reverse the decisions of lower bodies made in violation of the constitution and to sack the presidents of lower bodies for systematically not fulfilling their constitutional duties or for gross violation of financial discipline. The obkom now also has to approve the appointment and dismissal of the chief accountant of enterprise trade union committees. The Engineering Union introduced similar amendments at its Congress in the same month, including providing control over the finances of primary organisations.

problem'. For example, the sub-regional organisation of the health workers' union in the Komi-Permyatsk Autonomous Okrug was moribund, largely because of an inactive president. Union density had fallen to 50 per cent, against 80 per cent in the rest of the Perm' region, affiliation fees had not been paid in full since 1992 and in 1998 the organisation was suspended by the obkom. The obkom president went to Komi-Permyatsk and met with directors of health establishments, which led to the re-establishment of a number of trade union organisations. The union paid for six directors to visit Perm' to discuss the organisation of a trade union conference and the election of a new president, which was achieved shortly afterwards.

The FNPR trade unions still admit managers to membership,[1] and some unions make a virtue of managerial participation in union business. For example, in Perm' one-third of the seats at the plenums of the health workers' union are occupied by heads of establishments (chief doctors), which the union president justified as follows:

> That means that when a decision is taken at the presidium of a district or city committee, where the chiefs of the territory sit, and he himself has taken that decision, then I know that he will carry it out… If we work without close contact with the chiefs we will not achieve anything.

According to the president, the trade unions and employers are objectively allies because their aims (of extracting money from the regional administration) coincide. In Ul'yanovsk, three of the nine members of the regional executive of the health workers' union are chief doctors. However, the President of the Kemerovo teachers' union noted the absurdity of such a situation:

> My dream is to create a council of education employers, even a board of directors of schools. Though in itself that sounds strange – to 'create'. They should unite themselves, maybe even leave our trade union and receive the status of civil servants. And we can conclude a collective agreement with them.… Now the collective agreement is signed between the president of the trade union committee and the director, who is a member of our trade union. Is that really normal?

---

[1] Directors of establishments in the public sector are in an anomalous situation, since they are both the employees of the local administration and the employers with regard to their own establishment. It is not uncommon for the relevant trade union to defend public sector directors in the event of dismissal, securing compensation or reinstatement, or in the calculation of their pension rights. According to the Saint Petersburg tripartite agreement for the health service, directors of establishments who are union members can only be sacked with the approval of the regional trade union (the union managed to get this point into the agreement because the President of the City Health Committee, a good friend of the union, was under threat of dismissal at the time). The Ul'yanovsk health workers' union even successfully defended a chief doctor who had been fined for failing to pay holiday pay on time, on the grounds that he had not received the funds.

The chemical workers' union rejected a call to exclude management from membership by a massive majority at its 1995 conference. The miners' union, the most militant of the FNPR unions, rejected a similar proposal at its 1996 congress, primary group leaders arguing that if the mine director remained a union member they could compel him to attend union meetings to explain himself.[1] However, the Law on Trade Unions gives the union this power in any case, while the idea of a union president demanding the director's attendance at a union meeting is almost as far-fetched as the idea of the director responding to such a demand for fear of losing his union membership!

There are alternative trade unions active in most regions, but these are almost invariably tiny groups that play no significant role at the regional level. Only in Saint Petersburg and Leningrad region are the alternative trade unions involved in the regional tripartite agreement, but they were severely weakened by internal divisions in 1999. In Sverdlovsk the trade union organisation *Mai* became very active in regional politics at the end of the 90s and in Astrakhan the regional leader of the *Zashchita* trade union secured election to the State Duma from the constituency in 1999. Otherwise, the alternative unions are significant in spurring the traditional unions to action, but are not serious competitors for influence at the regional level.

In principle, the regional committees of the branch trade unions service their primary groups, while the primary role of the federation is to co-ordinate and unify the forces of member organisations to defend the rights of trade union members, primarily through its interaction with the regional administration. However, in practice there is not a clear division of functions and there is some duplication of effort, with the regional federations providing services for primary groups which the obkoms cannot or do not provide.

There tends to be a considerable amount of tension and mutual recrimination between the federation and the obkoms. The obkoms believe that the federation's primary task is to deliver the support of the regional administration for the unions and their members, and complain vehemently when they are not able to do so, often deriding the results of regional social partnership. The federations believe that the obkoms should be establishing union organisations in non-union workplaces, servicing their primary organisations and ensuring that the latter act more independently of management in defending their members and negotiating effective collective agreements, and blame the obkoms for the weakness of the trade union at the workplace.

This tension is reinforced (or, perhaps, underpinned) by the competition for scarce resources. Following the abandonment of democratic centralism, each structure has to justify its existence to its affiliates and the membership at large in order to induce

---

[1]   In connection with FNPR's application for affiliation, ICFTU strongly recommended that FNPR should not allow enterprise directors to be members of elected bodies or to serve as delegates at Congresses.

their member organisations to remit and, ideally, to increase their affiliation fees. This means that the regional federations are keen to prove themselves to primary organisations, while the obkoms are equally concerned to keep such competitors out. In some regions the preoccupation with generating revenue has gone so far that our colleague Vladimir Ilyin likens the regional trade union bodies to commercial firms seeking to maximise their revenues by selling their services to all-comers (Ilyin, 2001). In interviews, many obkom and primary organisation leaders explicitly relate their willingness to pay fees to the services they receive.

Many in the oblast federations blame the decline in trade union strength on the abandonment of democratic centralism, which has weakened trade union discipline and solidarity and prevents the federation from replacing ineffective obkom officials. The FNPR General Council has repeatedly identified the weakness of FNPR's territorial organisations as an obstacle to influencing enterprise trade unions. The solution to this problem preferred by the FNPR leadership is to unify the regional trade union apparatus by assimilating the obkoms to the regional federations, but this solution has faced stiff opposition from the branch unions. The compromise has been to recommend merging the regional organisations of related branches of the economy, while the General Council has also recommended that the practice of primary organisations affiliating directly to the regional federation or to the central committee of their branch trade union, by-passing its territorial organisation, should cease (*Vesti FNPR*, 1–2, 2001, p. 44). The IVth Congress of FNPR in November 2001 again recommended trade union mergers as a means of consolidating the trade union forces, particularly at the regional level. However sensible such a rationalisation might be, trade union mergers are notoriously difficult to achieve, with personal rivalries and financial questions compounding the problem.

## Trade union membership

Table 4.1: Membership of FNPR Trade Unions

| Date | Membership | Density |
| --- | --- | --- |
| I Congress: September 1990 | 54 million | 70 per cent |
| II Congress: October 1993 | 60 million | 86 per cent |
| III Congress: December 1996 | 45 million | 69 per cent |
| June 1999 | 37 million | 58 per cent |
| November 1999 | 34 637 700 | 54 per cent |
| January 2002 | 36.9 million | 51 per cent |

Source: FNPR Reports

Membership of the FNPR trade unions has fallen by about half since the late 1980s (Table 4.1), with considerable variation between branches and regions, but it has stabilised since around 1998. Although FNPR's records may not be entirely accurate, its claims are broadly supported by survey data, though many respondents in surveys do not know whether or not they belong to a trade union or to which union they belong. It should be noted, however, that reported membership figures are inflated by the inclusion of students in professional and vocational institutions and pensioners, who do not pay dues (or pay at a reduced rate) but who boost the numbers to increase the weight of the unions in tripartite negotiations. The reported membership of 36.9 million at the beginning of 2002 included 2.4 million non-working pensioners and about 3 million students. On the other hand, a further 0.8 million people belonged to trade unions that had collaboration agreements with FNPR without being affiliated. The membership of the alternative unions, which do not publish credible membership figures, is and always has been very small.

During the early 1990s there was a wave of resignations from union membership, particularly among managerial and professional personnel and skilled workers, and the withdrawal of GMPR in 1992 took about 1.5 million members away from FNPR, but by 2001 resignations amounted to a loss of only about one per cent of the membership each year, with 1.5 million new members, almost half of whom were students, reported as joining in 2001 (*Report to the FNPR Executive, May 2002*). Most of the membership decline has been a result of the decline in employment in traditional enterprises and organisations, the dissolution of trade union branches, particularly in smaller establishments, and the rise of the new private sector, in which union penetration is minimal. In some cases, trade union branches have been dissolved on the initiative of the employer, who absorbs the trade union functions into the management apparatus, but most employers have been happy to keep the trade union as a useful buffer between management and the labour force, carrying out management functions at the employees' expense. The majority of trade union branches which have dissolved have done so because they had become moribund and nobody could be found to serve as trade union officers or committee members (this implies that the director is indifferent to the presence of a union, since the director can always find a manager willing to take the post of trade union president). This was particularly the case in branches, such as trade and construction, in which privatisation led to the dismemberment of large organisations into a large number of small companies. Some union branches have been lost through simple bureaucratic incompetence: for example, in Samara the branch in a large furniture factory should have been transferred from the timber industry union to the union of workers in municipal industry, but the paperwork was not completed and the branch, with 5000 members, ended up lost in limbo.

## Membership dues

Trade union dues amount to one per cent of the wage (with concessions for the lowest paid, students and pensioners), checked-off from the salary automatically, and transferred to the trade union by the employer. In the soviet period the distribution of trade union dues was strictly controlled from the centre, with primary groups in the mid-80s retaining an average of 67 per cent of the dues and the remainder being transferred to higher bodies according to the central norms. With the abandonment of democratic centralism, higher bodies retained norms which defined the proportion of the dues which should be transferred to each level, but it no longer had the levers to enforce the transfer of dues according to those norms. Moreover, the norms were set by trade union conferences and congresses dominated by representatives of primary trade union organisations who were very reluctant to hand over more than the bare minimum to higher bodies, which they suspected of dissipating and misusing their funds. Attempts by regional and federal bodies to increase the proportion of dues remitted have so far been almost entirely unsuccessful, though the GMPR Congress in February 2000 decided to increase the amount remitted by primary organisations from 20 per cent to 25 per cent. Although the higher bodies could constitutionally suspend defaulters, they were loathe to do so because suspension was not a serious threat unless the defaulters felt that the services provided by the higher bodies merited the fees that they paid, while in most cases they felt that they were just supporting an apparatus which provided them with no tangible benefits.

The IIIrd Congress of FNPR in 1996 set a target for primary organisations to remit 50 per cent of dues by 2000. A resolution of the General Council in March 1999 more realistically recommended that primary organisations should retain at most 75 per cent of the dues paid, the remainder being transferred to regional branch organisations which should retain 20 per cent for their own use and that of their district and city committees, while the remaining five per cent should be divided between the central committee of the branch union, the regional trade union federation and FNPR, two per cent of the dues to be paid to FNPR by the branch union and a further sum, linked to the number of members, being paid to FNPR by the regional federations. In practice, according to FNPR, by the mid-90s primary organisations were retaining 80–5 per cent of their dues (Gritsenko, Kadeikina and Makukhina, 1999, p. 339).[1] Delegates at the IVth Congress in November 2001 again passed a resolution calling on primary trade union organisations to remit at least 50 per cent of dues to the appropriate trade union bodies, though this was hardly likely to have any effect.

[1]   Regional organisations report a similar level of retention of dues by primary organisations, but in the ISITO survey of trade union presidents the reported retention by the primary group amounted to only 69 per cent of the dues income, about the same as reported by VTsSPS in 1985. Part of the difference is probably accounted for by payments by primary organisations to city and district committees – the discrepancy is greatest in the health, education and coal-mining unions, which have such sub-regional organisations.

The problem of the payment of dues became acute during the 1990s as a result of the non-payment of wages: if workers were not being paid their wages, the union could hardly demand that the employer nevertheless should transfer the union dues.[1] Some employers took advantage of the situation simply to withhold the dues, which demanded that the union pursue the question of payment through the courts, but many primary organisations also realised that the higher bodies had no effective sanctions to enforce the payment of dues, so the incidence of non-payment of dues far exceeded that which resulted from the non-payment of wages and persisted even when wages began to be paid again at the end of the 1990s, cumulative arrears to the federation in many regions amounting to more than the annual budget. The largest and most prosperous enterprises, in particular, had no need for the services which the impoverished obkom could provide, and so could often see no reason to pay dues to the latter. The non-payment of dues by primary organisations to their obkoms meant that the latter did not transfer their dues to the regional federations and central committees and, ultimately, to FNPR, though many obkoms also withheld dues even when they had money coming in.

In 1999 FNPR received about 10 million roubles in income from membership dues, which was only 52 per cent of the amount expected. According to the budget, dues should have amounted to 77.6 per cent of FNPR's income of almost 25 million roubles ($1 million), but in fact they amounted to only 38 per cent of the total income of just over 15 million roubles. Thirty-one branch trade unions and five regional federations were in arrears, the Interior Ministry trade union and three regional federations having paid nothing, while the giant Agro-Industrial Workers' Union had paid only 1.7 per cent of the sum due (*Vesti FNPR*, 1–2, 2000, p. 48). FNPR had few sanctions against debtor organisations, although the Association of Trade Unions of Co-operative Enterprise Workers and the Interior Ministry trade union were expelled from membership of FNPR in 1999 for the non-payment of dues, and FNPR resolved to suspend the representatives of debtor organisations from membership of the Executive. In February 2001 the Federation of Branch Trade Unions of Stavropol'skii Krai was expelled from FNPR for non-payment of dues and for breaking off interaction with FNPR. On 1 September 2001, only two of the 43 branch trade unions and 27 of the 78 regional federations were fully paid-up, the Agro-Industrial Workers' Union again having paid only two per cent of the fees due. The average payment of all branch unions was 49 per cent and of regional federations was 72 per cent of the amount due, to give an overall average of 51 per cent (data from Organisational Department of FNPR).

---

[1]   In Ul'yanovsk this issue led to tension between the Federation and the budget-sector trade unions. The Federation had not pursued the non-payment of trade union dues by the regional administration on the grounds that the money was being used to pay wages, but the budget-sector unions, especially education, wanted to pursue the issue vigorously.

A substantial proportion of the expenditure of FNPR and of the regional trade union federations is covered not by their income from dues, but from their 'other' income, income from property and commercial activity. The Moscow Federation of Trade Unions derived between a third and a half of its income from 'other sources' between 1996 and 2000. The proportion of the income of the Leningrad and Saint Petersburg Federation accounted for by dues fell from 70 per cent in 1999 to 29.4 per cent in 2000 as it increased its 'other income'. Federations in less prosperous regions rely more heavily on their income from dues, but they still derive between 20 and 30 per cent of their income from their property. This gives these higher bodies a lot of independence from their members and gives rise to accusations that they are more concerned with managing their assets than servicing their members. In response, member organisations may stop remitting dues, making the Federation even more reliant on its other income. This is why the Komi Federation had to rely on 'other income' to cover more than 80 per cent of its much reduced spending in 1999.

## Trade union property

In the soviet period the trade unions had enormous property holdings. Following the collapse of the Soviet Union, the Executive Committee of VKP resolved on 22 September 1992 to transfer to FNPR ownership of much of its property located on the territory of Russia, including 690 tourist bases, 813 sanatoria, 277 administrative and social buildings, 657 sporting and physical cultural facilities, 113 training and educational establishments, 29 construction organisations and 79 buildings in the course of construction (Deputy President of VKP at the meeting of the FNPR General Council, 14.03.96, *Profsoyuzy i Ekonomika*, 4, 1996, p. 41, cited Milovidov, 2001, p.3. The report to the General Council of FNPR, 23 May 2001, gave slightly different figures). VKP nevertheless retained some of the most valuable assets. The value of the property acquired by FNPR on its foundation was estimated at 5.3 billion roubles at January 1992 prices (this was an historic cost valuation, bearing no relation to the commercial value of the assets, estimated in 2001 at $6 billion, generating an annual income of $300 million). Following Klochkov's failed attempt to retain the property in the hands of FNPR, almost eighty per cent of this property (according to the original valuation) was distributed to the regional organisations of FNPR over the following years (Report to FNPR General Council, 23 May 2001, *Vesti FNPR*, 5–6, 2001, pp. 60–72).

The right of VKP and FNPR to inherit the property of the soviet trade unions had come under insistent challenge from the alternative trade unions, in particular from Sotsprof, on the grounds that this property had been acquired using public funds. Yeltsin's Decree 2284 of 24 December 1993 required the State Property Committee to investigate the sources of financing of the property of social organisations, including the trade unions, but the trade unions were able to show that, over the period since 1971, 85 per cent of financing had come directly from trade union funds.

The property rights of the unions were finally confirmed by the 1996 Law on Trade Unions.

The biggest beneficiaries of the distribution of VKP's property were FNPR itself and the Moscow Federation of Trade Unions, which shared the bulk of the commercially valuable assets. The assets retained by FNPR were devolved to a series of joint-stock companies, in the majority of which FNPR had only a minority and in many only a small minority holding (in some the state had a shareholding in recognition of the role of state financing in the construction of the relevant assets). As part of this process, property rights in many establishments were assigned to other organisations, something that FNPR puts down to its lack of knowledge and experience. FNPR and the regional federations have subsequently been trying to re-establish their ownership rights to many establishments through the courts.

FNPR and the regional federations have inherited the premises that were occupied by their predecessors. FNPR occupies a large building complex on Leninskii Prospekt in Moscow and the Federations generally own large and prestigious buildings in the centre of their respective regional capitals. These premises are still occupied by the trade unions, with part of the premises provided either free of charge or for a rent to some of their respective branch trade union organisations. However, the slump in membership and income of the trade unions and the loss of their principal state functions has led to a sharp reduction in the size of the union apparatus and so of the size of the premises they require and that they can afford to maintain. The result is that they are able to lease out part of their premises to business organisations, so that typically the union headquarters building will be occupied not only by union offices but also by travel agencies, computing and electronics suppliers, casinos, bars, hairdressers and so on. The rental of the buildings can provide the organisation with a significant income, although in many regions this income is much reduced as offices turn out to have been disposed of on long leases at low rents, often to associates of former trade union officers. Moreover, the income has to cover the costs of maintenance and repair of the premises.

The most valuable assets, after their own premises, are the trade union hotels and hotel complexes. These include hotels in the centre of the large cities associated with the regional and national union headquarters, originally designed to accommodate delegates to conferences and union meetings, those associated with trade union residential training centres, and those in prestigious tourist resorts. Since the trade unions do not publish systematic accounts of their property holdings and transactions, considerable suspicion has attached to these deals, with allegations ranging from incompetent management of the assets of the trade unions to outright corruption.[1] It

---

[1]   FNPR published a report on its assets in 2001, under pressure from some of the branch unions, when there was a fear that it would be used as an issue in the attempt to unseat Shmakov at the forthcoming Congress. At the same time FNPR established a Commission of the General Council on property questions and created a Department for Trade Union Property within its apparatus (*Vesti FNPR*, 5–6, 2001).

appears that many of these assets have been dissipated, with trade union shareholdings being diluted or the investments lost altogether through bankruptcy of the companies to which they had been assigned. Trade union informants generally assert that the value of these assets has been considerably exaggerated since many of them were in a poor state of repair, requiring very substantial expenditure on renovation and maintenance to restore them to profitability.

Much the same can be said of the most numerous assets owned by the trade unions: the vast network of sanatoria, sporting and cultural facilities and holiday resorts, whose deplorable physical condition in most cases belied their high valuation on the books. Many of these facilities were sold, privatised or transferred to the ownership of municipal authorities, amidst suspicions that trade union officers, their families and their associates were benefiting personally from these transactions. One-fifth of the sanatoria and tourist facilities were sold or transferred to state bodies to raise money to pay for maintenance and repair of the remaining facilities and for the needs of FNPR and its regional organisations. More than half the sporting facilities were transferred to municipal ownership because the unions could not afford to maintain them. Most trade union educational facilities are retained to provide training for trade union officers and activists, but the regional federations cannot afford to maintain the facilities so that the training centres have usually been spun off into independent companies which have to supplement their revenue by renting out their premises and/or providing courses for the public.

In addition to their income from the management and disposal of trade union property, the trade unions have been heavily engaged in commercial and financial activity, particularly in the fields of tourism, finance and insurance. This was a direction of trade union development that had been pioneered by the alternative trade unions, many of which developed close relations with criminal structures as a result. Most of the commercial and financial activities of the regional trade unions appear to have ended in failure, but FNPR and VKP still own very profitable enterprises, most notably their tourist companies and the trade union bank, *Bank Solidarnost'*, although FNPR claims to have lost heavily in the banking crises of November 1994 and August 1998.

FNPR and most branch trade unions and regional federations have reasonably up-to-date office equipment: telephones, computers, fax, photocopiers and cars, but many obkoms have no more than a telephone and a few old typewriters, and depend on the federation for the use of fax, photocopying and email facilities. The more prosperous have their own fax machine and a photocopier, some (usually obsolete) computers and a car, although at best there may be only one member of the staff who knows how to operate the computer and the car may be laid up in the garage because the obkom cannot afford to employ a driver. The trade unions do not have the skills and equipment needed to make systematic use of electronic communications. It was reported to the FNPR General Council in July 2001 that only one-quarter of regional federations and fewer than half the branch trade unions even had an email address (*Vesti FNPR*, 1–2, 2001, p. 43).

Although much of the property of the trade unions has been dissipated, there is no doubt that VKP and FNPR still control substantial assets and enjoy a considerable income from their exploitation, the disposal of which is a strictly controlled secret known only, at best, to the members of their Executive Committees who nominally control the assets. The branch trade unions at federal and regional levels have very few assets, largely confined to their own office equipment and, in some cases, their offices, so that they rely almost entirely on income from dues to cover their spending. From the point of view of the fulfilment of their trade union functions the significance of these assets is that they enable FNPR and many of the regional federations to live quite comfortably without having to rely on their share of membership dues, which makes them potentially much less responsive to the needs and aspirations of their affiliated organisations and the wider trade union membership. Moreover, it is often alleged that for many trade union officials the exploitation of the property of the union takes priority over the fulfilment of their trade union functions, so that many see themselves as businessmen first and trade unionists second, or even see their trade union activity merely as a means to accumulate resources.

## The trade union apparatus

The reduction in income of the trade unions and the withdrawal of their state functions has led to a substantial reduction in the size of the trade union apparatus at all levels. The biggest reduction in the size of the trade union apparatus was a result of the state's withdrawal of the administration of the social insurance fund from the trade unions and its transfer to a new state body in 1994. In the first instance, since the new state body had no staff to replace the 100 000 trade union officers who had administered the distribution of social insurance, the relevant trade union officers were simply sworn in as state officials, but later these staff were transferred from the trade unions to the state administration altogether, although benefits financed by the insurance fund are still distributed through the trade unions. The Social Insurance Fund continues to be organised on branch lines, so that in co-operating or negotiating with the social insurance administration regional trade union officials are negotiating with their former colleagues.

The apparatus was also reduced by the withdrawal of the administration of health and safety from the trade unions and establishment of a State Labour Inspectorate, which was staffed by transferring 90 per cent of labour inspectors from the trade unions (FNPR, 1996, p. 56) and was financed from the Social Insurance Fund.

Other staff reductions were dictated by the decline in membership and in remittances from primary trade union organisations. In some cases these were associated with the abandonment of some of the traditional functions of the trade union, particularly in relation to the organisation of socialist competition and other activities related to the stimulation of production, and the decline in the scale of welfare provision. On the other hand, the regional trade union organisations have acquired new functions, particularly in relation to social partnership and the provision of legal advice, which they have to fulfil on top of their continuing functions of servicing primary organisations and their ongoing involvement in social and welfare provision at the regional level.

The reduction in the size of the trade union apparatus at regional level has sometimes been dramatic. The majority of obkoms have only 3–4 staff – we found one obkom reduced to the president, who worked from his small apartment – and some of the smaller obkoms have simply dissolved. At least one member of staff is required to keep the accounts and another is usually needed as a secretary-receptionist, so the majority of regional branch trade union committees have only one or two officers to negotiate at regional level and to service all of their primary groups. Limited staff and equipment makes it very difficult for the obkom to keep in touch with its primary organisations, particularly in regions in which its members are dispersed over a wide area (many regions cover an area of more than 100 000 square kilometres, the size of Bulgaria – the largest, Yakutia, covers more than three million square kilometres, the size of India). Typically, the President of the obkom will make occasional sorties out into the region, perhaps spending two days on a bus to reach a district capital, but the obkom will usually only maintain close relations with primary organisations located in and around the regional capital.

The larger unions can afford a larger staff, although some, like the teachers and health workers, are in very low-paid branches, with correspondingly small dues, with a large number of widely dispersed primary groups. Although there are economies of scale, the resources available are still very limited. For example, the health workers' union in the relatively prosperous Samara region had 16 staff in 1990, but this has now been reduced to 7: the president, a secretary/receptionist, two people in the finance department, one in the organisation department and two in the socio-economic department. The union also has two computers, a printer and a car, but the four officers have to negotiate at regional level and service 75 000 members in 242 primary groups.

The regional federations draw a smaller share of a bigger pot than do the branch trade unions, as well as having a certain amount of property income, and can afford a correspondingly larger staff which can provide support, especially for the smaller branch unions and for primary groups which have no branch organisation of their own in the region. The Samara Federation, for example, which had a staff of 112 in 1990 has a staff of 30 today, servicing a membership of over 850 000 in almost 5000 primary groups. The trade unions in Perm' taken together had a staff of 289 in 1990, which has been reduced to 70.5 today, of whom 43 work in the Federation. The Komi Federation, which had a staff of over 100 in 1990 and which today derives the bulk of its income from rental and commercial activity, has only 12 people left. The Moscow

Federation, by contrast, still has a staff of 77 at the City level, with further staff at the district level, while the branch union committees in Moscow are equally well staffed.

In many cases the staff of the trade union organisations is supported by permanent commissions, comprising representatives of affiliated organisations, which take responsibility for various aspects of the work of the regional organisation, but the actual conduct of the work is still the responsibility of the apparatus.

The obvious economies of scale in trade union organisation have led to suggestions from Federation officials that the branch obkoms should be abolished, so that all primary organisations affiliate directly to the Federation. A suggestion to this effect was floated by the Samara Federation in the spring of 2000, but received a very negative reaction. Officers of the regional branch unions do not favour such a development, insisting that a division of labour works best in which the Federation handles relations with the regional authorities and general trade union issues while the obkom handles issues specific to the branch. While this may be true in principle, the relationship does not necessarily work out so well in practice. As we saw above (p. 86), in July 2001 FNPR proposed the merging of obkoms in related branches to achieve economies of scale.

## Who are the trade union officers?

In the soviet period the trade union was notorious as the 'graveyard of cadres' to which incompetent managers and Party officials were consigned to see out their careers, with the most incompetent of all being further demoted to positions in the management of the trade union tourist complex. However, trade union work could also be a step in an upward career trajectory in which former managers who proved themselves in trade union work could expect promotion to a Party or more senior management position. Despite their relatively low status, trade union officers were formally equated with senior state officials and enjoyed comfortable salaries and all the perks of a *nomenklatura* position.

With the collapse of the soviet system, trade union officials lost their privileges and most experienced a steady decline in their relative salaries, while the prospects of further career advance were cut off by the collapse of the Party-state. In this context it is not surprising that some trade union officials should seek to exploit their position to augment their salaries and guarantee their future economic security, but such opportunities were pretty well exhausted by the mid-nineties. In general the limited career prospects have made trade union work fairly unattractive, while the decline in the size of the apparatus has meant that there have been limited career openings. The result has been that the trade union apparatus has been steadily ageing, with little turnover of personnel and a limited infusion of new blood, with many trade union officials having been in post for many years (or even decades), in sharp contrast to the rapid turnover which has been a feature of most other social and political institutions. In Kemerovo, for example, one-third of regional committee leaders are pensioners, with three-quarters over 50 and none under 40. Well over half the delegates to the 2000 Kemerovo Regional Federation Conference, mostly presidents of trade union committees, were over 50. In a survey undertaken by the Moscow Federation of Trade Unions over half the trade union presidents were over 50, and more than half had worked in their enterprise for more than 20 years (Tatarnikova, 1999). Mikhail Shmakov reported to the FNPR General Council in February 2001 that 20–30 per cent of trade union leaders at various levels were over pension age.

The typical career pattern of a soviet trade union official did not necessarily involve extensive trade union work: many officials were transferred to trade union positions from Party or managerial jobs and very few had come up from the shop floor. In keeping with their background, many officials had higher education and had undertaken a wide range of Party and trade union training courses to provide them with the requisite bureaucratic competence and keep them abreast of the Party line. Examination of their biographies shows that 10 per cent of regional and branch trade union leaders in post in 1999 had been transferred to those positions directly from other spheres while 43 per cent had previously held only one trade union position. Only ten per cent of these had come to their position from an enterprise trade union committee, the remainder having come from another position in the regional or branch apparatus. Only 14 per cent had come to their positions by advancing up the trade union career ladder from having been an official of the workplace trade union (Burlutskaya, 2001, p. 11). Although there was a big turnover of branch and regional trade union leaders at the beginning of the 1990s, the majority have been regularly re-elected since, closing off the career prospects for their deputies, who might otherwise have hoped to step in to their shoes.[1]

The close relationship between the regional trade union president and the regional administration fostered by social partnership means that the traditional career advance of a regional trade union leader into the state administration is not completely blocked. For example, the first head of the Komi Federation became First Deputy Prime Minister of the Republic in 1993, then Deputy Head of the Republic for Social Questions and is now President of the Republican State Council. The President of the Murmansk Federation resigned to become Deputy Governor of the region in 1997 and the President of the Chuvash Federation became First Deputy Prime Minister of his Republic in 1999. In 2000, the President of the Leningrad and St Petersburg Federation of Trade Unions, Yevgenii Makarov, resigned suddenly to take up a post as Deputy for Social Questions to Putin's plenipotentiary for the North-western Federal District; the President of the Karachaevo-Cherkessk Republican trade union federation left to become head of the Republican government; the President of the

---

[1]   Apart from 1994, when one-fifth of regional leaders were replaced following the change in the FNPR leadership, the turnover of branch and regional trade union leaders since 1991 has been about five per cent per annum (biographical data from Gritsenko, Kadeikina and Makukhina, 1999).

Ryazan' Federation left to become deputy head of the oblast administration; the President of the Magadan trade unions became Chief Federal Inspector for the oblast.

The background of the president and deputy presidents of FNPR is typical of that which is characteristic of the branch and regional trade union leaders. Now in their fifties, most have worked full-time in the trade unions for between ten and twenty years, reaching high office in the period of perestroika, but only one of the seven (Aleksei Surikov) is reported as ever having held a position in a workplace trade union organisation (Gritsenko, Kadeikina and Makukhina, 1999, pp. 551–2). Mikhail Shmakov, President of FNPR, a former research engineer, had been appointed as the President of the Moscow defence industry union in 1986 and in 1990 became President of the Moscow City trade union council, which then became the Moscow Federation of Trade Unions, before being elected President of FNPR in 1993. Two of his deputies are former heads of branch unions, both of whom had taken that position in 1991 (Vitalii Bud'ko from Kuzbass, a former underground miner who had worked in the apparatus of the coal miners' union since 1979, and Aleksei Surikov from Yaroslavl', who had worked in the apparatus of the automobile and agricultural machinery workers' union since 1980), one is the former head of a regional federation (Vyacheslav Goncharov from Ryazan', a former Komosomol and Party worker who had been appointed President of the Tula Federation in 1991); one, Tatyana Frolova, had been in trade union work since 1980 and came to FNPR from the Moscow Federation, where she had been a department head (she replaced Yevgenii Osinkin, former Deputy President of the Moscow Federation who had previously been trade union boss of the giant ZiL auto plant in Moscow, who had also come to FNPR with Shmakov but who died suddenly in September 2000) and one, Viktor Pugnev, who had worked in the apparatus of VTsSPS since 1982 and whose background was in construction and trade union tourism. Andrei Isaev, who was elevated to an Honorary Vice-Presidency in 2001, is an exception. He had been a leader of the informal movement *Obshchina* and an activist of KAS-KOR, an anarcho-syndicalist workers' information network established at the end of the 1980s. Isaev had become Shmakov's ideological mentor in the early 1990s and was appointed editor of *Solidarnost'*, the newspaper of the Moscow Federation (now the official mouthpiece of FNPR), before moving to FNPR with Shmakov in 1993.

The decline in the size of the trade union apparatus and the low turnover of trade union officers since the collapse of the Soviet Union has meant that there have been few opportunities for enterprise trade union presidents to advance to higher levels of the trade union apparatus. The ISITO survey of trade union presidents in May 2001 found that trade union presidents are predominantly managers or former managers. Their average age was 47, over a third being pensioners or approaching pension age and they had worked in the same enterprise or organisation for an average of 18 years (see below, p. 215). Thus, there is little evidence that there is a reserve of new blood in the workplace trade union organisations whose advance is blocked by the secure tenure of the regional trade union officials. The evidence rather suggests that workplace trade union leaders tend to be former managers and specialists who have been found a comfortable niche by senior management to work out their remaining careers before retirement.

Most of the specialist staff of the trade union apparatus at all levels have long trade union careers with the professional skills appropriate to the traditional functions of the trade unions in the administration of the social and welfare apparatus, the organisation of 'mass-cultural work', socialist competition and so on. Most of the trade union staff responsible for social insurance and health and safety were transferred to the state bodies which took over responsibility for those functions in the mid-1990s, although they tend to maintain informal relations and collaborate closely with their former colleagues. With the acquisition of the new functions of participation in social partnership and the protection of workers' rights the trade unions have tried to recruit economists and lawyers, but the low status, low salaries and limited career prospects of trade union work have made it difficult to attract people with the appropriate professional skills.

In view of the skills, experience and capacities of the staff of the trade unions, it should hardly be surprising that they have sought as far as possible to retain their traditional functions and to perform their new functions in traditional ways.

## Trade union expenditure

The allocation of expenditure is a good indicator of the priorities and activities of trade union organisations.[1] In the soviet period trade union spending was roughly equally divided between 'mass-cultural work' (culture, physical culture and sport), material assistance and the maintenance of the trade union apparatus. This allocation of resources has been largely maintained at enterprise level, but at regional level there has been a radical change in the structure of the trade union budget as a result of the sharp reduction in financial resources and the loss of the trade unions' social and welfare assets. In 1988 the Komi Trade Union Federation spent 73.7 per cent of its income on 'mass-cultural work', 5.5 per cent on material assistance and 20.6 per cent on its organisational and management expenses. Over the period 1996–2000 the Komi Federation spent 97.3 per cent of its much depleted income on organisation and management (84.9 per cent on wages alone), 0.5 per cent on material assistance and nothing on mass-cultural work. In 2000 the total expenditure of the Federation amounted to only a little over \$14 000 to service 238 000 members.

The scope for discretion in spending depends very much on the wealth of the Federation. The Komi Federation is one of the most impoverished, with few member

---

[1]   Many trade union organisations are very sensitive about releasing information on expenditure, particularly that on their wages. The account in this section is based on more or less complete information on the proportional allocation of spending of seven regional federations and 17 regional branch organisations obtained by our colleagues from various sources.

organisations remitting fees, but other federations typically spend between 75 and 85 per cent of their income on organisation and management, with the wages of the apparatus accounting for between a quarter and a half of the total budget. A typical provincial Federation, such as Perm' or Samara, with around 800 thousand members has an income of rather less than $100 000 a year, Kemerovo, with 618 000 members, had an income of $37 000 in 1999. The Moscow Federation, with 2.9 million members, has an income of rather more than one million dollars a year, about the same as FNPR itself, and the Leningrad and St Petersburg Federation, with a membership of 1.1 million, had an income of about $360 000 in 2000. Nevertheless, even the richest federations still spend relatively little on the traditional items of expenditure, with most federations spending between four and nine per cent of their budget on mass-cultural work, and a very small amount on material assistance (Moscow being the exception, devoting 10 per cent of its budget to material assistance). Despite the high priority given to training, expenditure by the federations is only between two and six dollars per thousand members per year, which will pay for one day's training in a union training centre.

The prosperity of regional branch trade union committees depends very much on the number employed in the branch, the level of their salaries and the extent to which primary groups remit their dues. An obkom with a large membership in a well-paid branch, such as metallurgy, will often have a much larger income than the regional federation, while an obkom with few members in a poorly paid branch with a high level of non-payment will barely be able to cover the salary and office expenses of its tiny staff. Even in the best-paid branches the obkom will usually have a much lower income than its largest primary organisations. Obkoms typically spend about two-thirds of their income on organisational and management expenses, with between a third and a half of the total covering the wage bill. Some continue to spend a substantial amount of money (up to half the budget) on mass-cultural work, while others spend very little under this heading. There is a similar very wide variation in the amount spent on material assistance, with some branch organisations devoting a quarter of their budget to helping those in need and others spending almost nothing. There is no discernible pattern in this variation by branch or region, nor is there an immediately obvious relation to the strategic orientation of the trade union committee. Some committees that denounce the preoccupation of primary trade union organisations with their social welfare functions nevertheless devote a significant part of their budget to performing just such functions, presumably in response to pressure from their primary organisations. The branch committees tend to spend a slightly higher proportion of their budgets on training than do the federations, although spending on training is still substantially less than it was in the soviet period and than is recommended by FNPR.

It is important in considering the way in which trade unions perform their functions to keep in mind the very limited human and financial resources that the regional trade union organisations have available to them to implement the strategic policy decisions of FNPR and the Central Committees of the branch trade unions and to respond to the pressures for support from primary organisations. In the face of the pressures to which they are subject and the constraints they are under it is not surprising that many regional trade union officers take a very passive approach to their work. If they just sit in their offices, there is plenty to keep them busy all day, reading the papers, opening the post, answering the telephone and fielding inquiries from visitors, the monotony broken by occasional meetings and business trips. This is why the problem of regional organisation, particularly at the branch level, is often seen as a personnel problem and higher levels are anxious to recover their powers to replace ineffective officers at lower levels.

# 5

# The Legal Framework of Industrial Relations

The soviet industrial relations system was marked by the extent to which the rights and responsibilities of employees and the trade unions were enshrined in law, with the Labour Code providing a comprehensive framework of regulation of the terms and conditions of labour and extending unprecedented rights and protection to trade union bodies, while the plan and collective agreements enjoyed juridical status. The Soviet Union prided itself on the fact that the legal rights and protection accorded to labour were the most advanced in the world. But this progressive appearance concealed a variety of features less favourable to workers. First, detailed legal regulation was required precisely because the Communist Party was not prepared for voluntary joint regulation of employment to take place. The latter would have entailed granting autonomy to workers' organisations and employers and thus would have challenged the Party's political monopoly. Second, the law by no means constituted an obligatory framework for labour relations: instead, it served as a discretionary instrument for confining managerial authority within the limits of Party policy. Finally, legal protection, and the role of the trade unions in monitoring the observance of workers' legal rights, was not defined in terms of the protection of workers' interests but in terms of the need to develop the productive powers of labour.

Since collective mobilisation of workers was the regime's worst nightmare, it is not surprising that, despite its collectivist rhetoric, the Party did not provide a legal framework for any kind of collective action or independent organisation. The 1972 Soviet Labour Code provided only for individual labour disputes and individual court hearings. Since the regime could not delegate the more detailed aspects of employment regulation to autonomous social institutions, it tried to regulate every possible detail of the employment relationship in every possible situation by law. The Labour Code minutely prescribed the terms and conditions of employment to be enjoyed by soviet workers. Alongside its well-known provisions protecting workers against arbitrary dismissal,[1] the code also laid down pay norms and tariff scales; the (strict) conditions under which employees could be transferred to different posts; the length of the working day; the normal length of the working week; the length and timing of rest periods, meal breaks, days off and vacations, including special privileges for certain categories of worker; restrictions on night work, shift work and overtime; the payment due for any extra work undertaken; detailed health and safety

---

[1] For a commentary see Hendley, 1996, pp. 52–62.

provisions, and so on. Meanwhile, the plan and collective agreements also enjoyed legal status. This comprehensive legal framework provided a 'safe' (from the Party's perspective) channel of conflict resolution. The trade unions and enterprise legal advisors could take up the cases of individuals whose legal rights had been violated. This provided some check on managerial arbitrariness without constituting any kind of political threat.

Indeed, even the law was not permitted to challenge the 'leading and guiding role of the Party'. As Kathryn Hendley argued in her study of Soviet labour law, the Party élite did not want to be constrained by law; they did not want to establish an autonomous power in society which could challenge their pre-eminence. Thus, 'in the hands of the Party élite, the law became a flexible tool.... Law proved incapable of restraining the powerful' (Hendley, 1996, p. 4). It is therefore not surprising that studies of soviet labour relations have shown that there was 'no consistency in the enforcement of law in the workplace' (Shelley, 1984).

The final argument – that the law was not designed to protect workers, but to further the building of communism – can be illustrated with regard to the protection against dismissal that we have already discussed briefly above (pp. 19–20). Legal protection against arbitrary dismissal was not provided in the interests of the individual worker, but in the interests of the soviet system of rule. The workplace, rather than the household, was the basic unit of soviet society, and integration into a labour collective was the primary means by which the individual was supposed to be integrated into society. The last thing the Party wanted to see was malcontents and deviants being thrown out of the enterprise onto the street where, beyond supervision and control, they would supposedly degenerate into hooliganism and criminality.

Protection against dismissal was a part of the set of policies designed to compel management to employ the less desirable elements of the labour force, alongside the requirement to employ released prisoners, new high school and college graduates, 'parasites' directed to work by the MVD and/or labour recruitment bureaux and quotas of disabled workers. In the same way, the strict legal limitations on the hours of work, the banning of overtime, limitations on shift and night work, rights to rest during the working day and holiday entitlements were all designed to check the tendency of management to seek to achieve the plan by intensifying labour and lengthening the working day to the detriment of the health of the labour force, rather than by organising work more rationally. At the same time, the irrationality of the soviet system meant that the plan could only be achieved by precisely such measures, particularly during the regular storming at the end of the month. Thus the contradiction between the extensive legal rights and protection enjoyed by workers and the reality of their situation was only an expression of the fundamental irrationality of the soviet system as a whole.

## Post-soviet changes to the legal framework: an overview

It might have been expected that the collapse of the soviet system would have been accompanied by an extensive revision of the legal regulation of the terms and conditions of labour and of the rights of trade unions to bring them into line with the changing economic and social reality. However, apart from the 1992 Law on Collective Agreements, some minor amendments to the Labour Code and *ad hoc* and inconsistent Presidential decrees and government resolutions, the legal framework of industrial relations until the end of 1995 remained that of the soviet period.[1] This is partly because this framework, which had proved its worth as a means of defusing conflict and regulating labour relations, was deeply embedded in the practice and expectations of trade unionists and workers. Thus the new alternative trade unions which emerged after 1987 continued to work within the traditional framework, seeking to achieve their aims not by building a membership-based organisation, but by employing lawyers and appealing individual cases to the courts, taking disputes out of the workplace and into the labyrinthine procedures of the soviet legal system. While trade unions and workers' organisations lacked the strength to enforce their rights within the workplace, the legal codification of those rights presented few limitations on employers. And while trade unions and workers' organisations continued to pursue disputes through the courts on an individual basis, with long delays and largely without effect, they were unlikely to develop effective workplace organisation.

Article 226 of the Labour Code, as amended in 1992, continued to define the trade union essentially as a part of the state: trade unions represent the interests of their members, but their rights are defined primarily in relation to their participation in the formulation, implementation and monitoring of labour legislation and their management of the state welfare and social insurance system. The extensive powers enjoyed by the trade unions were and remain powers delegated to them by the state to perform state functions rather than powers won by the trade unions in pursuit of their members' interests. The state has taken over some of these powers, for example in relation to the control of social insurance and the establishment of a state labour inspectorate, but the trade unions continue to administer the distribution of social insurance benefits and monitor health and safety and the law provides for the continued collaboration of the trade union with the new state agencies in monitoring the observance of labour law and health and safety regulations.

A second reason why reform of labour and trade union legislation was constantly postponed was the struggle for power and influence between the new and the old trade unions, new legislation being one of the daggers that the government could hold

---

[1]   Soviet law continued to apply in Russia, despite the collapse of the Soviet Union, unless it contradicted the Russian Constitution and until it was replaced or amended by appropriate Russian legislation. The proliferation of contradictory laws, decrees and resolutions after 1991, in the sphere of labour as elsewhere, provided enormous scope for legal interpretation.

over the unions. Following the 1993 Duma election, however, the situation somewhat stabilised, with the new unions having been marginalised and the traditional unions turning their attention away from politics towards the more routine defence of their institutional interests. The discussion of draft laws continued for a period of two years. Some of the drafts issuing from the Ministry of Labour in 1994 massively reduced the rights of trade unions and the protection accorded to employees, even managing to unite the leaders of the new and the traditional unions in their condemnation of the drafts, but it seems that these were intended more as shots across the bows of the traditional trade unions at a time when there was still some anxiety in government circles that they would constitute a significant oppositional force. During hearings and debate through 1995 final versions of the laws were agreed, and at the end of 1995 and beginning of 1996 new laws were introduced concerning trade unions, the settlement of collective labour disputes and, as a revision of the 1992 law, collective agreements, all of which at least maintained and in some cases strengthened the legal rights of trade unions and employees, but government hopes of revising the Labour Code were thwarted. The most contentious issue in the debates around the new labour legislation concerned not the rights of workers but the rights of trade unions, and in particular the privileges enjoyed by the unions affiliated to FNPR over the alternative unions. FNPR emerged as the unequivocal victor in all of these debates.

The general view outside the FNPR trade unions was that the new framework of industrial relations marked the triumph of the FNPR trade unions, which now enjoy a strongly privileged position as the legally sanctioned representatives of employees within a tripartite industrial relations framework. The Law on Trade Unions and the Law on Collective Agreements confine the right to participate in institutions of social partnership at the federal level to All-Russian trade unions, excluding most of the alternative unions. At enterprise level the privileges of the FNPR trade union undermine attempts of employers in private enterprises to substitute their own house 'trade unions', but also restrict attempts of workers to establish their own forms of representation, typically in the form of strike and workers' committees. Similarly, the Law on Collective Labour Disputes recognises the legitimacy of properly organised strikes, with due notice and following a conciliation period, but only in the case of *collective* disputes, i.e. those concerning collective agreements. All disputes concerning issues not included in the collective terms of labour are regarded as individual labour disputes, even if they involve all the employees in an enterprise, which have to be pursued through the channels of resolution of individual disputes and strikes in such cases do not enjoy the protection of the law. Thus participants in wildcat and unofficial strikes or strikes over the non-payment of wages, where that is not included in the collective agreement, enjoy no legal protection.

The introduction of new labour legislation potentially marked an important step forward, since the continued operation of the inappropriate legislation of the soviet period contributed to the discrediting of the law. For example, the late soviet law on strikes made it almost impossible to hold a legal strike, which meant that the law was widely ignored, but then implemented arbitrarily. Similarly, the use of contract and more flexible forms of labour, which have become widespread in the new private sector, have had no legal foundation, while the protection provided by the Labour Code was flouted even more blatantly than in the soviet period. Indeed, there was a widespread but completely unfounded assumption on the part of many private employers that the Labour Code applied only to state employees.

The revised legal framework continued the soviet tradition of providing Russian workers with the most favourable conditions of labour and trade union organisation of any country in the world. Given the depth of the crisis of the Russian economy and the appalling conditions under which so many Russian workers work, this gave rise to considerable doubt about the extent to which this legislation, like its soviet predecessors, would in fact be implemented and respected. The strength of legal protection is, as in the soviet period, not an indicator of the achievements of employees but of the weakness of employee representation, of the extent of the subordination of trade union organisation to enterprise management and of the inaccessibility of legal redress. The problem from an industrial relations point of view is that, as in the soviet period, this bureaucratic-legal framework provides a mechanism of tension management through the fragmentation and bureaucratisation of conflict. It does not provide any effective mechanism of employee representation and conflict resolution. The result is that, as in the soviet period, when conflict does erupt and overflow the bureaucratic channels provided there are no effective institutional mechanisms through which such conflict can be peacefully negotiated and resolved.

In this chapter we will briefly review the current state of labour legislation in Russia and comment on the most significant changes introduced by the new Labour Code, which was signed into law on 30 December 2001.[1]

## The Russian Constitution

The rights of labour are recognised in the Russian Constitution, adopted on the basis of the referendum of December 1993, which is the basic law of the Russian Federation. The Russian Constitution continues the soviet tradition of defining the protection of labour, including minimum wages and social protection, as a responsibility of the state. However, as against the Brezhnev Soviet Constitution, which defined the right and obligation of every soviet citizen to work, the Russian Constitution defines labour as free. The soviet right to work is replaced with the right to 'protection from unemployment', which means simply the right to receive unemployment benefit and the job placement services of the Federal Employment

---

[1]   This chapter has drawn heavily on the thorough commentaries on the 1995–6 laws: Shalaev, Gritsenko and Snigireva, 1996; Snigireva, 1996 and Burnova et al., 1996.

Service free of charge. In addition to the 'right to protection from unemployment', Article 37 of the Constitution defines the 'social-labour rights' of the population as the right freely to dispose of one's capacity to labour, to choose the form of activity and occupation; the right to work in conditions corresponding to requirements of health and safety; to be rewarded for labour without any kind of discrimination and not below the minimum pay laid down by federal law; the right to engage in individual and collective labour disputes, using the means for their resolution, including the right to strike, laid down by Federal Law; the right to rest; the right to social protection of the old, sick, disabled, loss of breadwinner and for bringing up children; the right to housing; the right to the preservation of health and medical support; the right to a healthy environment; the right to education; the right to free creativity and others. The Constitution also defines the right of association, including the formation of trade unions to defend the interests of employees and the use of all methods in defence of those interests, including the right to strike, which are not in violation of the law, although the trade union rights of certain categories of employees (such as the military, internal affairs, federal security service, customs, tax police and judiciary) are restricted by corresponding legislation.

A very important feature of the Russian Constitution from the point of view of labour legislation is that it incorporates international law and the international agreements of the Russian Federation into the Russian legal system, rights established under such international agreements having precedence over Russian legislation. This means, in particular, that those ILO Conventions endorsed by Russia form part of the basic Russian labour legislation, with priority over all other legislative acts.[1]

## The Russian Labour Code

The Russian Labour Code until the end of 2001 remained that of the Soviet Union which came into effect in April 1972, as subsequently amended. The major amendments to the Code were those adopted by decree of the Presidium of the Russian Supreme Soviet in February 1988 and by Russian federal laws of 25 September 1992 and 24 November 1995. However, these amendments were concerned primarily with the application of the Labour Code to changing property and contractual forms rather than with making substantive changes to the rights and protection of workers. Thus, for example, it became necessary to define employment on the basis of individual labour contracts and to specify that the Labour Code applied to all those employed on a contractual basis, regardless of the form of property, while it does not apply to those who contract to provide goods and services,

---

[1]    The ILO Bureau made a number of recommendations in relation to the new Labour Code in Memoranda in response to requests for clarification from the Russian government (10 October 2001) and from KTR and VKT (13 November 2001) regarding the potential violation of ILO Conventions, in particular in relation to the payment of wages in kind, the right to free association and the right to strike, but all of its recommendations were ignored.

who are considered to be self-employed and beyond the application of the Labour Code.[1] The main substantive change to the Labour Code was in relation to the ending of centralised wage regulation, which meant the removal of the clauses concerning the determination of pay norms and the tariff scale, payment systems outside the public sector now being determined at enterprise level and embodied in the collective agreement reached with the trade union. Similarly, the articles concerning the powers of the general meeting and the council of the labour collective (STK), a body embracing both management and employees, which had been incorporated into the Labour Code in 1988, were repealed in 1992 in view of impending privatisation.[2]

Government attempts to introduce a radically new Labour Code were blocked by opposition in parliament and from the trade unions, until a draft agreed between the government and FNPR, but vigorously opposed by the left parties and the alternative unions, was adopted by the State Duma in December 2001 (see above, pp. 64–68). Significant changes introduced by the new Labour Code will be noted in this chapter.

The Labour Code defines a contract of employment as an agreement between the employee (singular) and an employer which specifies the profession, qualification or post and the terms of employment of the employee, which must be no less favourable than those laid down by the law and the operative collective agreement. In the soviet period it was not usual to sign individual contracts, since the terms and conditions of employment were already specified in law and collective agreements, so the contract was implied in the act of hiring the person to a particular post in a particular subdivision of the enterprise. As the law and collective agreements increasingly refer only to the minimum conditions of employment, individual contracts have become more significant as a codification of the terms and conditions of employment of the individual employee. The 1992 amendment to the Labour Code specified that every employee should have a contract of employment, which was only valid if it was concluded in a written form, but many workers still have no such contract. Since the

---

[1]   This provided a familiar loophole for those employers wishing to flout the provisions of the Code with impunity by labour-only sub-contracting. The 2001 Labour Code closes this loophole by extending its application to all employees, whatever the contractual form of their employment. Indeed, where the old Labour Code referred to a 'labour agreement (contract)', the term 'contract' is deleted from the new Labour Code.

[2]   In practice the situation remained confused, since some of the previous legislation concerning the powers of the STK remained in force and other legislation, such as the 1992 Law on Collective Agreements, referred to representative bodies of employees without specifying their form. The situation was only clarified with the new legislation on collective agreements, labour disputes and trade unions in 1995–6, which finally reduced the responsibilities of the STK to some residual self-management functions and participation in the management of production. The 2001 Labour Code has removed altogether the section dealing with the labour collective – indeed the term itself does not appear in the new Code, but a Law on the Labour Collective was introduced into the Duma by the Liberal Democratic Minister of Labour, Kalashnikov, as a means of undermining FNPR, and was subsequently reintroduced by the Communists.

individual contract cannot legally provide worse conditions than those laid down by law and the corresponding collective agreement, individual labour contracts are in theory to the advantage of the employee and are usually welcomed by Russian workers.[1] For this same reason, however, the conclusion of individual labour contracts is still the exception in Russia, covering only about 10 per cent of the labour force, though about twice as many in the new private sector (Clarke, 1999c), most workers enjoying no more rights than are specified by law and the collective agreement.

Contracts of employment are in general of indefinite duration, although a non-renewable probationary period of three months (up to six months by agreement with the appropriate trade union, a qualification dropped from the new Labour Code, which extends the six-month probation only to heads of organisations and their subdivisions and which also rules that the terms of probation must be specified in advance) may be specified. Short-term contracts of up to five years can be concluded, but only where 'the character of the work, the conditions of its fulfilment or the interests of the employee as well as situations immediately stipulated by law' (Article 17) make it impossible to conclude an indefinite agreement.[2] This restriction of the use of contract labour was introduced in 1992, in conformity with ILO recommendation 166 of 1982, because employers had been transferring their entire labour force onto fixed-term five-year contracts which they used to prevent

[1]   However, many were ignorant of this provision of the law so that many employees, particularly in the new private sector, have been made to sign individual contracts which illegally define terms inferior to those specified in collective agreements and even in the Labour Code. Many of those hired in small and private businesses are illegally hired on the basis of a verbal agreement.

[2]   This restriction on fixed-term contracts is retained in the new Labour Code, which removes the 'interests of the employee' as a justification for a fixed-term contract, a term which is obviously open to gross abuse, specifies that state control bodies (the state labour inspectorate) should adjudicate the legitimacy of a fixed-term contract and forbids fixed-term contracts where the intention is to limit the rights of the employee. However, restrictions are removed where the employer is a private individual or a small business with fewer than 40 employees (25 in trade and services); to replace a temporarily absent employee; for temporary work (up to two months) or seasonal work; for work abroad or in the Far North; for work in connection with accidents and emergencies; where employment is based on an extension (e.g. reconstruction) or expansion (for up to one year) of the usual activity of the employer; where the organisation has only been established or the work expected to last for a particular period of time; for those employed to teach particular types of courses; for those employed in a second job; for pensioners or those who can only work temporarily for medical reasons; for artists, performers and sportsmen; for scientists, teachers and others who have taken a temporary job on a competitive basis; in the case of election to a post or in direct connection with the work of an elected body; for directors, deputy directors and chief accountants; for people placed in temporary work, including public works, by the employment services; or in other cases specified by federal law (Article 59).

employees from leaving their jobs voluntarily, while the employer always had the threat of dismissal or redundancy in his hands.[1]

The provisions of the Soviet Labour Code restricting the transfer and dismissal of employees remain in the Russian Labour Code. Thus, the administration cannot normally require an employee to perform duties not stipulated in the contract of employment, nor transfer an employee to other duties without his or her written consent. The 1992 amendment to the Labour Code also excluded the traditional soviet disciplinary measure of the transfer of an employee to lower-paid work. These are significant restrictions on the rights of management since the normal duties of an employee are quite narrowly defined by occupation or profession, grade, skill and location. In general, management is only free to transfer an employee to another job of the same skill and professional requirements and rates of pay and in the same location as the existing job.[2] However, alterations in the conditions of employment are permitted in connection with organisational changes, provided that the employee is given two months notice of such a change.[3] Temporary transfers for up to one month, without reduction of pay, are also permitted in the case of production necessity, including the absence of particular employees. In the case of a stoppage the employee can be transferred for the duration of the stoppage, or for up to one month to another enterprise in the same place, without reduction of earnings. In none of these cases is it permissible to transfer a skilled worker to unskilled work, a restriction dropped from the new Labour Code. In practice transfer was rare in the soviet period and was almost always on the initiative of the employee, so the legislation was largely irrelevant (Hendley, 1992). More recently the transfer of workers has become a common practice in the case of the structural reorganisation of the enterprise or as an alternative to redundancy, in which case transfer is permitted by the law. The transfer of skilled workers to unskilled work paid on time-rates became a common practice as a means of protecting their earnings in the face of the fall in production and production stoppages (Clarke and Donova, 1999). Whatever the legal position, such employees are hardly likely to object to the practice.

The Russian Labour Code also retained most of the limitations on the right of the employer to dismiss employees that existed in the Soviet Code. In general, employees other than senior managers could only be dismissed other than on disciplinary

---

[1]  An indefinite contract could be terminated by the employee by giving two weeks notice in writing, but a fixed-term contract could only be terminated on the grounds of incapacity or violation of the terms of the contract or collective agreement on the part of the employer. This latter restriction is removed from the new Labour Code.

[2]  The new Labour Code specifies that a transfer does not require the employee's agreement if it does not involve a change of function or a 'significant' change in the conditions of the contract (Article 72).

[3]  The new Labour Code allows the employer to introduce short-time working for a period of up to six months, after consultation with the representatives of the employees, as a means of avoiding mass redundancy, without giving the required notice (Article 73).

grounds or in the case of redundancy or if they were unable to carry out their specified duties, if it was impossible to transfer them, with their agreement, to other work and if the corresponding elected trade union body agreed to their dismissal. The trade union still had the right to demand the dismissal or transfer of any manager 'who is responsible for the violation of labour legislation, not fulfilling his or her responsibilities under the collective agreement, manifesting bureaucratism or permitting red-tape'. This right is retained in the new Labour Code, but only in relation to violations of the law or collective agreement. Disciplinary grounds for dismissal specified in the Labour Code were limited to the employee's systematic failure to perform his or her duties without good reason and following a warning, absenteeism (absence from work for more than three hours) without good reason, intoxication at work and theft of public property from the workplace. Since 1992 disciplinary dismissals have not required the agreement of the trade union, the person dismissed having the right to appeal directly to the court.[1]

The grounds for dismissal are one of the biggest changes in the new Labour Code, which includes a more extensive list of grounds for dismissal than in previous versions. Employees can be dismissed for failure to perform their duties for various reasons, for serious breaches of health and safety rules, for wilful loss of or damage to property, for revealing 'commercial secrets' or for reasons laid down in their labour contract, and the agreement of the trade union to redundancies or dismissal is not required, although in certain circumstances the opinion of the trade union should still be taken into account and the trade union committee can appeal the dismissal of a trade union member on the grounds of redundancy, inadequate qualification for his or her post or failure to fulfil his or her duties. Additional rights of the trade union to sanction dismissals can be specified in the collective agreement.

An employer is entitled to dismiss employees in the event of the liquidation of an enterprise or redundancy, but the Labour Code specifies in detail the categories of employees to be given precedence in this event and stipulates that those subject to dismissal should have priority in filling vacancies elsewhere in the organisation. In the case of redundancy the trade union must be notified at least two months in advance (three months in the case of mass redundancy) and those subject to redundancy must be notified and offered alternative work in the same enterprise at least two months in advance, the Employment Service being informed of the details of those subject to redundancy at the same time.

The Russian Labour Code retained the soviet restrictions on the length of the working day, the normal length of the working week, the length and timing of rest

---

[1]   This was another of the cases at the end of 1992 when the government failed to listen to the new unions, which had relied heavily on the legal protection from dismissal that they were able to offer their members, both to attract members and to protect their activists. With the amendment to the Labour Code the activists of the new unions faced a much lengthier battle through the courts every time they were dismissed, for example for absenteeism when attending a union meeting.

periods, meal breaks, days off and vacations, including specified privileges for particular categories of worker, restrictions on night work, shift work and strict limitations on overtime working, and specified the additional payment due in the event of the need to work overtime or on days-off or in the event of short-time working, transfers, work stoppages and so on. It retained virtually intact the articles of the Soviet Labour Code related to norm-setting and to various forms of compensation and deductions from pay, on labour discipline and the responsibilities of the employee, on health and safety, on the protection of women and young people. In short, despite the 'transition to a market economy', the legislative regulation of the terms and conditions of labour, other than rates of pay, inherited from the soviet period has remained largely intact.

Although the Labour Code now defines the statutory minimum terms and conditions of labour, which can be improved upon in collective agreements or individual employment contracts, in a situation of deepening economic crisis this minimum remains at best the norm in most branches and enterprises.[1] In practice it continues to be violated systematically and with impunity because workers fear for their jobs and do not want to lose earnings. For example, the Labour Code severely restricts overtime working and prescribes that those working overtime should be paid time-and-a-half for the first two hours and double-time for subsequent hours, but a household survey conducted by ISITO in May 1998 found that two-thirds of respondents worked overtime but only 10 per cent were paid at an enhanced rate, with 60 per cent being paid nothing at all for the additional hours worked (Clarke, 1999b, p.84). Employers equally flout the guarantees of work in safe and healthy conditions with impunity. Indeed, so prevalent was such work that the Soviet government had introduced supplementary payments for those working in harmful conditions, which in 1999 were received by 43 per cent of industrial workers, 40 per cent of those in transport and 31 per cent of those in construction (Goskomstat, 2000b).

## The 2001 Labour Code

The Labour Code passed by the Duma in December 2001 differs radically from the old in its definition of the basic principles of labour legislation. The old Labour Code related labour legislation not to the rights and interests of the worker but to the need to 'support the growth of labour productivity, improve the quality of labour, increase the effectiveness of social production and on this basis to support the material and cultural level of the life of the toilers, strengthen labour discipline and gradually transform labour for the well-being of society into the first vital need of every able-bodied person' (Article 1). The new Labour Code defines its tasks in terms of providing state guarantees for the rights and interests of employees (and employers)

---

[1]   Many collective agreements in fact specify terms inferior to those provided by the Labour Code (Chetvernina and et al., 1995, p. 7; Tatarnikova, 1999).

within a framework of social partnership and to this (very limited) extent meets the long-standing demand of FNPR for a Federal Law on Social Partnership.

The new Labour Code retains many of the protective and regulatory features of its soviet predecessor, and in other cases makes some modifications to the terms or extension of the provisions of the previous Labour Code, some of which are in favour of the employee, but in general gives much more discretion to the employer, who no longer requires the agreement of the trade union to such things as the determination of working hours and shift patterns, overtime working, the redeployment of labour, the revision of norms or the definition of disciplinary rules, although in some cases its opinion should still be taken into account and failure to reach agreement can be the pretext for a collective labour dispute. The new Labour Code retains largely intact the traditional restrictions on working hours, overtime, night work, work in harmful conditions, the regulation of rest breaks and holiday entitlements (the minimum holiday is increased from 24 to 28 working days), including the privileges and restrictions on the work of women, the disabled and young people and incorporates the benefits accorded to those working in the North of the country prescribed by previous legislation, although some relaxation of the restrictions on overtime and the deployment of women's labour is allowed 'with the written permission of the employee'. The benefits and protection accorded to women with young children are now extended to single fathers or guardians. The new Labour Code still prescribes enhanced rates of pay and benefits for overtime, working on holidays and days-off and for work in harmful conditions and retains largely intact an extensive range of concessions and restrictions for particular categories of employee and relating to particular circumstances.

It has been estimated that the total cost to employers of the benefits incorporated in the new Labour Code represents an increase of about eight per cent over the cost of the provisions of the old Labour Code, largely because of the incorporation of additional holiday entitlements and of benefits to inhabitants of the Northern Regions, with the cost of providing trade union facilities and of benefits to those undergoing training being substantially reduced and most other benefits not being significantly changed (Maleva et al., 2001, p. 38).

The main changes in the new over the old Labour Code are the removal of some of the restrictions on the flexible deployment of labour and on the right of the employer to dismiss the worker, and the regulation of many features of the terms and conditions of employment by the collective agreement and contract of employment where previously the permission of the trade union was explicitly required.[1] In many respects this is a progressive development in removing one of the links that tied the trade union to management. The trade union in the past routinely approved

---

[1]   In some cases, the employer is required to take into account the views of the trade union and if the trade union, after consultation, continues to reject the employer's proposals, this is ground for a collective labour dispute (Article 373).

management decisions, even if they were deleterious for the workers, whereas they will now have to justify themselves to their members by defending their interests on the basis of their collective organisation rather than through bureaucratic and juridical procedures. On the other hand, the need to seek the permission of the trade union was certainly a constraint on the unbridled exercise of power by the employer which has now been removed.

The new Labour Code provides some significant improvements in the position of workers in areas which have been the focus of conflict at the workplace. It retains the requirement that wages should be paid at least fortnightly but now prescribes the payment of interest on unpaid wages and entitles workers to stop work, without pay, if their wages are delayed by more than fifteen days, until such time as the wages due are paid, although some categories of workers (military forces, law-enforcement agencies, emergency services and vital pubic services) are excluded from this provision (this responds to a demand of the unions because of the enormous difficulty involved in organising a legal strike against the non-payment of wages). However, the new Labour Code permits the payment of up to 20 percent of wages in kind, as provided for by the collective or labour agreement and with the written permission of the employee (although payment in the form of alcohol, narcotics, poisons or arms and ammunition is forbidden). The new Law improves the provisions of the old Labour Code regarding payment when the worker is not able to achieve production norms, produces defective products or in the event of a stoppage which is not the fault of the worker, all of which have been the source of conflicts in unstable Russian conditions.

The most dramatic enhancement to the terms and conditions of labour offered by the new Labour Code is the specification that the minimum wage (and the lowest grade on any wage scale) cannot be lower than the subsistence minimum for an able-bodied adult, a long-standing demand of the trade unions. This would have a dramatic impact, were it to be implemented, since, according to Goskomstat's earnings survey in October 1999, 40 per cent of employees earned less than the subsistence minimum. The lowest grade on the Unified Tariff Scale (ETS), which governs the salaries of all public employees, in 2000 was less than one-tenth of the subsistence minimum. Moreover, the minimum wage refers only to the basic wage, without any bonuses, whereas on average the basic wage accounts for less than a third of earnings (Tatarnikova, 1999, p. 33, but see footnote 2, p.180). The new Labour Code qualifies this clause by noting (Article 422) that the method and period of introduction of such a minimum wage will be established by a Federal Law. Such a draft law, providing for a minimum wage of 60 per cent of the subsistence minimum in 2002 and 100 per cent in 2003, was passed on its first reading by the State Duma the day after the July vote on the Labour Code, but Putin immediately made it clear that such legislation represented an intrusion on the authority of the President and that the minimum wage would be set not by federal law but by the budget within the limits of financial possibilities. This will undoubtedly provide a prime focus for conflict in the future.

While the new Labour Code reduces the legal rights of the trade union to approve management decisions, reduces employment security and provides scope for unscrupulous employers to extend working hours, it retains intact the bulk of the soviet protective labour legislation and so does not mark a significant break with the traditional juridical regulation of industrial relations in favour of their regulation through collective bargaining. Moreover, while it explicitly assigns to the State Labour Inspectorate many of the control functions which were previously performed by the trade unions, the union retains the right to monitor the observance of labour legislation and the employer has the obligation to respond promptly to its representations. All-Russian trade unions are permitted to establish their own technical and labour inspectorates authorised by the trade union with the agreement of the government executive bodies responsible for labour. They have the right of access to any establishment in which they have members to carry out an inspection.

The new Labour Code weakens the alternative unions in three principal respects. First, the right to participate in the negotiation of a collective agreement is only given to the 'primary organisation' of an All-Russian trade union (Article 37), but most alternative trade union organisations do not qualify as primary organisations within an All-Russian  structure. Second, in negotiating a collective agreement where there is more than one trade union primary organisation, if the different organisations do not set up a joint negotiating body within five days, the interests of all employees will be represented by the trade union which organises the majority of the labour force, which makes it very easy for the established union to exclude an alternative trade union organisation from participating in collective bargaining.[1] Similar provisions apply in the case of higher level agreements. Third, a decision to call a strike must be confirmed by a majority vote of a meeting attended by two-thirds of the labour force or their representatives, making it almost impossible for the alternative unions, which typically organise particular groups of workers, to call a legal strike.

The new Labour Code incorporates Articles previously included in the Law on Trade Unions, the Law on Collective Bargaining and Agreements and the Law on Collective Labour Disputes, with only minor changes. However, apart from these changes, the new Labour Code does not supersede the latter Laws and the significant changes will be referred to in the following sections.


## The Law on Trade Unions

The 'Law on Trade Unions, their Rights and Guarantees of their Activities', was passed by the State Duma on 8 December 1995, signed by the President on 12 January 1996, and came into force with its publication in *Rossiiskaya gazeta* on 20 January 1996, replacing the Soviet law of 10 December 1990. Under the law, a trade

---

[1]    FNPR in fact proposed a conciliatory amendment for the December hearing which allows any excluded unions subsequently to join the negotiations.

union is a 'social organisation', which is one of the five types of 'social association' defined by the Law on Social Organisations, passed by the State Duma on 14 April and signed by the President on 19 May 1995, which regulates the formation of trade unions on the basis of the holding of a congress to adopt a constitution and establish a governing body and a supervisory-revision body.

The Law on Trade Unions was only passed after extensive controversy and debate. Until the Soviet law of 1990, introduced after the first wave of strikes in the Soviet Union, there was no defined legal procedure for the establishment of a trade union, the first of the new alternative trade unions having registered as social associations under the 1930s law which provided for the setting up of voluntary organisations such as sports clubs. The 1990 law still did not envisage the existence of alternative trade unions, and was therefore interpreted as applying equally to all trade unions, however small, with no provision for determining bargaining and recognition rights in the event of a dispute. Such ambiguity suited the new alternative trade unions, which could claim parity with the former state trade unions, but also proved very disruptive of attempts to develop an industrial relations framework.

The urgency of revising the law had already been recognised in a decree of the Presidium of the Russian Federation in 1991. Not surprisingly, the formulation of the new law proved very contentious, as the new unions saw the attempts of the traditional unions to set stiff conditions for recognition as an attempt to freeze them out. Various attempts to revise the law were thwarted as the new union leaders used their access to the presidential apparatus to block and veto various drafts of the law. The new State Duma elected in December 1993 began work on the task again, but still it took two years of deliberation to produce a law acceptable to all parties. These deliberations involved not only Duma deputies, but also specialists who had been involved in formulating the previous laws and representatives of various trade union bodies, several of which had been formulating drafts of their own. More than 40 trade unions sent delegates to a meeting on 31 March 1994 at which it was decided to set up a working group to prepare a single draft law. This included representatives of some of the new trade unions, but not of the more radical alternative unions such as NPG and Sotsprof, although the latter later submitted its own draft law to the working group. These unions continued to oppose the draft law, and in the final vote on the law in the Duma it was opposed by representatives of the more liberal fractions, including Gaidar's *Vybor Rossii*, Shakhrai's *Press*, and Yavlinsky's *Yabloko*.

Despite some reservations, FNPR regarded the law as an important victory, although there was also some opposition from the ranks of the FNPR unions themselves, some of whom argued that the draft law restricted the opportunities of trade unions, who had more rights under separate laws.[1] However, the majority view within the FNPR unions was that legal protection for union rights was necessary,

---

[1]   An earlier version, even more favourable to FNPR, had been passed by the Duma in April 1995, but vetoed by Yeltsin following protests from KTR.

particularly because the trade unions had already lost a series of rights which they had had in soviet times, including their rights to administer social insurance, their rights in monitoring health and safety regulations, their rights to approve the dismissal of workers and their right to consultation in the process of privatisation (Davydov introduction to Shalaev, Gritsenko and Snigireva, 1996, pp. 8–9).

The general philosophy of the law on trade unions is

1)  that of social partnership within a framework of tripartism. Article 15.1 declares that relations of trade unions with employers and state bodies are 'constructed on the basis of social partnership'.

2)  voluntarism, the law specifying the minimum of obligations on trade unions, leaving them to regulate their internal relations, including conditions of membership, forms of government, formation of primary groups and designation of their representatives according to their own constitution, which has only to meet a set of formal requirements. Unlike other social organisations, it is not necessary for a trade union to register in order to function as a trade union (under the previous law it had to register its constitution). This means that the state cannot refuse registration to any trade union, unlike other social organisations. However, registration as a juridical subject (as defined by Article 48 of the Civil Code) is necessary if the union is to own and administer property, including holding a bank account. This is a substantial burden for small primary organisations since the process of registration is complex and the financial records that have to be maintained for the tax authorities require the employment of an accountant. For this reason many primary organisations do not register and their accounts are maintained by the relevant obkom, which provides the service for a fee.

The sources and use of trade union funds are determined by its own constitution, so that unions can engage in entrepreneurial activity to achieve aims specified in their constitution, nor is any restriction on the independent financial activity of unions permitted. This makes illegal the frequent cases of local authorities trying to take over facilities owned by the unions (buildings, sanatoria, sports and cultural facilities). Unlike other social organisations, there is no financial control of executive bodies over the resources of the union, apart from those resources associated with entrepreneurial activity. This control is conducted on the basis of the union's constitution, by its revision commission, as was the case under the Soviet Law of 1990. It is therefore illegal for executive bodies, for example, to carry out financial investigations of the sources of income of trade unions, as has happened on occasion.[1]

---

[1]  According to FNPR, union funds are nevertheless controlled through the reporting requirements of the statistical agency, Goskomstat, and the tax inspectorate and by various other means (ICFTU, 1996, p. 106).

3) equality of rights of all trade unions under the law. However, the law gives the right to participate in general tariff agreements only to 'all-Russian trade unions', which are defined as those unions which operate on the territory of at least half the subjects of the Russian Federation (a definition already included in the Law on Social Organisations), or which organise at least half the workers in one or several branches. The significance of this definition is that only all-Russian trade unions have the right to participate in collective bargaining and to conclude branch tariff agreements at the Federal level, to be represented in the Russian Tripartite Commission, to participate in the examination by state bodies, local authorities and employers of all legislative acts affecting the social-labour rights of employees (until the 1993 Constitution trade unions also had the right of legislative initiative and the right to participate in the management of the state social funds, including social insurance, employment, health insurance and pension funds). The significance of this definition is reinforced by Article 4 that defines the rights of trade unions as pertaining 'within the limits of their authority'. This means that most of the new alternative trade unions, apart from those affiliated to VKT (the All-Russian Confederation of Labour) and KTR (the Confederation of Labour of Russia), have no legally guaranteed right to participate in trade union activity at the federal level and, under the new Labour Code, have almost no right to represent their members in collective bargaining.

4) welfare corporatism: although the trade unions have lost many of their former state functions, the law still defines their rights and responsibilities in relation to labour and social issues within a corporatist framework.

**Trade union rights and status**

In relation to the previous law there is some narrowing and closer specification of the definition of the activity of trade unions, from the earlier 'defence of the labour and socio-economic rights' of employees, which still appeared in the Labour Code, to the 'defence of their social-labour rights'. The same change is made in the Law on Collective Agreements. These social-labour rights are broad, although considerably narrowed from those defined by the old Soviet Constitution, now being defined in Article 37 of the Russian Constitution (above, p. 106).

The Law clarifies and strengthens the rights and status of the trade union in a number of respects. Until the end of 1990 trade unions were to represent and defend the interests of all those working in the relevant branch of the economy, but under Article 226 of the Russian Labour Code they were defined as representing the socio-economic and labour rights only of their members. This difference had little significance when virtually every employee belonged to the same branch trade union. However, with the emergence of alternative trade unions, together with the ambiguities in the 1992 Law on Collective Agreements, this led to a chaotic situation in a number of industries where competing trade unions each sought to apply the terms of its collective agreement to its members alone, so that rates of pay and benefits depended on the union to which an employee belonged.

The new law restored the *status quo ante*, defining trade unions as representing and defending the collective rights and interests of employees independent of their trade union membership, in the event of their delegating their representative authority in a proper manner, but defending the individual rights of their members alone. The same amendment was made to the Law on Collective Agreements, and brings Russia into line with ILO recommendations and international practice in this respect. At the same time, trade unions are now defined as the only legitimate representatives of the employees in collective bargaining. This ends the confusion of responsibilities between the trade union and the labour collective in forming collective agreements, a confusion which was not especially significant when all members of the labour collective were also members of the trade union, but which becomes absurd if and when a trade union excludes managers, who are members of the labour collective, from its ranks.[1] This clause also makes illegal the practice of employers in many private and privatised enterprises of excluding trade unions and unilaterally dictating the terms of the collective agreement in declaring wage-setting to be a management prerogative.[2]

The Law defines a primary trade union organisation as being established, as a rule, within one enterprise or organisation, regardless of the form of property, and its status is not changed by a change in the organisational form or ownership of the enterprise or organisation. This deals with those not infrequent cases in which management of privatised enterprises had dissolved the trade union unilaterally on the grounds that employee-shareholders do not require a trade union, or in which a new owner sought to dissolve the trade union on the spurious grounds that the former organisation no longer exists.

In addition to the removal of most of the powers of the labour collective, the Law declares that the existence of any other representative body of employees cannot be used to impede the activity of the trade union, while trade unions can put forward their candidates for election to any other representative body of employees in the organisation. This effectively means that, in the presence of a trade union, no other bodies can claim representative status. The only exception is the provision for the formation of strike committees, which are defined in the Law on Collective Labour Disputes as self-management bodies delegated by a general meeting, in the absence

---

[1]   The labour collective comprised all those working in the enterprise or organisation on the basis of a labour contract. Technically it therefore normally excluded the chief executive, who in a state enterprise worked on a civil contract with the state and in a private enterprise had a contract with the shareholders.

[2]   It is indicative of the status of trade unions in Russia that many private sector employers, as well as their employees, regard the annual shareholders' meeting and the shareholders' council as an appropriate substitute for the trade union in a privatised enterprise where the employees hold a majority of shares.

of the trade union, to lead a strike, and which cease to exist when the strike ends or is declared illegal (unless anything else was specified in the meeting which constituted it).[1]

The powers that the state gives to the trade unions, the state can also take away. Under the previous law a trade union could be dissolved on a decision of its members, or banned on a decision of the Supreme Court for certain specified serious violations of the law. The 1996 Law provides for the banning or suspension of a union for a period of up to six months on a decision of the Supreme Court, on the submission of the Procurator, for violation of the Constitutions of the Federation or its subjects or of Federal Law. Under the Civil Code (Part 2 Article 61) a trade union or primary group can be liquidated as a juridical subject by a decision of its members, or by a decision of a court for a series of reasons, including acting without proper authority, acting in violation of the law or other judicial acts, or systematically acting in violation of its established aims. This is clearly a serious threat to a trade union, since the Civil Code does not specify how serious or how trivial the violation need be for the Procurator to initiate a case for the union's liquidation. The case of the Federation of Air Traffic Controllers' Unions (FPAD) in 1992 was not auspicious: proceedings for the liquidation of FPAD on the grounds of its participation in an illegal strike were initiated in November 1992, although the grounds expanded in the course of the trial to include the charge that the union had illegally involved itself in political activity by demanding the establishment of a federal air traffic control system, the charge that the tariff agreement signed with the government in May 1992 was illegal because it had been signed under duress, and that the strike had imposed financial loss on the industry. After a farcical trial, which was boycotted by the union leaders, the charges were thrown out, but the union was warned by the judge that a further strike would result in the union's liquidation (Clarke, Borisov and Fairbrother, 1995, pp. 339–71).

## The unions as a privileged interlocutor with government

Although the trade unions have had many of their state functions taken away from them since 1991, the 1996 legislation reaffirms their right to participate in the management of various state bodies, to draw on state funds for various activities, and to monitor the implementation of various legislative and administrative acts. Under the Law on Social Organisations, trade unions have the right to engage in political activity and to participate in elections, provided this is included as an aim in their constitution, although the 1991 presidential decree banning political activity in the workplace remains in force.

---

[1]   The new Labour Code provides for a representative other than a trade union to represent the employees in collective bargaining, participation in management and the resolution of individual labour disputes, but only where no primary trade union exists.

All-Russian trade unions have the right to participate in the consideration of all legislative acts concerning labour conditions, and have the right specifically to participate in the working out of state employment programmes and propose measures for the social protection of members made redundant. Trade unions have retained their legal right to participate in the development of social programmes, the working out of measures for the social defence of workers, defining the basic criteria of the standard of living indices and the indexation of wages and have the right to monitor the implementation of law in this sphere.

Although trade unions no longer dispose of social insurance funds directly, they have the right to participate equally with the other social partners in the management of state funds such as health, social insurance and pension funds (i.e. to enjoy representation on management bodies in equal numbers with government and employers) and have to agree to the constitution of those funds (a new provision – previously the constitutions had been determined by the government on its own). Unions have the right to participate in the formation of a state programme on questions of the protection of labour and the environment and in the preparation of normative acts relating to the protection of labour, industrial injury and the environment.[1]

State funds can also be drawn on by the trade unions for various purposes. State budgetary funds are available for partial financing of trade union education and research establishments, as laid down in the Law on Education signed by the President on 13 January 1996. The former right of trade unions to participate in 'health-improving work' for members and their families using state social insurance funds is restored, the funding for this to be determined by the insurance fund after consultation with the trade union. Moreover, non-members can mandate the union to carry out such functions on their behalf.

Responsibility for much of the health and safety inspection which was delegated to the trade unions in 1933 has been transferred to the Federal Labour Inspectorate, set up under the Ministry of Labour by Presidential decree of 20 July 1994 on the basis of the Basic Law on Labour Protection of 6 August 1993, with powers defined by amendments to the Labour Code in July 1995. However, trade unions retain the right to monitor the implementation of the law and the activity of state bodies in a wide range of spheres. Unions have the right to participate in the investigation of industrial accidents and the defence of the rights and interests of members of the trade union in conditions of work and safety, compensation for industrial injuries and other questions relating to protection of labour and the environment. In the event of violations threatening the health and safety of employees a trade union body has the right to demand immediate correction of these violations and refer the case to the federal inspectorate. The trade union for the first time acquired the unambiguous right

---

[1]   References to the environment are a widening of the sphere of trade union activity, also included in the law on the protection of the environment.

to demand that work stop until a decision is taken by the state inspectorate and to require employers immediately to carry out its demands. Trade unions can participate in the evaluation of the safety aspects of all existing and planned production processes and machinery. The legislation on the protection of labour specifies the creation of a joint committee for labour protection with equal representation of employers and trade unions in all enterprises employing more than ten people, endorsed by a resolution of the Ministry of Labour of 12 October 1994.[1]

The trade unions have the right to monitor employment and the observation of employment and labour law by employers, including of the terms of labour contracts in organisations in which members work. Employers have to respond within a week to notification of violations, informing the union of the results of their investigation and the measures they are taking. To do this, trade unions have the right to create their own labour inspectorate, which will co-operate with state bodies of control. They have the right of unimpeded access to organisations to check the fulfilment of labour law, including the laws on trade unions and collective agreements. Trade unions have the right to all relevant information, and a new right to require employers or state bodies to attend meetings to explain the information provided.

### Rights in relation to management

Trade unions enjoy extensive rights in relation to management, although the new Labour Code dilutes these, as noted above. Their soviet-era rights in relation to changes in the terms and conditions of employment, including dismissal, have been retained. Any steps which will lead to job losses or a deterioration in working conditions must be notified at least three months in advance to the appropriate trade union, with whom negotiations must be conducted concerning the observance of the rights and interests of their members. This right was also included in the 1990 Law, although rarely observed by employers. The 1996 law added any change in ownership or property form among those steps which might lead to a notifiable job loss or deterioration in working conditions. Trade unions have the right to propose to local authorities the postponement or temporary prevention of mass redundancies.

Until the new Labour Code was introduced in 2002, the cancellation of labour contracts with trade union members on the part of employers was still only permissible on the basis of prior agreement with the corresponding trade union bodies and in cases prescribed by the law or collective agreement. The growing use of foreign contract labour in Russia led to the introduction of a clause in the law which specifies that the recruitment and use in the Russian Federation of foreign labour

---

[1]   All of this more or less corresponds to the Programme of Action of the Council of FNPR on the protection of labour for 1993–5 adopted at the XVth Plenum of the General Council of FNPR in May 1993. These rights are somewhat watered down in the new Labour Code.

power is only permissible after taking account of the views of the corresponding Russian trade union (although such views can, of course, be completely ignored).[1]

As noted above, trade unions have extensive rights of access to the workplace and to information to enable them to monitor the implementation and observance of a wide range of legislative and normative acts. Trade unions also for the first time acquired a legal right to participate in privatisation – a little late, as the privatisation process was more or less complete. Nevertheless, they have the right to representation on privatisation commissions and on committees for the management of state property. This allows trade unions to monitor the process of privatisation and in particular to prevent employers from surreptitiously changing decisions taken by labour collective meetings without reference back to those meetings.

The most dramatic strengthening of the trade unions' legal rights in the 1996 Law was their right to representation, if delegated by the employees of the organisation, on all corporate management bodies. Although the Labour Code included Articles (227, 228 and 235) on employees' participation in management, these were a residue of the enthusiasms of perestroika, vague provisions seeking to encourage employees to propose methods of improving production and to participate in the management of the social and welfare apparatus which have been removed from the new Labour Code. The Law on Trade Unions was the first legal reference to trade union participation in management bodies, and confirmation of some of the rights assigned by the Law on Trade Unions was included in the final version of the new Labour Code (Articles 52 and 53). At the same time, participation of trade union representatives in the work of any other representative body does not deprive the union of the right to turn directly to the employer on any question affecting the interests of trade union members. In practice, this does not appear to be a right of which trade unions have often availed themselves. Although the trade union president is sometimes represented on management bodies, it is usually as a senior member of management, responsible for social and labour questions, rather than as representative of the employees.

Employers have wide-ranging obligations to facilitate the work of the trade union: the employer is obliged to provide free use of equipment, premises, means of transport and communications necessary for their work in accordance with the terms of a collective agreement (the new Labour Code restricts this obligation to those with more than 100 employees). Employers can give the trade union the free use of premises, buildings and other objects such as holiday centres necessary for the organisation of rest, cultural and physical-cultural work with employees and members of their families, but the employer remains responsible for the maintenance and repair

---

[1]  The drafting of cheap labour from former Republics of the Soviet Union is becoming a serious problem in several regions, particularly in the construction industry, and its banning is already included in a number of collective agreements, while some regional agreements specify that its use is only permitted in consultation with the trade union.

of these facilities, unless otherwise specified in the collective agreement. These obligations are the same as those defined in the Labour Code, although the Law on Trade Unions relates them to the collective agreement. This is an important modification since the new trade unions had used the provisions of the Labour Code to demand facilities even when they had only a handful of members. Reference to the collective agreement makes it possible for employers to deny facilities to alternative trade unions. Similarly, management checks-off union dues on the basis of a written request from the individual workers within the terms of the collective agreement,[1] with no obligation for a renewal of these agreements with the introduction of the new law. This gave legal form to government explanation 20/XII–1993 and finally thwarted the demand of the alternative unions for a re-registration of union membership, denying the alternative unions access to check-off facilities unless they can secure provision for it in the collective agreement. The law also provides for the transfer of money from non-members to the trade union to pay for social and welfare benefits provided by the trade union under the terms of the collective agreement, with funds being distributed in proportion to union membership if there is more than one trade union.[2]

The Law defines stiff penalties for employers who do not fulfil its terms. Under the Labour Code unions can demand disciplinary sanctions against any managers who violate labour law or rules on health and safety, and the organisation has to report steps taken within one month. Under the Code of Administrative Violations the union could demand administrative sanctions, with a fine of up to 100 minimum wages for people violating labour law, and under the Criminal Code it could demand criminal sanctions: any person impeding the activity of a trade union is punishable by one year of corrective labour or a fine of up to fifty minimum wages or dismissal. Article 30 of the Criminal Code increases the maximum fine to 500 minimum wages for serious violations of labour law. On the demand of the union the employer *must* annul the labour contract of any person responsible for violation of the Law on Trade Unions or failing to carry out his or her responsibilities according to the collective agreement. In the Labour Code this power was available only to trade union bodies no lower than the *raion* (district) level, but the Law on Trade Unions and the Law on Collective Agreements extended the power to any trade union body. The main innovation of this part of the law is that it gives trade unions the right directly to initiate sanctions against employers' representatives.

[1]   According to the Labour Code, union dues should be transferred to the union without delay, but it has become common for management to retain union dues and use them for their own purposes (ICFTU, 1996, p. 106).
[2]   In the past, organisations had to transfer 0.15 per cent of the wage fund to the trade union for 'mass-cultural and physical cultural work', now widened to 'socio-cultural and other work'. This has been maintained in the new Labour Code, but without specifying how much money should be transferred. If there is no collective agreement this can be negotiated by particular agreement.

Privileges for trade union officials are normally defined in the collective agreement. On the other hand, trade union officials have wide-ranging legal protection against any kind of victimisation or disciplinary sanction without the agreement of the trade union, although this protection has been weakened somewhat in the new Labour Code. The only sanction prescribed against trade unions is that for failing to call off an illegal strike once it has been declared unlawful, while individual trade union members can be disciplined for involvement in an illegal strike.

## The Law on Collective Bargaining and Agreements

The liberalisation of the labour market, with the removal of a large part of the statutory and administrative control of payment systems and of the terms and conditions of work, has meant that collective bargaining and collective agreements have in principle become much more significant in determining the pay and working conditions of employees.

The Law on Trade Unions specifies the right of trade unions to conduct collective bargaining and conclude collective agreements in the name of the employees and in conformity with federal law. Trade union representation in such activities, including cases in which there is more than one trade union, will be determined taking account of the number of members in the trade union. The legal framework for collective bargaining is provided by the Law on Collective Bargaining and Agreements.

The Law on Collective Bargaining and Agreements, originally introduced in 1992, has been extensively revised, the new version being signed by the President on 24 November 1995. A further Law on the Russian Tripartite Commission for the Regulation of Social-Labour Relations was passed by the State Duma on 2 April 1999 and regulates social partnership at the Federal level. Some provisions of the Law have been over-ridden by the new Labour Code. Most significantly, the new Labour Code gives privileged rights of representation to 'All-Russian trade unions'; prescribes that the recognised representative represents all employees and not merely its own members; stipulates that a single collective agreement should apply to all employees of an organisation and prescribes that collective agreements are concluded by the trade union organisation and no longer have to be confirmed by a meeting of the employees. This considerably strengthens the hand of the traditional trade unions in relation both to the alternative unions and to their own members.

The new version of the Law on Collective Bargaining clarified a number of points which remained ambiguous in the earlier version: the law now refers to 'social-labour relations', where the previous law referred more narrowly to labour relations, which makes it clear that virtually any relevant issues can be included in a collective agreement. The term 'employees of the organisation', who enter into a collective agreement with their employers, replaced the term 'labour collective', which expressed the unity of interests of labour and management. The previous version of the law allowed 'any representative body delegated by the employees' to sign a collective agreement, which allowed the new alternative unions to propose and negotiate a collective agreement even if they had only a handful of members; the new version only allowed such forms of representation in the absence of a trade union representing a majority of the labour force, while the new Labour Code privileges the primary organisations of All-Russian trade unions. A new clause forbade representatives of employers to participate in the negotiations on the employees' side.

The law allowed for a range of agreements, from collective agreements (*dogovori*) between employees and employers through various kinds of higher level agreements (*soglasheniya*): general, regional, branch (inter-branch) tariff, professional tariff (a new category, dropped from the new Labour Code), territorial and other. The agreement can be two or three party, but those involving budget financing must include representatives of the executive powers and, under the new Labour Code, should 'as a general rule' be concluded before the relevant budget is set (Article 47).

Collective agreements (*dogovori*) last from one to three years. On expiry they remain in force until amended or replaced with a new agreement, although under the new Labour Code such prolongation requires the agreement of the parties. Agreements remain in force through reorganisations of the enterprise, but when there is a change in ownership the agreement only remains in force for three months, during which time negotiations for a new agreement may begin. Agreements may include no-strike clauses, conditional on fulfilment of the agreement. If an individual labour contract is worse than the collective agreement the latter applies, if the collective agreement is worse than an applicable branch agreement the latter applies.

Employers are required to conduct collective bargaining with trade union bodies if the latter initiate such bargaining. The Law on Trade Unions stipulates that employers are required to *conclude* collective agreements on terms agreed by both parties, a stipulation which is not included in the Law on Collective Agreements, which prevents what had become a common practice in cases of dispute of employers refusing to sign a new collective agreement on the pretext of disagreement over one term of the agreement. The new Labour Code prescribes that agreement must be reached within three months.

Employers have to make available all necessary facilities for the preparation of the enterprise collective agreement, including means of communication of the draft agreement to all employees. It is illegal to withhold necessary information on the grounds that it is a commercial or state secret. Participants in the negotiation are obliged to keep such material secret. The draft must be discussed by employees in subdivisions and revised in the light of their comments. The final draft has to be put to a meeting of the employees. Once concluded, the employer has to register the agreement with the appropriate state body within seven days, which will monitor the agreement and report on terms which violate the law. An annual reporting conference has to be held.

When there are several trade union bodies, any of them can initiate negotiations for a collective agreement. Then within five calendar days they have to form a single representative body to conduct negotiations, work out a single draft and sign a single collective agreement. If it is not possible to reach agreement on the formation of a unified body, under the Law on Trade Unions a general meeting of employees could adopt the most attractive draft and empower the people who drew up that draft as their representatives to negotiate the agreement and present it for confirmation to a general meeting. Under the new Labour Code (Article 37), the employees will be represented by the primary organisation that represents the majority of the labour force. Trade unions excluded in this way retain their rights subsequently to participate in the negotiations. If no trade union represents a majority of the labour force, the mandating of the employees' representative is referred to a secret ballot at a general meeting of employees. Non-union members can delegate their authority to a trade union body. The new Labour Code only recognises a collective agreement concluded at the level of the organisation or an organisational subdivision, which removes the former right of representatives of a particular group of employees to conclude a collective agreement independently in the name of those employees or propose it as an addendum to the agreement. This made it possible for the workers of a specific profession, typically represented by one of the alternative trade unions, to negotiate separately to secure their own particular interests.

The trade union has the right to monitor the implementation of the collective agreement. Should the employer violate the terms of the collective agreement, the trade union has the right to report these violations to the employer, who must respond within one week, failing which the disagreement will be reviewed in accordance with federal law. Under the law on collective agreements the union can refer the matter to the court, or demand that the employer punish or dismiss those people responsible for the violation of the agreement or seek to resolve the disagreement through the procedures laid down by the law on the resolution of collective labour disputes.

Higher level agreements (*soglasheniya*) are only reached by trade unions and, as noted above, only All-Russian unions can sign general and branch agreements, which effectively excludes many of the new unions. Where there is more than one trade union, each could negotiate a separate agreement on behalf of its own members, the most favourable to the workers then prevailing. Under the new Labour Code a single negotiating body has to be formed and, as noted above, in the event of failure to agree, the largest trade union has exclusive bargaining rights.

A tariff agreement applies to all those employers, employees and government bodies who have authorised the participants in the agreement to negotiate in their name. If at the federal level a professional or branch tariff agreement is signed covering at least fifty per cent of employees in the branch then the Minister of Labour can extend its application to all employers, even if they did not sign it. In this case, if an employer or employers' representative does not give notice of a refusal to be bound by the agreement within thirty days of its receipt then the agreement applies to that employer. These are important stipulations where employers' organisations are undeveloped, but we do not know of any cases in which they have been invoked.

## The Law on Collective Labour Disputes

The Law on Procedures for the Resolution of Collective Labour Disputes was passed by the State Duma on 20 October 1995, signed by the President on 23 November 1995, and came into force with its publication in *Rossiiskaya gazeta* on 5 December 1995, replacing the 1991 Soviet law on Procedures for the Resolution of Collective Labour Disputes (Conflicts) , which had in turn replaced Gorbachev's 1989 Law on Strikes that had been introduced as a panic measure following the 1989 miners' strike. Since then a whole series of laws, decrees and other normative acts had emerged contradicting one another, with some subjects of the Russian Federation (e.g., Tatarstan, Bashkortostan) having introduced their own laws. The working out of the drafts began in the State Duma in March 1994. A commission, which included trade union and employer representatives, was set up to review three different drafts and various proposals put forward, and parliamentary hearings took place in December 1994. The 2001 Labour Code introduced a few provisions which over-ride or clarify those of the Law on Collective Labour Disputes.

Collective labour disputes arise as a result of the inability to reach agreement in negotiations concerning collective conditions of labour established in a collective agreement or any legal acts and in cases in which the employer refuses to conclude, amend or carry out a collective agreement or, under the new Labour Code, to take the trade union's views into account following consultation. This is distinct from cases of disputes with the employer where workers unite in support of their individual labour rights. These are defined as individual labour disputes of each individual employee with the employer, since the conditions of work of each is determined by each person's individual labour contract, governed by Articles 201–19 of the Labour Code (56–84 of the new Labour Code). Only if the issue, e.g. of timely payment of wages, is included in the collective agreement can it be the subject of a collective labour dispute and so, ultimately, the pretext for a legal strike. If the dispute concerns one subdivision (shop or department) then this can be a collective labour dispute if other subdivisions support it; otherwise, it is an individual labour dispute.[1]

The law lays down strict procedures for the resolution of collective labour disputes. The trade union at the appropriate level is normally the representative of the employees in such a dispute, in conformity with its constitution, which is thereby given juridical force (although an initiative group can serve as representative at enterprise level, on the conditions defined above).

The demands must be put forward by workers at a meeting by majority vote (or by a trade union body). Employers have to provide premises for a meeting of workers to

---

[1]   Every enterprise employing more than 15 people must have a Labour Disputes Commission (KTS) to which disputes that cannot be resolved through immediate negotiation with management are referred. The position of the trade union in such individual disputes is ambiguous: on the one hand, union representatives are normally members of the KTS, on the other hand, the union is supposed to help the complainant make his or her case to the KTS.

put forward their demands and cannot impede the process. Where similar demands are put forward by various representatives they can form a single body to participate in the resolution of the dispute. The demands can be registered with the Service for the Settlement of Collective Labour Disputes (hereafter called the conciliation service) which has been established as a division of the Ministry of Labour throughout the Russian Federation.[1]

Employers have to respond to the workers' demands within three days or those of a trade union within one month. A conciliation commission is established as an obligatory stage in the procedure within three working days of the start of the dispute, comprising equal numbers of employer and employee representatives. It must consider the case within five working days of its establishment. If this fails to agree then the dispute moves on to mediation and/or arbitration. A mediator may be appointed by the conciliation service if the parties cannot agree within three working days of notifying the service of mediation. The mediator can demand necessary documentation from the employer and must review the case within seven working days. Arbitrators must be brought in within three working days of the ending of a review by the conciliation commission or the mediator. An arbitration body comprises three people, cannot include parties to the dispute and must review the case with the parties within five working days. If the employer refuses to participate in a conciliation commission the case goes directly to arbitration. If the employer refuses arbitration the employees can go on strike.[2] Any agreement reached between the parties has compulsory status and is monitored by the parties.

Employees can strike if the employer refuses conciliation or conciliation does not lead to a resolution of the dispute or an agreement is not fulfilled by the employer. Participation in a strike is voluntary: nobody can be compelled to participate or not to participate in it. Representatives of employers do not have the right to organise or participate in a strike, an important (if unenforceable) clause since many strikes in Russia are supported and often initiated by employers as a means of putting pressure on government or local authorities. Under the Law on Collective Labour Disputes, a strike may be called by an appropriate trade union body or by a meeting of the whole labour force or a delegate conference, which must vote in favour by a majority of the participants at a meeting attended by at least two-thirds of those eligible, but the new Labour Code requires any decision of a trade union body to call a strike to be confirmed by such a meeting or delegate conference, or by a petition signed by a

---

[1]   The Service took some time to establish. It was created by government resolution 730 of 30 July 1993, and its powers defined by resolution 1133 of 4 November 1993, and then confirmed, following the introduction of the revised law on labour disputes, by government resolution 468 of 15 April 1996. It has a wide range of responsibilities for monitoring labour disputes and providing conciliation, mediation and arbitration services.

[2]   Under the new Labour Code, arbitration is compulsory in organisations in which strikes are prohibited, otherwise it only takes place if both parties agree in writing to abide by the decision of the arbitrator.

majority of the labour force, at every establishment affected (Article 411). This restores the requirement of the Gorbachev strike law, a condition that was almost impossible to meet, so that virtually all strikes referred to the courts under the Gorbachev law were declared illegal.

A single one-hour warning strike can be called after five days of conciliation (the first time such a type of strike has been recognised in law), with employers being given three working days written notice. Ten calendar days notice must be given of an impending strike and the notice must include a list of disagreements which are the basis of the strike, the date, time of start and duration of the strike and the expected number of participants, the body heading the strike, nominees to participate in the conciliation procedure and proposals for the minimum necessary work to be carried out during the strike. Employers notify the conciliation service of an impending strike. The whole procedure does not have to be repeated for the renewal of a suspended strike, but employers and the service have to be given three working days notice of such a renewal. A body elected specifically to head the strike is dissolved on resolution of the dispute or the ending of the strike unless otherwise specified in a resolution of the meeting that formed it.

In any strike, a minimum of necessary work must be carried out in organisations which affect the safety of people, providing for their health or the vitally important interests of society, the work to be agreed within five days of the announcement of the strike or decreed by government body. All parties must act to ensure the preservation of social order during the strike, protect the property of the organisation and the continued working of machinery and equipment whose stoppage would pose a threat to life and health.

A strike is illegal if

a)  it was announced without giving due and proper notice or taking account of the period, procedure and requirements laid down for conciliation, mediation and arbitration.

b)  if it presents a real threat to the basis of constitutional order or the health of other people.

c)  if the strike involves members of the military forces, law-enforcement organs, organs of the federal security services if this threatens the defence of the country or the security of the state (federal law also excludes certain other categories from the right to strike, including the railways (under the law on federal railway transport of 25 August 1995) and state officials (under the law of 31 July 1995 on the foundations of state services of the Russian Federation)). The previous law also excluded civil aviation and various other branches. The pilots' trade union, PLS, took the matter to the Constitutional Court, when a series of strikes was ruled illegal, on the grounds that the strike ban violated the right to strike prescribed in the Russian Constitution. The court ruled against PLS on 17 May 1995 on the grounds that the rights of citizens could be limited by federal law if they impinged on the rights of others, but recommended that alternative channels be available to employees who were not permitted to strike. The 1996 Law provides for the reference of such disputes to the President for decision, which must be provided within ten days (amended to the Government in the new Labour Code).

d)   if the minimum of necessary work is not carried out.

The strike only becomes illegal when it has been judged to be such by the appropriate court. In such an event, the strikers must return to work the day following notification of the court's decision to the body heading the strike. If the strike presents an immediate threat to life and health the court can postpone or halt it for 30 days (under Article 208 of the Civil Code, apart from those to the Supreme Court, appeals must be heard within ten days). In situations of particular significance for the vitally important interests of the Russian Federation or separate territories the President and government have the right to halt the strike until the question has been resolved by the appropriate court, but not for more than ten days.

If a trade union does not stop a strike after it has been declared illegal, it is liable to repay from its own funds the losses caused by the strike to the extent determined by the court.

Participation in a strike is not a violation of labour discipline and participants cannot be punished or moved jobs, until or unless the strike has been declared illegal, from which time it can be treated as a breach of discipline, with penalties up to dismissal for absenteeism under the Labour Code. Employers have the right not to pay workers on strike, but they can be paid by agreement. Under the Labour Code, non-participants in a strike who are unable to work as a result of the strike are paid not less than two-thirds of scale salary (increased under the new Labour Code), and may be transferred to other work, as for a stoppage which is not their fault.

Lockouts are banned for the first time in Russian law. Employers who violate any of the provisions of the law or refuse to participate in conciliation or fail to fulfil an agreement are liable to disciplinary sanctions and fines of up to 50 minimum wages.

The new version of the Law made it much easier for a trade union to hold a legal strike, provided that it adhered to the detail of the procedures laid down by law, a gain reversed by the new Labour Code. However, the requirement of a two-thirds quorum and a majority voting for an unofficial strike makes it as difficult for such a strike to come within the law as it was in the past, quite apart from the unlikelihood of a spontaneous strike following the prescribed bureaucratic procedures. This is very important because the overwhelming majority of strikes, apart from the mass actions which have sometimes marked the coal-mining and education branches, have been unofficial spontaneous actions. However, the law clearly states that participation in a strike cannot be considered grounds for disciplinary sanctions under the Labour Code until or unless the strike is declared illegal by a court. This means that the law in theory gives protection to wildcat strikes, and that the employer has to get the strike declared illegal before being able to take disciplinary steps against those who remain on strike. But in Russia reality and the law are often a long way apart from one another. On the other hand, while everybody is guaranteed the right to strike and is protected from disciplinary sanctions for participating in a strike, not every work stoppage is a strike. Article 2.6 of the law defines a strike as a 'temporary deliberate refusal of employees to carry out their work responsibilities (in full or in part) *with the aim of resolving a collective labour dispute*' (my italics). This means that a solidarity strike, a stoppage of work with political demands, or a stoppage of work with demands which do not relate to the collective terms and conditions of work, is not a strike and participants can be punished for absenteeism under the Labour Code.[1]

## Conclusion

The legal framework of Russian industrial relations retains many features of the soviet framework, though selective innovation has occurred. The implications of the post-1991 framework are as follows. First, the legal changes that have occurred have served to preserve the institutional dominance of the FNPR. Little has been done to ease the establishment and growth of alternative trade unions, and, though the traditional unions have lost some of their functions, they have not faced anything approaching a legislative assault on their position. Second, legal regulation of employment continues to be very detailed. This has facilitated the reproduction of the 'law book' approach of unions to defending their members' interests. Indeed, given half a chance, the trade unions would opt for even more comprehensive legal regulation: most regional federations devote a lot of time to lobbying for regional laws on topics as diverse as housing policy and employers' associations, while the FNPR is also active in pressing for increased legal regulation of a variety of matters at the federal level. Finally, the law has defined a legal framework for the development of 'social partnership'. The FNPR has preserved the status of a privileged interlocutor with the state, and has the right to participate on a number of state bodies including, for example, the management bodies of the health, social insurance and pension funds. The law on collective agreements, meanwhile, facilitates the negotiation of both bipartite and tripartite agreements at a variety of levels, thus potentially allowing voluntary regulation to extend legal provisions. This theoretically provides unions with an opportunity to redefine their role as active defenders of workers' interests within a framework of 'social partnership' or 'neo-corporatism'. The question, which the next chapter turns to consider, is whether they are capable of doing so.

[1]   Absenteeism is defined in the Labour Code as absence from work for three hours (increased to four in the new Labour Code). The alternative trade union *Solidarnost'* in Samara developed the practice of the two-hour strike to avoid disciplinary sanctions.

# 6

# Social Partnership

One of the defining characteristics of the post-communist Russian trade union movement is its adherence to 'social partnership'. It is almost impossible to open a union publication without encountering the term; it is impossible to talk to a Russian trade unionist about her movement without the topic arising at some point. Where did this ideology of social partnership come from, and what do contemporary Russian trade unionists mean when they talk about social partnership? What does social partnership mean in practice and what are its implications for the development of trade unions and industrial relations in Russia? This chapter will consider the first of these questions by way of introduction, before turning to the more complex topic of the practice and implications of social partnership.

## The origins and meaning of *'sotsial'noe partnerstvo'*

The commitment to social partnership as the framework for the activity of the Russian trade unions was established at their inception. The 1990 Founding Congress of FNPR adopted a resolution defining the basic tactics of the trade unions as involving the negotiation of general, tariff and collective agreements, to be backed up by demonstrations, meetings, strikes, May Day celebrations and spring and autumn days of united action in support of the unions' demands in negotiations and to enforce the subsequent fulfilment of the agreements. The official history of FNPR stresses that this was

> an extensive programme for the formation of social partnership as a particular type of social-labour relations, an effective mechanism of civilised regulation of those relations (Gritsenko, Kadeikina and Makukhina, 1999, p. 341).

With a changing balance between confrontation and collaboration, this has been the basis of trade union strategy ever since the signing of the first agreement with the Russian government in February 1991 and the first trade union 'day of unity' in March 1991.

The doctrine of social dialogue has long been the staple of the ILO, and the ILO certainly influenced the development of social partnership in Russia.[1] Nevertheless,

---

[1] 'Social dialogue', like social partnership, is a rather imprecise term. As Hyman has pointed out, it has a variety of meanings from collective bargaining to a normative orientation towards conflict avoidance (Hyman, 2000, p. 1). As will be seen, *'sotsial'noe partnerstvo'* is an equally capacious term.

the official FNPR history downplays external influences, claiming that soviet trade unions had a long history of engaging in social partnership, arguing that the FNPR adopted it as a programme as a result of 'many years of positive experience' in the administration of socio-economic processes at enterprise, regional, branch and national level (Gritsenko, Kadeikina and Makukhina, 1999 p. 341). The authors assert that

> In conditions of centralised administration of the economy with only state property, social partnership between enterprise administrations and different forms of worker participation in the administration of production... existed in the USSR (ibid., p. 506).

From this perspective, 'social partnership' has built on the traditional bureaucratic structures of participation of trade unions in management: the collective agreement at the level of the enterprise; collaboration of branch trade unions with the structures of economic management in relation to such issues as 'socialist competition', 'rationalisation and innovation', norm-setting, wage and bonus scales, health and safety, certification, training and retraining and the recruitment and retention of labour; the collaboration of regional trade union organisations with local government in considering issues of housing, social and welfare policy; and the involvement of the national trade union federation in the consideration of labour and social legislation and the formulation of the government's wages, social and labour policies.

Most of the current administrators and ideologues of social partnership within the union movement are more cautious about links to soviet practice, however. For example, Vladimir Kiselev, the head of the department of social partnership and the trade union movement at the FNPR's Academy of Labour in Moscow, in an interview in June 2001, did emphasise the fact that Russians had come to realise the importance of social partnership themselves:

> You can't deny the influence of the ILO. But for all that, Russian people, they all the same prefer to act when they understand for themselves the necessity of it. So here, on the one hand, of course, of course, we learnt from the ILO, we looked at the ILO conventions... but the initiative was taken when we understood that it was really impossible to do without it [social partnership].

But this did not lead him to argue that social partnership had domestic roots. Indeed, he argued strongly that social partnership did not exist in the past since the leading role of the Communist Party in the Soviet Union meant that equality of rights (*ravnopravie*) between the parties was impossible:

> There was co-operation between the Communist Party and the trade unions naturally ... but it wasn't social partnership from the point of view of equality of

> rights in relations…. Here in the Soviet Union… – I remember it well – they talked of social partnership in negative terms. Yes: 'Social partnership develops in the West. In the West, where trade unions are yellow, venal trade unions. They betray the interests of the working class.'

Similarly, Galina Strela, the head of the department of social-labour relations and defence of workers' economic rights at the FNPR (which is essentially the Federation's social partnership department), when interviewed in June 2001, stressed the break with past practice implied by contemporary social partnership:

> First of all, I must say we came up with practically nothing new in the theory of social partnership. In principle we adhere to the ideology which has been developed by the International Labour Organisation. In our country, of course, in our past practice there were several differences – although there were agreements, collective agreements were concluded, the practice was different. Why? Because all labour relations were regulated by law. Strict legal regulation.

So what do the Russian trade unions mean by 'social partnership' and how does it differ from their past relationship with the Party-state? As a concept, social partnership 'has many available meanings' (Hyman, 2001, p. 38), which is perhaps why it has become such a popular term. It has been used to describe a wide variety of arrangements, some, to quote Hyman again, 'more "collaborationist" than others' (ibid.). In its Russian incarnation *'sotsial'noe partnerstvo'* is no more precise. At the most basic level the term is used to refer simply to tripartite negotiations. As one member of the Academy of Labour said of tripartism and social partnership, 'in practice no one particularly distinguishes between these concepts, here tripartism and social partnership – it's one and the same'. More specifically, however, it is used to refer to the network of negotiations and agreements which have developed in post-communist Russia. Strela, for example, asked for a definition of social partnership, outlined the system of agreements at enterprise, branch, regional and national level and continued 'all this system of negotiations and conclusion of agreements and collective agreements we call the system of social partnership. Why? Because we say that we maintain the principle of social partnership; above all… we are oriented to reach agreement'.

Kiselev, who is something of a social partnership guru within the FNPR fold, also viewed social partnership as referring to the system of negotiations and agreements, but saw it as having two additional meanings, one of which is hinted at in Strela's comment quoted above. First, he claimed that social partnership was a specific form of social-labour relations, the essence of which was finding a balance between the interests of the different sides, while the final point of his three-fold definition was that it was an ideology aimed at social peace and harmony (*soglasie*).

The reference to social peace does not mean that FNPR renounces resort to strikes and demonstrations in support of its aims but, chastened by the experience of 1993, it sees social partnership very much within the framework of conflict avoidance. Shmakov made his position clear in his report to the meeting of the General Council attended by Putin on 16 February 2000, 'the trade unions consider a strike to be a "failure" of social partnership. *Either social partnership or class struggle!'* (*Vesti FNPR*, 1–2, 2000, p. 10, original emphasis). When interviewed in June 2001 the leading specialist for the group on defence of workers' interests in the FNPR legal department made a passionate statement of his belief in social partnership, which was very much based on the normative definition of the concept as a means of conflict avoidance:

> Social partnership is our main method and form of work. To move from confrontation... to negotiation. The process of negotiation is the basis of our activity... To transform all conflictual situations into negotiations, to sit round the table and come to an agreement. You've got to learn it, it's an art, it's a science. But we as trade unions don't see another way – we only see that... It's the basis of our activity. We can't imagine any confrontational situations and their conflicts being resolved other than through this [negotiation]. Everything else for us is excluded.

To conclude, social partnership in Russia is an adaptation of the idea of social dialogue. The 'system' of social partnership comprises the network of negotiations and agreements which supplement the legal regulation of labour relations. But the argument developed in this chapter is that social partnership continues the close collaboration of trade unions with management and the state in the regulation of labour relations which marked the soviet period. The key distinguishing feature of social partnership from the perspective of the trade unions is that it should be based on the equality of rights of the social partners: neither government nor employers should be able to dictate the terms and conditions of labour, but should conclude agreements with the full participation of trade unions. The trade unions do not exclude the use of 'strong methods' when their point of view is not given adequate consideration, but, as the analysis of this chapter will show, in practice the trade unions offer the other social partners social peace in exchange for what is in many cases little more than their 'respect'.

As we will see in the rest of this chapter, the emphasis on equal rights is more an aspiration than a characterisation of the reality of social partnership in Russia. In practice, the adoption of the strategy of social partnership marked a break more in the rhetoric than in the substance of the activity of the trade unions. The withdrawal of the Party from intervention in the economy and the marginalisation of the trade unions under perestroika forced independence on the trade unions and at the same time deprived them of the underpinning of their authority. 'Social partnership' with government and employers promised to provide the trade unions with a new prop, enabling them to retain or reconstitute their traditional functions on a new foundation, the state replacing the Party as the guarantor of their authority, the guarantees being embodied in formal legislation and in negotiated agreements which, the trade unions insist, should be legally binding.

The turn to social partnership depended on the willingness of the other social partners to collaborate in the exercise. 'Social partnership' provided a useful instrument for the federal and regional governments in their attempts to maintain social peace in a period of rapid and destabilising economic and social change and to prevent the trade unions from providing the nucleus of an effective oppositional force. While employers in traditional enterprises in the 'productive sphere' had routinely signed collective agreements in the past, it proved much more difficult to extend 'social partnership' to the new private sector and to encourage employers to participate in the institutions of social partnership at regional, sectoral and federal levels. Thus, in Russia the institutions of social partnership were constructed from the top down, even before a distinct class of employers had come into being, to provide a framework within which the trade unions, often with the support of the employers, could press their demands on the state.

The structure of social partnership is similarly constructed from the top down, with an order of precedence running from the General Agreement between government, employers and trade unions; through branch tariff agreements between sectoral trade unions, government and employers; regional agreements with the regional administration and regional branch tariff agreements with the regional employers' representatives and the relevant branch of the regional administration; to collective agreements between the trade union and employer at the enterprise level. Over the past decade there has also been an increasing number of sub-regional agreements signed with municipal authorities who are responsible for the delivery of public services.

The framework for social partnership in post-soviet Russia was established by Presidential Decree No. 212 of 15 November 1991 'On Social Partnership and the Resolution of Labour Disputes (Conflicts)'. This decree provided for the establishment of a Russian Tripartite Commission for the Regulation of Social-Labour Relations (RTK) and similar commissions at branch and regional levels. The RTK was established on 24 January 1992 and its powers and duties were specified in Government Resolution No. 103, February 1992 'On the Russian Tripartite Commission for the Regulation of Social-Labour Relations'. The constitution of the Commission was modified by amendments on 5 February 1993 and 21 March 1994 and was finally given a secure legal foundation with the Federal Law 'On the Russian Tripartite Commission for the Regulation of Social-Labour Relations' of 1 May 1999.

The Tripartite Commission stands at the apex of a system of general, branch, regional and sub-regional tripartite (or bipartite) agreements and enterprise collective agreements, whose constitution was determined by the 1992 and 1995 Laws on

Collective Agreements. The Tripartite Commission draws up an annual General Agreement between the government, trade union and employer representatives and monitors its implementation, as well as settling collective labour disputes and disagreements arising in the conclusion and implementation of branch (tariff) agreements. Regional tripartite commissions perform a similar role at regional level. These bodies are also supposed to participate in the resolution of labour disputes by giving advice, recommending mediators and experts, nominating arbitrators and so on, although some of these functions have been taken over by the conciliation commissions established at regional level under the Ministry of Labour.

The first partnership agreements at Federal and regional levels pre-dated Yeltin's 1991 decree, but once the framework was put in place the negotiation of agreements at these different levels developed very rapidly (Table 6.1).[1] The institutionalisation of negotiations at all these different levels meant that social partnership was quickly transformed from a slogan into a concrete form of practice, and one which structured the activity of the trade unions at all levels.

Table 6.1: Agreements of various types signed each year, 1993–2000

|  | 1993 | 1994 | 1995 | 1996 | 1997 | 1998 | 1999 | 2000 Jan to June |
|---|---|---|---|---|---|---|---|---|
| General Agreement | 1 | 1 | 1 | 1 | 1 | 1 | 1 | 1 |
| Federal branch (inter-branch) tariff agreements | 62 | 51 | 60 | 60 | 51 | 48 | 58 | 58 |
| Regional agreements | 68 | 74 | 77 | 76 | 78 | 77 | 77 | 77 |
| Regional branch (inter-branch) tariff agreements | 241 | 498 | 673 | 964 | 1 420 | 1 423 | 2 062 | |
| Territorial (sub-regional) agreements | 62 | 176 | 371 | 430 | 466 | 684 | 827 | |
| Collective agreements (thousands) | 68.8 | 105.3 | 123.1 | 147.5 | 146.0 | 146.6 | 144.6 | |

Source: Ministry of Labour of the Russian Federation

Although the FNPR apparatus and the Federal government had a common interest in establishing a framework of social partnership, the relationship has never been a stable one. On the one hand, there have always been forces in the presidential apparatus that have favoured a confrontation with the former official trade unions. On the other hand, the FNPR leadership has repeatedly come under pressure from

[1]  The rapid increase in the number of collective agreements signed reflects the extension of the practice to the non-productive sphere, particularly health and education, which did not conclude collective agreements in the soviet period, rather than any dramatic increase in the strength or activism of enterprise trade unions.

activists in its constituent branch and regional trade union organisations to present a more concerted opposition to the government in pressing the interests of their members.

## Social partnership at the Federal level: the history of the Russian Tripartite Commission and the General Agreement

The first problem FNPR faced in its attempt to insert itself into the system of social partnership established by Yeltsin's 1991 decree was to establish its authority as representative of the employed population. The challenge to FNPR's claims came from two directions. On the one hand, the alternative unions claimed that the FNPR trade unions were only pseudo-unions and demanded that FNPR should suffer the fate of the Communist Party, with the nationalisation of its property, the removal of its legal privileges and a re-registration of trade union membership. On the other hand, the government itself challenged the legitimacy of FNPR in insisting that it was the government, not the trade unions, which represented the interests of the mass of the population. The first two years of the Tripartite Commission were dominated by squabbles between the alternative and FNPR unions over their rights of representation and between FNPR and the government over the content and implementation of the General Agreement.

The first co-ordinator of the Tripartite Commission, Gennadii Burbulis, had a reputation as a steadfast opponent of FNPR, while the alternative trade unions, and in particular Sotsprof, were embedded in the Ministry of Labour, headed by Aleksandr Shokhin, which hardly boded well for FNPR's prospects of social partnership. Immediately after his nomination, Burbulis declared that 'all those present are united by a single interest: to achieve the irreversibility of reform and the mastery by workers of a new consciousness (that is, first learn to adapt to market conditions, then demand something from the government)'. Challenging FNPR's claim to be the defender of the interests of the population in the face of radical reform, Burbulis insisted that 'there is no organisation more interested in defending the interests of the toilers than Yeltsin's government, and that is why it needs professional, competent, honest support'. As negotiations for the first General Agreement dragged on, Burbulis blamed FNPR for its failure to agree to the government's proposals: 'There are forces which speak on behalf of the toilers, but which in reality do not represent them and have no connection with them'.

The first dispute in the RTK concerned the composition of the trade union side of the Commission, when the government gave three seats to the tiny Sotsprof trade union federation, two more to other alternative trade unions, and only nine seats to FNPR, which was insufficient to give FNPR the two-thirds of the votes on the union side required to constitute a decisive majority, but FNPR had no levers to enforce its claim to more effective representation. The employer side of the Tripartite Commission was dominated by the ministerial and former ministerial bodies which were responsible for the state enterprises that still employed the overwhelming majority of the population. The most important non-state employers' organisation was Arkadii Vol'skii's Union of Industrialists and Entrepreneurs, which only had one seat on the RTK, but three other Commission members sat on Vol'skii's Council. Vol'skii's organisation was hardly more an employers' association then any of the other bodies represented on the employers' side of the RTK. The organisation was dominated by representatives of large state enterprises and had emerged out of the industrial departments of the Central Committee apparatus when the latter lost their role after Gorbachev withdrew the Party's economic functions. As we have already seen (p. 40), it also had very close relations with FNPR and VKP.

The Tripartite Commission was active in early 1992 and met regularly, although the FNPR unions became increasingly frustrated at the government's attempts to exploit divisions between themselves and the alternative unions and at the government's failure to submit key policy issues and legislation to the Commission.[1] The employer and worker representatives adopted a common programme in negotiation with the government, but the 1992 General Agreement was signed on 25 March by only three of the FNPR representatives and the alternative unions, the other six FNPR representatives refusing to sign on the grounds that the Agreement offered them only rhetoric in exchange for a no-strike pledge and that the government's commitments were at variance with the pledges made to the IMF only days earlier, although FNPR itself subsequently endorsed the agreement (Teague, 1992, p. 21). The agreement committed the parties to the development of a 'socially oriented market economy', including privatisation and price liberalisation, the government promising social protection, including a minimum wage, the employers promising to refrain from mass layoffs or plant closures and the unions committing themselves not to strike. However, the agreement included no mention of the level of the minimum wage or benefits, as had been demanded by FNPR.

Once the General Agreement was signed, the Commission had largely served its purpose as far as the government was concerned. By July the Council of FNPR was denouncing the government for its failure to discuss crucial policy changes within the Commission and its failure to carry out point after point of the agreement, asking what sense there was in negotiating a new agreement for 1993 when all agreements remained only on paper. In the autumn, Sotsprof withdrew its signature from the Agreement in protest at Yeltsin's decree on social insurance, which eventually endorsed FNPR's continued control of social insurance funds (above, p. 40).

The Tripartite Commission was used by the government as the means of resolving the miners' strikes in March 1992 and intervened in a further series of strikes in May,

---

[1]   The first key issue of disagreement concerned the new Law on Collective Agreements, where the government rejected FNPR's draft, which gave negotiating rates to the majority union (eventually implemented in the 2001 Labour Code), in favour of that of Sotsprof, which gave negotiating rights to any properly constituted trade union (Teague, 1992, p. 20).

but it resolutely kept out of the air traffic controllers' dispute later in the year. This dispute marked the turning point in the relationship between the government and the alternative trade unions, when the government first failed to respond to the union's demands and then, having forced the union into a short strike, the government tried (unsuccessfully) to liquidate the union through the courts on the grounds that it had called an illegal strike (Clarke, Borisov and Fairbrother, 1995, pp. 339–71). At the same time, the Tripartite Commission was effectively suspended, while the government held occasional bilateral talks with FNPR.

The marginalisation of the alternative unions was confirmed with the announcement of the composition of the Tripartite Commission for 1993, with all the Sotsprof representatives being thrown off, the Independent Miners' Union (NPG) members then withdrawing in solidarity. FNPR saw the opportunity of increasing its legitimacy through active participation in the Commission, which the government equally saw as the means of neutralising FNPR by persuading it to commit itself to the principles of social partnership. The greater attention paid by the government to FNPR at the expense of the alternative trade unions was not a result of the strength of FNPR (or of its equality of rights), but of its potential role in the developing conflict between Yeltsin and the Supreme Soviet. FNPR's attempts at mass mobilisation in order to press its claims had been a dismal failure, with derisory turn-outs, but its alliance with Vol'skii presented a more serious challenge to the government, as it threatened to constitute an effective centre-left opposition to the government's reforms.

A General Agreement was signed by both sides on 29 March 1993 in which the government agreed to the FNPR's central demand by committing itself to bringing the minimum wage closer to the subsistence minimum, although the government refused to agree to the FNPR demand that the minimum wage be set at 6000 roubles from 1 April, to be linked subsequently to inflation, and that the government should set a target maximum rate of unemployment of 3.5 per cent. Once the Agreement was signed, however, the government made only a token effort in the direction of raising the minimum wage, which was soon reversed by inflation,[1] and made no further efforts to fulfil the agreement or to consult with the trade unions, leading to growing frustration on the trade union side which played its part in fuelling the political polarisation over the summer. In August 1993, as part of its growing confrontation with parliament, the government appealed to workers and trade union members over the heads of the FNPR, which responded with an angry statement accusing the government of crudely violating the General Agreement and the co-ordinator of the Tripartite Commission, now Deputy Prime Minister Shumeiko, who rarely attended meetings, of avoiding his responsibilities.

[1]   The government raised the minimum wage to 4275 roubles in April and to 7740 in July, but by September it had fallen back to the relative level of March, before the increase, and was not raised again until December, just prior to the Duma election.

Following Yeltsin's confrontation with the Supreme Soviet in September 1993 and the subsequent change in the leadership of FNPR, the Tripartite Commission resumed in March 1994 as though nothing had happened, under a new co-ordinator, Yurii Yarov, reaching a General Agreement on 8 April. The alternative trade unions had hoped to be rewarded for their support of Yeltsin in the allocation of seats on the Tripartite Commission, but their hopes were disappointed as the government resumed its conciliatory approach to the FNPR unions, while the change of leadership of the FNPR equally implied a willingness to participate in conciliation. The leading alternative trade unions, NPG and Sotsprof, walked out of the discussions around the composition of the Commission because they were not satisfied with the alternative unions' proposed allocation. In the end, for 1994 the workers' side of the Commission had 28 seats, of which 20 were assigned to FNPR affiliates, six to unions belonging to the FNPR's Consultative Council, which had been set up in May 1993 to tie non-affiliates in by offering them patronage and protection, one to the metallurgists, who had withdrawn from FNPR at the Federal level, and the leader of one of the alternative pilots' unions, Alfred Malinovsky, who was by then working closely with the FNPR aviation union. However, while FNPR strengthened its position on the Tripartite Commission, the Commission was being sidelined by Yeltsin's 'Memorandum of Civic Accord' of March 1994, which fulfilled the same role as the Commission, while seeking to broaden the framework of social partnership. With their participation in the Memorandum of Civic Accord, the alternative unions declared the Tripartite Commission redundant, the trade union side subsequently continuing to be dominated by FNPR. At the end of 1995, when the General Agreement for 1996–7 was ready to be signed, the alternative trade union federation, VKT, demanded admission to the Commission, but its demand was not satisfied at that time.

The RTK was fairly inactive through 1994–5, as Yeltsin relied on his Memorandum of Civic Accord and occasional bilateral meetings with FNPR, but under Yarov's chairmanship the RTK was developed from a confrontational forum into a self-sufficient bureaucratic organisation, its apparatus rooted in the apparatus of the Vice-Premier, so that subsequent personnel changes (Ilyushin, Sysuev, Matvienko) had no impact on its character as a quasi-governmental structure. The main function of the RTK has been the negotiation of the General Agreement (annual until 1995, biennial since 1996) and the biannual monitoring of its fulfilment, which has become a bureaucratised process of government consultation with the trade unions on labour and social issues in which the employers' representatives play a very limited role. In this respect it is not very different from the traditional subordinate role played by VTsSPS in the consideration of social and labour policy in the soviet system. The trade unions are consulted at the government's discretion, their views may or may not be taken into account and they have no effective sanctions to press their position on the government. The General Agreement is very different from the traditional soviet planning documents in that it has no executive status, but is merely a statement of wishful thinking.

The General Agreements have tended to be declaratory and very general, laying down the broad lines of the government's economic and social policy and the common aspirations of government, trade unions and employers, with no means of enforcing the agreements reached. Although it is only the government that has the power to realise most of the terms of the Agreement, nearly all the obligations are assumed not by the government, but by the joint efforts of the parties to the Agreement. The significance of this formulation is that it refers policy development to subsequent tripartite discussion, particularly in the Tripartite Commission, rather than to unilateral government action. Many items oblige the parties to do no more than 'give consideration to', 'prepare' or 'bring forward proposals to', 'work out a draft law', 'take steps to', 'continue working on', 'consult with the trade unions about' measures and programmes 'to address a problem', 'improve a situation', 'rationalise the provision' or 'modernise the organisation' of something, without prescribing what, if anything, the government is actually to do. (This, as will be seen, is also a prominent feature of the regional agreements.) Many items of the General Agreement are subsequently reported to have been fulfilled because there has been further discussion of the issue in the Tripartite Commission or because FNPR has participated in government commissions or merely put proposals to the government. Many obligations, particularly those relating to the employers, are deferred to the negotiation of branch tariff and collective agreements, where the parties are mandated to take various factors into account or to take steps to do various things.

Negotiation of the General Agreement is also constrained by the fact that it is conducted after the budget has been prepared, so has to take place within existing budget constraints. The General Agreement for 2000–1 was the first to be signed before it came into force, in December 1999. Although the budget for 2000 had already been adopted, President Putin promised to take its terms into account in forming the 2001 budget, which was not a great commitment since most of its very few substantive concessions were already constrained by 'the economic constraints of the state' or 'the limits of budgetary possibilities'.

The priorities of the trade union side in negotiating the General Agreement have been to secure the government's commitment to a realistic minimum wage and social benefits, acceptable wages in the budget sector, guarantees regarding the level and increase in unemployment and the regular payment and indexation of wages and benefits. The trade unions' demands are, in general, inconsistent with the government's restrictive budgetary and macroeconomic policies, which therefore regularly become the focus of attention. The government has generally resisted making 'unrealisable' promises, confining itself to rhetorical declarations and qualifying its commitments by reference to budgetary constraints but, despite the largely rhetorical character and unenforceability of the General Agreement, the fact that negotiations can be quite tough indicates that it has at least some ideological and political significance. Moreover, although the unions' gains have been very limited, they have undoubtedly been able to have an influence on the detail of government social and labour policy and legislation in small but significant respects.

The 1995 General Agreement committed the government to introducing a comprehensive employment programme and raising the minimum wage closer to the subsistence minimum by the end of January, but by its April 1995 'day of action' FNPR was able to charge that the government had taken no steps to implement the agreement, while wage delays, which the government had promised to reduce, were growing ever larger and the promised increase in the basic wage in the public sector had been financed by reducing differentials. The General Agreement for 1996–7 continued the tradition of wishful thinking in recommending that budgetary funds should be found to ensure that the average wage in the budget sphere should not fall below 85 per cent of the average industrial wage and once more recommended bringing the minimum wage and the basic wage for budget organisations into line with the subsistence minimum, to no effect as budget sector pay and the minimum wage continued to be eroded by inflation.

The General Agreement for 1998–9 was signed on 26 January 1998. The government and employers committed themselves to paying off wage debts in the first half of 1998 and also recognised the need to introduce a series of legislation, including a law to compensate those who had lost from non-payment of wages and benefits. FNPR registered two disagreements, including the need to bridge the gap between the minimum wage and the subsistence minimum, which the government had this time refused to endorse. In the event the key points of the agreement were not fulfilled. The promised indexation of budget sector pay was not realised in 1998, and in 1999 was only partially achieved by compressing pay scales in order to keep within the budget. The result was that the commitment to bring the level of pay in the budget sphere closer to that in industry was not met as the relation fell from 51–3 per cent to 45 per cent. Similarly, unemployment, which it was anticipated would be kept below 10 per cent, increased to 12 per cent. Wage debts, far from being liquidated in the first half of 1998, continued to increase. FNPR had no sanctions as a result of the non-fulfilment of the agreement, but could only seek to include the unfulfilled items in the next agreement.

Negotiations for the 2000–1 General Agreement were tough, with threats not to sign it at all, but it was signed on 16 December 1999 with a memorandum of disagreement from the unions concerning the means to increase budget sector wages. The Agreement followed the tradition of its predecessors in outlining the intention of all parties to work together to secure the growth of the national economy, higher investment, an increase in the standard of living, a rise in employment and a reduction in inflation, but the government made virtually no substantive concessions in the Agreement and the only obligations of the employers were to increase the coverage of employers' associations, and to meet their legal obligations to sign agreements and not impede the legitimate activity of the trade unions. The continued recovery of the economy in the wake of the August 1998 financial crisis meant that the macroeconomic indicators, apart from that for inflation, were realised, but this was hardly an achievement of social partnership, or even of government policy, but a result of the forced devaluation of 1998 and the increase in world energy prices. According to Resolution 1-15 of the FNPR Executive on 27 February 2001, the key failures in the first year of the agreement concerned the government's reform of electricity tariffs, which would increase the cost of living, and, above all, the government's unilateral introduction of the Unified Social Tax, which directly violated a number of principles endorsed by the General Agreement. The main achievement for the trade unions was the consolidation of the participation of FNPR in the system of labour and health and safety inspection through agreements with the relevant inspectorates at the Federal level.

In the run up to the 2000 Presidential election, Acting President Putin and a coterie of Ministers attended the regular meeting of the FNPR General Council on 16 February, an unprecedented event, and Putin expressed his commitment to continued social partnership, though he warned the unions that while the trade unions were justified in pressing for increases in pay and minimal social guarantees and it was inevitable that they should make demands on the government, such demands should be as close as possible to the real economic situation in the country, since to make unrealistic demands only stirred up social tension.

The 2002–4 General Agreement was signed on 20 December 2001. Although the budget had already been set, the government promised to increase budget sector wages by at least 50 percent during 2002. The trade union side registered two disagreements, the first with the refusal of the government to commit itself to bring the minimum wage into line with the subsistence minimum during 2002 (the government only undertook to discuss the issue in the Tripartite Commission in drawing up the draft budget for 2003–5), the second with the refusal of the government to agree to incorporate projected social spending under the Law on the North into the annual consideration of the budget. The unions had little expectation that the government would implement any promises that it might make to increase the minimum wage, but at least if the commitment were to be included in the General Agreement the unions could make the government's failure to implement it the pretext for a legal labour dispute.

The Tripartite Commission barely met through 1998, as a result of the frequent government changes and the developing financial crisis, but FNPR continued bilateral discussions with the government and employers. The Commission resumed its work in October 1998, on the insistence of FNPR, and since then has met about ten times a year, usually with one major item on the agenda of each meeting.[1] Most of the work

---

[1]  In addition to its biennial consideration of the fulfilment of the General Agreement, the principal topics considered at the 2000 meetings were: government wage policy; the problem of unemployment; the draft law on employers' associations; amendments to the tax code and

of the Commission is carried out in its working groups, whose terms of reference correspond to the sections of the General Agreement, which draft and monitor the fulfilment of the General Agreement and consider draft legislation and other relevant issues. Sometimes *ad hoc* working groups are established to deal with particular issues, as happened in 1999, for example, in relation to the conflict in the Vyborg Cellulose-Paper Combine (Pulaeva and Clarke, 2000). Over the years it has become a much more bureaucratised structure, in which detailed discussion of legislation and government policies and programmes takes place, instead of the platform for demagoguery that it provided in its first years. Nevertheless, the problems that faced the RTK in its earliest years remain barriers to its effective functioning today. These are the problems of representation; of the status of decisions of the RTK and the enforceability of commitments entered into; of the failure of government to submit items for discussion; and of the small size of the apparatus servicing the Commission.

### The social partners at national level

The problem of representation concerns all three parties. We have already seen the conflicts between FNPR and the alternative trade unions which have surrounded the representation of the trade union side and, while the resolution of the issue since 1993 has been favourable to FNPR, there is still no unambiguous basis of trade union representation. Under the 1999 Law only All-Russian trade union structures are entitled to representation on the Commission, which excludes Sotsprof from membership, each being entitled to one member. GMPR, the metallurgists' union, reaffiliated to FNPR in 2000 primarily in order to retain its representation on the RTK. In 2001 FNPR unions held 24 of the 30 seats on the trade union side of the Commission, with the other seats being distributed among FNPR allies and alternative trade union federations, VKT and KTR each having one seat.

On the employers' side, the RTK was established before mass privatisation, when the overwhelming majority of workers were still state employees, so the employer representatives in the first RTK were primarily representatives of ministries and quasi-ministerial bodies, using their position to press their branch interests on the government, and a number of self-styled employer representatives, mostly claiming to represent entrepreneurs and small businesses (which tend to be non-union), who were selected by government patronage. With privatisation the weight of employer representation has shifted in favour of private employers, but there are 60 registered

the introduction of a Unified Social Tax; the basic directions of the government's socio-economic policy; pension reform; tariff policy for electric power and revisions to the Criminal Code relating to the non-payment of wages. Meetings in 2001 considered revisions to the Labour Code and the issue of tax liabilities in relation to the payment of wages; employment policy; the law on employers' associations; the government's medium-term economic programme; the government's programme for health and safety; pension reform; problems of the North; medical insurance; 2002 budgets of social funds; Russia's entry into the WTO and the 2002–4 General Agreement.

All-Russian employers' associations and several hundred at regional level, about half of which are active, as well as a substantial number of branch organisations.

A Co-ordinating Council of Employers' Associations (KSOR) was established in November 1994 as an umbrella organisation and reconstituted on a more substantial basis as the Co-ordinating Council of Employers' Associations of Russia (KSORR) in March 2000. In 2001 KSORR had 26 members, consisting of Volskii's Russian Union of Industrialists and Entrepreneurs and six other All-Russian employers' associations (the Union of Public Associations of Entrepreneurs and Leaseholders, the Congress of Russian Business Circles, the Association of Privatised and Private Enterprises, the Association of Joint Ventures and International Associations and Organisations, the Russian Chamber of Commerce and the Union of Employers in Small and Medium Business), 12 branch organisations (covering light industry, engineering, shipowners, coal, river transport, mining-metallurgy, construction, agro-industry, road transport, bakers, atomic energy and paper), six large holding companies and the Moscow Chamber of Commerce. KSORR is a member of the International Employers' Organisation, and as such represents Russian employers at the ILO. The first declared function of KSORR is 'to co-ordinate and represent the interests of employers and their associations in the conclusion of the General Agreement' (www.ksorr.ru) and members of the council dominate the employers' side of the RTK. With the consolidation of KSORR the Russian employers have begun to play a more significant and coherent role in tripartite negotiation and in lobbying the Duma. Nevertheless, the majority of the employer representatives still represent producer rather than employer interests, with little interest in labour and social issues, using their position to get access to government and to press their individual and sectional interests. It is indicative of the status of KSORR that its formation had to be cleared by the anti-monopoly commission.

The trade union and employer representatives tend to have a common interest in such fundamental issues as the regeneration of the national economy and easing the burden of taxation in order to permit increasing employment and rising living standards. As FNPR President Mikhail Shmakov noted, 'in preparing the tripartite General Agreement we find that we have much more in common with the employers than with the government' (*Obshchaya gazeta*, 27.7–2.8.1995). The most important employers' organisation continues to be Vol'skii's Union of Industrialists and Entrepreneurs (RSPP). As we have seen, RSPP was originally a producers' organisation rather than an employers' organisation, which had a close alliance with FNPR from 1992–5. In November 2000 the RSPP was given a new lease of life when it was effectively taken over by the 'oligarchs' who control the commanding heights of the Russian economy, to become their 'trade union', giving rise to the expectation that it would tend more to support the government than the trade unions in the Tripartite Commission. However, this development did not enhance the authority of KSORR, which had also been hoping to enlist the oligarchs but which was seen as being dominated by one of those giant conglomerates, Potanin's Interros.

The government is doubly represented on the Commission. On the one hand, the Co-ordinator of the Commission is the First Deputy Prime Minister. On the other hand, the government side is represented by officials of various interested ministries, chaired by the Minister of Labour. As in the case of the employers, the government side of the Commission is fragmented as representatives press their ministerial interests, in some cases as employers, the general position of the government being represented by the Co-ordinator of the Commission rather than by the government side. Negotiations within the Commission do not, therefore, consist in the government mediating between employer and employee representatives, but tend to take the form of collaboration between employer and employee representatives, sometimes with support from particular representatives on the government side, to press their policy demands on the government. As Frank Hoffer, formerly Labour Attaché at the German Embassy and later ILO Workers' Representative in Moscow, commented

> The tripartite commission is more a forum for presenting social policy concepts to government than a body in which the state participates, as a neutral third party, in settling labour relations between labour and management (Hoffer, 1997, p. 43).

## The enforcement of agreements

The problem of enforcement of agreements has two components. On the one hand, commitments entered into by the employer representatives are not binding on most employers since the basis of employer representation is undefined. The trade unions have long pressed for legislation on employers' associations which would define both the basis of employer representation and the status of the commitments they enter into. A draft Law on Employers' Associations was eventually given its first reading in the Duma in December 2000, but the draft law still does not address the central issues of representation and enforcement of commitments. On the other hand, the commitments entered into in the General Agreement and the decisions of the RTK have no legal status in the sense that no mechanisms are provided for their enforcement and no sanctions are provided for in the case of their non-fulfilment.

Although the government is committed to submitting policy and legislative proposals related to labour and social questions to the RTK, this commitment has no clear juridical foundation and the government is under no obligation to take the views of the RTK into account. Moreover, the resources available to the RTK to service its activities are very limited – the staff of the RTK was reduced to one person in May 2000. The RTK and General Agreements, therefore, provide more of a ritual manifestation of a commitment of government and trade unions to social dialogue than a substantive foundation for social partnership. As Mikhail Shmakov commented in an interview in January 1999, the Tripartite Commission 'at the moment is still mainly a club for the exchange of views, and does not serve as the basis for the fulfilment of commitments undertaken', though he contrasted the situation with that in the regions, where he claimed that regional administrations do not run away from their commitments (*Vesti FNPR*, 1–2, 1999, p. 58). The accuracy of this claim will be examined below.

The Tripartite Commission and the General Agreement provide the formal framework of collaboration between the government and the trade unions, but there is also extensive collaboration between FNPR, the branch unions and the government on a less formal basis, through consultation with government officials, trade union participation in ministerial commissions and working groups and trade union representation on the governing bodies of the various off-budget funds. Such collaboration is often based on long-established personal relations between trade union and government officials and reproduces the traditional participation of the trade unions in the elaboration of social and labour policy not so much as representatives negotiating on behalf of their members, but as specialists with considerable experience and expertise in their fields.

FNPR has sought to secure the government's fulfilment of the commitments entered into in the General Agreement through its regular Days of Action and May Day demonstrations but, despite FNPR's extravagant claims about their turnout, these have not had a significant impact on the government. FNPR has repeatedly observed that 'the effectiveness of this form of defence of our interests is sharply reduced by the weak recognition of the need for solidary actions' (FNPR, 1996, p. 41).

Finally, as already noted in Chapter 3, FNPR has placed increasing emphasis in its activities on lobbying the State Duma over the passage, amendment and rejection of legislation which affects the social and labour interests of its members, in conjunction both with its days of action and with its attempts to persuade the government to include promises of support for such legislation in the General Agreement. Over the period 1996–2001, FNPR commented on and proposed amendments to 65 Federal laws and participated in seven parliamentary hearings (Naboishchikov, 2001).

## Social partnership at the branch level: branch tariff agreements

Branch tariff agreements are signed covering virtually all branches of the economy. To an even greater extent than with regard to the General Agreement, in lobbying and negotiating branch tariff agreements the trade unions represent not so much the interests of the worker in opposition to the employer, as the interests of the branch in relation to the government. In many industries the employers are happy to leave the trade union to do their work for them and do not participate in the structures of social partnership, while in others they take a back seat. Thus, the majority of tariff agreements are bipartite, involving only the government and the trade union, with only about one-fifth being signed by private employers' representatives, and the proportion of the latter has been in decline.[1] In the defence industry, the tariff agreement is signed with government agencies which have no role as employers, and the number of employers refusing to recognise the agreement has increased year by year (FNPR, 2001a). The tariff agreements for the oil and gas industry do not involve any of the private conglomerates that dominate the industry, but are signed exclusively by the union and the Ministry of Fuel and Power. The tariff agreements for public sector employees, such as health and education, are signed with the corresponding Ministries, but do not involve the Ministry of Finance and so cannot include any commitments which have budgetary implications. Thus tariff agreements still tend more to reproduce the traditional interaction between branch trade unions and the appropriate ministerial structures than the outcome of collective bargaining between employers and employees.

The absence of employers' organisations is a reflection of the weakness of the trade unions. In an attempt to find social partners some of the branch trade unions, sometimes with government support, have been very active in sponsoring the formation of branch employers' associations. The chemical workers' union had been one of the first to press the need for a Union of Industrialists and Entrepreneurs as an interlocutor with FNPR as early as 1990, and in 1996 was the initiator of the formation of the Union of Chemical Industry Employers with whom to sign a branch tariff agreement. In 1997, the Mining-Metallurgical Trade Union similarly sponsored the formation of the Association of Industrialists of the Mining-Metallurgical Complex of Russia (AMROS) to provide a counterpart, since the State Committee for Metallurgy, with which it had previously signed agreements, had been dissolved. The role of the government side in tariff agreements is also ambiguous. The Ministry of Labour is a signatory of about half the tariff agreements concluded, but it plays the role of consultant in the negotiation process rather than that of representative of the government ready to assume the appropriate obligations and, in particular, to guarantee the financing of the tariff agreement in those branches which are budget-funded or rely on government subsidies.

Branch tariff agreements are potentially much more significant for union members than is the General Agreement because they include more concrete specifications of the terms and conditions of employment specific to the branch. However, employers and the government are very cautious about conceding significant increases in wages or improvement in the terms and conditions of employment beyond those specified by the law. Almost all tariff agreements include a section on wages, which establishes a minimum wage for the branch and sometimes includes an obligation on employers to give priority to the payment of wages over other outlays, but very few agreements make any reference to pay scales, and even fewer specify the level of wages, leaving this to the collective agreement, though some provided for the partial or even

---

[1]   Alternative trade unions sign tariff agreements in the coal-mining (NPG) and aviation (FPAD, PRIASGA, PARRRSR) industries.

complete quarterly indexation of wages to compensate for inflation. In 1998, all but three, and in 1999 all but one tariff agreements established a minimum wage higher than that laid down by the law, though still ridiculously low. In the 1999 agreements governing the construction and timber processing industries the minimum wage was related to the regional subsistence minimum, though in the case of construction this was only a recommendation,[1] but in many agreements the real value of the minimum wage had been reduced since it did not take account of the previous year's inflation. Some agreements included the aspiration to raise the minimum wage towards the subsistence minimum (details of tariff agreements are provided in FNPR, 2001a).

Over the 1990s employers have increased wage flexibility by steadily reducing the tariff component of wages (according to FNPR, to around 30 per cent) and increasing the proportion accounted for by bonuses and premia. This not only increases workers' insecurity, but also means that they lose out on all those payments, such as payment for stoppages, which are related to the tariff wage rather than to actual earnings. It has long been a priority of the trade unions to increase the proportion of earnings accounted for by the tariff and many have tried to introduce this question into their branch tariff agreements. In the 1999 tariff agreements for the timber, atomic energy and mining-metallurgical industries it was agreed that the tariff should account for at least 50 per cent, and in defence and aviation at least 70 per cent, of the wage. A number of tariff agreements in 1999–2000 included clauses defining the terms of compensation for delays in the payment of wages, while others referred this concession to the collective agreement.

In the budget sector, wages are defined by the government, which sets the Unified Tariff Scale (ETS), but the tariff agreement can provide for various bonuses and premia, particularly those to be paid from non-budget revenues.

Tariff agreements may include a range of other concessions. They may provide various benefits, such as additional vacation for those working in harmful conditions or allowances for special clothing and so on. Several tariff agreements increase the rate of pay in case of temporary lay-off to 100 per cent of the tariff wage and many include provision for bonus payments to those approaching retirement. The 1999 tariff agreements for construction and light industry set limits to the pay of management, related to the average wage and size of the enterprise. Agreements may provide compensation above that provided for by the law in case of redundancy. They may specify minimum levels of expenditure on health and safety measures (for example, in engineering this is set at three per cent of the wage bill and in atomic energy at 0.5 per cent of production costs).

---

[1]   The 1995–6 branch tariff agreement for the iron mill workers specified that the minimum wage, including all supplements, should be no less than the regional subsistence minimum, but qualified this by noting that if the employer could not afford to pay, then the collective agreement should set a lower minimum wage (cited Hoffer, 1997, n. 101, p. 47).

The coverage of the tariff agreements is restricted by the limited coverage of employers' associations. According to the Law on Collective Agreements, the terms of branch tariff agreements are binding only on those employers who have delegated their rights to a signatory employers' association, although if the agreement covers more than half those employed in the branch the Ministry of Labour can extend the application of the agreement to all employers who do not register their refusal to be covered by the agreement in writing within thirty days. Limited coverage means that tariff agreements provide a point of reference for workplace collective bargaining rather than a binding commitment on most employers. Moreover, some of the concessions included in the agreement are only recommendations and other items have to be specified in the collective agreement, so enterprise trade union committees are encouraged to use the tariff agreement as a guide in drawing up the enterprise collective agreement, often incorporating some or all of the points of the tariff agreement into the latter. The effective application and enforcement of the tariff agreement is therefore a matter of the diligence of the enterprise trade union committee.

The branch trade unions press their interests not only through negotiated agreements, but also through lobbying government and organising demonstrations, days of action and even, occasionally, strikes. However, the demands put forward by the branch unions in these actions are almost invariably demands concerning the branch, directed at the government, rather than demands regarding the terms and conditions of employment directed at the employers. In many cases the employers, tacitly or overtly, support these actions. For example, the Agro-Industrial Workers' Union campaigns in collaboration with the industry body, the Russian Agro-industrial Union, and the Agrarian Party of Russia for increased budget support for the branch and for an improvement in the ratio of agricultural to industrial prices. The defence industry workers' union campaigns for the government to pay its debts for military procurement and to adopt a long-term procurement policy. The aviation industry union similarly campaigns for the payment of government debts and for the adoption of a long-term state programme for the industry. The coal miners' union campaigns for increased budget subsidies for the industry, for the payment of subsidies due, and for a properly financed programme to mitigate the social impact of mine closures, while the health and education workers lobby for increased budget funding and for the payment of budget allocations due for their branches.

Specialists from the branch trade unions also continue their traditional practice of participating extensively in the formulation and implementation of policies specific to their branch, particularly in the areas of health and safety, training and retraining and the qualification and accreditation of employees. The Deputy President of the civil servants' union declared that 'there must always be a trade union representative on the commission for the attestation of civil service jobs' (ASTI, 34, 2001).

## Social partnership at the regional level

Russia is a federation of 89 regions (oblasts, krais, republics and the cities of Moscow and St Petersburg), each of which has its own regional government, headed by an elected Governor, and elected legislature which has the power to pass regional laws, within limits set by the Constitution and federal legislation, and to set a regional budget. In a context in which the financing and administration of most public services and the implementation of federal programmes have largely been devolved to the regional level, and each region has its own social and economic specificity, the development of social partnership at the regional level has assumed increasing importance.[1] Given that the trade unions have found their influence so limited at federal level, this development has been strongly encouraged by FNPR. Regional trade union federations are judged above all by the quality of their regional agreement and the coverage of collective agreements in their region.[2]

The first regional social partnership agreements were signed at the beginning of the 1990s and by the middle of the decade covered virtually every Russian region. The timing of the introduction of social partnership in different regions depended partly on the interest of the trade unions in such a development, but more on the willingness of the regional authorities to involve themselves in the process – things which in turn depended on the political situation in the region. For example, the leaders of the Komi Federation of Trade Unions claimed that theirs was the first regional agreement to be concluded in Russia (it was concluded in 1991 on a bipartite basis between the Rebublican Council of Trade Unions and the Council of Ministers of the Autonomous Soviet Socialist Republic of Komi).[3] The impetus to conclude such an agreement came from the attempt to respond to the demands put forward by the miners in the Pechora coalfields in 1989, many of which had been addressed to the Komi republican government. The regional trade union council assembled these demands and sent them on to the Soviet government, whose reaction was very negative, so the

---

[1]  Public opinion appears to see the regional administration, rather than the employers or the Federal authorities, as the main counter-agent of the trade unions. VTsIOM asked in a nation-wide poll in September 1993 how unions should realise their defensive functions: 43 per cent said unions should secure the resolution of problems through local government, 24–7 per cent that they should turn to the central authorities, 13–16 per cent that they should actively participate in the work of the tripartite commission (Klopov, 1995).

[2]  Regional social dialogue is also gaining in importance within the EU. The Commission has recently called for the negotiation of 'territorial employment pacts', and tripartite agreements have been negotiated in at least some of the regions of the majority of member states (Hyman, 2000, pp. 24–7). In this sense, Russia, with its well-developed institutional architecture of regional social partnership, could even claim to be in the vanguard of employment relations.

[3]  In fact this was pre-dated by a 1990 bipartite agreement in Moscow (Gritsenko, Kadeikina and Makukhina, 1999, p. 343). A regional agreement was concluded in February 1991 in Leningrad Oblast between the *oblsovprof* and the *ispolkom* of the oblast Congress of People's Deputies.

trade union council decided to concentrate its efforts on its own republican government, which refused to sign the proposed agreement on the grounds that there was no precedent for such a thing, although they eventually signed a bipartite regional agreement in 1991. Meanwhile, in Kemerovo oblast, the other centre of the miners' movement, regional social partnership was not initiated until 1998. The first Governor, Mikhail Kislyuk, a leader of the 1989 miners' strike appointed to his position by Yeltsin, refused to have any dealings with the FNPR trade unions on the grounds that they were pro-Communist and anti-reform, and tried, unsuccessfully, to expropriate their building, collaborating instead with the Independent Miners' Union (NPG) and the regional Workers' Committee, to both of which he assigned offices in the regional administration building. It was not until Aman Tuleev replaced Kislyuk in 1997 that the regional administration established relations with the FNPR trade unions and the first regional agreement was signed only in 1998.

The first generation of agreements were generally bipartite. In the mid-1990s, following mass privatisation, there was a move to include employers in the regional agreements. Some regions moved rapidly from bipartite to tripartite agreements (employer representatives were included in the St Petersburg agreement for 1992, while the first regional agreement in Perm' was concluded in 1992, already on a tripartite basis), while others took somewhat longer (for example, the first tripartite agreement in Samara region was only concluded in 1997, three years after the first bipartite agreement), but by 2001 all agreements were, at least formally, tripartite. Meanwhile, while the first agreements had a duration of one year, in the late 1990s there was a tendency for agreements to be concluded on a two-year basis. The Komi republic moved from annual to biannual agreements in 1998, for example. The Leningrad Federation moved in 1999 to a three-year framework agreement, to coincide with the gubernatorial term, with annual appendices negotiated in co-ordination with the budgetary process.

Alongside regional agreements, regional tripartite commissions were established to provide a bureaucratic framework for social partnership and conflict resolution, with schedules for conclusion and monitoring of agreements, rules of conduct in case of non-agreement, implementation plans and so on. In the absence of a specific federal law on social partnership, some regions established their own laws, some of which, such as those in Novosibirsk and Tula, were modelled on the Moscow Law on Social Partnership which was passed in 1996, though others are less far-reaching. Now 53 regions have such laws, while a further 20 are considering them, and 8 have laws on the regional tripartite commission (FNPR, 2001b). Meanwhile, social partnership agreements are also spreading to town and district level.

Social partnership has become an established part of the regional political landscape. The trade unions have been keen sponsors of the process, while regional authorities have generally co-operated in building the requisite institutions. In a small number of cases the enthusiasm of the authorities has even matched or exceeded that of the trade unions. But what is the elaborate machinery of regional social partnership designed to achieve? And does it serve the purpose for which it was ostensibly designed? The rest of this section focuses on this question, looking first at the formal objectives of social partnership and the degree to which they are met, and then turning to consider the informal aims of its sponsors and the degree to which these are realised.

### The formal aims of regional social partnership

The stated aims and tasks of regional social partnership differ slightly from region to region, but the key goals are very similar. To take a typical example, the 1998 Kemerovo Oblast Law on Social Partnership sets out the purpose of social partnership as being: to provide an effective means of regulating social-labour relations; to carry out collective negotiations; to improve labour legislation; to conclude agreements and to prevent collective labour disputes. Within such a framework each institution is generally given a set of specific tasks. To take a different example, though Samara oblast does not have a law on social partnership, in 1997 the region adopted regulations (the *polozhenie*) and standing orders (a *reglament*) to govern the operation of its tripartite commission. The regulations set out the main task of the commission as being: to provide for the equal (*ravnopravnoe*) co-operation of the three sides in working out the general principles regulating social-labour relations in Samara oblast; to carry out collective negotiations and prepare the draft of the tripartite agreement; to develop social partnership in Samara Oblast and to co-operate with the participants in regional branch tariff agreements to regulate disagreements arising between them.

As these examples reveal, the broad aim of regional social partnership is said to be the regulation of 'social-labour relations'.[1] This is to be carried out on the basis of *ravnopravie* (equality of rights) of the three sides, and is to be achieved through collective negotiation and collective agreements. The process will serve to 'develop social partnership' or, in the more stark Kemerovo version, 'prevent collective labour disputes'. Some of these goals are clearly met in a formal sense: negotiations are carried out and agreements are signed. But it is less clear whether social partnership serves to regulate social-labour relations, whether it is carried out on the basis of *ravnopravie* and whether it serves to prevent conflict. This section considers these questions by looking in turn at the social partners, the content of the agreements, and enforcement mechanisms.

### Who are the social partners?

The three parties in regional agreements are supposed to enjoy equal rights in negotiations, but reality falls well short of this ideal. As will become clear in this section, this is partly due to the nature of the three 'partners'. The employee and

---

[1]   'Social-labour relations' have a wider scope than 'labour relations', specified by the definition of 'social-labour rights' in Article 37 of the Constitution (see above, p. 106).

government representatives in regional social partnership are clear: the regional federation of trade unions and the regional government, generally represented by its department or 'ministry' of labour.[1] The representation of the employers in regional social partnership, however, has proved more problematic.

Since employers have few common interests at the regional level, it has proved even more difficult to establish employers' associations at the regional than at the branch or federal levels, even with strong encouragement from the regional administration and trade unions. Securing the co-operation of employers generally requires the judicious use of carrots and sticks by the regional authorities. In Kemerovo Oblast, for example, state orders are informally used to encourage participation, while such inducements are openly used in Moscow, where point 1.17 of the 2001 city agreement lays down that in placing orders the city government should 'take into account the participation of an enterprise attempting to receive an order in the system of social partnership'.[2] In Sverdlovsk, too, the government takes into account the existence of a collective agreement in deciding on the allocation of benefits to enterprises. In most cases, where there is no regional employers' association, surrogates are found in various producers' organisations or even the individual directors of large enterprises. Sometimes, as in Moscow City, Sverdlovsk and St Petersburg, the regional branch of the Union of Industrialists and Entrepreneurs is co-opted to serve as the employers' representative.[3] Alternatively, a number of different organisations representing producers, entrepreneurs, small business and so on may be drawn in as employer representatives. Elsewhere, as in Kemerovo, where there is no regional employers' association, large employers are simply invited to the sittings of the tripartite commission:

At the moment, what we do is invite the managers of the largest enterprises in the oblast, but with every meeting the group of managers changes, and so there's nothing real to rely on. But, all the same, we're going along with it in order to get the largest enterprises involved in this process. The other goal is to provide an

[1] The dominance of the FNPR trade unions at regional level is rarely contested by the alternative unions, which generally do not have effective regional bodies. In Leningrad and St Petersburg region the alternative unions participate in the regional agreement, where they work in collaboration with the Leningrad and St Petersburg Federation of Trade Unions. Alternative trade unions participate in the Tripartite Commission in Primorskii krai, Tambov, Ivanovo and Vladimir oblasts and did so in the past in Perm'.

[2] This policy is the subject of dispute since it contravenes federal anti-monopoly legislation.

[3] As at the Federal level, this organisation has very close connections with the trade unions. The Union of Industrialists and Entrepreneurs and the Leningrad and St Petersburg Trade Union Federation collaborate in the regional social-political organisation *Yedinstvo radi progressa* (Unity for progress – ERP), established in January 1994, which is the vehicle for lobbying for industrial regeneration and for the trade unions' political activity in the region. The Moscow Federation signed a similar co-operation agreement in 2000.

example for the other enterprises (Specialist, Kemerovo Oblast Department of Labour).

There is a similarly shifting system of employer representation in Ul'yanovsk oblast, where each agreement has been signed by a different contingent of employers. The number of employers included has at least increased: the first tripartite agreement in 1994 was signed by only five employers, while the 2000–1 agreement was signed by the leader of the Council of Industrial Employers which unites over 30 large Ul'yanovsk enterprises, of the more than 18 000 enterprises registered in the region. Nonetheless, widening the participation of employers in social partnership is acknowledged to be necessary and the aspiration formed point 6.4 of the 2000–1 Ul'yanovsk regional agreement.

In other regions, the regional authorities and/or trade unions have had more success in encouraging the formation of regional employers' associations. For example, in Samara the trade unions raised the question of employer representation early on, but it required the authority of the administration to address the issue. In 1996 the regional administration invited representatives of more than 100 enterprises to a meeting regarding the development of social partnership, where they were encouraged to involve themselves in the process, and, specifically, to form an employers' association. This meeting took place in the year of the first elections for the governorship in Samara, and since it was clear that the (appointed) incumbent was likely to win, the enterprise managers were anxious not to displease him.[1] Shortly after the meeting, in October 1996, the Samara Oblast Union of Employers (SRSO) was created, including representatives from both light and heavy industry. At the end of November 2000 this organisation had 193 members and covered approximately 17 per cent of those employed in the oblast (though the organisation itself prefers to stress that it covers 57 per cent of industrial employees). The vast majority of the firms involved are large or medium enterprises.

The forced nature of employers' participation in the system of social partnership might appear to imply that they are 'weak' in relation to the other parties. Certainly, it highlights the capacity of regional governments to influence them. The employers' side in social partnership could also be said to be 'weak' in the sense that employers generally lack properly constituted representation. Often the employers who sign the agreement have no real claim to represent anyone other than themselves (as in Kemerovo, for example) and even employers' associations represent only a small minority of employers. Since the obligations assumed by the employers in the regional agreement only apply to those employers who have delegated representative rights to the association in the negotiation of the agreement, these obligations have no immediate relevance for the majority of employers. The employers' associations also

---

[1]   It is equally the case that the meeting on social partnership was a good occasion on which to firm up support among the so-called 'directors' corpus'.

tend to have a limited ability to govern the actions of their own members, making their commitments even less significant. But the most important point regarding employers' involvement in regional social partnership is that – except to the extent that non-involvement risks incurring the displeasure of the regional authorities – it is irrelevant to them. In Sverdlovsk, for example, the Svedlovsk Oblast Union of Industrialists and Entrepreneurs (SOSPP), cites its priority as being to secure 'rational state protectionism to defend commodity production and business'. It lists 'the development of relations of social partnership … with the aim of reducing social tension' seventh and last on its list of objectives. It is clear that the inclusion of this point is merely a courteous nod in the direction of prevailing norms. Such polite indifference to social partnership on the part of employers above all reveals that they do not see the trade unions as a serious threat: that is, the absence of effective employers' associations is a sign of the weakness of the trade unions rather than the employers.

What of the trade unions? Unlike the employers' associations, the oblast federations of trade unions are representative, nominally accountable to their members and keenly interested in social partnership. The legitimacy of trade unions' representation of the interests of the employed population is generally not contested, although sometimes their claim to represent the interests of the whole population – which the unions justify on the grounds that the non-working population are dependants of those in work – is questioned.[1] The main problem of the union side concerns what Franz Traxler calls 'governability' (Traxler, 1995) that is, the unions have very little ability to deliver or mobilise their membership.

Added to the generic problems faced by all levels of the Russian trade union movement, the regional federations of trade unions have particular difficulties in this regard. The regional federation attempts to unite the whole range of branch trade unions. Clearly, the interests of these branches do not always coincide. To take the most obvious example, budget sector trade unions are generally more interested in regional social partnership than other branch unions since they are more dependent on securing concessions from the regional authorities. Moreover, their interests are in raising regional taxation to increase the funds available to their employers, while industrial unions see the punitive levels of taxation as a prime cause of low wages and the non-payment of wages and want regional resources to be devoted to investment rather than public services. Given that the extent to which unions with different agendas will support each other is limited, a regional federation has to tread carefully when presenting its case. It can issue few credible threats in the course of negotiations. Indeed, even in rare cases where all the branch trade unions in a particular region are united on a particular issue, the obkoms themselves are unable to organise anything more than token protests – symbolic pickets of the regional

---

[1]  In Leningrad oblast, for example, the Deputy Governor proposed that there should be another party in the tripartite commission to represent the non-working population.

parliament or co-ordinated meetings within individual labour collectives are the most common forms of action. This inability to mobilise severely limits the extent to which the regional federations are able to translate their numerical strength into bargaining power.

The strongest of the three parties in regional social partnership is undoubtedly the regional government. Generally, social partnership is a resource which the regional authorities can use to strengthen their control over their territories – something which they do to varying extents. At the most basic level, social partnership provides a mechanism for maintaining social peace. Although regional authorities are generally not in awe of the trade unions, they are worried by spontaneous outbursts and enlist the support of employers and trade unions in containing local conflicts. Employer co-operation is probably more important in controlling the latter than is trade union assistance, since spontaneous protest is usually the result of problems such as non-payment of wages. Engaging the employers in social partnership is one way of attempting to keep their behaviour within some kind of reasonable bounds, though, as will be seen, informal mechanisms of control are far more important in achieving this than are the formal channels of complaint and conciliation available within the framework of social partnership. Typically, if conflict breaks out, the regional trade union organisation will seek to persuade the regional administration to pressure the employer to make the concessions required to settle the dispute, sometimes supporting an appeal of the employer for financial support from the regional administration, for example in the form of grants or loans to permit the payment of wage debts. Nevertheless, signing employers up for social partnership does mean that they can be reminded of their commitments if and when the regional authorities see fit: that is, social partnership provides a useful normative framework which can be mobilised according to the demands of the situation.

Meanwhile, promoting social partnership is a sure way of eliciting trade union co-operation. This is useful to regional governments because trade unions can act as an important channel for discontent, and the regional federations can act as mediators in the worst conflicts. As a head of department from the Sverdlovsk Federation of Trade Unions put it:

> After the revolution of the 1990s there were many different forms [of protest] – rallies, different kinds of outcries. That is, active forms of workers' resistance. But it could have been resolved through negotiation. It's easier to reach agreement with workers' representatives, of course, and that means the trade unions. Then you've got one partner and not ten uncoordinated individuals. The government's not stupid. It's better to work with the trade unions than to be in conflict with them… People in the oblast are in that regard quick to catch on.

In short, having the trade unions on side is a useful insurance policy. In addition to this, social partnership is perceived as a 'calling card', a tripartite commission being the hallmark of a stable and 'civilised' region in which it is safe to invest.

The dominance of the regional authorities among the social partners is highlighted by the fact that their economic, social, welfare and employment policies and aspirations form the core of the regional agreements. The trade unions, as will be seen, can have some impact on these at the margins, but for the reasons discussed above they are unable to secure anything but minor concessions on these issues. The involvement of the employers, meanwhile, is little more than a formality. In this sense, the regional social partners are a long way from being equal. To a more or less considerable extent, social partnership at the regional level reinstates the traditional relationship between the regional Party committee and the regional trade union federation, although today the regional authorities have much more discretion than they had in the past.

## The content of the regional agreements

To what extent do regional agreements serve to 'regulate social-labour relations'? Voluntary regulation of industrial relations through collective agreements generally serves to supplement legal regulation in two ways. First, by laying down a set of specific procedural rules governing the interaction of the parties, and, second, through the inclusion of substantive measures not already foreseen in the law. Any trade union worth its salt aims to gain additional benefits for its members through the process of negotiation, and it may also try to widen its rights to negotiation, consultation and information. Collective agreements usually provide useful additional regulation of the employment relationship since, while the law tends to provide all-purpose rules,[1] agreements focus on the specificities of particular environments (be they workplaces, industries or regions). Do the regional agreements in Russia extend the regulation of labour relations? Are they, as commentators such as Vladimir Kiselev have implied, a means through which regional differences are addressed (Kiselev, 2000)? This section attempts to answer this question through an analysis of the content of regional agreements.

[1]   As has been seen in Chapter 5, however, soviet labour law was very specific and detailed. This was necessary since voluntary regulation was not an option in a country in which the Communist Party had a political monopoly and autonomous organisation was banned. Democratic states, by contrast, are generally content to allow joint voluntary regulation of the employment relationship: although the extent of legal regulation varies from country to country, the law is not intended, as in the soviet case, to regulate in advance every possible situation. Rather, it provides a (more or less detailed) basis on which further regulation can occur. The insistence of the Russian trade unions on retaining and even extending the minute soviet legal regulation of labour relations is a clear indicator of their limited bargaining power in collective negotiations at all levels.

Regional agreements tend to have a similar structure and content. The issues usually covered are: the development of the regional economy, employment policy, pay, health and safety (and sometimes environmental policy), social defence of the population and the development of social partnership. These may be arranged differently, but there are few significant variations in subject matter between agreements. For example, the 2001–2 Sverdlovsk oblast agreement has sections on: economic policy; employment and the development of the labour market; 'social guarantees, labour rights and measures for the social support of the population'; pay; health and safety and the environment; and the development of social partnership. The 2001–2 Samara agreement, meanwhile, has two fewer sections since it deals with economic policy ('the development of production') and employment in the same section, while pay and health and safety are also combined (the environment is omitted). But despite this superficial difference, in essence the same topics are covered. Each section of an agreement contains obligations applying to all three partners, as well as specific provisions obliging one or two of the parties.

The first section of a regional agreement expresses the aspirations of the regional administration to promote local production and growth, to stimulate restructuring, attract investment and so on. Most such provisions are general in nature, though the agreements often contain commitments to support particular local industries. For example, agreements in Perm' oblast have contained commitments to support light industry and textiles, Sverdlovsk oblast agreements have included commitments to support the wood, motor and weapons industries, St Petersburg and Leningrad to support the shipbuilders, while in Kemerovo oblast commitments have been made to the coal and construction industries (Germanov, 2001).[1] The sections on employment likewise begin with the ambitions of the regional authorities to create jobs, while they also set out a series of measures to ensure the smooth functioning of the regional labour market (most of which, as will be seen below, are already contained in existing legislation). Duplication of legislation is also a feature of the sections on health and safety.

The sections on social support of the population, meanwhile, lay out the spending priorities of the regional authorities (though not usually precise spending plans),[2] and the social obligations of the other partners. Regional administrations usually commit

---

[1]  This support varies in nature. To take one example, the 2001–2 Sverdlovsk oblast agreement exempts the wood and motor industries from two forms of road tax.

[2]  Any genuine negotiation over the allocation of the budget was impossible in the early agreements, the vast majority of which were concluded after the regional budget had already been set. The trade unions have pressed for agreements to be concluded either prior to or in tandem with the budgets, and the new Labour Code prescribes that this should 'in general' be the case (Article 47). Although Moscow City has concluded agreements before the budget for some time, and Perm' oblast did so in 2000, these are still very much the exception. The significance of this change, however, depends on the ability of the trade unions to exert pressure on the regional administration during the course of the negotiations – something which, as has been seen, they are ill-equipped to do.

themselves to continue financing free education and health facilities, and outline their plans to support the most needy. The commitment to maintain price controls on certain key items also features in this section of some agreements, as does the duty of the regional government regularly to calculate and publish a regional subsistence minimum. The obligations of the other social partners in this section mainly concern the maintenance of what is left of the social, cultural and everyday services provided by the soviet enterprise in the past. Although most of these facilities have now been transferred to the municipalities, trade unions and employers are often charged with the upkeep of those which remain. Another venerable soviet tradition which employers and trade unions are called on to maintain is the organisation of prophylactic holidays for children. In addition to this, this section occasionally contains obligations to carry out particular projects such as the building of a school or medical facility (point 4.12 of the 2000–1 Ul'yanovsk agreement is an example of such an undertaking).

The most important section from the perspective of the trade unions is the section on pay. FNPR has recommended its priorities for the negotiation of branch, regional and collective agreements for several years. The most important of these priorities have been to raise the minimum wage for full-time workers to the level of the regional adult subsistence minimum; to bring wages in the budget sector closer to the level of industrial wages; to increase the proportion of wages accounted for by the basic wage, to reduce reliance on unstable and discretionary bonuses; to secure the regular payment of wages, with appropriate penalties for delayed payment; and to increase the share of wages in total costs. Many regional agreements pay at least lip-service to some of these priorities.

According to the FNPR's information regarding 1999–2000 agreements, the Moscow, Vologda, Astrakhan and Udmurtiya agreements obliged employers *to work towards* paying the lowest-paid workers at the level of the subsistence minimum (FNPR, 2001a, p. 7), and this type of aspiration is found in a number of other agreements. The 2000–1 Sverdlovsk agreement does actually oblige non-budget sector employers to raise the wages of full-time workers to the level of the subsistence minimum, though the trade unions do not expect to see this implemented. The head of the socio-economic defence department of the Sverdlovsk Federation of Trade Unions remarked with regard to this provision:

> We proposed 70 per cent [of the subsistence minimum], but the metallurgists' [trade union] said – let's make it 100 per cent. I sit there, keep quiet. It's clear that they are not going to pay it, but it exists as a reference point [*no orientir est'*].

Meanwhile, the agreements usually contain similar indications of the need to increase the wages of budget sector workers. In the mid-90s many regions supplemented the pay of budget sector workers from the regional budget, and this was often included in the regional agreement, but in most cases these commitments have been watered down over the years as regional budgets have come under pressure. Thus, for example, in Samara, budget sector workers enjoyed a 50 per cent pay boost in 1998, reduced to 40 per cent in 1999 and 15 per cent in 2000, before being eliminated altogether from the 2001–2 agreement, which promised only to 'continue the practice of increasing the pay of employees in budget establishments and organisations, depending on the resources of the regional budget'. The 2001–2 Sverdlovsk agreement obliges all parties during the discussion of the 2002 budget to introduce a proposal into the oblast Duma to raise average budget sector pay to 60 per cent of the average level of pay in the oblast (point 87). Trade unions in other oblasts have had problems in obtaining commitments even this concrete. For example, the Perm' trade unions attempted to include a provision in the 2000–1 regional agreement 'to secure for budget sector workers average pay no lower than the oblast average'. What was eventually included in the agreement, however, was a provision 'to implement a gradual increase in the average pay in the budget sectors, with the final aim of its nearing the level of average monthly pay in the oblast towards the end of the term of the agreement' (point 1.2.2). The Leningrad and Saint Petersburg health workers, by contrast, have been much more successful in preserving their regional supplements not through the regional agreements but through frequent protest actions.

Overall, what is most striking about the agreements is their generality, the unenforceability of many of their provisions, the extent to which they defer, rather than initiate, action, and the extent to which they reiterate, rather than extend, existing federal or regional legislation. In any given section of an agreement, a large proportion of the provisions will be either unenforceable statements of good intent or forms of deferring action. The most concrete points in the agreements, meanwhile, tend to be those which either repeat existing legislation or oblige the parties to provide certain information at pre-determined intervals. To take just one example, the section on pay from the 2000–1 Ul'yanovsk oblast agreement contains 12 points concerning either employers, the regional administration or both. Of these, half are deferrals of action, one is an unenforceable statement of good intent, and five are in principle enforceable (a comparatively high proportion). But of these five, one (point 3.3) obliges the regional administration to pay wages on time, while another (3.10) obliges employers to do likewise. That is, the agreement obliges the parties to obey one of the most basic provisions of the Labour Code! Meanwhile, the remaining three points assume that employers will not always meet their obligations in this regard. One (3.7) obliges the administration to use the appropriate legal mechanisms to bring managers to book in cases of wage delays, another (3.9) obliges employers and trade unions to work out and ensure the fulfilment of a timetable for payment in cases of wage delays, while point 3.12 lays down that when wage delays occur, employers are forbidden to pay members of the administration before they pay workers.[1] Some

---

[1]  This provision does at least have the merit of addressing workers' grievances. Rumours that managers are being paid on time while depriving workers of wages have a tendency to

regional agreements, such as that of Sverdlovsk mentioned above, have sections on pay which are more concrete than this, but the general tenor of this agreement is by no means exceptional.

A sprinkling of unenforceable expressions of good intent is present in all agreements, though there has been a tendency to weed these out over time. The 'good intent' provisions are unenforceable in the sense that it is impossible to determine on the basis of outcomes whether or not they have been fulfilled. A typical example of this from the pay and health and safety section of the 2001–2 Samara regional agreement is the obligation of all sides:

> 2.1 To implement a consistent policy, aimed at the creation of conditions for the reestablishment of the role of pay as the basic (main) source of income of the population, the increase of its relative weight in the general income of the population, [and] the consistent movement of the minimal level of pay of organisations of all types [property forms] towards the level of the subsistence minimum of the working age population.

Far more frequently encountered than this type of provision, however, is the sort which defers action in one way or another. Such provisions are the stock in trade of agreements. Deferral takes many forms – some of which promise some kind of tangible outcome and some of which guarantee virtually nothing. Belonging to the former category are those provisions which oblige the parties to prepare draft laws on certain issues, or which mandate trade unions and employers to ensure that certain points are included in enterprise collective agreements. For example, the 2001–2 Samara agreement obliges all sides to co-operate in the working out and passing of draft laws on 'the basis of industrial policy in Samara Oblast', on 'innovation and scientific-technical policy in Samara Oblast' (point 1.4), on social partnership and on employers' associations (point 4.2). Meanwhile, mandating the trade unions and/or employers to include certain points in enterprise collective agreements is widespread. The Ul'yanovsk agreement for 2000–1, for example, obliges employers to guarantee the inclusion in collective agreements of measures aimed at creating and preserving jobs, giving priority in hiring to those made redundant and unemployed citizens especially in need of help, and towards the creation of conditions for the professional training and retraining of redundant workers (point 2.10). The main characteristic of such provisions is that they serve to displace regulation to another level, be it to the higher level of law or the lower level of the enterprise. They do not serve in themselves to regulate 'social-labour relations'.

circulate in cases of non-payment, and are the cause of often explosive resentment. The problem is that proving whether or not such payment has taken place is very difficult – managers have many means of concealment at their disposal. For an example of the tension caused by such suspected injustice see Ashwin, 1999, p. 118.

The forms of postponement which are no guarantee of anything are those which oblige the parties to 'look at the question of' something, or to 'take measures' or 'co-ordinate action' to achieve something. For example, the 1998–9 regional social partnership agreement of Komi Republic committed the republican government to 'take measures to stabilise the socio-economic position in the republic' (point 1.1); the employers to 'implement measures over the preservation and creation of jobs' (point 3.10) and all three partners to 'co-ordinate action to ensure the timely payment of wages and other payments foreseen in the law' (point 4.1). The most important feature of such 'obligations' is that they can be 'fulfilled' without anything actually being achieved! Slightly more substantial are the common injunctions to 'work out and realise a programme' to achieve some or other objective, though such provisions still constitute deferrals of action.[1] Indeed, an agreement cannot specify in advance the contents of the prescribed programme, and there is no guarantee that the programme will not recommend the launching of another programme, or a law, or the conclusion of yet another agreement.

Added to the clauses which defer action are those that are redundant. These clauses are usually expressed in an enforceable and direct manner, their only defect being that they are already included in existing legislation. Large parts of the sections on employment and health and safety comprise such provisions. As Igor' Germanov has noted, sections on employment and the labour market usually include provisions from the federal law 'On the Employment of the Population in the Russian Federation', common examples being the provisions from the law which oblige employers to inform the Federal Employment Service regarding vacancies or forthcoming redundancies and to guarantee a certain quota of jobs for those especially in need. Meanwhile, Germanov also shows that sections on health and safety not only incorporate large sections from the law, they also commonly include points specifically obliging employers to obey the law. Five out of six points obliging employers in the health and safety section of the 2001–2 Sverdlovsk agreement are copied from the law. The same can be said of five out of seven points obliging employers from the same section of the 2001–3 Kurgan agreement, eight out of twelve in the 2000–1 Perm' agreement, four out of seven in both the 2000–1 Ul'yanovsk and Tatarstan agreements, and both of the provisions obliging employers in the 2001–2 Samara agreement (Germanov, 2001). The St Petersburg regional agreement for 1997–8 included a point committing the parties to observe the General and branch tariff agreements, which led some employers to reject the application of this agreement to their enterprises.

---

[1]  An example of this type of provision is point 100 of the 2001–2 Sverdlovsk oblast agreement which obliges all parties to 'work out a plan of measures to improve working conditions and health and safety in Sverdlovsk oblast during 2001–3 and to guarantee its realisation'.

The incorporation of sections of existing legislation and of obligations to abide by the law is an indication of the extent to which Russian employers ignore, or often do not even know, their most basic legal obligations. The reiteration of legal provisions in unenforceable agreements seems a particularly futile attempt to secure employer and government compliance with the law, and one which highlights the unions' preference for bureaucratic over active methods of achieving their aims, since in principle, if not in practice, it transfers responsibility for the enforcement of the law from the trade union to the tripartite commission. What can be said for certain is that this practice does not extend the regulation of labour relations in the regions. At most, it serves to remind the parties of their legal obligations.

The obligations of the trade unions contained within the agreements likewise have a tendency to be otiose. These effectively instruct the trade unions to behave as trade unions! For example, the section on pay and health and safety from the 2001–2 Samara oblast agreement instructs trade unions, among other things, to: initiate the preparation and conclusion of collective agreements; work on increasing trade union membership; attempt to ensure that wages are paid on time and that wage debts are eliminated; provide members with essential legal advice and to carry out 'constant social monitoring of the fulfilment of collective agreements, laws and other normative legal acts regarding work and workplace safety'. The fact that the trade unions are mandated to perform their role in this way by agreement with employers and the state is worthy of comment. No doubt the unions see this as legitimising their activity, but at the same time, this can also be seen as a continuation (albeit in a modified form) of the soviet tradition of state prescription of the trade union role. Indeed, many of the agreements do call on the trade unions to perform functions derived from the soviet past, even restoring their Leninist role of contributing to increasing production and strengthening labour discipline. For example, the 2000–1 Ul'yanovsk oblast agreement obliges trade unions and employers to work out measures to stabilise and develop production and 'strengthen labour discipline' (point 1.23), as does the Samara agreement for 2001–2 (point 1.39). Meanwhile, the Komi regional agreement for 1998–9 laid down that trade unions should 'carry out work to involve workers in processes of management and of raising the effectiveness of production' (point 1.13). In August 2001 the Minister of Labour, Aleksandr Pochinok, proposed the reintroduction of Honour Boards and socialist competition in a letter to the Governor of Krasnoyarsk, a suggestion which was endorsed by the region's tripartite commission for the consideration of enterprise directors (*RIA-Press-Line*, 4 September 2001).

This analysis of the content of regional agreements has painted a rather gloomy picture of the achievements of regional social partnership, but each agreement usually includes a few points which the unions perceive (or can at least portray) as victories. For example, a useful concession achieved by the Komi Federation of trade unions was that those afflicted by wage delays would not be liable for fines for late payment of rent, electricity and other bills. In the Belgorod and Tomsk regional agreements, the employers agreed to index wage debts (FNPR, 2001a). Meanwhile, other federations have made progress over pay increases. The case of Sverdlovsk has already been mentioned. The Kemerovo federation also made gains in the 2001–3 agreement including: a point providing extra pay for young specialists working in the budget sector (point 4.11); a point obliging employers to limit differentiation of workers' and managers' wages (point 4.15); and one (point 4.14) obliging employers to 'take measures' to increase the tariff component of wages to not less than 50 per cent (excluding the regional coefficient) and to equal the subsistence minimum by the end of 2001, though the latter point, as pointed out above, can be fulfilled without its formal 'aim' being met.

Often the achievements of the trade unions are limited to the inclusion of points that we have categorised as forms of deferral. For example, asked about union successes in the 2000–1 agreement, the head of the socio-economic and legal department of the Ul'yanovsk federation listed ten. Of these, six were obligations contained in the agreement to develop programmes or to draft laws. Two were points increasing union or worker rights to consultation – though one of these was a rather symbolic (and very soviet) point obliging employers to take into account the opinion of the labour collective when conferring state decorations on workers. The most concrete achievements he listed were the inclusion of a point allowing for the re-nationalisation of property privatised in an illegal manner (point 1.13), and the fact that more deadlines had been included in the agreement, something which he considered would facilitate monitoring. This level of attainment is lower than in some other regions, but it is not exceptional. It should also be noted that, as the case of the Sverdlovsk minimum wage highlights, the federations do not necessarily expect their achievements on paper to translate into practice.

Finally, it should be stressed that paper 'victories' are not necessarily won through union strength. It is arguable that social partnership agreements contain more concrete provisions in regions such as Sverdlovsk, Kemerovo and Moscow where the political authorities are, for their own reasons, more committed to the process. In Sverdlovsk, Governor Eduard Rossel' has recently been promoting social partnership as part of his 'turn to the people'. Meanwhile, in Kemerovo, Governor Aman Tuleev is the main mover behind the development of social partnership, and has used it to strengthen his control over the region after the disorder caused by the summer 1998 'rail wars' during which the Trans-Siberian railway was blocked by workers in protest at wage delays. Likewise, in Moscow, Mayor Yurii Luzhkov has strongly promoted social partnership. Indeed, he was awarded an honorary professorship by the FNPR's Academy of Labour in 1996 in recognition of his achievements in this area.[1]

---

[1]    In his speech in honour of this occasion, FNPR President and former President of the Moscow Federation of Trade Unions, Mikhail Shmakov, was careful not to give the impression that social partnership had been handed to the Moscow unions on a plate, but he

Indeed, in those regions where social partnership is most advanced the unions are often accorded a role in the performance of state functions. This gives the unions the chance to retain or resume the state social welfare and regulatory functions which they performed in the soviet era, distributing state benefits to employees and monitoring the performance of employers on behalf of the regional administration, but it also serves as a means of incorporating trade unions, neutralising them as a potential source of opposition. In Kemerovo oblast and Moscow City the trade unions participate in highly developed forms of state-dominated corporatism, the Moscow Federation of Trade Unions sometimes being described as the social welfare department of the Moscow City administration. This is reflected in the respective regional agreements. The Kemerovo agreement, for example, mandates the unions to monitor elements of the spending of the regional budget, specifically in the unions' traditional area of expertise – prophylactic medical care (point 5.32 of the 1998–2000 Agreement). The 2001 Moscow agreement mandates the trade unions to work with the city government in the realisation of the city-funded 'Youth of Moscow' programme (point 3.42); to participate in working out programmes for the development of sport, education, culture and public health (point 3.43), to organise the annual New Year's celebration for children in the Kremlin (point 3.45) and to give workers suffering from certain illnesses free holiday vouchers paid for by the social insurance fund (point 3.46).

Such forms of collaboration are common, if less extensive, in other regions, without being included in the regional agreement, although they may well be discussed in the regional tripartite commission. It is normal for the unions to collaborate with the regional offices of various state inspectorates to monitor the observance of health and safety and labour legislation, to work closely with the regional department of the social insurance fund, to participate in the elaboration of regional employment programmes and to sit on the management boards of the regional social funds. For example, the Leningrad oblast and St Petersburg city administrations have delegated the right to monitor conformity to health and safety and ecological legislation to the trade unions, which trains state inspectors and conducts inspections jointly with the state inspectorates. The trade union federation claims to participate in the elaboration of all aspects of the policy of the city government, apart from the budget; represents member organisations in a wide range of bodies dealing with issues of housing, tariffs and prices; participates in the protection of consumer rights through ten district inspectorates of trade union control; co-operates with the administration in setting up local departments of the Social Insurance Fund to establish regional programmes for children and young people;

could not avoid acknowledging that the understanding of the mayor and the 'practical work' of the Moscow city government had been crucial to the success of social partnership in the capital (Shmakov, 1996). Others, however, were less cautious in their praise for this 'best of mayors' and his 'concern for the people' (Andrievskaya, 1996).

manages cultural and sporting facilities; uses social insurance and local budget funds for cultural and leisure activities; is very active in the summer campaigns preparing children's holiday camps; holds seminars for camp directors and inspections of the camps; helps primary organisations with the transfer of housing to the municipality and is represented on the management bodies of the various social funds. The construction, energy, transport and all the budget sector unions collaborate closely with the city committees responsible for their branches. For example, the President of the regional health workers' union sits on virtually every government committee relating to the health service and the union collaborates in the elaboration and implementation of all aspects of health policy. The industrial unions have fewer possibilities for such collaboration, since the city does not have committees with specific responsibility for their branches, but they maintain close relations with other departments of the city administration, particularly the economics and finance committee, the housing committee, the environmental committee and the tax and law-enforcement agencies.

## Coverage and enforcement of regional agreements

This section examines two questions. First, given the patchy representation of employers, to whom among this group can the agreement be said to apply? And, second, which mechanisms ensure (or fail to ensure) the enforcement of the agreement?

According to the Federal Law, as noted above, the obligations undertaken by the employers' side in regional agreements apply, at best, to employers who are members of the signatory organisations. In addition to the measures noted above to induce employers to join their employers' organisations, some regions have attempted to extend the coverage of the agreement through regional legislation. Thus, in a few regions, such as Leningrad Oblast, the regional law on social partnership (1998) includes a mechanism through which the agreement can be extended to all employers. This is an ideal to which many trade unions aspire. In Kemerovo oblast, the trade unions have been attempting to introduce a clause into their law on social partnership which would mean that all employers would be bound by the agreement unless they registered a formal rejection. The Perm' *oblsovprof* also proposed such a clause for their regional law 'On Social Partnership', but the idea was rejected by the regional administration.

Twenty-five regions have local laws on employers' associations in place or in preparation (FNPR, 2001b). More generally, the regional federations see the passing of a federal law on employers' associations as the answer to their problems which, they think, would encourage membership of employers' organisations and facilitate their regulation. FNPR had a number of objections to the original draft of the Law, which was thrown out by the Duma in May 1999. The new draft, prepared in collaboration with FNPR, does nothing to extend the application of agreements to non-signatory employers and is unlikely to do much to help the trade unions. As Strela wisely remarked with regard to the draft law:

> What I want to say is that it's a good law, but it won't give us trade unions anything. Why? Well, some might think that as soon as that law is accepted all the employers will run into the employers' association. Nothing of the kind. Today all those who wanted to unite have already organised. Some will then join them... but absolutely not because of a law coming out. They will join at the time when trade unions are strong and they have to defend themselves.... In that law it's not going to say that membership is obligatory – it will be voluntary membership.

The enforcement mechanisms of the agreements are no better defined than is the coverage. Often, as in the case of Samara, there are no penalties foreseen for non-fulfilment of the agreement. This means that the trade unions are forced to rely on a 'name and shame' approach.[1] This, for example, was the answer of the head of the socio-economic department of what in Perm' is still known as the *oblsovprof* to a question regarding the use of penalties for non-fulfilment:

> Up to now it hasn't happened. We try morally and otherwise... to point out that a side didn't fulfil [something] and for all that take measures in order to enforce it... At the level of the enterprise we have many examples when they even brought up the question of sacking, of dismissal, of financial penalties. That's more [clearly]... prescribed in legislation. But in questions of the agreement it's... still a matter of dispute... it's still necessary to introduce changes into federal law.

Usually, the monitoring within the tripartite commissions is very formal: a percentage of fulfilment for each point is noted and everyone promises to do better next time. In short, the agreements lack teeth.

The main means of securing employer compliance with the agreement are informal and are in the hands of the regional authorities. If the employers fail to fulfil the terms of the agreement, or refuse to involve themselves with the system of social partnership, then the administration has very potent levers at its disposal. Enterprises depend on all manner of grants, subsidies, licences and permits which can be given and withdrawn at the whim of the regional administration. Their work can be disrupted by regular fire, health and safety and sanitary inspections and the levying of fines and administrative penalties for the violations that will inevitably be found. The most powerful weapons of all are the initiation of bankruptcy procedures in the case of enterprises in financial trouble, or the threat to send in the tax police, whose

---

[1]   A proposed regional law in Sakhalin would publicise details of the salaries of all directors of enterprises in receipt of budget funds who are more than three months in arrears in the payment of wages.

investigations effectively freeze an enterprise's financial transactions. This, for example, is an extract from a letter of 14 April 1998 from the Samara oblast administration to an enterprise management which was systematically failing to pay wages on time:

> According to the data of the oblast state statistical committee, wage delays are systematically allowed to occur at your enterprise…. I draw your attention to the fact that, in accordance with the law 'On Insolvency (Bankrupcy)' brought into force on 1 March 1998, the presence of delays in payment higher than the sum of 500 minimum wages for a period of three months is a basis for alerting the arbitration courts to a case of bankruptcy, and for the bringing in of outside administration. I consider it essential to warn you that, in the case of your failing to take sufficient measures to liquidate the wage debt, the oblast administration, as a participant in the tripartite agreement, will initiate the action foreseen in the aforementioned law.

This is certainly a strong argument for obeying the terms of the agreement. But reliance on such informal levers means that the enforcement of the agreements is essentially determined by the discretion of the regional administration.

**The regional tripartite commission**

Tripartite Commissions have been established in 70 federation subjects. Where commissions have not been established it is because of the absence of a regional trade union organisation (some smaller regions are represented through the trade union federation of a larger neighbour) or, more often, of any employer representatives. Sub-regional tripartite commissions have been established in cities and rural districts, particularly in the Republics of Mordovia and Chuvashiya and in Samara, Bryansk, Kirov and Moscow oblasts. Regional commissions have between seven and 15 representatives on each side and generally meet quarterly.

As at the federal level, the tripartite commission provides the institutional framework for the everyday interaction of the social partners, negotiating and monitoring the fulfilment of the tripartite agreement, considering the policies of the regional government and reviewing draft legislation. The character and role of the tripartite commission is determined by the regional administration, which controls the frequency of meetings and provides administrative support, which enables it to control the agenda and the supply of information to the parties. Negotiation of the regional agreement is usually delegated to working groups, with contentious issues being brought back to the commission and sometimes referred to the regional governor for resolution. In some regions, the trade union federation occasionally organises pickets and demonstrations in support of its demands, but the effectiveness of such measures is doubtful and in general the trade unions have to accept the decisions of the governor. In some regions the tripartite commission does little more than meet once or twice a year to negotiate and monitor the regional agreement, but in other regions it is a more active body, considering proposed regional legislation, government policies and resolutions and addressing problems around the non-payment of wages and benefits, job creation, support for particular sectors of the economy, the state of transport, health, education and communal services in the region and intervening to resolve conflicts in enterprises. Relations between the trade unions and the administration are usually better at regional than at federal level, because the two can often find common ground in blaming the federal government for their difficulties and in appealing to the federal government for a solution. Essentially, the significance of the tripartite commission depends on the importance attached to it and the role assigned to it by the regional governor.

While much of the work of the tripartite commission is bureaucratic, and consultation with the trade unions is often largely formal, it can confront the trade unions with major problems, particularly in balancing the interests of the various branch unions. Each branch union expects the federation to represent its interests in negotiation with the regional administration, but these interests are often inconsistent or conflicting, with the main division being between industrial unions, which want to see the administration devoting its resources to investment and employment programmes, and the budget sector unions, which want to see increases in spending on public services. In some regions the budget sector unions accuse the federation of ignoring them in favour of the industrial unions, in other regions the charge is the reverse, while in some regions both accusations are levelled at the federation.

One of the most contentious issues is that of charges for electricity, public transport and municipal services, which regional administrations have being trying to increase under pressure from the federal government and the International Financial Institutions. The problem is that increasing the tariffs increases the cost of living for the mass of the population, but is also represented as the only means of maintaining or increasing the wages of the workers in the relevant branches. In St Petersburg, for example, the trade union federation protested vehemently at an increase in energy tariffs, which had been introduced without discussion with the trade unions in June 2000, picketing the government offices for five days and securing a promise that there would be no further increase before the autumn. However, when the government submitted proposals for increased fares for urban transport to the Tripartite Commission, the Federation registered its objections, but participated in the approval of the increases on the grounds that it could not stop the increases, but wanted to preserve at least the semblance of social partnership. The Federation's participation in the approval of these increases discredited the Federation, created widespread discontent among the branch unions whose members would suffer the consequences and led the alternative unions to dub the Tripartite Commission 'the Commission for Increasing Tariffs'. The Samara Federation had a very similar experience with fares for local transport, successfully resisting an increase in 1999 with pickets and a court victory, but approving such an increase in 2000 on the grounds that it was the only way to increase wages in the branch.

The employers generally play a very minor role in the tripartite commissions at the regional, as at the federal, level. In some regions, particularly Leningrad and St Petersburg, the unions and the employers work closely together,[1] but in others, such as the Komi Republic, the unions complain that the employers invariably back the regional administration, while the employers complain that the trade unions and the Republican government always try to take all the credit for the achievements of the agreement, while the employers are constrained by branch tariff agreements signed at the federal level without reference to them. As the executive director of the Komi employers' federation commented at the conference of the Republican Trade Union Federation

> I think… that we have the right to expect the support of the trade union federation because although the branch tariff agreements handed down from above are good, without co-ordination with our regional agreement, with the trade union committee and employers, on the ground they sometimes turn into impractical rules.

## Relations with the regional legislature

As at the Federal level, the regional trade union organisations have increasingly turned their attention to regional legislative bodies, lobbying over the regional budget, seeking the adoption of regional legislation that will favour the trade unions and their members, participating in regional elections in support of sympathetic candidates, establishing lobbies of sympathetic deputies and seeking to elect trade unionists to the regional legislature, usually in collaboration with one of the regional power blocks. In many regions the trade union federation has a co-operation agreement with the regional legislature which allows the union leaders to comment on draft laws, participate in parliamentary commissions and even to address parliamentary hearings. In some regions the trade unions have recovered their right of legislative initiative, which enables them to propose regional laws in their own name. The legal department of FNPR has prepared 70 different information booklets to support the legislative activity of its regional organisations.

In general, lobbying of the regional legislature has not often been crowned with success because the trade unions are no more significant a political force at regional than at federal level. The majority of regions have adopted or are considering laws on social partnership and ten have passed regional laws on trade unions which give the

---

[1]   The continued participation of management in trade unions can make for very close relations: in Sverdlovsk, the executive director of the association of directors of light industry enterprises is also the president of the regional branch trade union committee!

unions additional powers, over and above those provided by Federal law. Member organisations have reported to FNPR a total of 142 regional laws affecting social and labour rights which have been adopted with their participation or on their initiative. Over a third of these cases are accounted for by Bashkortostan, whose trade unions have participated in the adoption of 52 Republican laws, 13 of which had been proposed by the trade unions (Naboishchikov, 2001). The trade unions in the Arctic regions have been very active in pressing for the introduction and implementation of special legislation providing extra benefits and protection, backed up by federal budget funding, for those living and working in the North. The Komi Federation claims that the trade unions were responsible for the 1990 and 1991 Laws on the North, though the regional authorities claim not even to know of the participation of the unions and insist it was their achievement. Similarly, each claims all the credit for the 1993 Law on the North, ignoring the claims of the other. Nevertheless, FNPR has consistently made support for the Northern population a priority, incorporating guarantees into the General Agreement and including a section relating to those working in the North in the new Labour Code.

## Social partnership at the sub-regional level

The devolution of budgetary and administrative responsibility for a wide range of public services and the municipalisation of housing and enterprise social assets has given municipal authorities a much greater role and has led to the development of social partnership at the sub-regional level. In some cases, particularly in education, municipal agreements are used in place of a proliferation of collective agreements in individual institutions. The barriers to this development are the same as the barriers at higher levels, most notably, the absence of employers' organisations at the sub-regional level, the unwillingness of municipal authorities to enter into meaningful agreements and the unenforceability of agreements that are reached. A big burden is placed on sub-regional agreements, since they are often called upon to compensate for the weaknesses of collective agreements and regional branch tariff agreements.

Development of social partnership at the district level in Leningrad oblast began in 1996 when the Leningrad and St Petersburg Federation of Trade Unions began to establish Co-ordinating Committees in the districts, with a view to adding an appendix to the regional tripartite agreement for each district, to persuade the regional government to pay more attention to local problems. However, the process developed slowly, being established in only nine out of 29 districts, with only four tripartite and two bipartite agreements having been signed by 2000.

There have been no such developments in Saint Petersburg, because the city is divided into 111 micro municipal authorities, but in Moscow the Federation of Trade Unions decided to extent tripartite agreements to the level of the administrative *okrug*, which lies between the City and the district administrations, in 1995. The first such organisation was established in the South *okrug* in 1997 and another established for the Southeast *okrug* in 2000. The Presidents of the *okrug* councils are appointed by the Moscow Federation and they collaborate closely with the *okrug* administration in implementing the social, labour and welfare policies and administering the employment programme of the Moscow City government.

In Sverdlovsk, despite the enthusiasm of the regional administration, the development of social partnership at the sub-regional level has been impeded by the tacit opposition of the branch trade unions and the lack of local trade union leaders willing to take on the work, so only six sub-regional agreements have been signed with municipal authorities, where the head of the local administration was keen to do so, and social partnership at the sub-regional level amounts to little more than this. In other regions, such as Perm' and Samara, social partnership at the sub-regional level is more highly developed. In Samara, the regional federation has established co-ordinating councils in every city and in one rural district, and pays a small bonus to the presidents of the councils. In 2001 there were territorial tripartite agreements in seven cities and two rural districts and a bipartite agreement in one rural district. In Perm', there are 50 local co-ordinating councils which provide a framework for social partnership at the municipal level and for communication between the federation and primary organisations, which is not to the liking of many of the branch unions, but the effectiveness of the local councils is impeded by a lack of finance and personnel, only six having full-time officers, paid 500 roubles (less than $20) a month for their efforts.

## What is the point of social partnership?

The above analysis of social partnership at the Federal, branch and regional levels provides little evidence to suggest that social partnership serves to regulate labour relations. Amid those provisions which duplicate legislation, defer action or displace regulation to another sphere, there are few points in the agreements which develop the existing regulatory framework. Meanwhile, as has been seen, the current enforcement mechanisms are so weak as to allow the social partners to violate the agreements with impunity. The minimal role of the employers in the institutions of social partnership means that agreements are essentially between the trade unions and the government. The occasional disciplining of wayward employers is generally accomplished through informal mechanisms rather than through the formal apparatus of social partnership, while it is the administrative power of the federal and regional government, as opposed to the social power of the trade unions channelled through the institutions of social partnership, which serves to bring employers into line.

FNPR recognises the limitations of the system of social partnership. Every year the General Council adopts resolutions which recognise the weakness and non-fulfilment of agreements at all levels and exhorts trade union organisations at every level to make greater efforts, but to little or no avail. The evidence supports the withering assessment of social partnership made by one of the FNPR's prominent internal critics in an interview in June 2001:

We've got a General Agreement, for which the FNPR is usually praised. We've got branch tariff agreements. We've got a whole series of regional agreements... We've got collective agreements – the only thing we haven't got is pay. We've got it all, all, all, but then we've got wage delays or low pay. And what's the point of it all? ... It's an imitation of energetic action. They write papers. Moreover, they produce these papers themselves. It's like Parkinson's Law. These party [sic] workers exist and they find work for themselves: come on let's have a law on social partnership, let's have a tariff agreement, conclude a [collective] agreement. That is, for the sake of the bit of paper. And the fact that they [the agreements] are not fulfilled – that's only in tenth place.... If they concluded an agreement and they got a result – that would be understandable. But if you write something and there's no result – then the question is, what for? ... It's all completely meaningless work from a social perspective.

There is some scepticism about the value of social partnership within the responsible trade union apparatus. This, for example, was the comment of the head of the legal department of the Sverdlovsk Federation of Trade Unions:

I'm not against the tripartite agreement. But they write down hundreds of demands and only a few are fulfilled. They conclude an agreement and that's it – no one does anything. And what if we didn't have the agreement? Wouldn't everyone do the same [as they do now]?

One of the staff of the Samara Federation of Trade Unions was likewise unconvinced of the merits of the regional agreement, saying 'We've been concluding the agreement for three years – it's already time for it to have borne some kind of fruit. But there aren't any particular results'. Although not all those involved in social partnership share this scepticism, it is difficult even for the most committed to deny that there are reasons to doubt the efficacy of the current agreements.

So what is the point of social partnership from the perspective of the trade unions? The critic quoted above saw the 'imitation of energetic action' as a means through which the unions could 'prove themselves'. There is some truth in this. With the collapse of the administrative-command system the higher trade union bodies lost many of their previous functions as decision-making powers were devolved to the enterprise. Nevertheless, they have to prove their usefulness to the primary trade union organisations whose dues sustain the apparatus. On the other hand, FNPR and the regional trade union organisations are not as dependent on the remission of trade union dues as are the branch union structures, since they have their property and 'other' income to fall back on. Moreover, it is at the level of the primary and regional branch trade union organisations that the greatest scepticism about social partnership is expressed, precisely because they see no tangible results from the huge investment of time, money and effort. In the ISITO survey of presidents of primary trade union organisations in May 2001, only a small number gave a negative assessment of their regional federations, but two-thirds of respondents were not able to give any evaluation of the work of the regional federation in the tripartite commission or in the social support of the population, suggesting that it was irrelevant to them. The trade union president of one Leningrad enterprise commented 'It looks beautiful, but in reality the agreement does not work'.

The scepticism of the branch trade unions at the regional level is shown by the fact that most obkoms do not actively involve themselves in the process of preparing regional agreements. In Komi, the president of the federation complains that he receives very little support over the preparation of the agreement, while in Sverdlovsk only a quarter of the obkoms submitted any suggestions for the 2000 agreement. Those that did were small, budget or depressed sector unions. This pattern is also found in other regions. Industrial unions such as the chemical or metal workers have a tendency to see the agreement as relevant only to budget sector workers since their branch tariff and collective agreements provide much more favourable terms than those which might be included in the regional agreement. Many obkoms, like some of the federation staff quoted above, are critical of the declarative nature of the agreements. One president of a Komi republican committee, for example, saw the agreement as little more than gesture politics: '"Look how important we are, going to the tripartite commission, meeting with ministers"… Well so what? Where's the concrete gain from it? Who [does it benefit]?' Less typical, though indicative, is the position of the Samara construction workers, which is one of opposition to the whole concept of social partnership. The obkom vice-president claims that social partnership is 'a fig leaf on the body of wild capitalism. It's not a compromise, but a complete sell-out'. He publicly criticised the position of the Federation at its November 2000 Conference, and called to have its work declared unsatisfactory. In his speech, which was met with great applause, the vice-president argued that:

> The oblast federation of trade unions, for all its energetic action, is very reminiscent of a mouse on a wheel: it uses up a lot of strength with the complete illusion of moving forward, but it doesn't move from the spot…
>
> The Federation proclaimed its course of social partnership, created with its own hands the employers' association, thus strengthening the organisation of its main opponent (I can't bring myself to call them partners).
>
> Taking into account the fact that the leadership of the federation has turned out to be incompetent in ideological, political and organisational terms, that its present policy basically leads to the discrediting of the idea of a trade union as an agent of struggle and a defender in the eyes of workers, we propose: to declare the work of all the leading organs of the FPSO unsatisfactory.

He insisted that real social partnership could only be achieved if the trade unions put unremitting pressure on the employers and the authorities:

It is necessary radically to change the strategy of the trade-union movement. Neither to reject the idea of social partnership, nor to make it an end in itself as we do today, but to exploit the method of total pressure on the employers, state bodies and local government. It is necessary, first of all, ideologically, politically and organisationally to rally trade union organisations for a struggle for their rights. Real partnership (in the full sense of equal rights) will not begin until labour collectives, by their powerful protest actions and civil disobedience, will compel, or will put the authorities and employers in a situation in which they will be compelled to invite the trade unions and offer compromises and concessions in return for social peace. For now that is not the case – the administration and the employers do not take the demands of the trade unions seriously. The experience of the last few years clearly proves it. And to shut our eyes to it means – to betray the interests of the workers.

Although most union leaders are more sympathetic to the idea of dialogue *per se*, the Samara construction workers are far from alone in their view of regional tripartism as energetic action signifying nothing but, although their representative's speech was well-received, the usual vote of confidence in the Federation was carried overwhelmingly.

The importance of social partnership for FNPR and the regional federations does not lie so much in the substantive gains which the trade unions might achieve as in the recognition of their legitimacy which is accorded to them by the state through their incorporation into the institutions of social partnership as the recognised representative of the employed population. From this point of view social partnership has an important ideological role to play, not only for the trade unions but also for federal, and especially regional, government. The weakness of the party system in Russia means that the executive appeals directly to the population, over the heads of the legislature and political organisations, on the basis of its populist claims to represent the interests of the people. Tripartite agreements in this framework represent a social contract not between trade unions and employers, but between the government and the people, with the trade unions serving as the government-anointed representatives of the people, a familiar role which they are very happy to perform (Perfilev, 2000). This is why the General and regional agreements embrace a wide range of issues which do not apparently have any direct relevance to the regulation of labour relations, but do concern the well-being of the population as a whole.

The collaboration between trade unions and government 'in the service of the people' has more than a purely ideological significance. It is institutionalised in a more or less extensive framework of collaboration, more highly developed at the regional than at the federal level and in some regions more than others, through which trade union representatives participate in the consideration of state policy and collaborate in the exercise of state functions, from the administration of the social insurance fund and the monitoring of health and safety, through the implementation of employment and training programmes, to the organisation of sporting and cultural events and the celebration of festivals. Branch and regional trade union organisations even collaborate on occasion in the traditional way with their corresponding governmental partners in the intra-governmental bargaining for resources, the participation of the trade union legitimating the claims of the regional administration or ministerial body to speak not on its own behalf but on behalf of those who depend on it for their livelihood and well-being. Social partnership thus provides the rhetorical framework which has legitimated the reconstitution of many of the traditional forms of exercise of state power and the trade unions' retention or recovery of many of their traditional functions.

# 7

# The Functions of Russian Trade Unions

In previous chapters we have looked at the role of the law and of institutions of social partnership in the regulation of social and labour relations, and we have outlined the human and material resources available to the trade unions to carry out their role. In this chapter we will review the functions of the Russian trade unions and outline the ways in which they use the resources available to them to carry out those functions. We will start by looking at the new functions assumed by the trade unions in the 'transition to a market economy' of negotiating over issues of wages and employment. We will then look at the ways in which the trade unions have sought to perform their traditional functions, of the social protection of workers and 'mass-cultural' work, in new circumstances, before looking finally at their activity in organisation and recruitment.

## Wage determination

The primary function of trade unions is usually to negotiate over wages and working conditions. We have seen that in the Soviet Union the trade unions had very little role to play in the determination of wages. Wage scales and piece-rate norms were centrally determined according to the 'scientific' evaluation of the demands of the job, with supplements for working in remote regions or harmful conditions, in the elaboration of which trade union specialists would participate, while the level of wages was set by considerations of the macroeconomic balance and plan priorities. A minimum wage was in place which set a floor round about a minimum subsistence level. In practice, there was some scope for managerial discretion in the allocation of work and payment so that wages earned by an individual worker depended very much on individual informal bargaining in the workplace.

Perestroika saw some devolution of the powers of determining wages and employment to the enterprise administration. With the collapse of the soviet system this devolution was completed, raising the question of the role of the trade union in negotiating or approving the decisions of management. In practice the change was not as dramatic as it might at first appear, because wage scales have largely been preserved intact and earnings in practice have still been determined primarily by individual informal bargaining, so that the trade union has continued to play little role in wage determination. The public sector wage scales, which cover about a quarter of all employees, continue to be set by the government with little reference to the trade unions, although there is scope for regional governments to supplement wages from the local budget and for local negotiation over the scale of bonuses and for payment from non-budget funds, such as fees for private medical treatment or payments from state medical insurance funds in the health service.

The majority of state and privatised enterprises in the 'productive sphere' continue to use the traditional skill grades and wage scales, at least as their point of reference.[1] Moreover, although the majority of large enterprises continue to operate within the framework of collective agreements, since actual earnings depend primarily on the distribution of work and bonuses, the pay of individual workers is determined by the discretion of line managers rather than by any agreement, so that wage bargaining continues to take the traditional form of negotiation of divisional chiefs with the enterprise director over the allocation of wage funds and individual informal negotiation of workers with line managers over the allocation and grading of work and the payment of discretionary bonuses. The scope for managerial discretion (and the instability of wages) has increased as the proportion of earnings accounted for by the scale wages has declined at the expense of the proportion accounted for by bonuses and premia.[2] This has considerably increased the flexibility of wages (Standing, 1996, pp. 119–21) and also devalued many social guarantees, such as payment for temporary lay-offs, which are related not to average earnings but to scale pay. The principal issue which faces the trade union, and which potentially falls within the remit of the branch tariff and collective agreements, has been the indexation of wages to compensate for the unrelenting rise in the cost of living.

The wages strategy of the trade unions has had three components. First, lobbying at federal level to secure increases in the statutory minimum wage and increases in the lowest grade on the public sector pay scale, and collaboration with the government (under the 2000–1 General Agreement) in the up-dating of the soviet-era Unified Tariff Handbook of Workers' Jobs and Professions and the Unified Skills Handbook for Managers, Specialists and Clerical Workers, which even the new Labour Code defines as the reference point for enterprise pay scales (Article 143). Second, the negotiation of minimum wages and wage indexation in branch tariff agreements. Third, encouragement of primary trade union organisations to negotiate a minimum wage at least at the level of the subsistence minimum, to negotiate an increase in the

---

[1]   In the 2000 round of the Russian Labour Flexibility Survey, covering 308 industrial enterprises, 23 per cent still used the state tariff scale and a further 45 per cent used it as the point of reference for their payment system (Tsentr issledovannii rynka truda, 2001, p. 28).

[2]   FNPR claims that the scale component accounts for an average of only one-third of earnings (e.g. Tatarnikova, 1999, p. 33). Goskomstat's earnings survey in October 1999 reported the scale component of wages in a series of occupations in industry, construction, transport and communications. This averaged 58 per cent for the reported occupations, ranging from a low of 26 per cent for oil drillers to a high of 86 per cent for air stewards (Goskomstat, 2000c, Table 4.49). The average for a slightly different set of occupations in 1993 was the same, although the variance was a bit greater. The Russian Labour Flexibility Survey found over the period 1994–2000 that in those industrial enterprises paying bonuses (the majority), the bonus accounted for around 40 per cent of average earnings, with a slight increase over time (Tsentr issledovannii rynka truda, 2001, p. 30).

scale component of earnings at the expense of bonuses, and to include provision for wage indexation. In addition to attempts to raise the minimum wage and to increase wages to compensate for inflation, the trade unions have sought compensation for the delayed payment of wages and in some cases have sought to include clauses in branch and collective agreements which limit the size of differentials.

As we saw in Chapter 6, even when FNPR has managed to incorporate guarantees to raise the minimum wage in the General Agreement, the government has reneged on its commitment and the real value of the minimum wage (and the first point on the public sector ETS) was steadily eroded by inflation, falling to six percent of the miserly subsistence minimum by June 2000. FNPR had more success in its lobbying the legislature, securing a modest and progressive increase in the minimum wage from 2000 and the incorporation into the new Labour Code of the provision that the minimum wage should be no less than the subsistence minimum, though with little expectation that this provision would be implemented. Laws on the indexation of wages and pensions passed in the early 1990s were also systematically ignored.

Most branch tariff agreements set a minimum wage for the branch which is higher than the statutory minimum, though in most cases far below the subsistence minimum, and many include some provision for the quarterly indexation of wages to take account of inflation while a few also provide for the indexation of wage debts (a provision that has been incorporated into the new Labour Code), but the limited coverage of tariff agreements means that these provisions have to be incorporated into the enterprise collective agreement and enforced by the primary trade union organisation. The trade unions have similarly proved unable to secure realisable wage gains in regional agreements.

In the end, the buck stops with the primary organisation because it is only here that the trade union has any chance of negotiating an enforceable agreement to secure acceptable wages. However, as we will see in the next chapter, primary trade union organisations lack the will and bargaining power to intrude on management discretion in wage determination. The collective agreement may provide for regular increases in pay, usually 'subject to the economic possibilities of the enterprise', but this will nearly always be an expression of the wages policy of management, rather than an achievement of the trade union. Trade union leaders are easily convinced that the enterprise cannot afford to pay a living wage, while the threat of redundancy inhibits workers from pressing wage demands in depressed enterprises, so that 'exit' prevails over 'voice' as high rates of labour mobility enable the more skilled and enterprising to get higher wages by changing jobs. In this context, trade union leaders see the most effective method of increasing wages, or even getting wages paid at all, to lie in the traditional forms of collaboration with the employer in the attempt to increase production, improve quality, expand sales and by lobbying local and national government for support. Such an approach was expressed by Yevgenii Makarov, then President of the Leningrad and Saint Petersburg Trade Union Federation, in his speech to his regional trade union conference in March 2000, in which he said

A breakthrough in wages – that is our historical mission. This is where we have to show ourselves. It is very difficult work. At every enterprise, it is necessary to keep abreast of the state of affairs in the economy, to study and to carry out measures to increase the economic efficiency of the separate enterprises, to keep and to create new jobs.

The metallurgical trade union in Sverdlovsk has made the revival of socialist competition a priority direction of its activity, now called 'economic rivalry', one of its officers explaining,

We have to resolve socio-economic questions. We watch how production is doing. If there is no production there will be nothing to distribute… our task is production, to participate through the system of trade union activists. We must help in the development of production.

## Employment protection

The trade unions have seen a halving of their membership over the 1990s, associated with the collapse of employment in the traditional sectors of the economy. The issue of jobs is a pressing one both for trade unions and for their members, but it is always one of the most difficult to address. FNPR has sought to incorporate target levels of unemployment and guarantees of job creation and retraining programmes into the General and regional agreements, has sought to defend the existing levels of redundancy compensation and statutory notice laid down by the Law on Employment and has worked closely with the Federal Employment Service in the formulation and implementation of its programmes, but trade union action has had little impact on unemployment at the macroeconomic level. Many regional trade union organisations work more or less closely with the regional administration and employment service in the formulation and implementation of regional employment policy, but action at the regional level can have only a limited effect.[1] As in the determination of wages, the buck is passed to the enterprise trade union organisation to negotiate employment guarantees at the level of the workplace.

[1]   FNPR reported at its IVth Congress that, at the instigation of the trade unions, many regions had introduced local laws reserving a quota of jobs for the disabled and young people and some regions had introduced laws on the use of immigrant labour. In several regions the trade unions had successfully appealed to the regional administration to persuade enterprises to postpone or to phase mass redundancies, and many regional and branch agreements required the authorities to take steps if unemployment rose above an acceptable level. Programmes to maintain employment had also been adopted in ten branches of the economy (FNRP, 2001).

Management has almost complete discretion in the deployment of labour and in its employment policy. The restrictions on the transfer of workers embodied in the Labour Code are a dead letter – faced with the choice between transfer and redundancy very few workers will insist on their rights under the Labour Code to remain in the same job. Management can get rid of surplus employees with few constraints: the threat of disciplinary proceedings, short-time working, administrative vacation, the non-payment of wages and the mere threat of redundancy provoke large-scale voluntary quits without having to invoke laborious and expensive redundancy procedures, which are required only to get rid of those who are determined to hold on to their jobs at any price. Thus the sharp fall in employment over the 1990s was achieved largely by natural wastage as people left low-paid jobs in declining enterprises to seek out better opportunities elsewhere. Even at the end of the nineties, fewer than one in twelve separations were officially the result of redundancy and only a quarter of the unemployed had suffered redundancy from their previous jobs (Goskomstat, 2000a), although many of those officially recorded as voluntary separations had in fact been pushed out by employers anxious to avoid having to make redundancy payments.

The issue of redundancy is always a difficult and divisive one for trade unions, because employers often present redundancies as the only means of maintaining or increasing the wages of those who remain. FNPR recognises the dilemma and recommends its member organisations to ensure that if they do permit redundancies, the collective agreement should make this conditional on wages being raised for those who remain and on all possible measures being taken to facilitate the re-employment of those made redundant, proposing that the decision should 'only be taken at a general meeting of the employees on the basis of a recommendation of the trade union committee' (FNPR Executive Committee, 17 September 1997, *Vesti FNPR*, 9–10, 1997, p. 10).

Redundancy is a particularly difficult issue for Russian trade unions since the trade union is integrated into the management of the redundancy process, having the legal right to be consulted over redundancies and being responsible for approving the selection of those who will be subject to redundancy. It is very rare for the trade union to oppose redundancies in practice and in the selection of candidates for redundancy it tends to follow the management priority of retaining the most productive employers rather than defending those, such as single parents, with the most to lose and those, such as those approaching retirement, with the least prospect of re-employment. The collective agreement might set a limit to the proportion of the labour force which can be made redundant in any one year but, in general, the trade union priority is not to resist redundancy but to facilitate the redeployment and re-employment of those subject to redundancy, in some cases even taking on the personnel functions of redeploying and retraining workers. The unions try to ensure that those made redundant receive the benefits to which they are entitled, while the union may be able to incorporate additional benefits in the collective agreement, such as time-off to look for a new job, for those made redundant and the agreement may provide for the retraining and internal transfer rather than dismissal of redundant employees, and for a freeze on new hirings, encouragement of early retirement and voluntary leave and an overtime ban to reduce the scale of redundancy.

## Social protection and the enforcement of labour rights

The Russian trade unions proclaim their primary function as being to secure the social protection and defend the social and labour rights of the working population in the transition to a market economy, including the right to employment and the right to the timely payment and an acceptable level of wages which we have just considered. In accordance with the rhetoric of social partnership, the trade unions proclaim the significance of general, branch tariff and regional agreements in securing the social protection of their members. However, as we have seen, these agreements include few substantive guarantees and the trade unions have no effective means of enforcing the commitments entered into by their partners in such agreements. This has led them to fall back on the traditional mechanisms of the legal and administrative regulation of labour relations.

In the post-soviet period the trade unions have sought to preserve, extend and improve the legislative and administrative regulation of the terms and conditions of employment with some success, as has been detailed in earlier chapters. However, such legislation is not worth the paper it is written on if it is not observed and enforced in the workplace. Similarly, as we have seen, federal and regional agreements have no force if their terms are not also included in the enterprise collective agreement. Responsibility for enforcing the labour rights of union members therefore falls on the primary trade union organisations and their presidents.

Employers have even more incentive to violate workers' rights than they had in the soviet period and they are no longer subject to Party control. According to the official data of *Rostrudinspektsiya*, by the end of the nineties there were around two million violations of labour legislation by employers every year and, according to FNPR's analysis, one in four employers sacks workers for trade union activity, almost half promise to give workers material incentives for refusing to join a trade union and one in three facilitates the creation of various kinds of anti-trade union structures (Naboishchikov, 2001). The unions therefore have to find other means of seeking to ensure that employers respect the individual and collective rights of their members. According to Russian legislation, the enforcement of labour rights is through individual disputes procedures within the workplace, supplemented by individual court action, while strikes are only legal, following exhaustive procedures, in pursuance of a collective labour dispute. The institutional industrial relations and legal framework is, therefore, one which structures and strongly reinforces the trade unions' predilection for defending the interests of workers on the basis of the juridical enforcement of laws and agreements on behalf of individuals or groups of individuals, rather than on the basis of collective organisation and collective action.

The dependence of the enterprise trade union on the administration, and in many cases the limited knowledge of the trade union officers, mean that the trade union in the workplace is often as reluctant actively to protect the rights of its members as it was in the soviet period. As we will see in the next chapter, the trade union committee prefers to seek to resolve individual cases through informal negotiation with management, only reluctantly invoking the disputes resolution procedures and appealing to the courts only as a last resort. As in the soviet period, the systematic violation of workers' rights may only come to light in the event of an accident or if workers protest, sending letters and petitions to higher authorities or holding demonstrations, pickets or strikes.

The failure of primary trade union organisations to negotiate and enforce effective collective agreements and to defend their members' legal rights means that much of the burden of doing so falls onto the regional trade union organisations. Regional trade union organisations seek to strengthen the work of primary organisations by encouraging and helping the negotiation of collective agreements, providing training and advice to presidents of primary organisations and providing legal advice and support for individual union members, including in the conduct of court cases. In the case of conflicts in enterprises, the regional trade union organisation can assist in the resolution of conflicts by offering its services as a conciliator or by putting pressure on the employer, either directly or through its connections in the regional administration. The regional organisations also take responsibility for establishing new union branches in non-union workplaces. In principle the servicing of primary organisations should be the responsibility of the obkoms, but the lack of resources (and indolence) of the latter means that the federations often also take on these functions. We will consider each of these dimensions of the work of the regional trade union organisations in the following sections.

**Support for the negotiation of collective agreements**

Primary responsibility for encouraging primary groups to negotiate and improve the quality of collective agreements falls to the regional committees of the branch trade unions, encouraged and assisted by the regional federation. The principal form of support comprises the provision of model collective agreements to primary organisations and the provision of training and guidance materials to presidents of trade union committees, much of which is based on materials prepared by FNPR, the branch trade union or the regional federation. Primary organisations are particularly encouraged to incorporate (or improve on) the provisions of the regional and branch tariff agreements in concluding their collective agreements. The obkom and federation also provide advice to trade union presidents, particularly in legal matters, may review drafts of collective agreements and in the event of a dispute with the employer may support the trade union committee in its negotiations. In some cases the regional branch organisation may negotiate collective agreements on behalf of their primary organisations, as is the case, for example, in the Leningrad fishing industry. In the education sector in Leningrad collective agreements are negotiated directly with the municipal administration by the local trade union co-ordinating committee.

Neither the obkoms nor the presidents of primary organisations have much interest in or commitment to the negotiation of collective agreements, preferring to concentrate on their more familiar social welfare functions, and in many cases, ostensibly through lack of time and resources, the obkoms do not even circulate material prepared for them by higher bodies to the primary organisations, just leaving them lying around in the office to be taken by anybody interested. With their limited resources even the most active obkoms are not able to provide much support to primary organisations and their main efforts are exhortative, their priority being to increase the number of collective agreements reported rather than to improve their quality (only about two-thirds of regional federations even complete their annual returns to FNPR on the conclusion of collective agreements, and those that do often have to estimate the figures because the obkoms have not reported to them). Their provision of advice and support is mostly reactive, when a trade union president telephones or calls into the union office, rather than proactive. Although the obkoms are heavily criticised for the inadequacy of their work, the more active among them feel that their efforts have led to a steady improvement in the quality of collective agreements.

As we saw in the last chapter, in some regions the regional agreement includes commitments on the part of the employers and the regional administration to encourage the conclusion of collective agreements. In Moscow and Kemerovo, the existence of a collective agreement is a requirement for receiving various kinds of support and contracts from the government. This is also an important stimulus to the formation of new trade union organisations, since employers need a trade union with which to conclude a collective agreement.

## Training for trade union activists

In the soviet period there was an extensive and well-organised system of training for trade union activists, much of which was devoted to lecturing them on the policies and priorities set by the Party and VTsSPS, the organisation of socialist competition and their production tasks and informing them of changes in legislation or regulations. With the collapse of the Party-state much of this training lost its purpose, while the decentralisation of the union structure and the loss of income meant that trade union bodies at all levels were reluctant to spend money on training. However, from the middle of the nineties much greater priority was attached to training as a means of attempting to improve the competence of activists and stimulate the activism of trade union primary organisations. Training came to be one of the means of increasing the 'discipline' and 'solidarity' of trade union organisations, strengthening the 'trade union vertical' in the absence of democratic centralism.

Trade union training was traditionally provided through regional or inter-regional trade union training centres funded by the regional federation. In many regions the training centres were closed and in others they were devolved into independent self-financing organisations which charged for their services. On the one hand, most trade union organisations could not afford the fees charged for training, finding it much cheaper to provide training using their own resources. On the other hand, the training centres were not financially viable providing training only for trade unionists and so offered training to employers and to the regional administration and developed courses for the general public (in languages, accountancy, law, IT or any other topic for which they could create a demand). The trade union centres also provide all the training of arbitrators for the Ministry of Labour. By 1996 the number of regional training centres had fallen from 70 to 43, while less than a quarter of the capacity of those that remained was used for trade union training (FNPR, 1996, p. 93).

The Leningrad Zonal Training-Methodological Centre, one of the largest inter-regional centres, trained 8000 trade unionists in 1990, which fell to only 764 in 1993, but since then has increased to around 1500 a year, although all courses now have to be paid for. Training is also provided for employer representatives, although trade unionists pay lower fees. The Sverdlovsk regional training centre used to train 10 000 trade unionists a year, but in the first semester of 1999–2000 only 305 of its 2360 students were following trade union courses, while there were 800 students following courses on social insurance and 200 following courses on health and safety (including employer representatives and state officials). The Centre also offers courses in English, accountancy, computer literacy and various professional courses targeted primarily at state officials. The 2000 regional agreement provided funding for the Centre from the regional budget, but the money was never forthcoming.

Training is generally financed by the organisation sponsoring the trainee. In some regions, such as the Komi Republic, the federation no longer finances any training at all, but in others, such as Leningrad and Saint Petersburg it funds priority areas, such as the training of new trade union presidents. Training is also provided through various internationally supported training programmes, particularly those of the ILO, the Friedrich Ebert Foundation and programmes supported by the Nordic trade unions. In order to save money, most obkoms provide training for their primary group presidents using their own resources, sometimes bringing in outside specialists from the federation, the regional training centre or the regional administration.

Most trade union training is provided as an ancillary to trade union meetings: for example, many branch unions hold monthly meetings for presidents of trade union committees, part of the day being devoted to training, particularly updating presidents on changes in legislation or in trade union policy. Special courses are often provided for responsible officers, particularly in labour law, social insurance and health and safety inspection. Particular attention is usually paid to the training of newly elected trade union presidents.

FNPR has two higher educational establishments, the Academy of Labour and Social Relations in Moscow, which receives government funding secured under the General Agreement and has established a network of 19 subsidiaries based on regional training centres, and the Trade Union Humanitarian University in Saint Petersburg, which also has regional affiliates. These are supposed to provide advanced training for senior trade union officers and specialists. However, financial constraints severely limit the number who take advantage of these opportunities and the trade union students have often been outnumbered by state officials being trained on the basis of agreements with the Ministry of Labour, *Rostrudinspektsiya* and the Pension Fund. The Saint Petersburg Humanitarian University has a quota of 1000 places for trade unionists, but at the end of the nineties had only 14 trade union students because the unions could not afford the fees. By the IVth Congress in November 2001, FNPR could report that the number attending courses organised by the Academy of Labour had increased twenty-fold, to around 20 000 (FNPR, 2001b). The Academy of Labour also conducts research and has collaboration agreements with the Committee on Labour and Social Policy of the State Duma and a number of ministries.

The forms and methods of training are usually traditional: a formal lecture with the distribution of photocopied instructional materials, which encourage passivity and bureaucratism, but more active forms of training ('ILO methods') have been introduced through an ILO-sponsored training-the-trainers programme, with the support of the Norwegian trade unions, which trained more than 300 trainers between 1997 and 2001 (FNPR, 2001b). These are often unpopular with older trade union officials, who would rather sleep through a lecture than be expected to engage in role-play, but are enthusiastically embraced by the more active and younger trade unionists.

FNPR sees training as an important means of preparing the next generation of trade union leaders, and in July 2001 the General Council proposed that a minimum of four per cent of the trade union budget should be spent on training, with further financing being secured from employers and local authorities. This is about twice the amount currently being spent by most regional federations and about four times what is being spent by obkoms and enterprise primary organisations.

## Provision of legal advice

The provision of legal advice to presidents of primary organisations and members is one of the most time-consuming activities of the regional trade union organisations and provides virtually their only contact with ordinary members. In the soviet period workers could turn to the enterprise lawyer for legal advice, but today this channel has been closed off, while very few primary trade union organisations have their own legal specialist, although developing the legal competence of primary organisations is a priority aim of trade union training. In principle union members should appeal in the first instance to their own trade union committee, but in many cases they go directly to the regional offices of their branch union or the federation or even to FNPR in Moscow.

The legal department is usually the largest department in the regional trade union apparatus, and is accorded a much higher priority than any other department. In Sverdlovsk, for example, seven of the 22 staff of the Federation are lawyers, and the regional trade union organisations as a whole employ a total of 26 lawyers. In Samara, six of the 30 staff of the Federation are lawyers and the obkoms employ a further 11. Still, the most common complaint from regional trade union organisations is that they cannot afford to employ a sufficient number of labour lawyers to meet their needs.

Regional trade union offices have fixed hours at which they will receive personal callers, and also receive written and telephone applications for help and advice. These applications may come from trade union primary group presidents (and sometimes from employers), but many of the requests for advice come from members of the public who may or may not be union members and concern such things as redundancy and dismissal, compulsory leave, the non-payment of wages or injury benefits, the miscalculation of wages or, especially, of pension entitlements, entitlement to benefits and vacation vouchers, but they may also involve non-work-related problems such as housing problems, problems with payment for communal services, criminal cases or even marital disputes. Individuals may receive advice and be sent on their way, they may be referred back to their primary organisation, or the regional trade union organisation may take up their case. Most complaints arise out of ignorance or misunderstanding of the law on the part of management and can be remedied by informal intervention, but occasionally, particularly in dismissal cases, they can lead to a formal dispute which may be referred to the court.

Individual cases take up a great deal of the time of the regional trade union organisations' lawyers. For example, the Leningrad and St Petersburg federation receives more than 10000 personal inquiries a year, almost half of which concern legal issues, around one-fifth health and safety issues, one-eighth social issues and four per cent concern housing problems. The legal department of the Sverdlovsk Federation receives 2–3000 people a year and has about 20 telephone inquiries every day. The Samara Federation receives about 9000 appeals a year. In Kemerovo region in 1999, the regional trade union organisations as a whole received 16479 individual appeals, of which 4390 were to the regional federation, resulting in 1200 legal cases, of which 123 were conducted by the federation, with a 93 per cent success rate, and 279 collective and 1976 individual labour disputes, mostly handled by the branch union committees, 86 per cent of which were successful. As a result of the unions' efforts 140 people were restored to their jobs and 24 managers were disciplined, of whom 10 were sacked, for violations of labour legislation. According to FNPR's figures, across the whole of Russia during the period 1997–2000, trade union lawyers gave legal advice to 862 166 people and supported members in 174 517 court submissions, 50 000 court cases, 117 539 individual and 7500 collective labour disputes, three-quarters of each being resolved successfully (FNPR, 2001b).

Some complainants appeal directly to FNPR, which received more than 17 000 individual appeals between 1998 and 2000 and in 2000 conducted further investigations in response to more than 250 written appeals. The main issues dealt with by FNPR were complaints about wages and the non-payment of wages; dismissal, particularly in connection with redundancies, and transfers; unfavourable entries in the labour book or failure to hand over a labour book; the legality of temporary labour contracts; pension and housing issues; and compensation for industrial injury (Naboishchikov, 2001). This was almost double the number of appeals compared to the period 1994–6, when more than a third of cases concerned dismissal (FNPR, 1996, pp. 11, 78).

Many trade union lawyers think that the preoccupation with individual cases is a distraction from what should be their main task of defending the collective interests of the workers, but the weakness of primary trade union organisations and their reluctance to engage in collective action reinforces the continued individualisation of the regulation of labour disputes. Moreover, the regional trade union leadership tends to see this work as very important for the public image of the trade unions as organisations to which those in trouble (and not only union members) can turn. The provision of legal advice is generally seen very much within the framework of the traditional view of the trade union as a welfare agency solving individual problems.

### Action through the courts

Primary trade union presidents are reluctant to pursue grievances against the employer through the courts because of their fear that the employer will regard this as a provocative step, much preferring to rely on informal negotiation to resolve disputes. However, if such means fail the case may be referred to the court, in which case the assistance of the regional trade union organisations – the obkom if it has a competent lawyer, otherwise the federation – will be sought. Appeal to the courts is often sufficient to persuade the employer to settle, without the need for a hearing.

The defence of workers' rights through the Russian courts is a cumbersome and laborious process and its results are unpredictable. Win or lose, appellants are often subsequently victimised by the employer. If they win, workers often have to return to court to secure enforcement of its judgement and if they lose, they have to work through trade appeals procedure. Given the limited resources available to the trade unions, for this reason alone they are reluctant to support an appeal to the courts, despite the fact that such appeals are successful in the overwhelming majority of cases, and most workers have to handle their own cases without any help from the union. In the second half of the nineties the Leningrad and St Petersburg Federation submitted an average of over 500 cases to court each year on behalf of appellants, but only represented the appellant in an average of 24 cases each year. According to

FNPR figures, over the period 1998–2001 trade union lawyers assisted in the formulation of 105 000 applications to court and represented the appellant in 50 000 cases, of which three-quarters were resolved in the appellant's favour. They also submitted an average of 1000 cases a year to the prosecutors and the labour inspectorate to proceed against individual managers for violation of labour legislation. The trade unions managed to overturn the dismissal of 4000 people and secure the disciplining of 1500 managers of various levels. FNPR itself submitted 3370 cases in this period, including 6 cases which went to higher courts, as well as successfully defending 11 trade union activists accused of holding illegal meetings and 52 accused of blocking transport links in connection with protests against the non-payment of wages (Naboishchikov, 2001).

Trade union lawyers also appear in a variety of other court hearings, particularly bankruptcy cases, to protect the interests of their members, and in cases of contested ownership of the enterprise, where the legality of privatisation, for example, may be challenged, and the union is supporting one or the other party to the dispute, usually the existing management against an outside owner. In a number of regions the trade unions have successfully conducted court actions to prevent increases in communal service charges.

Court action has been one of the principal forms of activity of the alternative unions, the AFL-CIO-sponsored Free Trade Union Institute providing a comprehensive legal advice service, the availability of which is one of the attractions of the alternative unions to those seeking support in a dispute with their employer, particularly because the alternative trade unions refuse to sanction the dismissal or redundancy of their members. In the early nineties many of their court actions were to defend alternative trade union activists who had been victimised by their employers or to compel an employer to recognise their trade union organisation, but in the middle of the decade they pioneered the use of the courts to secure the payment of unpaid wages. Court action is also an important means by which the alternative trade unions advertise their existence and, in the absence of effective collective organisation, is often the only means by which they can put pressure on employers.

The FNPR unions soon took up this use of the courts. The delayed payment of wages is a violation of the Labour Code but, unless the regular payment of wages is explicitly included in the collective agreement, it is not a legitimate pretext for a collective labour dispute, and so for strike action. Nevertheless, wildcat strikes in response to delays in the payment of wages were common, and such strikes would often be settled by the payment of those involved in the strike, although usually at the expense of other workers. Quite apart from the legal barriers to their endorsement of wildcat strikes, the trade unions generally regarded such actions as unproductive, preferring to address the question of non-payment of wages through collaboration with employers, particularly to lobby for funds to pay wages, and through legal channels. In many cases, employers did not have the cash to pay wages because, as we have seen, the tax authorities had first claim on their bank accounts. In these circumstances the employers were not averse to being sued for the payment of wages because a court judgement would give the payment of wages precedence over the payment of taxes. Many trade unions therefore became involved in mass legal actions on behalf of unpaid workers, which had to be repeated monthly, in which the trade union would secure the judgement but then, if the money were forthcoming, would also have to arrange the payment of the recovered wages to the individual complainants, usually in collaboration with the enterprise's wages office. This use of the courts over the non-payment of wages is one reason for the enormous growth in the number of court actions in the late 1990s, so that by the end of the decade cases regarding violations of labour law took up almost a third of the time of the civil courts (Naboishchikov, 2001). Between 1993 and 1998 the number of such cases submitted to the courts increased from 94 thousand to 1.5 million, 1.3 million of which concerned wages, 850 000 concerning non-payment, while FNPR lawyers were assisting in around 25 000 cases a year. This is one reason why FNPR regards the further development and rationalisation of the legal services of its member organisations to be a priority direction of development of the trade unions (*Vesti FNPR, 3–4, 2000*, pp. 7–42).

From around 1997 the courts appear to have become much more receptive to hearing labour-related cases, with fewer delays and more favourable judgements, providing an incentive for employees and trade unions to take their cases through the courts rather than engaging in more militant actions. In some regions this development was encouraged by the regional administration, but we have no evidence of such intervention at the Federal level.

## Conflict resolution

The involvement of the regional federations in social partnership commits them to seeking to maintain social peace in the region. However, the regional federations have little direct contact with primary trade union organisations so rarely get involved in the early stages of conflict, often only finding out about a conflict through reports in the mass media, and generally are reluctant to get involved in conflict resolution. A round-table of presidents of trade union committees in the Leningrad and St Petersburg regions proposed the establishment of a co-ordinating committee by the Federation to help in cases of conflict, only to discover that such a committee had been in existence for several years, but had been so inactive that nobody had heard of it. Member organisations were not happy about the Federation's inaction in the event of conflicts and insisted on an amendment to the constitution in 2001 which requires the Federation to 'organise and co-ordinate the conduct of collective actions, including strikes, and to support the collective actions of member organisations'.

If a collective conflict comes to the attention of the obkom or the federation, an officer may visit the workplace in order to mediate in the resolution of the dispute. Social partnership in Russia commits the unions to seek to resolve disputes within the framework of the law and collective agreements, so the regional organisation will usually seek to channel the dispute into the conciliation and arbitration procedures provided for by the law, often itself assuming the role of arbiter rather than that of defender of its members. For example, in the Komi Republic, the Federation heard indirectly about a dispute in the local aviation company, KomiAvia, but called for an inquiry rather than supporting the labour collective on the grounds that the Federation was not in possession of all the facts as it had not been represented at the conference of the labour collective at which the dispute had arisen. If the regional organisation considers that the workers' complaint has no legal justification, it may even end up supporting the employer, particularly if it has good relations with the employer and/or the employer has the support of the regional administration. In some cases a conciliatory approach can be successful: in Komi again, an attempt by a director in Ukhta to suppress the local branch of the oil and gas union was successfully resolved through the republican tripartite commission when other unions had ignored the oil and gas union's appeal for solidarity.

The more active obkoms are generally more inclined to support the workers in dispute, sometimes even in the face of opposition from their own enterprise trade union organisation, and may seek to mobilise their contacts in the regional administration to put pressure on the employer if a dispute cannot be resolved amicably. However, the obkoms usually have only relatively low-level connections in functional departments of the regional administration and so may appeal to the regional federation to use its contacts on their behalf. The obkoms regard such intercession on their behalf as one of the most important functions of the federation and the failure of the federation to deliver is often a source of grievance on the part of the obkoms.

In general, in the case of collective conflicts, the regional trade union organisations have a difficult line to tread. While their primary obligation might be to support their members in dispute, though their members are often opposed by their own enterprise trade union committee, they also have a commitment to the employers and the regional administration to maintain social peace, which leads them to prefer administrative pressure and bureaucratic and judicial channels of conflict-resolution over direct action. Moreover, the regional trade union organisations will not want to compromise their relationships with their counterparts in the regional administration for the sake of one group of members in conflict. Thus, they will be very wary about supporting workers in opposition to an employer who has the support of the regional administration. On the other hand, it is sometimes convenient for the regional administration to use a labour conflict as a pretext to remove a director who is not in its favour.

## Monitoring the observance of health and safety and labour legislation

Although the existing labour and health and safety legislation gives workers a very high degree of protection in principle, in practice the means of enforcement of the legislation are very limited, with only a small proportion of legal violations being challenged by primary trade union organisations or uncovered by individual labour disputes. The transfer of the trade union functions of health and safety inspection to the new state body, *Rostrudinspektsiya*, not only deprived the trade unions of many of their powers of enforcement and led to the transfer of the personnel responsible from the regional trade union apparatus, but also led to the virtual collapse of the system of voluntary inspectors in enterprises. While the trade unions needed the support of *Rostrudinspektsiya* to retain their powers of enforcement, *Rostrudinspektsiya* needed the trade unions to provide the network of voluntary inspectors that it required to function effectively. Thus the ground was prepared for the trade unions to recover their state functions in monitoring the observance of health and safety legislation.

The trade unions became increasingly concerned at the threat to the health of workers presented by the breakdown of the traditional system of trade union control, the deterioration of plant and equipment and the reduction in spending of enterprises on health and safety measures. Official statistics do not suggest any significant increase in the incidence of industrial injury, but this is most likely a result of the closure of the most archaic production facilities and a decline in reporting associated with weaker control. In 1999 there were 153 110 reported industrial accidents, with 5370 fatalities, but this compares with 432 000 reported accidents in 1990, of which 8393 were fatal. However, in 1999 *Rostrudinspektsiya* uncovered 1090 accidents, of which more than 140 were fatal, which had not been reported by the employers (*Vesti FNPR*, 7–8, 2000, pp. 23, 31). The incidence of reported industrial accidents fell from 6.6 per thousand workers in 1990 to 5.2 per thousand in 1999 and 5.1 per thousand in 2000, although the decline in employment meant that the incidence of reported fatal accidents, which are harder to cover up, had increased from 0.129 per thousand workers to 0.144 per thousand in 1999 and 0.149 in 2000 (Goskomstat, 2000b; Goskomstat, 2001).

The strategy of the trade unions in dealing with issues of health and safety and the monitoring of the observance of labour legislation has involved a number of different dimensions. At the federal and regional levels FNPR has sought to develop collaboration with the Ministry of Labour and *Rostrudinspektsiya*, involving the provision of training for state inspectors by the trade union training institutions and the collaboration of regional trade union organisations with state inspectors in carrying out inspections of enterprises. The number of such inspections increased between 1999 and 2000, from 6.9 to 8.4 thousand (FNPR, 2001b). The 2000–1 General Agreement included a commitment on the part of the government to expedite such collaboration and to consider financing trade union inspectors from the state Social Insurance Fund. Following the transfer of staff in 1994, the number of trade union technical inspectors has continued to fall, with half the regional and branch unions having no technical inspector on their staff in 1999, the total number having fallen from 84 to 46 in three years (*Vesti FNPR*, 7–8, 2000, p. 28). In many regions the administration has delegated the right to monitor conformity to health and safety and ecological legislation to the trade unions. Branch trade unions have sought to include clauses specifying the minimum acceptable level of expenditure on health and safety in their branch tariff agreements and encourage primary organisations to include similar provisions in their collective agreements.

Inspections of establishments by trade union inspectors and joint commissions generally reveal a very large number of violations of labour and health and safety legislation and regulations. For example, in 1999, according to the reports received from 38 regional and 12 branch trade union organisations, 17.4 thousand inspections had revealed 89.1 thousand legal violations. Trade union inspectors had issued instructions to stop work in 5361 cases and 3491 managers had been sanctioned, of whom 238 were dismissed for violations of health and safety and ecological legislation. Many fewer cases were investigated as a result of industrial accidents (9677, of which 1108 had been fatal) or labour conflicts (2619, 74 per cent of which were resolved in favour of the workers) (*Vesti FNPR*, 7–8, 2000, pp. 21–36). The trade unions take this as a sign not only of the negligence of employers, but also of the ineffectiveness of primary trade union organisations, which have not raised these issues on their own initiative. However, the primary trade union organisations come under conflicting pressures. On the one hand, higher trade union bodies press them to secure the enforcement of health and safety legislation. On the other hand, compensation for working in hazardous conditions provides a significant addition to the wages of a substantial proportion of the labour force, many of whom would rather receive a bonus for working in harmful conditions than see the money spent on removing such conditions. Thus, in 1999, while 2619 conflicts were reported from 38 regions regarding the violation of health and safety legislation, there were 14 329 complaints regarding unsatisfactory working conditions and the failure to pay appropriate compensation (*Vesti FNPR*, 7–8, 2000, p. 30). Primary organisations, in their negotiations over the collective agreement, tend to give priority to securing compensation for their members over increased spending on health and safety measures.

The regional trade union organisations have given a high priority to appropriate training for officers of primary organisations and distribute a wide range of handbooks to help them in their work. At the end of the 1990s FNPR made the restoration of the system of voluntary inspectors in enterprises a major priority, although it often proved difficult to find people willing to take on the task. In 1999, 38 regions reported that they had recruited 160 thousand voluntary inspectors (*Vesti FNPR*, 7–8, 2000, p. 24). When violations are identified in enterprises the trade union may appeal to the obkom for support and the threat of reporting the violation to *Rostrudinspektsiya* is often sufficient to secure the employer's compliance. The threat of an inspection is often a useful lever which the trade union can use to pressure the employer in unrelated disputes.

## Informational-analytical work

The federal and regional trade union organisations attach considerable importance to their informational-analytical activity, which provides the centre with a means of communicating with trade union activists in the attempt to maintain a degree of direction of their activity in the absence of the former relations of hierarchical subordination. The regional trade union organisations generally consider that informational activity is the most effective way of retaining members and increasing membership, to disseminate information and advice and to make the members aware of the things that the regional apparatus is doing for them. However, financial constraints mean that the scale of this activity is much reduced from the soviet period.

Today FNPR has lost control of its daily newspaper, *Trud*, instead relying on the fortnightly newspaper inherited from the Moscow Federation of Trade Unions in 1996, *Solidarnost'*, to communicate with its members. However, despite all the efforts of FNPR to persuade primary organisations to subscribe, the circulation of *Solidarnost'* is very small, with a print run of 28 700 in October 2001, just before the crucial Congress – less than one copy per ten primary organisations. FNPR also publishes a bi-monthly journal for activists, *Vesti FNPR*, which contains resolutions and reports from FNPR and the branch unions, the journal *Profsoyuzy i Ekonomika* and the *Biblioteka profsoyuznogo aktivista*, each issue of which focuses on a particular issue relevant primarily to trade union officers, such as collective bargaining, implementing social partnership or defending jobs. FNPR also maintains a website, www.fnpr.ru, as do a small number of regional and branch trade union organisations.

Most branch and regional trade union organisations no longer have sufficient funds to produce their own newspaper, as they did in the past, instead producing information bulletins for their member organisations, and holding press conferences and issuing press releases which are rarely reported in the media. In some regions, the federation has made an arrangement with one of the regional newspapers to publish a monthly or weekly trade union supplement. In the past, many larger enterprise trade union organisations published a factory newspaper, which was under the control of the Party Committee but could still be an important source of information for union members. Today many factory newspapers have ceased publication, others being controlled by management. FNPR and the branch trade unions publish a substantial number of handbooks and informational material on such issues as labour legislation, collective agreements, health and safety and so on for the guidance of their activists, and these are circulated by the regional federations and obkoms, but the lack of 'discipline' means that many such publications never reach their intended recipients.

## Social welfare and mass-cultural work

While FNPR and its regional organisations set themselves the priority task of defending the terms and conditions of employment of their members in the transition to a market economy, enterprise (and many regional) trade union organisations still give priority to their traditional social welfare functions, usually referred to as defending the 'social guarantees' of the employed population. These conflicting priorities underlie much of the tension between enterprise trade unions and higher trade union bodies, not least in that expressed in conflict over the allocation of trade union funds. Enterprise trade union organisations want to hold on to as much of their dues as possible, to spend on social welfare and the provision of material assistance to their members. The regional trade union organisations (and more active trade union presidents), on the other hand, decry this misuse of resources, insisting that trade union funds should be used to defend the labour rights of union members, and can best be so used by transferring funds to the regional organisations to employ more staff, particularly lawyers and economists, to enable them to strengthen the negotiation and enforcement of regional laws, regulations and agreements. As one Leningrad official put it, 'In sum, we are not a trade union, but a mutual assistance fund'. The following is typical of the views of the regional trade union federations, here expressed by the chief accountant of the Perm' *oblsovprof* in a speech to its Plenum:

> Social cultural measures, and not labour relations, is the basic activity of the trade union committees, and we cannot do anything to get away from that... While our trade unions occupy themselves with social welfare, culture and physical culture we will never have normal trade union work because all the money goes on that.

Nevertheless, the provision of social and welfare benefits to their members is still a central part of the trade unions' function. On the one hand, these are the principal benefits which trade union members expect to derive from their membership. On the other hand, this is the preferred sphere of activity of many trade union officers, who look back nostalgically to the days when they controlled a huge social and welfare infrastructure. The trade unions provide advice to their members on both work and personal problems, distribute sick pay, provide material support to cover the cost of funerals or exceptional medical expenses, help their members resolve their housing problems, organise child care, provide subsidised places for children in summer holiday camps, provide and organise sporting facilities, provide subsidised vacations and rest breaks in sanatoria to their members and a whole host of other benefits and facilities. Today the unions continue to collaborate closely with the Social Insurance Fund, most of whose staff are former colleagues, which could not function without the trade unions' continuing to distribute the benefits financed by the Fund. The regional trade union organisations also collaborate closely with the regional administration and with enterprises in planning and managing social and welfare programmes, particularly the annual provision of camps for children during the long school summer holidays, and in providing training for managers of tourist, social and welfare facilities.

Material support is provided primarily from trade union funds, while the other benefits are financed, as they were in the past, jointly by the social insurance fund, the trade union, employer and local administration. The biggest problem facing the trade unions today is the inadequate financing of this sphere of activity and their main task is to supplement the limited resources of the trade union with funding from the other sources.

Privatisation and economic pressures have led many enterprises and trade union organisations to sell-off, transfer to the municipality or simply to close down their social assets. This has exacerbated the inequality of provision of the soviet period: Large and prosperous enterprises have been able to preserve their social assets and finance the social welfare activity of the trade union from enterprise funds, while less successful enterprises have lost their social assets and rely primarily on the Social Insurance Fund and the regional and municipal administration to maintain their social welfare provision, but provision from the Social Insurance Fund has also been sharply reduced. For example, the chemical workers' union used to distribute 37 vouchers per thousand workers each year, but now receives only between five and 10 per thousand members a year. Nevertheless, FNPR reported at the end of 2001 that the trade unions still had around 600 resorts, providing holidays for six million members and their families, as well as two thousand cultural centres, more than two thousand libraries, almost six thousand artistic clubs and around 50 thousand sporting establishments. Almost two and a half million people received treatment in trade union sanatoria (FNPR, 2001b).

Most mass-cultural work is still the responsibility of the enterprise trade union organisations, but the latter expect to receive organisational support from regional trade union bodies and expect the latter to secure continued access to social insurance funds and funding from the regional administration. In some regions, the regional trade union federation has established joint-stock companies jointly with the regional administration to own and manage their social and welfare facilities. However, trade union facilities have been considerably reduced and many are in a deplorable condition. By 1999, only 32 of the 3.2 thousand operating permanent children's out-of-town holiday camps were in trade union hands (*Vesti FNPR*, 1–2, 2000, p. 62), although two thousand were still operated by the trade unions, providing holidays for three million children (FNPR, 2001b).

At the Federal level, the battle to maintain social insurance funding, and to maintain the proportion of that funding allocated for vouchers for holidays and rest-homes, particularly for children's summer holidays, has been an on-going one for FNPR. Until 2000 the battle was pretty successful: spending from the Social Insurance Fund actually increased in real terms between 1992 and 1996, and was subsequently at least maintained as a proportion of GDP (though the cost of vouchers has soared ahead of the general rate of inflation). The number of adults taking vacations in resorts fell by more than half between 1992 and 1998, before increasing slightly in 1999, but the number of children holidaying in summer camps increased from 4.3 million in 1992 to 6.2 million in 2000 (Goskomstat, 2000c; Goskomstat, 2001). These holidays might be good for the moral health of the children, but they are often not so good for their physical health – in 2000, mass outbreaks of intestinal disorders were reported in camps in 17 regions and there were a number of accidents, some fatal, which FNPR attributed to the inadequate quality and training of staff (*Vesti FNPR*, 1–2, 2001, pp. 18–19).

The introduction of a Unified Social Tax in 2001 threatened to result in a substantial reduction in the resources at the disposal of the Social Insurance Fund, while proposed reorganisation of the Fund threatened to undermine the branch basis of its administration which would impede collaboration between the Fund and the branch trade unions.[1] For these reasons FNPR campaigned vigorously against the introduction of the new tax (see above, p. 62) and has pressed regional organisations to negotiate increased funding from the local budget for social and welfare benefits and primary organisations to negotiate increased employer contributions in their collective agreements to compensate for the loss of social insurance funding. The expenditure of the Social Insurance Fund was maintained at the 2000 level through 2001 by running down its reserves, but the cut in the budget for 2002 was expected to lead to a two-thirds cut in the provision of holiday vouchers (Report to FNPR Executive, 25.09.01).

The financing of children's vacations is often a principal point of contention between the trade unions, often supported by the employers, and the regional administration. For example, in 1999 the Perm' regional administration sought to reduce its commitment to finance children's summer holidays from 270 000 places agreed the previous year to 250 000. The trade unions insisted on the provision of 315 000 places, which was supported by the employers, but after lengthy and heated negotiations the administration only agreed to retain the previous year's allocation, which the unions and employers accepted as a minimum figure. In Moscow City negotiations are much easier, because Mayor Luzhkov takes great pride in his care for the city's children. The Moscow Federation of Trade Unions still operates 350 children's camps which provide vacations for 400 000 children every year.

The regional trade union organisations organise trade union celebrations, particularly the May Day demonstrations, and in some regions the distribution of new

---

[1]   The Social Insurance Fund collected dues from employers amounting to 5.4 per cent of the payroll. FNPR had successfully warded off attempts to reduce the rate to four per cent before the introduction of the ESN, in which the feared reduction was achieved through the back door. A cut in the budget of the Insurance Fund would hit 'mass-cultural' work disproportionately because benefits such as pensions and sick pay have a prior claim on the funds.

year presents to children and presentations to veterans on Victory Day, while the branch unions organise the celebration of the annual holidays in honour of their respective professions, but much other mass-cultural work, such as the organisation of sporting and cultural events, has disappeared unless the unions can get financial support from commercial sponsors or the regional administration. Finally, the regional trade union organisation often still has responsibility for maintaining the waiting list for public housing and allocating newly available housing units in those regions in which municipal housing construction continues or has been resumed.

## Organisation and recruitment

Despite the sharp decline in membership over the 1990s, the trade unions do almost nothing in the sphere of organisation and recruitment, expecting that the benefits of trade union membership will be self-evident to employers and employees if the unions continue to perform their basic functions. The absence of trade unions in the new private sector is accepted more or less as a fact of life. The regional federations regard organisation and recruitment as being the responsibility of the branch unions, but the branch unions claim to have their hands full servicing the existing membership and don't consider it worth the effort to try to establish small branches.[1] The vast majority of new trade union organisations represent the re-establishment of defunct branches rather than the creation of branches in new private enterprises. In Sverdlovsk, for example, large and medium enterprises account for almost 80 per cent of total employment, the remainder working in 25 900 small enterprises, of which only 850 have trade union organisations. The regional officials claimed that new branches were being established, but nobody could cite a single example. An officer of the Ul'yanovsk construction union explained why they don't bother with small organisations:

> They have got their projects – and they work. If there is no project – everyone disperses and the business is closed. Well, what do we want them for? Such an organisation just gives us endless trouble that we don't need, it will bring us 10 roubles a month and we will have to make an effort for them.

The unions responsible for the branches which are dominated by the new private sector, such as retail trade and services, are among the weakest of the unions, including some like the 'Union of Workers in Co-Operatives and Enterprises of Other Forms of Ownership' or the 'Union of Small and Medium Businesses' whose

---

[1]   There are exceptions to the rule. The obkom of the Perm' health workers' union makes a point of its work with primary groups and sometimes sends teams out into the region to re-establish defunct organisations and set up city and district committees. The energetic President spends much of his time on the road, making 70 trips to primary groups in 1998 and 126 in 1999.

regional organisations are often little more than empty shells for those pursuing their own personal or commercial aims.

Occasionally a group of disgruntled workers will arrive at a regional trade union office to inquire about setting up a trade union organisation. However, it is very difficult to establish a trade union organisation in the face of opposition from the employer, who can easily intimidate or (illegally) dismiss those attempting to establish the trade union. Those setting up the union are therefore advised to do so in secret in the first instance, and not to try to recruit managers to membership. Once the primary organisation has been established, a regional official will inform the director that he or she has a trade union and demand the rights provided by the law, of premises and facilities and the negotiation of a collective agreement. In foreign-owned enterprises the regional trade union organisation may call on the support of the International Trade Secretariat to which the relevant branch union is affiliated, but even with international support it can prove difficult to make headway, particularly in notoriously anti-union companies. In the Coca Cola plant in Yekaterinburg, a new union branch was soon destroyed by management intimidation, despite strong support from IUF (Petrova, 2000). In the well-publicised case of Macdonalds in Moscow, which was also supported by IUF, the union managed to establish a toehold, despite strong management repression, and won a court case over recognition, but the management refused to conclude a collective agreement despite the intervention of the State Duma – and despite the fact that the Moscow government has the controlling interest in the company (Vesti FNPR, 1–2, 2001, pp. 56–60). In the case of Neste, a Finnish-owned chain of filling stations in Leningrad region, a trade union organisation was eventually established on the initiative of the workers after the Russian union, with the support of ICEM, appealed to the Finnish trade union federation, which got a lot of publicity for the case in Finland, resulting in the replacement of the director of the Russian subsidiary by one more favourable to the trade union (ISITO St Petersburg branch, 2000). After a short honeymoon period, a new director, who could see no place for a trade union, arrived and the union was once more engaged in a struggle for survival (*Solidarnost'*, 25, July 2001, p. 1).

The establishment of new primary organisations is as likely to be on the initiative of the employer, who requires a partner to handle social problems and with whom to negotiate a collective agreement, as it is on the initiative of a disgruntled workforce, and the organisational efforts of the trade unions are primarily directed at employers to persuade them of the usefulness of having a trade union, rather than trying to mobilise the employees. The normal procedure would be for an officer of the obkom and the enterprise director together to identify a candidate to be president of the union and for the director to organise a meeting of the labour collective at which the trade union branch would be established and the nominee elected president. The greatest hopes are pinned on persuading the regional administration to press employers to negotiate collective agreements, and so establish union branches.

The need to strengthen their efforts in organisation and recruitment and to change the expectations of the membership is widely recognised. As a primary group president expressed it at the conference of the Leningrad health workers:

Work in this direction has been insignificant. I do not remember any measure devoted to the most acute problem – trade union membership. The present trade-union consciousness is a heritage of the previous socialist period. Present membership in the trade union is, in the overwhelming majority of cases, either due to the socialist tradition, or to a feeling of collectivism ('I will do the same as everyone else'). Membership of a trade union is not a conscious act. It is necessary to get rid of the former mercantile-consumer approach to membership. The trade union is growing old, the former motivation of membership is disappearing (material assistance, holiday vouchers, etc.), and at present we have little to offer in its place. We need new methods of management, new ideas and, certainly, new young people – bearers of these ideas and conceptions.

The trade unions have become increasingly aware of the problem of their ageing membership and the need to bring young people into the trade unions. Andrei Isaev, the chief ideologist of FNPR, has argued that the problem is at least in part one of the unions' failure to propagate an ideology appropriate to their new status which can appeal to the idealism of young people, believing that such an ideology can be found in the commitment to 'economic democracy' made by FNPR at its IIIrd Congress in 1996 (*Vesti FNPR*, 3–4, 1999, pp. 68–70). Organising young people and drawing them into trade union work has become a major priority of FNPR. Following a series of conferences sponsored by FNPR, GMPR, ICFTU and various ITSs, a network of young Russian trade unionists was established in December 2000.

# 8

# Trade Unions and Industrial Relations in the Enterprise

The particular character of enterprise trade unionism, the 'labour collective' and enterprise paternalism in the soviet system was not just a matter of state policy or management strategy but was deeply embedded in the structure of social relations of the enterprise. This is why the reforms of perestroika, the disintegration of the soviet system and the collapse of the Party-state did not lead to any rapid or fundamental change in the role and functions of the trade union within the enterprise.[1] The 'transition to a market economy' and mass privatisation transformed the environment in which enterprises had to function, but similarly did not lead to any immediate or rapid changes in the internal organisation of enterprises and organisations. Adaptation to the limits of the market or budgetary funding was achieved primarily by the reduction of wages and employment, curtailing investment and spending on maintenance and health and safety, the disposal of enterprise social assets and increasingly by unpaid leave, short-time working and the non-payment of wages, rather than by any radical changes in technology or the organisation of production. The characteristic soviet forms of industrial relations persisted, but deteriorating living and working conditions provided new sources of conflict and a new challenge to the trade unions. In this chapter we will outline these changes before looking in more detail at the character and practice of trade unions at the enterprise level.

## Privatisation, the enterprise director and the labour collective

The disintegration of the administrative-command system made the transition to a market economy and the 'corporatisation', if not the 'privatisation', of state property inevitable (Clarke, 1992a). The first wave of privatisation took place between 1989 and 1991 through the formation of co-operatives and leasehold enterprises which were then transformed into closed joint-stock companies, owned by their employees. These enterprises retained their traditional management structures, with the shareholders' annual meeting at first being merely the meeting of the labour collective under another name, and the shareholders' council little different from the STK. The traditional administrative methods of controlling such decision-making bodies were supplemented now by plural voting, corresponding to the number of shares owned and proxies held by senior management.

---

[1] For detailed case study research into changes in shop floor organisation in Russian enterprises see Clarke, 1995; Clarke, 1996a; Clarke, 1996b; Clarke, 1996c.

The bulk of privatisation took place between 1992 and 1995, with the majority of large and medium enterprises choosing to privatise according to the 'second option', in which a controlling 51 per cent of shares were sold to the labour force at a heavily discounted price, the minority choosing the 'first option' in which non-voting shares were allocated to the labour force without charge. In both cases the unallocated shares were subsequently sold at auction. The effect, in both cases, was that at least in the first instance the control of the enterprise remained in the hands of the existing management, although to retain that control management had to ensure that it controlled the voting at the annual shareholders' meeting. The process of concentration of share ownership and the accumulation of outside holdings proceeded quite rapidly, but the majority of enterprises remained under management control with employees often enjoying significant voting rights (Clarke and Kabalina, 1995).

Outside owners took control of enterprises either by purchasing devalued shares or by buying shares, usually at knock-down prices, by tender or auction. Most outside owners were financial institutions or holding companies which had no interest in intervening directly in management, but only in subjecting the enterprise management to rigid financial constraints, their profits usually deriving from their control of supplies and sales through their own commercial subsidiaries. Towards the end of the nineties, the bankruptcy procedure enabled creditors to nominate a temporary director of an enterprise in administration, enabling them to enjoy the benefits of control without the perils of ownership.

Even where enterprises came under the control of outside owners, it was important for management to retain the support of the labour collective. This was primarily because the rights of private ownership were not regarded as being unconditional, while capitalist forms of corporate governance were not well-developed. The legitimacy of private ownership was conditional on the owners fulfilling the traditional obligations of the enterprise director, the legitimacy of managerial prerogatives being regarded as conditional on management being seen to do its best to provide good wages, benefits and working conditions. The support of the labour collective was particularly important where ownership was contested, one or another faction often mobilising the labour collective and appealing to political authorities in its support. Thus, privatisation in itself did not radically change the internal social structure and social relations of the post-soviet enterprise. The collapse of the Russian economy was much more significant than changes in ownership in determining the development of industrial relations and the role of the trade union.

## Globalisation and the collapse of the Russian economy

The purpose of the radical reforms introduced in 1992 was to secure the rapid integration of Russia into the world economy by liberalising prices and allowing them to reach world levels as rapidly as possible. Price liberalisation and fiscal and financial stabilisation would supposedly provide a favourable environment for a rapid structural adjustment of the Russian economy as domestic and foreign investment flowed into the branches of production which had been held back by the dominance of military production and heavy industry and by Russia's economic and technical isolation from the rest of the world: the extraction and processing of Russia's abundant fuels and natural resources, the production of processed foods, clothing and consumer durables, agriculture and the service sector.

The integration of Russia into the global economy indeed had a dramatic impact, but not in the direction intended by the radical reformers. Military industry, as expected, collapsed, and heavy industry declined by around half during the 1990s, but industries which were supposed to flourish in the free domestic market – food processing, light industry and the production of consumer durables – collapsed as much or more, with food processing down by almost half, consumer durables down by about three-quarters and textiles, shoes and clothing down by over 80 per cent between 1990 and 1995, with the decline accelerating again in 1996 as these industries were hit by foreign competition which became steadily stiffer as the exchange rate hardened (all data in this section is derived from Goskomstat, 2000b unless otherwise stated). Although domestic production and employment recovered somewhat with the devaluation following the August 1998 crisis and the big rise in oil prices, it was not expected that the recovery would be sustained for long.

The extraction and processing of fuel and mineral resources for export fared better. However, increasing exports were not achieved on the basis of new investment and expanding production, as these branches saw a fall in production of over one-third, with oil production down by a quarter and even the production of natural gas, Russia's principal export, falling. Metallurgy was protected from the decline which afflicted heavy industry as metals, particularly steel and aluminium, were diverted from domestic markets for export, although it saw a fall of over 40 per cent in output between 1990 and 1999. Overall, GDP at constant prices was halved between 1990 and 1998, while both agricultural and industrial production fell by slightly more than half.

The decline of traditional industrial enterprises was supposed to be compensated by the expansion of a new private sector. However, the growth of employment in the new private sector, largely confined to trade and services, by no means made up for a 40 per cent decline in employment in industry and construction during the 1990s and small business growth had ground to a halt by the mid-90s, the increase in employment in new businesses being matched by the decline in established facilities. Even in the largest cities, by the end of the 1990s the new private sector accounted for no more than 20 per cent of employment (Clarke and Kabalina, 1999).

With such substantial surplus capacity and an uncertain future, it is hardly surprising that industrial investment held little appeal for either domestic or foreign investors. Capital investment fell continuously by almost 80 per cent between 1990 and 1998, with only a modest recovery following the August 1998 crisis. Many industries saw no investment at all in technical re-equipment or reconstruction and a substantial proportion of the investment that did take place was piecemeal replacement and repair of individual pieces of plant and machinery. The result is reflected in the ageing of industrial plant. The average age of industrial plant and equipment in the soviet period was about nine years, but by 1999 it had increased to over 18 years, about two-thirds having been installed before the beginning of perestroika. Far from being regenerated by the transition to a market economy, the Russian economy was still capitalising on the deteriorating legacy of the past.

Great hopes were placed in the regenerating powers of foreign investment, which was supposed to introduce not only advanced technology but also capitalist management techniques. However, foreign direct investment between 1994 and 1999 amounted to only $3 billion per annum, against an estimated capital flight of $20–25 billion per annum. In 1999, 23 per cent of foreign investment went into oil and metallurgy, 20 per cent into trade and catering, commerce and finance and 15 per cent into the food processing industry, with only a trivial amount in the remaining industrial branches. Over a quarter of all foreign investment was in Moscow City.

With such low levels of domestic and foreign productive investment there was very little scope for technology transfer or the introduction of new production and management methods as a result of the integration of Russia into the world economy. Even when foreign investors bought Russian companies, this was often the prelude not to productive investment but to using the enterprise as a conduit for the export of raw materials or to simple asset-stripping (OECD, 1996). Where productive investment did take place, expatriate managers might fill the senior positions but in general the foreign owner tried to disrupt the existing organisation of production as little as possible and continued to work with the traditional trade union organisation.

With minimal new investment, the prosperity of an enterprise depended much more on its legacy from the past and its external circumstances than on its ability to marshal its own resources. Prosperous enterprises were primarily those which enjoyed a favourable market situation as a result of a relatively modern capital stock, access to lucrative export markets or monopoly powers endorsed by local authorities or criminal structures. These enterprises were able to pay relatively high wages, retain their social and welfare infrastructure, hire the most skilled and energetic workers and enforce strict labour discipline. Those enterprises in less favourable conditions were unable to increase wages in line with inflation or to maintain their social and welfare infrastructure, so that they could not retain the best workers and suffered from high labour turnover, while they were not able to enforce labour discipline, having to tolerate widespread theft, absenteeism and drunkenness. Management in the more prosperous enterprises could use the levers of wages and social and welfare provision to encourage the growth of productivity and facilitate the reorganisation of production, while management in the less prosperous enterprises could only complain of the 'unmanageability' of the labour force.

While the lack of investment and the limited growth of the new private sector meant that there were no radical changes in the social organisation of production, the same factors did lead to a radical change in the labour market situation and so the individual and collective bargaining power of employees. Unemployment increased to about 12 per cent by the end of the decade, but an equivalent number of people, mostly the young and the old, dropped out of the labour market altogether, while others were put on short-time, laid-off temporarily or worked for months without pay. The uneven impact of the economic crisis meant that there were opportunities for some, while others faced a sharp deterioration in their real wages, wage inequality increasing from Scandinavian to Latin American levels. Those who were able to take advantage of the new opportunities readily changed jobs, so that labour turnover remained high throughout the 1990s, but those who were not competitive in the labour market stayed put, in increasing fear of losing their jobs despite their meagre rewards (Clarke, 1999a). Such a transformation of the labour market situation led to a radical shift in the balance of power between employer and employee, reinforcing the role of informal personal relations between manager and worker in the regulation of the employment relation. Where there were still shortages of skilled labour, those with the appropriate qualifications could bargain individually for good wages and working conditions, but those who did not have such competitive advantages were increasingly dependent on the goodwill of management, whose common response to complaints was 'if you don't like it, you can leave'. Thus individual 'exit' prevailed over collective 'voice' in the response of employees to unacceptable wages and working conditions. This has naturally had an impact on the potential role of trade unions in the transitional economy.

## Primary organisations after the collapse of communism

The primary trade union organisations are caught in a veritable vortex of countervailing expectations. These emanate from their three main interlocutors – the members, higher trade union bodies and management – each of which expects different things from the enterprise trade unions. To add to this confusion, both the members and the higher trade union organisations make demands on the primaries which are themselves contradictory.

As has been seen, after the fall of communism officers at the higher levels of the union movement quickly realised that their survival depended on their defining a new role for themselves. 'Social partnership' provided a framework for their survival at the cost of their dependence on the state, but their aspiration was to develop social partnership on the basis of an 'equality of rights', which could only be achieved if they could establish themselves as unchallenged representatives of a working population pressing its demands through active primary organisations.

Case study research at enterprises has found that officers at this level were also cognisant of the need to change, and many wished the unions to move to defending workers' interests (Ashwin, 1995). But the obstacles in the way of any such transformation were formidable. The demise of the Communist Party – though theoretically leaving the unions free to develop as they saw fit – immediately intensified the enterprise trade unions' dependence on management (Clarke et al., 1993, pp. 93–5). Workers at this point had very little reason to trust the trade unions which, as mentioned above (p. 32), initially sided with management and the political authorities in the struggles which preceded the collapse of communism. Thus, after the expulsion of the Party from the enterprise, the survival of the trade unions essentially depended on the willingness of management to tolerate their existence. This placed trade unions in a very difficult position. The only way to break out of their dependence on management was to secure the support of workers, but to court the workers was a risky enterprise. Given the deep barrier of distrust separating unions and the workers, such 'wooing' was unlikely to result in any rapid conquest. It was, on the other hand, very likely to alienate their only sure source of support: management (Ashwin, 1999, pp. 84–110). Enterprise unions therefore found themselves uncomfortably 'caught between pressurised and no longer predictable managers, and distrustful, disgruntled workers' (ibid., p. 99), with no easy exit in sight. Added to this, the trade unions also had to deal with the demands of their colleagues in the higher echelons of the union movement who realised that the survival of the union movement depended on consolidation of its rather shaky foundations.

The demands of management were at once the most simple and the most inexorable of those the enterprise unions faced. Essentially, managers did not want trouble. They wanted compliant trade unions which would act as mediators when required and would administer the diminishing social infrastructure of the enterprise.[1] What complicated the trade unions' relations with management, however, was that the two sides often appeared to share common interests. For, although the radical reform programme launched by Gaidar in 1992 transformed the external environment in which Russian enterprises and organisations operated, the reforms had no immediate impact on their internal organisation or the ways in which the labour force was managed. In general, directors sought to preserve the internal unity of enterprises in order to withstand external pressures and constraints.[2] As Vladimir Ilyin has argued on the basis of research in the coal, aviation, oil and gas and transport sectors, the 'contradictions between the interests of workers and those of the [enterprise] administration, while they are very significant, nevertheless take second place to the contradiction between the labour collective of the enterprise and the external administrative, and now even market, environment' (Ilyin, 1996, p. 67). It is therefore not surprising that the former official unions often served 'as an instrument of the struggle of labour collectives, headed by the directors, against the destructive policies of the post-Communist government which have, whether deliberately or not, led to

---

[1]    Though some more canny managers realised that distributing benefits could add to their own authority, and that giving this duty to the trade unions was a wasted opportunity to use patronage to further their own (rather than the trade union's) ends (See Ashwin, 1995, pp. 196–7 for an example).

[2]    For case study examples see Clarke et al., 1994 and Ashwin, 1999.

the collapse of production, the de-industrialisation of the country, unemployment and bankruptcy' (Ilyin, 1996, pp. 68–9). This 'one enterprise' approach offered the unions a way in which they could simultaneously serve the workers, who clearly had an interest in the survival of their enterprises, and management, who often relied on unions to press their case with the appropriate outside authorities.

Although such 'one enterprise' unionism served to ensure that some of workers' interests were represented, it did little to draw workers closer to the union. For *within* the enterprise the unions remained at best equivocal champions of workers' interests. Even the most active trade unions tended to hedge their bets (Ashwin, 1999, pp. 84–110), and took care not to mobilise workers against management. Instead, they sought to direct conflict outside the enterprise in the manner described above. Protests conceived within the 'one enterprise' framework were generally short-lived, formal affairs which were not intended to engage workers and certainly failed to do so.

So how have primary organisations retained their members? They have been helped by the somewhat contradictory demands of the workers. When asked in group interviews what trade unions are supposed to do, workers habitually chorus 'defend workers' interests' (Ashwin, 1995, p. 202) and denunciations of the failures of their unions in this regard spring easily to their lips.[1] At the same time, while workers may argue in interviews that defending workers' interests should be a union's primary task, on a day-to-day level they still expect the unions to perform social welfare functions such as providing benefits and financial assistance (Ashwin, 1999, p. 108). Indeed, the remaining benefits to be gleaned from the primary organisations play a crucial role in binding workers to the unions. Alongside this attraction, 'social work' has the great merit for the unions of not involving conflict with management. For this reason, as will be seen, enterprise unions have continued to devote a vast proportion of their resources to this aspect of their work (in terms of both time and money).

There are dangers in this, of course. These social welfare functions came under increasing pressure as the resources at the disposal of the trade union declined and the needs of employees escalated in the deepening economic crisis. A substantial part of the trade unions' own social assets, much of the enterprise social and welfare apparatus and the bulk of the housing stock of enterprises were privatised or transferred to the municipalities, while the removal of social insurance funds from trade unions' control drastically reduced the resources at their disposal. The trade unions' own funds could not keep pace with the escalating demands for material assistance, not only to cover the traditional costs of funerals or family sickness, but also to cover routine expenditures for services, particularly medical services, which had in the past been free, and to provide assistance for those suffering as a result of low pay, unemployment or the non-payment of wages. Nevertheless, it is very difficult for the unions to abandon these functions.

---

[1]   See Ashwin, 1999, pp. 107–8 for examples.

Alongside the pressures from management and members, which have been previously highlighted in the literature, enterprise trade unions also face expectations from the union hierarchy. These have not been considered previously, and formed an important aspect of the research on which this book is based. The higher organisations have several concerns with regard to the enterprise unions, which do not necessarily tend in the same direction. First, they have an interest in ensuring the retention of membership. Theoretically, this should lead them to regard with satisfaction the sterling efforts of their enterprise organisations on the social work front. But, retaining membership is at least partly an instrumental goal: higher organisations such as the obkoms, as has been seen, rely for their existence on members' dues and social work consumes a large proportion of the dues which are retained at enterprise level. The higher union bodies would ideally like to obtain more money from their primary organisations, and social work is a major barrier to the realisation of this dream. Finally, the FNPR's strategy of social partnership depends for its success on the activity of the enterprise unions, something which in turn implies another set of demands.

Embedded in the policy of social partnership are certain assumptions regarding the proper conduct of enterprise trade unions. These are again somewhat contradictory. On the one hand, the end of centralised economic management has increased the potential significance of collective bargaining, a tendency which will be much stronger following the revision of the Labour Code. Social partnership as a policy is in part a recognition of this: it seeks to replace legal regulation with voluntary joint regulation. Thus, the FNPR is attempting to enshrine collective bargaining as the cornerstone of the primary organisations' activity. In its annual resolutions on 'the tasks of trade union organisations for the protection of employees and members of their families', the FNPR Executive regularly stresses the need for its member organisations 'effectively to use the main instrument of struggle for the rights and interests of the workers – the system of collective agreements' (Resolution 3–3 of the FNPR Executive, 26 May 1999, *Vesti FNPR*, 5–6, 1999, p. 17). FNPR President Mikhail Shmakov has pushed this line strongly, FNPR even proclaiming that 'if there is not a collective agreement at an enterprise, then there is not a trade union organisation there either' (Gritsenko, Kadeikina and Makukhina, 1999, p. 505). Such statements recognise the importance of the collective agreement in achieving the unions' strategic aims: certainly, it is the agreement which is most easy to enforce, both in the courts, and through any form of protest. To take one example, the reliance of the FNPR on the bargaining efforts of its primary organisations reveals itself in the area of pay, where the higher level union bodies have encouraged primary trade union organisations in negotiating their collective agreement to realise the policy objectives of raising the level of the minimum wage towards the subsistence minimum, raising average pay in the public sector towards the average in industry, and of increasing the tariff component of wages to reduce managerial discretion in wage determination. Achieving such goals, however, would in many cases necessitate the mobilisation of workers' collective power against employers: hard-pressed employers are not going to grant such concessions out of the goodness of their hearts.

The unions' promotion of social partnership thus requires enterprise unions to develop their capacity for mobilisation and at least be prepared to countenance conflict with employers. But, on the other hand, the education and policy advice of the higher organisations serves to promote the 'law book' form of trade unionism that lies at the heart of FNPR's commitment to 'social partnership', which has the opposite implications. The advice of higher organisations to the primaries regarding how to proceed in cases of conflict is to use legal and bureaucratic methods: they never advise anything other than the most symbolic of protests. Such activity, while it does in some cases secure gains, or, more usually, redress on behalf of workers, does nothing to involve them. It also does nothing to further the sort of organisation required for successful collective bargaining.

The primary organisations are thus caught between opposing pressures. On one side, they face strong pressures from enterprise management, as well as to some extent from their own members and the FNPR itself, to engage in an accommodative form of trade unionism. Managers do not want conflict, union members contrive to reinforce the unions' tie to traditional 'social work', while the FNPR promotes a non-mobilisational, bureaucratic mode of action through its education and advice. On the other side, enterprise unions face pressures to move towards a more mobilisational model of trade unionism. Members claim to want their interests defended against management, while the FNPR needs the enterprise trade unions to give some substance to the policy of social partnership at the sharp end. As noted in chapter 6, higher level agreements often serve to displace regulation to a lower level, by including provisions obliging management and trade unions to insert certain points into their collective agreements. Such blithe mandating of unions and employers to include controversial clauses in their collective agreements serves to disguise the conflict of interests between workers and employers, which is only revealed when the clauses are either not included or not fulfilled. If social partnership is to mean anything, however, enterprise trade unions have to be prepared in the last instance to come into conflict with employers over the negotiation and fulfilment of collective agreements.

How are the enterprise trade unions responding to these conflicting pressures? The following sections consider this question by analysing in more detail the activity of the enterprise trade unions by drawing on case studies and the findings of a number of surveys. These include a survey conducted as part of our research project with ISITO of 1454 presidents of trade union primary organisations in nine Russian regions in May 2001 (referred to as the ISITO survey), a survey conducted by ISITO and funded by the Free Trade Union Institute of 4537 employees of nine enterprises in three regions in May 2001 (referred to as the FTUI survey), a survey of directors, trade union presidents and employees of 40 unionised enterprises which had not concluded collective agreements conducted in 1998 by the Moscow Federation of Trade Unions

(Tatarnikova, 1999: referred to as the MFP survey), and a survey of 246 enterprises in five regions conducted by the Centre for Labour Market Studies of the Institute of Economics of the Russian Academy of Science in January 1995 (Chetvernina et al., 1995: referred to as the CLMS survey). Data from further surveys conducted by the Centre for Labour Market Studies, including the Russian Labour Flexibility Survey (RLFS) conducted in industrial enterprises annually between 1994 and 1997 and in 2000 and a survey of 278 enterprises conducted in 1999, a follow-up to the 1995 survey, will also be referred to.[1]

## Trade union organisation

The trade union organisation in the enterprise comprises the trade union committee, headed by the president, who is elected by a trade union conference. In larger enterprises there will also be trade union committees in the various sub-divisions of the enterprise (Ashwin, 1999 pp. 111–9). Most of the work of the trade union is conducted by the president or within the trade union committee, with the membership having little involvement and little information about what the trade union actually does. Union dues are collected by check-off and it is the president and the union committee who decide how to allocate those dues, reporting back to the annual conference of the trade union. Although members of the trade union committee and representatives of subdivisions are required regularly to report back to and consult with the members in their workplaces, in most cases this is at best a formality, with meetings, if they take place at all, bureaucratically organised and poorly attended. Trade union conferences are also usually under the firm control of management and the trade union apparatus. As is usual in trade unions around the world, the members complain of the bureaucratism of the leadership and the leadership complains of the passivity of the members.

In many enterprises, the trade union is identified almost entirely with the president and even members of the trade union committee play a predominantly passive role. One indicator of the degree of involvement of the trade union committee is the frequency of its meetings (Table 8.1). There is a significant tendency for trade union committees in larger enterprises to meet more often than in smaller enterprises, which is understandable because in the latter the president is more likely to encounter committee members informally in the course of a normal working day. In some small enterprises the trade union committee meets only once a year, but in a substantial majority of enterprises the committee meets at least monthly.

[1]  We are very grateful to the Centre for Labour Market Studies for making this data available to us. The data from the ISITO and FTUI surveys is available through our project website www.warwick.ac.uk/russia/trade.

Table 8.1: Frequency of meetings of the trade union committee. Percentage distribution

| At least | Up to 50 employees | 51 to 100 employees | 101 to 500 employees | 501 to 1000 employees | More than 1000 employees | Total |
|---|---|---|---|---|---|---|
| Once a week | 2.2 | 1.6 | 3.5 | 2.9 | 7.8 | 3.5 |
| Once a month | 50.0 | 64.8 | 66.9 | 76.8 | 81.0 | 67.9 |
| Once a quarter | 34.8 | 24.3 | 23.5 | 18.8 | 11.2 | 22.6 |
| Twice a year | 7.9 | 3.6 | 3.7 | 1.0 | | 3.3 |
| Once a year | 5.1 | 5.7 | 2.5 | 0.5 | | 2.7 |
| Total | 100.0 | 100.0 | 100.0 | 100.0 | 100.0 | 100.0 |

Source: ISITO Survey

In the ISITO survey of trade union presidents we found that only one in five, mostly in larger enterprises, held the post as a full-time position, the remainder having to do their trade union work on top of their regular job (Table 8.2). Although trade union officers are protected by the law, a part-time president is particularly vulnerable to management pressure, but even a full-time president may depend on the management for his or her future career prospects. Smaller enterprises cannot afford to employ a full-time president, but quite often the president does not want to give up his or her regular job for fear of losing pay and professional skills and damaging his or her future career. It is rare for any other members of the trade union committee to hold a full-time trade union position, although some large branches employ full-time deputy presidents and a bookkeeper and in the largest enterprises there will be full-time officers heading the trade union committees in subdivisions of the enterprise. Part-time trade union officers are legally entitled to time away from their jobs on average pay to perform their trade union duties, but this has to be negotiated with management and is sometimes included in the collective agreement.

Table 8.2: Percentage (number) of branches with a full-time president, by size of branch

| | Up to 50 members | 51 to 100 members | 101 to 500 members | 501 to 1000 members | More than 1000 members | Total |
|---|---|---|---|---|---|---|
| per cent | 2 | 1 | 12 | 54 | 87 | 21 |
| N | 303 | 294 | 517 | 165 | 159 | 1438 |

Source: ISITO Survey

The dominance of the president means that the character and background of the president can play a determining role in the activity of the trade union. Trade union presidents are much better educated than the labour force they represent, 96 per cent in the ISITO survey having some post-school education, which is a reflection of the fact that most trade union presidents came to their posts from managerial and professional positions (Table 8.3), reflecting the perception of the trade union president as a member of the management team of the enterprise.[1] Indeed, when it comes to the election of a new trade union president, the candidate will often be nominated in consultation with management and the post is effectively a managerial appointment. Full-time presidents were more likely to have been workers than were part-time presidents, particularly in coal-mining and the timber industry, which accounted for two-thirds of the former workers in the sample (over half the part-time worker-presidents were accounted for by the construction industry). Clearly, those who came from or hold managerial positions are more likely to identify with management, and are more likely to be dependent on the director for their future careers. The managerial origin of trade union presidents also means that the trade union is more deeply embedded in intra-managerial conflicts than it is in conflicts between management and the workforce.

Table 8.3: Occupational status of part-time trade union presidents, and previous occupational status of full-time presidents

| | Part-time current position | Full-time Previous position | Total |
|---|---|---|---|
| Senior administrators and managers | 1 | 3 | 1 |
| Middle and junior managers | 20 | 38 | 24 |
| Professionals, senior specialists | 54 | 33 | 50 |
| Technicians, junior specialists | 21 | 10 | 19 |
| Clerical and administrative staff | 2 | 2 | 2 |
| Skilled manual workers | 2 | 12 | 4 |
| Semi/unskilled manual workers | 0 | 2 | 1 |
| Total | 100 | 100 | 100 |

Source: ISITO Survey

The dependence of trade union presidents on management is reinforced to the extent that they are paid not by the trade union but by the enterprise administration (Table 8.4). The vast majority of full-time presidents were paid out of union dues, although more than a quarter received some payment from the enterprise, while the vast

---

[1]   An unpublished survey of presidents of enterprise trade union committees in the spring of 1993 found that 95 per cent considered themselves to be a part of the management team (personal communication, Yurii Milovidov).

majority of part-time presidents were paid by the enterprise, with over a quarter receiving some payment from trade union funds. Those in larger enterprises were less likely to receive any payment from the administration, suggesting that they are more independent of the latter. Very few trade union presidents received any payment from obkom funds, the vast majority relying on the funds of their own trade union committee.

Table 8.4: Sources of payment of the trade union president

|  | Part-time | Full-time |
| --- | --- | --- |
| Enterprise | 71.1 | 7.1 |
| Trade union committee | 4.4 | 65.8 |
| Enterprise supplemented by trade union committee | 21.9 | 5.1 |
| Enterprise supplemented by obkom | 0.6 | 0.3 |
| Trade union committee supplemented by enterprise | 1.8 | 21.0 |
| Trade union committee supplemented by obkom | 0.2 | 0.7 |

Source: ISITO Survey

The position of trade union president has lost status and nowadays offers limited career prospects. The low status of the position is indicated by the fact that trade union presidents were disproportionately female when compared with the workforce they represent (Table 8.5), while the limited career prospects are indicated by the fact that over a third of presidents were close to or beyond pension age (Table 8.6). The mean age of the presidents in the ISITO sample was 47 and on average they had worked in the same enterprise for the past 18 years. Long experience of work in the enterprise means that the president is likely to know the enterprise well and to have an extensive network of informal connections to mobilise in the course of his or her daily work. On average the presidents had been in post for six years, although over a quarter had been in post since the soviet period.

Table 8.5: Percentage of female trade union presidents, and percentage of women employed in the branch

| Percentage of | Health | Education | Chemicals | Construction | Metallurgy | Coal-mining | Timber |
| --- | --- | --- | --- | --- | --- | --- | --- |
| Female presidents | 83 | 97 | 54 | 66 | 36 | 33 | 59 |
| Women employed in branch | 81 | 80 |  | 24 |  |  | 20 |

Source: ISITO Survey, Goskomstat

Table 8.6: Age distribution of trade union presidents

| Age group | Per cent |
| --- | --- |
| Under 30 | 4 |
| Thirties | 17 |
| Forties | 38 |
| Fifties | 30 |
| Over 60 | 10 |
| Total | 100 |

Source: ISITO Survey

## Trade union facilities

Trade unions are legally entitled to premises and facilities, but they have to claim these facilities from management. The power to provide or deny premises and facilities to the trade union committee gives the director considerable leverage over the trade union, which directors often use in the event of conflict with the committee. Trade unions in large enterprises were much more likely to have premises than those in smaller enterprises (Table 8.8) and they were much the best supplied with office equipment (Table 8.7). Some presidents who did not have their own equipment noted that they were able to use enterprise facilities. Access to a telephone is essential if the trade union committee is to be able to communicate with the regional or national offices of the trade union and a photocopier is essential for the circulation of information within the enterprise.

Table 8.7: Percentage of trade union committees having various kinds of equipment

| | Up to 50 employees | 51 to 100 employees | 101 to 500 employees | 501 to 1000 employees | More than 1000 employees | Total |
| --- | --- | --- | --- | --- | --- | --- |
| Have some equipment | 45 | 46 | 51 | 82 | 98 | 61 |
| Internal telephone | 15 | 18 | 29 | 54 | 77 | 36 |
| City telephone | 34 | 37 | 39 | 68 | 87 | 49 |
| Inter-city telephone | 5 | 10 | 17 | 29 | 66 | 23 |
| Computer | 6 | 9 | 11 | 19 | 53 | 17 |
| Photocopier | 6 | 13 | 9 | 13 | 39 | 14 |
| Fax | 4 | 6 | 7 | 7 | 16 | 8 |
| Automobile | 3 | 2 | 4 | 4 | 21 | 6 |
| Other | 1 | 1 | 3 | 8 | 5 | 3 |

Source: ISITO Survey
Other items mentioned included a typewriter, printer, video-camera, radio, television, piano, tape-recorder, accordion, safe, record-player.

Table 8.8: Percentage of trade union committees provided with premises

| Up to 50 employees | 51 to 100 employees | 101 to 500 employees | 501 to 1000 employees | More than 1000 employees | Total |
|---|---|---|---|---|---|
| 8 | 11 | 25 | 64 | 92 | 36 |

Source: ISITO Survey

## Trade union activities

A good indicator of the priorities of the trade union organisation is its allocation of funds to various activities (Table 8.9).[1] The overwhelming bulk of expenditure, net of salaries, is devoted to the traditional social and welfare activities of the trade union. The total income of the primary organisation (estimated from data on average wages, union membership and the percentage of dues retained by the primary organisation) in the case of a large enterprise, can be substantial: much more than is available to the regional trade union organisation, for example, so it is hardly surprising that large organisations have little need for the services of their regional organisations. The trade union organisations in the largest enterprises were spending on average $7000 per month on salaries, some of which would possibly be for staff of the social and welfare facilities, and $9000 per month on financial assistance to union members. Almost half of the income of primary organisations, net of wage costs, was devoted to providing material assistance to members and over a third was devoted to 'mass-cultural work' (providing vacations; organising celebrations, sporting and cultural events; giving new year presents and so on). Very little was spent on training and informational activity or on obtaining legal advice, for which primary organisations rely heavily on the regional trade union bodies. Almost nothing was devoted to the 'solidarity fund', which serves, among other purposes, as a strike fund.

Providing material assistance and organising mass-cultural work are very time-consuming activities and generally fill the working day of the trade union president and his or her associates. Quite apart from the organisational work involved, there is a constant stream of supplicants coming into the trade union office asking about the availability of vouchers for vacations, particularly for children in the summer, or pleading for financial help to arrange a funeral, purchase medicines, pay for an operation or carry out repairs to their home. Many people turn to the trade union for help with problems quite unrelated to work, for example, marital problems or trouble with the neighbours. This is the traditional work of the trade union, and trade union officers often remark that it is the most satisfying part of their job because they feel

---

[1]   This distribution of expenditure corresponds quite closely to that reported in the consolidated reports of expenditure of primary organisations by regional trade union organisations, except that the latter tend to show a higher level of spending on wages.

that they are able to provide people with real help. It is also the most congenial because it does not involve their having to make any demands of management and so avoids conflict.

Table 8.9: Percentage of trade union budget spent on wages and percentage distribution of budget spending net of wage expenditure by enterprise size

| Enterprise size | Wages of trade union officers | Material assistance | Mass-cultural work | Information | Training | Legal services | Management expenses | Solidarity fund | Other | Mean Income (roubles) |
|---|---|---|---|---|---|---|---|---|---|---|
| < 51 | 3.2 | 47.6 | 47.4 | 0.9 | 0.8 | 0.1 | 1.6 | 0.1 | 0.8 | 20 025 |
| 51 – 100 | 2.2 | 54.6 | 38.1 | 1.0 | 0.5 | 0.0 | 1.5 | 0.1 | 1.9 | 58 404 |
| 101 – 500 | 6.4 | 51.5 | 39.0 | 0.6 | 0.5 | 0.2 | 3.4 | 0.3 | 2.0 | 225 143 |
| 501 – 1000 | 20.9 | 48.6 | 33.4 | 2.0 | 1.5 | 0.6 | 5.9 | 0.6 | 4.9 | 1 034 523 |
| > 1000 | 29.9 | 39.7 | 34.3 | 2.0 | 2.7 | 1.4 | 6.2 | 1.3 | 7.7 | 8 373 666 |
| Total | 10.9 | 49.4 | 38.3 | 1.1 | 1.0 | 0.4 | 3.6 | 0.4 | 3.1 | 1 678 836 |

Source: ISITO Survey

Although many of the social assets formerly owned by enterprises and the trade unions have been privatised or transferred to municipal ownership, many remain. Three-quarters of the largest enterprises (over 1000 employees) in the ISITO survey had some social assets, with about a third each having a sanatorium, a health resort, a tourist base and sports facilities. Only one in five of the smallest enterprises had any social assets, usually a library. About 90 per cent of these assets were owned by the enterprise and only 10 per cent, most often the library, were at least partly owned by the trade union. However, trade union-owned assets are generally the property of the regional federation, not of the primary organisation, and some will also be provided by the municipal and regional administration with places acquired through the social insurance fund or even on a commercial basis, so that facilities are available even in enterprises which do not have any of their own. In this case the trade union president has to negotiate the terms of access to these facilities on behalf of his or her members.

Primary trade union organisations have come under considerable pressure from higher trade union bodies to downplay their social and welfare role in order to defend the wages, employment and working conditions of their employees. To what extent have trade union presidents taken these priorities on board? We asked presidents to rate the importance of a number of activities of the trade union on a scale from one to nine according to their importance, their responses suggesting that both traditional and new functions are, on average, rated of approximately equal importance. There is very little difference in the rating of the first four functions of the trade union: the traditional functions of maintaining social welfare benefits and providing material support and the new functions of preserving jobs and fighting for pay. Representing members in conflict situations rates well down the list, as does the traditional priority of the soviet trade unions of improving the economic indicators of the enterprise. Since most enterprises had very high union density, it is not surprising that few gave priority to attracting new members to the union. There is very little significant correlation between the rating of different items, so trade union leaders do not neatly divided into 'traditional' and 'modern'.

Table 8.10: Rating of importance of various trade union activities

| Activity | per cent who could not say | per cent of all respondents who rated of most importance | Mean Rating |
|---|---|---|---|
| Preservation of the privileges and guarantees of union members | 10 | 25 | 3.3 |
| Struggle for wages | 16 | 23 | 3.4 |
| Support for trade union members | 5 | 22 | 3.2 |
| Preservation of jobs | 15 | 19 | 3.4 |
| Safety and working conditions | 8 | 13 | 3.6 |
| Representing members in labour disputes | 14 | 11 | 4.2 |
| Improving the economic indicators of the enterprise | 27 | 11 | 4.9 |
| Attracting new members | 19 | 6 | 5.7 |
| Other | 96 | 1 | 5.4 |

Source: ISITO Survey. Eighteen percent of respondents did not answer the question at all. Seven percent gave an equal top-rating to two or more activities.

Trade union presidents were asked to nominate up to three difficulties which they faced in their work (Table 8.11). The most frequently cited barriers were the lack of specialist knowledge at the disposal of the trade union and the bad situation of the enterprise. This gives a good indication of the approach of trade union presidents to the defence of their members' interests. On the one hand, they identified with management's pleas that they could not afford to provide acceptable wages, benefits and working conditions for the employees. On the other hand, they regarded a lack of knowledge as the main barrier to their being able to achieve improvements, suggesting that they regarded negotiation as a matter of rational argument and enforcement of the law rather than a trial of strength between opposing forces. This interpretation is supported by the relatively low importance attached to a lack of support from the members and higher trade union bodies as barriers to their work.

Table 8.11: What do you see as the main difficulties for the work of your trade union organisation? (Select up to 3)

|  | Per cent |
|---|---|
| Inadequate knowledge of legal questions | 46.4 |
| Bad financial-economic situation of the enterprise | 42.9 |
| Inadequate knowledge of financial and economic questions | 42.5 |
| Opposition of administration, absence of real levers of influence | 28.4 |
| Lack of protection of trade union leaders from the administration | 25.2 |
| Lack of members' knowledge of their legal rights and means of their defence | 23.8 |
| Poor trade union office equipment | 23.1 |
| Lack of support and trust from ordinary members | 14.1 |
| Absence of necessary support from higher trade union bodies | 8.1 |
| Other (most cited was lack of time) | 3.2 |
| Difficult to answer | 4.0 |

Source: ISITO Survey

## Collective agreements

While most trade union expenditure is devoted to the traditional functions of social and welfare provision for employees, the other trade union priorities, jobs and wages, are served through negotiation with the employer and secured through their incorporation in the collective agreement. Collective agreements still tend to be formal documents drawn up jointly by the trade union committee and the enterprise administration with little overt conflict. Although shops may be asked to submit proposals for inclusion in the collective agreement, and the draft may be circulated for comment, negotiation of the agreement is a bureaucratic process that does not involve any mobilisation of the membership. The director will usually decide unilaterally whether or not to accept trade union proposals and the union will rarely contest the director's decision, although a memorandum of disagreement may be prepared as an appendix to the collective agreement. The FNPR report on the 1999–2000 collective agreement campaign noted that FNPR did not know of a single case in which a primary trade union organisation had taken any kind of action in support of its demands (FNPR, 2001a, p. 12).

FNPR has made the signing of collective agreements, as the cornerstone of the system of social partnership, a major priority and regional trade union organisations are judged by the extent to which they manage to persuade their primary organisations to do so. The preparation and signing of the collective agreement was a well-established ritual in the industrial sector in the soviet period, but in public services it is a more recent innovation. This is the principal explanation for the fact that the number of collective agreements signed each year has increased steadily through the 1990s. According to the Ministry of Labour's figures, 68 800 collective agreements were signed in 1993 and 144 600 in 1999. These figures are substantially lower than those issued by FNPR, a difference that is largely explained by the fact that the majority of collective agreements are signed for a period of two or three years and many are not registered with the Ministry of Labour.[1] According to FNPR, in 1999 a collective agreement was in force in 72 per cent of reporting enterprises, a big increase on the 60 per cent of the previous year. There were substantial regional variations, with Moscow oblast reporting 90 per cent penetration but the Komi Republic only 42 per cent (FNPR, 2001a). These figures relate only to enterprises with a trade union organisation, while trade union penetration of the new private sector is minimal,[2] so this figure considerably overstates the coverage of collective agreements – according to the Ministry of Labour data, only five per cent of all enterprises sign a collective agreement, although these tend to be the largest enterprises. Moreover, according to the Moscow Federation of Trade Unions, only 33 of the 1887 collective agreements signed in Moscow in 1995 were registered with the Moscow government (Tsentr issledovannii rynka truda, 1995). By 1998 the situation had improved somewhat, with 751 of 7719 collective agreements being registered (Tatarnikova, 1999 p. 5). The situation elsewhere is not as bad as in Moscow. In Samara, for example, 2160 of 3426 agreements were registered in 1999–2000.

Most enterprise collective agreements retain the traditional form, detailing management's plans for the next year in the spheres of the development of production, improvements in health and safety, training and upgrading of skills and the provision of social and welfare benefits, usually now with additional sections covering wages and employment, which were formerly the preserve of higher authorities. Although most agreements have been simplified in recent years, removing all of the rhetoric related to the building of socialism, socialist competition and much of the detail concerning changes in the production process, the installation of plant and equipment and so on, the tendency is still to take the previous year's agreement and insert new figures, usually with disclaimers, such as 'within the limits

---

[1]  Trade unionists repeatedly assert that a collective agreement that is not registered has no legal status. This, however, is not true. Registration merely brings the agreement within the framework of monitoring by the Ministry of Labour.

[2]  A Moscow survey in 1994 found that 27 per cent of new private businesses had collective agreements, a figure similar to that found in a survey of private sector service firms in St Petersburg (Tatarnikova, 1995; de Melo and Ofer, 1993), although the collective agreement would not necessarily be with a *bona fide* trade union. Some employees of new private enterprises are enrolled in organisations which call themselves trade unions but which are in fact insurance companies. These are a means of providing tax-exempt bonuses to employees. In a household survey conducted by ISITO in Moscow, Samara, Kemerovo and Syktyvkar in May 1998, 10 per cent of those working in new private enterprises said that their enterprise had a trade union organisation, against 85 per cent in state enterprises, 80 per cent in budget organisations and 75 per cent in privatised enterprises. In the 1999 CLMS survey, six per cent of private sector employers said that they had a trade union organisation, against 70 per cent of privatised and 83 per cent of state enterprises, although 12 per cent of private employers said that they had a collective agreement, half of which must be with non-union bodies.

of financial possibilities', to cover contingencies. The high degree of uncertainty and delays in the preparation of the General and branch tariff agreements has meant that collective agreements have tended to be signed later than in the past: whereas in the past the agreement for the following year would normally be signed by November, in many cases nowadays agreements are not signed until well into the following year. As one enterprise director was quoted as saying, 'Everything changes so fast, including the state minimum wage. I cannot sign concrete obligations in the collective agreement since I do not know in advance how the shops are going to work, what they are going to buy and for what prices, on the basis of which I can calculate my sales' (Kabalina and Monousova, 1995, p. 24). The formalism of the negotiation of the collective agreement is also indicated by the fact that the proportion being renewed, rather than renegotiated, each year has steadily increased.

In the ISITO survey of trade union presidents we asked a number of questions about collective bargaining and the collective agreement. Almost all large enterprises had a collective agreement and large enterprises were more likely than small enterprises to register their collective agreements (Table 8.12). The RLFS surveys from 1994 to 2000 similarly found that in their sample virtually every enterprise employing over 1000 people, but only about half those employing fewer than 100, had a collective agreement.

Table 8.12: Percentage of enterprises with a collective agreement and percentage of agreements which are registered by enterprise size

| Percentage | Up to 50 employees | 51 to 100 employees | 101 to 500 employees | 501 to 1000 employees | More than 1000 employees | Total |
|---|---|---|---|---|---|---|
| With an agreement | 77 | 83 | 82 | 90 | 98 | 85 |
| Of agreements registered | 61 | 73 | 80 | 89 | 91 | 80 |

Source: ISITO Survey

### Failure to conclude a collective agreement

Despite the pressure to conclude an agreement, 15 per cent of trade union presidents in the ISITO survey reported that they had not concluded a collective agreement. These respondents were asked why they had not concluded an agreement (Table 8.13). About a third regarded it as unnecessary, the majority of whom had complete confidence in their administration, but a quarter did not conclude a collective agreement because the administration refused to negotiate or the two sides were unable to agree, despite the fact that according to the law the administration is obliged to negotiate and to conclude an agreement if the trade union proposes to do so.

Table 8.13: Why is there no collective agreement in your enterprise? (Only one response allowed)

|  | Frequency | Per cent |
|---|---|---|
| It is not necessary because the administration does all it can for the employees | 55 | 26 |
| We were unable to agree a number of points with the administration | 29 | 14 |
| There was not enough knowledge and experience to draw one up | 28 | 13 |
| The administration refused to negotiate | 24 | 11 |
| A collective agreement is not important – it is a formality | 21 | 10 |
| There was no time to do it | 12 | 6 |
| Other reasons* | 40 | 19 |
| Total | 209 | 100 |

*The most common other reasons cited for failing to have a collective agreement were that the negotiations were protracted, it was a new trade union organisation or that the enterprise was going through a change of ownership.
Source: ISITO Survey

Just over half the directors of the enterprises in the MFP survey of enterprises with no agreement had a more or less negative attitude to signing collective agreements, 18 per cent being convinced opponents. Almost half the trade union presidents thought a collective agreement necessary, but more than a quarter thought that their enterprise did not need one at all. Those in privatised and private enterprises were more convinced of the need for a collective agreement. Only 28 per cent of trade union presidents had given official notification of their desire to enter negotiations while 31 per cent had raised the matter informally but had not insisted when the director did not support the idea and 41 per cent had never even suggested entering into negotiations.

The main reasons given by enterprise directors for the failure to sign an agreement were the financial situation of the enterprise, which made it impossible to undertake realisable commitments (46 per cent), doubts about the possibilities of such an agreement (39 per cent), the inertia of the trade union committee (15 per cent) and indifference of the employees (10 per cent). The main reasons given by trade union presidents for the failure to sign an agreement were doubts about the possibilities of such an agreement (53 per cent), the financial situation of the enterprise (33 per cent), unwillingness of the employer (23 per cent), the inertia of the trade union committee (23 per cent) and the absence of any proposal from outside (8 per cent). Doubts about the possibility of reaching agreement were explained alternatively by a strictly authoritarian management (characteristic of 18 per cent of the enterprises), which would not tolerate any independence on the part of the trade union, or traditional soviet relations of clientalism (characteristic of 64 per cent of the enterprises) in which the trade union president and director see their interests as identical in caring for the labour collective and combating external destabilising factors. In the former case, the director will not tolerate any intrusion on his (rarely her) authority, in the latter the director and trade union president see no need for a collective agreement, preferring to resolve problems informally on a day-to-day basis, so they either do not sign a collective agreement or, if they do, regard it as a pure formality.

Failure to sign a collective agreement in either case is the result of the abrogation by the trade union president of his or her responsibility to represent the interests of the employees. Both directors and trade union presidents in the MFP survey thought that the employees were happy with this situation. Around half the directors and trade union presidents thought that the majority of employees did not fully understand the significance of a collective agreement and 21 per cent of directors and 13 per cent of presidents thought that the employees had no interest in concluding a collective agreement. However, almost two-thirds of employees said that they thought a collective agreement was necessary, 18 per cent doubted that a collective agreement would change anything for the better, only 10 per cent thought it was not necessary and seven per cent did not know what it was. The enterprises without a collective agreement were marked by a relatively vulnerable labour force, with a predominance of female and older workers, whose fear for their jobs prevented them from actively pressing their views, and relatively low trade union membership, almost half the enterprises having a union density of less than 50 per cent, the decline being explained by a lack of confidence in the union among the employees. These enterprises also paid relatively low wages, which tended not to have been increased to compensate for inflation.

Although there was no collective agreement in these enterprises, almost two-thirds of directors said that they consulted with the trade union president over questions of pay, but only in 10 per cent of enterprises could anyone recall a case in which the trade union's opinion had prevailed. Almost a third of the enterprises had declared redundancies, but there was no consultation with the trade union over employment matters in almost half the enterprises and in 80 per cent of enterprises neither the director nor the trade union president could remember a single case of disagreement over employment issues in the past two or three years. In four of the nine enterprises in which there had been temporary lay-offs the employees had not been paid or had been paid less than the minimum prescribed by the Labour Code. Many of the enterprises did not provide the benefits prescribed by law for those working in dangerous or unhealthy conditions and provision of other social and welfare benefits had declined, although in 35 of the 40 enterprises the trade union president declared that there was a common understanding with management over social questions.

The survey found that neither enterprise directors nor trade union presidents had an adequate knowledge of their legal rights and obligations. More than three-quarters of the directors had either never heard of the Moscow City Law on Social Partnership or knew no more than the fact that it existed. Only one in five trade union presidents knew the basic elements of the Law, while 65 per cent had heard of it but knew nothing of its contents. Half the employers and almost half the trade union presidents did not know the provisions of their branch tariff agreement and over a third of employers and a quarter of trade union presidents did not know the provisions of the Moscow City Tripartite Agreement. Directors also had little contact with employers' associations: only a quarter of directors were members of any such organisation, while the majority had had no contact of any kind with any employers' organisation and three-quarters had no opinion when asked about the degree of authority of the Moscow Confederation of Industrialists and Entrepreneurs.

In the absence of a collective agreement, the most important reference points for resolving labour questions were the Labour Code, management instructions and the enterprise's own regulations, which were given about equal weight by both directors and trade union presidents, although in most enterprises the rules were interpreted flexibly. The terms of individual labour contracts had rather less and branch and regional tariff agreements and the Moscow Tripartite Agreement had much less significance. The significance of the Labour Code did not mean that enterprises adhered to its provisions, the researchers finding widespread violations, and the absence of a collective agreement did not mean that the terms and conditions of labour were defined in the employees' individual contracts: only 59 per cent of enterprises gave employees written contracts at all, although this has been a legal requirement since 1992, and most contracts did not include any detailed provisions regarding the terms and conditions of labour.[1]

The data overwhelmingly supports the conclusion that those enterprises which do not sign collective agreements are not those in which management shows a spontaneous concern for the well-being of their employees, but those with a vulnerable labour force and inferior wages and working conditions, in which the trade union president is unable or unwilling to press the claims of the employees against management. This conclusion is supported by analysis of the data of the ISITO survey of 4000 households in four cities undertaken in April and May 1998, which showed that wages in unionised establishments without a collective agreement were significantly lower than wages in unionised establishments which did have a collective agreement. Likewise, employees in unionised establishments without a collective agreement were significantly less likely to have a formal job definition and less likely to be paid for overtime working than those working in unionised establishments with a collective agreement.

## Negotiation of the collective agreement

Trade union presidents are provided with reams of documentation and advice to help them in negotiating their collective agreement. FNPR provides training materials and

---

[1]   It was estimated in 1995 that one-third of employees in small enterprises did not have a contract of employment (IEPPP, 1995). The ISITO household survey in May 1998 found that one-third of those working in individual or family businesses, and eight per cent of those in incorporated new private businesses, were employed illegally on a verbal agreement (Clarke, 1999c).

prepares general guidelines each year, while the branch unions prepare materials specific to their branch, which is supplemented by the regional Federations and obkoms. The obkoms also provide training sessions and, at least in theory, are available to give advice to presidents in the negotiation of the agreement. Nevertheless, trade union presidents say that they lack many of the skills and much of the knowledge required to engage in serious negotiations with their management counterparts. More significant than a lack of knowledge and skills, however, is the dependence of the trade union on management. As noted above, an authoritarian director will not tolerate any interference from the trade union, while a paternalistic director regards the trade union as the branch of the enterprise administration responsible for social and welfare questions, subject to the authority of the director, the trade union president sometimes also holding the relevant managerial position.

The 1995 CLMS survey found that the more the branch or regional trade union provided assistance, the more work was done on the collective agreement. The majority of trade union leaders could get assistance from the branch or regional trade union but 30 per cent of trade union leaders knew nothing about the content of their branch tariff agreement and 20 per cent only knew some general items, despite the fact that this was supposed to provide the framework for their negotiations. Seventeen per cent of collective agreements in industry and over one-third in state administration and in the budget sector were concluded without any discussion between management and the trade union at all. In two-thirds of cases the trade union considered that the administration provided full information required to draw up the agreement, but management gave no information in 10 per cent of state enterprises, 23 per cent of open joint-stock companies, 39 per cent of closed joint-stock companies, 55 per cent of co-operatives and two-thirds of private enterprises. Without information, which the employer is legally obliged to provide, it is impossible for the trade union to negotiate effectively, and yet the authors reported that they did not know of a single case in which the trade union had taken management to court over this. The union presidents also considered that they had people fully competent to conduct the negotiations, which is not surprising since the majority of union officials are drawn from management, two-thirds of them in this sample having higher education. The main area of bargaining was wages, followed by social questions and then labour protection, with employment only being an object of negotiation in a quarter of industrial enterprises (although the question of redundancy was included in 80 per cent of collective agreements), one in eight transport enterprises and less than six per cent in other branches. Where disagreements between union and management remained, these would be put to a vote of a general meeting and the union's position would usually prevail, but only because management does not take the agreement any more seriously than does the trade union (Chetvernina and et al., 1995). In a Ministry of Labour survey of 300 enterprises in 1993, one-third of the workers thought that a collective agreement did them no good at all, the majority believing that it served the interests of management more than those of the employees (*Profsoyuznoe obozrenie*, 9, 1994).

The clear impression from this research confirms the conclusion of case study research in enterprises, that the negotiation of the collective agreement is a formal bureaucratic process. In the best of cases a draft will be circulated through the enterprise to collect comments and suggestions, some of which may then be incorporated into the agreement, and there may be some discussion of the agreement at a general meeting, but it is very rare for there to be real conflict between trade union and management in the course of negotiations. The 1995 CLMS survey found that two-thirds of trade union presidents and the same number of enterprise directors thought that it was normal for the managers to be a member of the same trade union as this helps to avoid conflict (Chetvernina and et al., 1995). In the 1999 CLMS survey more than 80 per cent of trade union presidents thought that it was expedient for employees and the administration to belong to the same trade union.

Traditionally the draft of the collective agreement would be drawn up by a commission made up of management and trade union representatives participating on the basis of their professional skills and experience, rather than on any adversarial basis. In the ISITO survey of trade union presidents, in most enterprises the draft of the collective agreement was still prepared jointly by the trade union and the administration.

Table 8.14: Who prepared the draft of the current collective agreement?

|  | N | Per cent |
|---|---|---|
| Trade union | 244 | 20 |
| Administration | 20 | 2 |
| Trade union and administration together | 938 | 77 |
| Trade union and administration each produced a draft | 19 | 2 |
| Total | 1 221 | 100 |

Source: ISITO Survey

The negotiation of the collective agreement is a more conflictual process in large enterprises, but conflicts are usually resolved by compromise, with the trade union view rarely prevailing (Table 8.15).

The 1999 CLMS survey asked trade union presidents which items of the collective agreement had been the most difficult to settle. Not surprisingly, wage increases and wage arrears were the most contentious issues, although one in six presidents reported that there had been no conflicts (Table 8.16).

Table 8.15: How would you characterise relations with the administration in the process of preparation and adoption of the collective agreement?

| Percentage | Up to 50 employees | 51 to 100 employees | 101 to 500 employees | 501 to 1000 employees | More than 1000 employees | Total |
|---|---|---|---|---|---|---|
| Virtually no disputes or conflicts | 41 | 31 | 30 | 21 | 12 | 27 |
| Disputes usually settled in favour of the administration | 10 | 9 | 8 | 6 | 5 | 7 |
| Disputes resolved by compromise | 41 | 49 | 52 | 63 | 71 | 55 |
| Disputes usually settled in favour of the trade union | 2 | 6 | 2 | 3 | 3 | 3 |
| Some issues were unresolved | 6 | 5 | 8 | 8 | 11 | 8 |
| | 100 | 100 | 100 | 100 | 100 | 100 |

Source: ISITO Survey

Table 8.16: Points of the collective agreement giving rise to the most discussion in negotiations

| Collective agreement points | Percentage |
|---|---|
| Wage arrears | 34.6 |
| Wage increase | 37.2 |
| Social sphere provisions | 26.8 |
| No disputes | 19.5 |
| Work safety and conditions | 17.2 |
| Employment | 3.6 |
| Benefits | 2.7 |

Source: Centre for Labour Market Studies Survey, 1999

## Content of the collective agreement

Various surveys of the content of collective agreements have found that even the better agreements usually do little more than restate the provisions of operative labour legislation and the branch tariff agreement. At worst, collective agreements are confused and include provisions that are, illegally, inferior to those provided by the law and higher agreements. A substantial proportion of collective agreements are not registered with the Ministry of Labour. A survey of collective agreements registered with the Labour Department in Moscow in 1998, conducted by the Moscow Federation of Trade Unions, found that only half the collective agreements even identified the parties to the agreement correctly as the employer and employees, others referring to the administration, director, labour collective, STK or trade union as one or the other party. Quite a few collective agreements provided for the payment of wages only once a month, rather than fortnightly as required by the Labour Code. Many provided benefits inferior to those prescribed by tariff agreements or by the law for those working in harmful conditions, inferior payment in the event of stoppages and a shorter period of notice of redundancy than that laid down by the law. Some agreements defined only a maximum rate of benefits, with no guarantee of their payment, while many qualified provision by phrases such as 'if the funds are available', 'depending on financial possibilities' or 'if there are savings on the wages fund'. It should not be surprising that the majority of collective agreements made no provision for the indexation of wages, even though this is included in most branch tariff agreements, nor did they implement the recommendations of the Moscow City Tripartite Agreement to take steps to bring the minimum wage closer to the subsistence minimum. The majority of collective agreements included a no-strike clause in relation to the terms of the agreement, but some included a blanket abrogation of the right to strike under any circumstances (Tatarnikova, 1999).

The Russian Labour Flexibility Survey has asked about the points included in the collective agreements of industrial enterprises each year (Table 8.17). There do not appear to be any substantial changes over time. Most collective agreements in the survey contain some reference to wages, and over half make some provision for wage indexation, although this point is often qualified by reference to the ability of the enterprise to pay. This data suggests that collective agreements are quite comprehensive, but it does not give any indication of the content of the points, many of which are likely to be purely formal provisions. Since the format of the collective agreement is generally defined by tradition and the law, the exclusion of particular items is likely to be a deliberate choice of management. In the 1995 CLMS survey, trade union leaders defended the exclusion of reference to pay on the grounds of realism, since management would decide what to pay in any case. Many collective agreements tied pay scales to a multiple (typically three times) of the derisory state legal minimum wage as the scale minimum, leaving management the discretion to pay above this rate, and many which included an obligation to raise wages taking into account inflation, qualified this by reference to the financial possibilities of the enterprise (Chetvernina and et al., 1995). Only just over a third of trade union presidents in the 1995 CLMS survey and 43 per cent in 1999 considered that the collective agreement guaranteed the basic socio-economic interests of their members.

A survey of collective agreements in coal-mining enterprises in 1995 conducted by the miners' union found that many collective agreements included points in violation of the Labour Code, included contradictory provisions and did not incorporate the terms of the branch tariff agreement, or simply incorporated them in an idiotic way, for example where the tariff agreement provided for a range of alternatives to be made concrete in the collective agreement, the latter merely transcribed the list of alternatives (Sokova, 1996 pp. 233–52).

Table 8.17: Points included in collective agreements in industrial enterprises, 1994–2000

| Percentage of agreements including each point | 1994 | 1995 | 1996 | 1997 | 2000 |
|---|---|---|---|---|---|
| Basic rates, wages | 94.8 | 93.2 | 86.5 | 90.3 | 87.3 |
| Wage indexation | - | 56.8 | 53.4 | 45.8 | 63.4 |
| Bonuses | 87.0 | 81.1 | 82.4 | 76.4 | 80.3 |
| Benefits | 97.4 | 94.6 | 89.2 | 91.7 | 91.5 |
| Working time | 93.5 | 95.9 | 97.3 | 93.1 | 94.4 |
| Dismissal | 79.2 | 82.4 | 83.8 | 91.7 | 84.5 |
| Job transfers | 58.4 | 45.9 | 51.4 | 58.3 | 42.3 |
| Career development | 41.6 | 33.8 | 24.3 | 20.8 | 16.9 |
| Output norms | 66.2 | 63.5 | 58.1 | 66.7 | 45.1 |
| Redundancy | 59.7 | 52.7 | 59.5 | 66.7 | 57.7 |
| Health and safety | * | 100 | 100 | 98.6 | 98.6 |
| Social insurance | * | 79.7 | 75.7 | 70.8 | 76.1 |
| Training | * | 71.6 | 73.0 | 80.6 | 84.5 |
| Resolution of labour disputes | * | 83.8 | 81.1 | 87.5 | 84.5 |
| N | 384 | 472 | 493 | 186 | 308 |

*Not included in questionnaire
Source: Russian Labour Flexibility Survey

The officer responsible for collective agreements in the Leningrad and St Petersburg Federation of Trade Unions reported in an interview in 2001 that the quality of collective agreements in the region had been improving, with more of them taking into account the regional and branch tariff agreements, though few made use of the Federation's guidelines on intra-firm payment systems and many were still grossly inadequate. In one case, the collective agreement still included the holiday entitlement which had been the legal minimum until it was increased in 1992. Many collective agreements made no provision for indexation and some illegally worsened conditions in comparison to the law and relevant agreements, for example several specified the monthly payment of wages, reduced the payment for night work, set the minimum wage at the legal minimum (below that in the tariff agreement), underpaid for work stoppages, violated the legal restrictions on transfer to other work and the legal terms of redundancy.

The responsible officer in Sverdlovsk reported that their review of collective agreements found little use made of the regional tripartite agreement. In 1999 only one-third of the collective agreements included reference to the indexation of unpaid wages, even though this was provided for by a regional law. The survey of collective agreements signed in 2000 found the usual violations of labour legislation regarding such matters as the regularity of payment and inadequate payment for stoppages and administrative leave. In Tomsk, some collective agreements give the employer the right to cut wages in the event of financial difficulties (*Vesti FNPR*, 1–2, 2001, p. 48).

FNPR's review of 1999 collective agreements concluded that a growing number of collective agreements based themselves on branch tariff and regional agreements and were becoming more concrete in their content, particularly in relation to pay, health and safety, employment, training, retraining and social guarantees and included a range of benefits above those provided by the law, particularly in relation to financial assistance, retirement benefits, benefits for the birth of children, subsidised vacations and additional days of vacation and additional rights and benefits for those made redundant. But the review also noted that many collective agreements still did not provide for increasing wages in the face of inflation or for the indexation of wage debts, nor define penalties for the non-payment of wages, did not define rates of pay and conditions for overtime and short-time working and did not provide any restrictions on redundancies or administrative leave. Many collective agreements did not include the provisions on pay laid down by the relevant branch tariff agreement and only one in ten collective agreements included the pay scales of the enterprise. An increasing proportion of collective agreements were merely being extended rather than renegotiated and amended each year. Overall, collective agreements continue to be dominated by the traditional social and welfare provisions of the soviet period, with only a limited adaptation to the new conditions of a market economy in which the trade union represents the interests of employees as sellers of labour power to the employer. Indeed, some collective agreements continued the soviet practice of committing the employees to observing labour discipline, increasing labour productivity and working for the realisation of the production plans of the enterprise (FNPR, 2001a).

The weakness of collective agreements is not only a result of the inexperience and ignorance of trade union presidents, many of whom have been in post for a long time and have had extensive training. It is more fundamentally a result of the close collaboration between the trade union and the enterprise administration, so that the trade union president moderates his or her demands in accordance with the priorities of the enterprise administration. A symptomatic example of this relationship concerns the issue of the additional holiday entitlement for employees of the health service. Health workers were granted twelve days annual holiday in 1974, in addition to the basic legal entitlement of 12–18 days. In 1991 the Law on Social Guarantees defined the national minimum holiday as 24 days, but the Ministry of Labour ruled in 1993 that additional holidays continued to be based on the previous norm of 12–18 days, so that those formerly benefiting had effectively lost their previous privilege. This interpretation was endorsed by the Ministry of Health and the State Labour Inspectorate. However, a court in Yamalo-Nenetsk ruled in 1994 that the health workers were entitled to the additional 12 days on top of the minimum 24 days holiday, a ruling confirmed by the Supreme Court in 1996. Although in a few regions the regional administration agreed to implement the ruling, elsewhere employers have consistently refused to recognise the health workers' right to additional holidays, pleading an inability to pay, and this plea is generally met 'with understanding' by trade union presidents, who continue to sign away their members' rights in collective agreements. Recently, increasing pressure from the members has forced a growing number of employers to include the additional holiday entitlement in the collective agreement, often following a successful application to court by individual employees.

FNPR has recommended trade union committees to include the provisions of the old Labour Code in their collective agreements so that the terms of the Labour Code would remain in force even when the Code is amended. This is by no means an innovation, since studies of collective agreements over the years have repeatedly found that agreements have (hitherto redundantly), included provisions of the Labour Code. In the ISITO survey only five per cent of trade union presidents said that they did not include provisions of the Labour Code in the collective agreement and 55 per cent reported that their collective agreement included some provision for health and safety or working conditions superior to those already laid down by the Labour Code (Table 8.18), but one in six found it difficult to say whether they included provisions of the Labour Code, suggesting that they did not know what those provisions were.

Only 30 per cent of collective agreements in the ISITO survey included any provision for an increase in wage scales. The largest enterprises, those in metallurgy and those in Moscow City were significantly more likely to provide for a wage increase, and public sector organisations, where wage scales are set by the government, significantly less. Just over half of these collective agreements included some provision for the indexation of pay, as did a further 19 per cent of collective agreements which did not provide for any increase in pay scales, but still the majority of collective agreements made no reference to pay at all. Around half the collective agreements in coal-mining, chemicals and construction made no provision for wage indexation, despite the fact that the tariff agreements in these branches provide for quarterly wage indexation, suggesting that these employers did not intend to implement the tariff agreement.

In view of the painful history of the non-payment of wages it is notable that 86 per cent of collective agreements followed FNPR recommendations and included provision for the regular payment of wages. This is important because although the Labour Code lays down that wages should be paid twice a month, unless the item is included in the collective agreement the non-payment of wages cannot give rise to a collective labour dispute and, ultimately, to strike action to secure the payment of wages (the new Labour Code allows workers to refuse to work if they have not been paid for fifteen days – hitherto they have had to write individual declarations to the director to this effect). This clause was more likely to be included in the collective agreement of larger enterprises, but it was much less likely to be included in the agreements of educational establishments, despite the fact that the non-payment of wages has been most acute in the education sector and the educational workers' trade union has placed great emphasis on conducting disputes in accordance with the law. We can only presume that this is a result of the reluctance of the employers to make a commitment which they were still not confident that they could fulfil.

Only 11 per cent of collective agreements included provision for the indexation of unpaid wages, now provided for by the new Labour Code, with no significant differences according to the size of the enterprise. This is an important provision in the context of continuing inflation and wage debts that can extend back over years. It is striking that only eight per cent of chemical enterprises included such a provision, since the branch tariff agreement specifies that in the event of wage delays workers should be compensated according to terms to be defined in the collective agreement.

Eleven per cent of collective agreements set some limit to the percentage of the labour force which could be made compulsorily redundant, and a third of collective agreements prescribed benefits to be paid to those made redundant over and above those due under the law.

Collective agreements provided a wide range of welfare benefits, and foreign-owned enterprises were the most likely to make such provision, suggesting that welfare benefits are not just a feature of more conservative management but respond to the expectations of Russian employees within limits set by the economic situation of the enterprise, foreign-owned enterprises being the most prosperous. Almost half the collective agreements included provision for benefits and subsidies for vacations for employees and members of their families. Such provisions were more common in larger enterprises and most common in outsider-controlled and especially in foreign-owned enterprises, 10 of the 11 in the sample including them in their collective agreements. Almost as many, 44 per cent of collective agreements, provided subsidised medicines and 31 per cent of collective agreements provided subsidised transport, which might take the form of a works bus taking people to work or provision of employees with subsidised or free passes on public transport. This was again much more likely to be provided by foreign-owned enterprises (nine of the 11 in the sample). Twenty-one per cent of collective agreements provided subsidised food, which might take the form of subsidised canteen meals or subsidies for purchases of food in a company store. Again this was more common in large enterprises and in privatised, and especially foreign-owned enterprises. Eighteen per cent of collective agreements included provision for subsidised housing. In the past all large enterprises built their own housing which was allocated free to their own employees. Now very few enterprises are able to continue to build houses, but many still run their own hostels, which might be subsidised, and some provide subsidised loans to employees to enable them to buy their own apartments. Large enterprises were more likely to include some such provision in their collective agreements while foreign-owned enterprises were the most likely to provide housing subsidies, though the difference is not sufficient to be statistically significant. Seven per cent of presidents reported that their collective agreements included other benefits, most of which involved financial assistance for people such as pensioners, for funerals or for women on maternity leave or the provision of additional holidays.

Overall, according to the testimony of enterprise trade union presidents, this survey presents a more encouraging picture of the progress of collective agreements than previous research, suggesting that FNPR's impression that collective agreements have been improving is correct. Nevertheless, a collective agreement is not worth the paper it is written on if there are no effective means of enforcing its provisions.

Table 8.18: Percentage of collective agreements including the following provisions

|  | Per cent |
| --- | --- |
| Wage scale superior to that determined by the branch tariff agreement | 30.1 |
| Wage indexation | 34.7 |
| Regularity of payment of wages | 86.3 |
| Indexation of wage debts | 11.2 |
| Percentage of workers who can be subject to redundancy | 10.9 |
| Benefits to those made redundant additional to those in the Labour Code | 32.5 |
| Benefits and subsidies for vacations for employees and their families | 46.9 |
| Additional benefits and subsidies for the purchase of medicines | 44.3 |
| Benefits and subsidies for transport | 31.4 |
| Benefits and subsidies for foodstuffs | 20.7 |
| Provision of free or subsidised housing | 17.7 |
| Provisions for safety and working conditions superior to those in the Labour Code | 55.2 |

Source: ISITO Survey

## Fulfilment and enforcement of the collective agreement

The 1995 CLMS survey found that most directors did not take the collective agreement seriously – some did not even know whether they had one or not, a few who did have one thought they did not. Over a quarter of employees in enterprises with a collective agreement did not know that it existed, 40 per cent where the agreement was for more than one year. Thirteen per cent of employees in enterprises that did not have an agreement said that it did. Employees in industry and transport, the more educated and those in enterprises with alternative trade unions, where there is more likely to be conflict, were better informed.

Outside the state administration and social services fewer than a third of trade union leaders believed that the collective agreement was fully observed, over a half that it was partly observed, while over one-fifth in industry noted that there were a lot of violations of the agreement.[1] Moreover, in none of the closed joint-stock companies and only a third of the open joint-stock companies was the agreement reported to have been fully observed. The Labour Code was reported to have been systematically violated in 22 per cent and sometimes violated in 28 per cent of the closed joint-stock companies, with violations reported in a total of 51 per cent of open

---

[1]   In a Ministry of Labour survey of 9720 employees in June 1995, only two per cent of respondents reported that their collective agreement had been completely fulfilled (cited Hoffer, 1997, p. 50).

joint-stock companies and 46 per cent of state enterprises. However, this appeared to be a substantial overestimate of the degree of observance of the agreement.

Table 8.19: Points of the collective agreement most frequently violated

| Collective agreement points | Percentage |
| --- | --- |
| Wage arrears | 59.3 |
| Wage increase | 24.2 |
| Work safety and conditions | 21.4 |
| No violation | 19.5 |
| Benefits | 10.7 |
| Employment | 4.2 |
| Social sphere provisions | 2.1 |

Source: Centre for Labour Market Studies Survey, 1999, 113 enterprises with collective agreements

When directors were asked to specify which items were not observed, over 80 per cent in industry and construction noted that the items relating to wage payments and indexing had not been observed, 20 per cent that items related to working conditions had not been observed and 40 per cent in industry and 20 per cent in construction that items related to social benefits had not been observed. Trade union presidents were asked how they dealt with violations of the agreement. Over 80 per cent of violations were dealt with 'within the framework of social partnership', by discussions within the trade union committee, a meeting of the labour collective (18 per cent) or negotiation within the enterprise (54 per cent). In 17 per cent of cases the trade union did nothing at all about the violation (in four per cent it could see no point because management would take no notice), but in 10 per cent of cases in industry and 20 per cent in transport it claimed that it took more drastic measures, including taking the case to court (4 per cent of cases overall), picketing the enterprise or strike threats. (Chetvernina and et al., 1995). In the 1999 CLMS survey, in 96 per cent of cases trade union presidents reported that they had dealt with violation of the collective agreement through negotiation with the administration, 17 per cent had taken the issue to court, 15 per cent each to the State Labour Inspectorate and the branch trade union organisation and four per cent had responded with a strike. The 1999 survey again showed that the points on wages were much the most likely to be violated (Table 8.19), and this seems to be generally the case: in the RLFS for 1997 only two of the 22 enterprises which reported that they were committed to the indexation of wages under the collective agreement had in fact done so.

These findings correspond closely with our own experience and with the findings of the 2001 ISITO survey of trade union presidents. On more than one occasion, when visiting the trade union offices of an enterprise, nobody has been able to find a copy of the collective agreement and in one case one of us was given the president's personal copy when it was eventually found in the bottom of a drawer. In one hospital the trade union president confessed to a researcher that she had signed an agreement prepared by the chief doctor but did not know what it contained as she had not read it. All of the labour collective and trade union meetings to report on the fulfilment of the collective agreement that we have attended, including meetings in coal mines and large industrial enterprises which have alternative trade unions, have had the same format: representatives of management departments read in a monotone a detailed bureaucratic report on the fulfilment of the various terms of the agreement, sometimes specify areas in which the agreement has not been fulfilled and provide an explanation for this failure, usually related to the shortage of funds or the failure of a particular section to do its work properly. The chair of the meeting, usually the trade union president but sometimes the enterprise director, calls for comments from the floor. Most comments will relate to relatively minor items: the failure to repaint part of the premises, to repair a kindergarten, to install adequate ventilation, which may have been outstanding for years. Some may relate to the central issue of wages, which can lead to heated arguments on the floor as different sections press their own claims. The director and/or trade union president may promise to see to these matters, or to include them again in the agreement for the following year, and the chair of the meeting will declare it closed.

Almost half the trade union presidents reported in the ISITO survey that the agreement had been fulfilled in full by the employer, and only a handful, particularly in small enterprises and in coal-mining and construction, reported that it had hardly been fulfilled at all (Table 8.20). Of course, it is not difficult to fulfil an agreement if most of its substantive obligations are hedged with reservations, such as being conditional on the availability of funds. Thus, as reported by Chetvernina, when a collective agreement is 99 per cent fulfilled, the issues unfulfilled are almost certainly the crucial ones.

Table 8.20: Percentage reporting that the collective agreement had been fulfilled

|  | Frequency | Per cent |
|---|---|---|
| Fully | 604 | 49 |
| Partly | 607 | 49 |
| Not at all | 19 | 2 |
| Total | 1 230 | 100 |

Source: ISITO Survey

The presidents who said that their agreement had not been fulfilled in full were asked what they did about management's failure (Table 8.21). The findings are very similar to those reported by the CLMS surveys, with only one in twelve trade union organisations undertaking any active steps to secure the fulfilment of the collective agreement, such action being more common in coal-mining and metallurgy and not occurring in any of the foreign-controlled enterprises. Appeal to higher authorities (courts or higher trade union bodies) was more likely in larger enterprises and in coal-mining, while the union was more likely to do nothing in smaller enterprises. Those enterprises with a history of wage delays were more than three times as likely as those without to have turned to the courts or engaged in protest actions. It is noteworthy that primary trade union organisations are much more likely to appeal to outside bodies, which might influence the director through bureaucratic channels, than they are to mobilise their own members in protest.

Table 8.21: What did the trade union do as a consequence of management's failure to observe the collective agreement? Percentage undertaking each action

|  | With wage delays | Without wage delays |
| --- | --- | --- |
| Conducted negotiations with the administration | 80.5 | 82.1 |
| Appealed for support to higher trade union bodies | 30.3 | 19.4 |
| Appealed to the court | 15.3 | 4.8 |
| Conducted collective protest actions | 13.2 | 3.9 |
| Did nothing, because of the difficult financial situation of the enterprise | 8.7 | 11.8 |
| Did nothing since it is pointless to struggle with our administration. | 4.5 | 3.3 |
| N | 287 | 330 |

Source: ISITO Survey

## Relations with the administration

We have already noted the personal dependence of the trade union president on the enterprise director and of the trade union on the administration for facilities and resources. In the soviet period the nomination of a candidate for the post of trade union president would usually be agreed between the Party secretary and the enterprise director, and it is still usual for the director to play a role in the nomination of the trade union president, often in consultation with the regional trade union organisation. It is very rare, except in situations of endemic conflict, for a trade union president to be elected against the wishes of the enterprise director.

In the vast majority of enterprises and organisations senior managers, right up to the director, remain members of the trade union, and so eligible to attend trade union meetings and serve as trade union officers or delegates to trade union conferences: according to the RLFS data in 1997, the administration belonged to the trade union in 72 per cent of surveyed enterprises and in a further 23 per cent part of the administration belonged to the trade union. It is not uncommon for enterprise directors to be elected as delegates to the regional and national conferences of the branch trade unions and they sometimes serve on elected union bodies, particularly in the public sector.

We have seen that in the negotiation of the collective agreement relations between the trade union and the enterprise administration tend to be harmonious and collaborative, even when the administration does not fulfil the terms of the collective agreement. The MFP survey of enterprises with no collective agreement found very close relations between the director and trade union president in the majority of enterprises. Fifty-one per cent of directors met the trade union president every day, in 76 per cent of cases representatives of the administration participated in trade union committee meetings and in 59 per cent of cases the trade union president participated in management meetings. Only three per cent of directors and 13 per cent of trade union presidents reported any kind of difficulty in their mutual relations and two-thirds declared that they were engaged in constant collaboration based on complete mutual understanding. Just over a third of trade union presidents participated in collegial management bodies and a further 10 per cent did so on the basis of their professional post, but 20 per cent of directors said that they never consulted the union president. About half the presidents said that they were kept fully informed but 17.5 per cent of presidents said that they did not have access to the information they needed (Tatarnikova, 1999).

In the ISITO survey, trade union presidents were asked to assess their relations with the management of the enterprise. Relations were characterised as being significantly more conflictual in privatised enterprises under outsider and especially under foreign control. They were more conflictual in coal, metallurgy and construction than in other branches. There is no significant relationship between the age, length of service in the enterprise or length of office of the trade union president and the degree of conflict in relations with the administration, but relations were significantly more conflictual where the president was paid from trade union funds than where the president was paid by the enterprise, and trade union presidents who were or had been skilled workers were much more likely to describe relations as more or less conflictual, and those who were or had been managers more likely to describe relations as collaborative. Relations were more conflictual in enterprises with experience of wage delays, although even where the employees were still owed back wages, two-thirds of presidents described their relations as amicable or collaborative, and almost half so described their relationship even where current wages were not being paid (Table 8.22).

Table 8.22: How would you assess your relations as trade union leader with the management of the enterprise?

| Percentage distribution | With wage delays | Without wage delays |
| --- | --- | --- |
| Collaborative | 48.8 | 62.7 |
| Some conflicts but basically collaborative | 37.5 | 26.3 |
| Amicable | 4.4 | 2.2 |
| Conflictual | 2.9 | 4.0 |
| No relationship | 6.4 | 4.8 |
| N | 344 | 1093 |

Source: ISITO Survey

Trade union presidents were asked how much influence they had over the employer in a number of spheres (Table 8.23). Overall, presidents in larger enterprises considered that they had more influence than in smaller enterprises, otherwise there were few significant differences between branches, regions or by property form. Trade union presidents thought that they had much less influence on the level and regularity of pay than they had in their traditional spheres of activity of working conditions and the provision of social and welfare benefits, but a third of the presidents felt that they did not even influence the resolution of social welfare questions. We can conclude that close collaborative relations between the trade union president and management do not guarantee that the trade union will have a substantial influence on the living and working conditions of its members. Nevertheless, the pay-off from collaboration is suggested by the fact that presidents who characterised their relations as more or less conflictual were significantly less likely to have influence in the traditional areas of social welfare and working conditions while they were no more likely to have influence in relation to the level or payment of wages.

Table 8.23: Can your trade union organisation exert real influence on the resolution of the following problems in the enterprise in present conditions?

| Percentage distribution | Size of Enterprise | | | Total |
| --- | --- | --- | --- | --- |
| | Up to 100 employees | 101 to 1000 employees | More than 1000 employees | |
| *The trade union influences the level of wages* | | | | |
| Yes | 8.6 | 9.9 | 27.1 | 12.1 |
| On the whole, yes | 15.8 | 15.8 | 35.4 | 18.8 |
| On the whole, no | 22.2 | 27.2 | 26.6 | 25.6 |
| No | 53.5 | 47.1 | 10.9 | 43.5 |
| *The trade union influences the regularity of wage payment* | | | | |
| Yes | 10.7 | 21.6 | 42.0 | 21.5 |
| On the whole, yes | 20.5 | 22.2 | 35.4 | 23.7 |
| On the whole, no | 21.4 | 23.6 | 16.6 | 21.9 |
| No | 47.4 | 32.5 | 6.1 | 32.8 |
| *The trade union influences the payment of benefits* | | | | |
| Yes | 21.1 | 27.2 | 46.7 | 28.4 |
| On the whole, yes | 39.2 | 38.9 | 39.7 | 39.1 |
| On the whole, no | 13.2 | 15.7 | 10.3 | 14.2 |
| No | 26.5 | 18.2 | 3.3 | 18.4 |
| *The trade union influences working conditions* | | | | |
| Yes | 23.8 | 28.4 | 37.8 | 28.5 |
| On the whole, yes | 40.4 | 47.5 | 50.8 | 45.9 |
| On the whole, no | 21.9 | 16.3 | 9.3 | 16.9 |
| No | 13.9 | 7.9 | 2.1 | 8.8 |
| *The trade union influences redundancies and transfers* | | | | |
| Yes | 27.9 | 28.3 | 42.1 | 30.3 |
| On the whole, yes | 33.3 | 39.7 | 44.8 | 38.6 |
| On the whole, no | 19.7 | 18.6 | 10.9 | 17.7 |
| No | 19.1 | 13.4 | 2.2 | 13.3 |
| *The trade union influences the provision of special clothing* | | | | |
| Yes | 21.8 | 29.0 | 41.5 | 29.1 |
| On the whole, yes | 30.7 | 41.5 | 44.6 | 39.0 |
| On the whole, no | 17.2 | 17.5 | 10.4 | 16.2 |
| No | 30.4 | 12.0 | 3.6 | 15.7 |
| *The trade union influences social welfare questions* | | | | |
| Yes | 26.9 | 29.7 | 34.8 | 29.7 |
| On the whole, yes | 35.3 | 37.1 | 49.0 | 38.4 |
| On the whole, no | 17.9 | 19.9 | 13.6 | 18.4 |
| No | 19.8 | 13.3 | 2.5 | 13.5 |

Source: ISITO Survey

## Relations with members

Surveys have generally shown that the population as a whole has little confidence in trade unions, although they have usually rated them higher than politicians or private businessmen. There is a difference between the evaluation of trade unions as political actors and the evaluation of the activity of the trade union in the workplace. Nevertheless, a 1998 survey found that 58 per cent of union members did not trust their union officers to look after their interests at their place of work (Rose, 1998).

The ability of the trade union to represent the interests of its members depends on the communication between the leaders and the members and the identification of the members with their leadership. In the ISITO survey, trade union presidents were asked how often they met members in their workplaces (Table 8.24). They were much more likely to meet their members daily in small enterprises, and full-time presidents were less likely to meet members than those who combined their trade union post with their regular job. Nevertheless, there was quite a high level of interaction between the union president and the membership.

Table 8.24: How often do you meet with members in their workplaces

| Percentage Distribution | Up to 50 employees | 51 to 100 employees | 101 to 500 employees | 501 to 1000 employees | More than 1000 employees | Total |
|---|---|---|---|---|---|---|
| Every day | 91 | 83 | 75 | 61 | 47 | 72 |
| Several times a week | 5 | 10 | 13 | 23 | 24 | 14 |
| Several times a month | 2 | 4 | 9 | 13 | 25 | 10 |
| Less often | 2 | 3 | 3 | 3 | 4 | 3 |

Source: ISITO Survey

Presidents were also asked how often members turned to them concerning a number of issues (Table 8.25). Members were significantly more likely to turn to the union in larger than in smaller enterprises. The most common issues on which members turned to the union were social and welfare questions, wages and benefits. They were less likely to turn to the union on issues of working conditions, dismissal and special clothing, all issues which are more likely to face only particular categories of employee. In the CLMS survey more than twice as many people turned to the union with questions about social benefits than with questions about pay (Chetvernina, Smirnov and Dunaeva, 1995).

Although members consulted the trade union quite often about one issue or another in around half the enterprises, surveys consistently show that employees are much more likely to turn in the first instance to their managers than to their trade union when they face problems. In the 1995 CLMS survey, 41 per cent of employees saw their defender as the director and administration, 16 per cent themselves, 13 per cent the union and 13 per cent nobody. Union leaders were three times as likely as employees to see themselves as defenders of the interests of the employees, but just as many saw the director or administration as the employees' defender, nine per cent the worker him or herself and four per cent nobody. Directors saw the defensive role of the union as negligible. Almost two-thirds of employees and almost half of the enterprise trade union leaders thought the influence of the trade union in defending

Table 8.25: How often do members turn to the union on various issues?

| Percentage | Up to 50 employees | 51 to 100 employees | 101 to 500 employees | 501 to 1000 employees | More than 1000 employees | Total |
|---|---|---|---|---|---|---|
| **Wages** | | | | | | |
| Very often | 19 | 10 | 11 | 17 | 24 | 15 |
| Quite often | 28 | 22 | 25 | 31 | 37 | 28 |
| Not often | 27 | 39 | 40 | 39 | 29 | 36 |
| Hardly ever | 26 | 28 | 24 | 12 | 10 | 21 |
| **Benefits** | | | | | | |
| Very often | 3 | 9 | 7 | 10 | 13 | 8 |
| Quite often | 20 | 27 | 32 | 36 | 41 | 31 |
| Not often | 47 | 42 | 42 | 41 | 38 | 42 |
| Hardly ever | 29 | 22 | 19 | 14 | 8 | 19 |
| **Working conditions** | | | | | | |
| Very often | 3 | 4 | 4 | 2 | 6 | 4 |
| Quite often | 18 | 16 | 20 | 33 | 23 | 21 |
| Not often | 43 | 46 | 47 | 50 | 58 | 48 |
| Hardly ever | 35 | 34 | 29 | 16 | 12 | 26 |
| **Dismissal** | | | | | | |
| Very often | 2 | 1 | 1 | 3 | 1 | 1 |
| Quite often | 7 | 6 | 8 | 10 | 13 | 8 |
| Not often | 28 | 35 | 33 | 47 | 66 | 40 |
| Hardly ever | 64 | 58 | 58 | 41 | 20 | 51 |
| **Special clothing** | | | | | | |
| Very often | 2 | 2 | 7 | 7 | 11 | 6 |
| Quite often | 8 | 11 | 17 | 29 | 31 | 19 |
| Not often | 22 | 33 | 32 | 37 | 40 | 33 |
| Hardly ever | 68 | 55 | 44 | 28 | 19 | 42 |
| **Social welfare** | | | | | | |
| Very often | 10 | 8 | 13 | 21 | 19 | 14 |
| Quite often | 26 | 32 | 32 | 39 | 52 | 35 |
| Not often | 45 | 46 | 39 | 33 | 26 | 38 |
| Hardly ever | 19 | 14 | 16 | 7 | 3 | 13 |

Source: ISITO Survey

employees was insignificant, only a third of employees thinking that the union could ever fight for their interests. Over one-third of the employees saw the trade union as an aid to management in resolving production problems and strengthening labour discipline, one-third saw it as a means of defence against the administration and half of those questioned saw distribution as the most important function of the trade union (Chetvernina, Smirnov and Dunaeva, 1995). The 1999 CLMS survey produced rather similar results (Table 8.26), with more employees than in 1995 believing that they defend themselves or that nobody defends them. No employees had any confidence in the protective value of a labour contract, which is very significant in the light of the government's emphasis in the reform of the Labour Code, which put all the weight on the labour contract. Only 11 per cent of employees in unionised enterprises would turn to the trade union for help, almost four times as many turning to the employer (Table 8.27).

Table 8.26: Who defends the interests of employees?

| Percentage of each category | Enterprises without a trade union | | Enterprises with a trade union | | |
|---|---|---|---|---|---|
| | Employees | Employers | Employees | Employers | Union leaders |
| Director, administration | 43.9 | 66.0 | 34.7 | 62.4 | 26.7 |
| Trade union | - | - | 11.2 | 16.8 | 49.3 |
| Shareholders' meeting | 2.5 | 4.7 | 1.0 | 0.8 | 4.2 |
| STK | 0.5 | 0.0 | 0.1 | 0.0 | 0.0 |
| Micro-collective | 3.4 | 4.7 | 4.0 | 0.0 | 2.3 |
| Informal leaders | 0.9 | 2.8 | 0.5 | 0.0 | 0.8 |
| They defend themselves | 27.0 | 7.5 | 24.9 | 5.6 | 12.2 |
| Nobody defends them | 21.5 | 4.9 | 23.6 | 3.2 | 4.6 |
| Labour contract | 0.0 | 9.4 | 0.0 | 11.2 | 0.0 |

Source: Centre for Labour Market Studies Survey, 1999

Table 8.27: Where do employees turn for help in enterprises with and without trade unions?

| | Enterprises with a union | Enterprises without a union |
|---|---|---|
| To the employer | 40.4 | 49.5 |
| To the trade union | 11.2 | – |
| To the court | 7.9 | 5.1 |
| Nowhere | 34.8 | 39.4 |

Source: Centre for Labour Market Studies Survey, 1999

In the MFP survey of unionised enterprises without collective agreements, 80 per cent of directors and union presidents said that workers turned in the first instance to management and only in the second instance to the trade unions. Eighty per cent of workers said that they would turn to management if they had a problem, one-third said they would turn to the trade union committee, nine per cent to the court and four per cent to someone else (most often a lawyer but also including the President and 'bandits') and 14 per cent said that they would keep quiet so that things wouldn't get worse. The more senior and better-educated employees were more likely to turn to the enterprise director, rather than their immediate manager, or appeal to the court. The youngest and oldest employees were less likely to turn to the trade union, women, the young and the old more likely to keep quiet (Tatarnikova, 1999).

In the same survey, the majority of directors and trade union presidents thought that the trade union committee had the unconditional confidence and support of the employees, while only about one in five thought that people had little trust in the trade union, despite the fact that almost half the trade union branches in this survey had lost at least half their members, the main reasons given by those leaving the union being a lack of confidence in the union and in its ability to achieve anything.[1] Most trade union presidents thought that their trade union activity was adequate only in resolving urgent social problems and in organising mass-cultural and sporting activities, while only one in ten regarded their activity as very high in relation to the defence of employees' interests. They explained their inactivity in terms of the shortage of time, while 47.5 per cent said that they found it difficult to work because of the weak support of the members.

Directors and trade union presidents had a very similar perception of the work of the trade union committee, one in ten regarding it as excellent, around half as good, one-third as satisfactory and fewer than one in ten as bad. The employees, however, had a much less positive evaluation of the work of the trade union, almost a third regarding it as good but almost as many assessing it as weak. Their assessment of the president was similar, one-third believing that the president had authority in the collective and had influence over the director; one-fifth that the president knew how to stand up for the interests of the employees; one-fifth believing that the president did not want to enter into conflict with the employer and conducted a conciliatory policy; while one-fifth did not know anything about the activity of the president; seven per cent didn't know who the president was and four per cent thought that the president did not know how to (did not want to, was afraid to) defend workers (Tatarnikova, 1999).

In the 2001 FTUI survey of employees of nine enterprises, three-quarters of respondents did not know to which trade union federation their union was affiliated

---

[1]   A survey by the trade unions' scientific centre of Moscow metallurgical enterprises in 1993 found that one-third of those who had left their union had done so because they felt it did nothing for them, one-quarter because they were dissatisfied with the union's position on the transition to a market economy, one-quarter because they had not received help from a particular trade union body and one-fifth because they thought that the union was under the thumb of the administration (Krest'yaninov, 1995, p. 104).

and only two per cent knew the name of their national trade union president, although just over half the respondents knew the name of the president of their own enterprise trade union committee.[1] The majority rated their trade union committees reasonably highly, with an average score of 3.3 for the enterprise committee and 3.4 for the shop committee on a five-point scale, although more than two-thirds of members had not turned to the enterprise or shop trade union committee for help in the past year. Around one-third of respondents thought that the trade union could represent their interests and defend their rights, but almost half felt that on the whole it could not do so. Just over one-third thought that the trade union primarily defended the interests of all employees, 18 per cent that it defended the interests of particular groups of workers, 15 per cent that it defended the interests of management and nine per cent that it defended its own interests, with 22 per cent finding it difficult to say. Respondents did not see the weakness of their trade union leaders as the main problem impeding the activity of the trade union: 40 per cent attributed the difficulties to the difficult financial position of the enterprise, around one-third each to the passivity of the members, the absence of any levers of influence over the administration and the weakness of the legal basis of trade union activity and one quarter to the members' lack of knowledge of their legal rights. Around one-fifth cited the absence of support from employees, the conciliatory approach of the trade union committee and the lack of support from higher trade union bodies.

A sizeable minority of respondents said that they had participated in some way in the formulation of the collective agreement. Forty per cent of respondents said that the whole collective had participated in the consideration of the collective agreement, almost one-third said that they had themselves participated in consideration of the agreement and one in ten had made suggestions for the agreement or participated in its drafting. However, such participation is more likely to have involved putting forward particular suggestions than participating in the elaboration of a common negotiating position. Thus, workers did not know much about the agreement as a whole: two-thirds knew only the broad outlines of the collective agreement and more than a quarter did not even know whether or not there was such an agreement. Respondents were reasonably satisfied with the collective agreement, giving it an average rating of 3.5 on a five-point scale. Forty per cent of respondents thought that the collective agreement represented the interests of the whole collective, 19 per cent the interests of the administration, 16 per cent regarded it as a formality which reflected nobody's interests, while almost a quarter found it difficult to give an opinion.

---

[1]  Six of the nine enterprises had an alternative trade union organisation, which are usually more combative, stimulating the traditional union to display more independence and activism. However, there were few substantial differences between those enterprises with and those without an alternative union and, indeed, not many substantial differences between the evaluations of members of traditional and alternative trade unions. The small number of the latter meant that differences were generally not statistically significant.

Trade union members had much more confidence in the union's ability to carry out its traditional social and welfare functions than in its ability to represent their interests as employees. Fewer than one in five respondents believed that their trade union had any influence in increasing the level of pay, just over a third in relation to the regularity of payment, the preservation of jobs and improvement of working conditions, almost half in relation to the observance of the rights of workers made redundant, 43 per cent in relation to the observance of the workers' rights with regard to health and safety, 47 per cent in relation to the realisation of benefits to which they were entitled, 10 per cent in relation to the provision of housing, 60 per cent in relation to securing subsidised vacation vouchers, almost two-thirds in the organisation of mass-cultural work, almost one-third in relation to the resolution of problems of daily life and almost half in relation to the work and vacation regime.

Almost one-third of respondents had thought of leaving the trade union at some time. Half of these said that there would be no negative consequences of leaving the union, one in eight that it would lead to conflict with management and one in six each said that they would lose some material benefits and that they would have less protection. When asked why they were members of the union, around one-third said that they could see no advantage in being a union member, slightly fewer than one-third that they got particular privileges as a result of their membership and about the same number that they got material assistance through the trade union. Fewer than one in ten said that the trade union protected them from dismissal, protected them from managerial arbitrariness or sustained the level of their wages.

Overall, the evidence suggests that the unions continue to be seen by their members predominantly in traditional terms, as the providers of material assistance and social and welfare benefits, rather than as organisations which protect their rights or advance their interests. Most members do not participate in any trade union activities and regard the union as a service-provider, rather than as a membership organisation. Nevertheless, a significant minority do look to the union as the protector of their interests and, although the majority turn to management with their problems, in the event of conflict with management, workers do tend to appeal to the trade union, as we will see below.

## Relations with regional trade union bodies

Trade union presidents tend to look for support to the regional trade union organisations for advice and to resolve problems they cannot deal with themselves, particularly when that might involve conflict with the employer. In case of conflict, they expect the regional trade union organisation to exert pressure on the employer, either directly or by mobilising their connections in the regional administration, and such pressure can prove effective. The MFP survey of enterprises without collective agreements found that 10 per cent of presidents said that they received no support from higher trade union bodies and 37.5 per cent said that they did not get sufficient support.

Table 8.28: Assessment of various activities of the regional branch committee of the union

| Per cent rating the committee | Very bad | Bad | Satisfactory | Good | Excellent | Cannot assess |
|---|---|---|---|---|---|---|
| Training and methodological support | 1 | 5 | 28 | 36 | 10 | 19 |
| Legal advice | 1 | 5 | 24 | 39 | 15 | 17 |
| Negotiations with the administration | 2 | 6 | 20 | 25 | 7 | 40 |
| Help in courts | 2 | 4 | 11 | 15 | 5 | 64 |
| Support of collective protests | 1 | 3 | 15 | 25 | 9 | 47 |
| All-Russian actions | 1 | 4 | 17 | 33 | 11 | 35 |
| Participation in local tripartite commission | 0 | 2 | 16 | 21 | 9 | 51 |
| Help with collective agreement | 1 | 4 | 19 | 31 | 16 | 29 |

Source: ISITO Survey

Table 8.29: Assessment of various activities of the regional trade union federation

| Per cent rating the committee | Very bad | Bad | Satisfactory | Good | Excellent | Cannot assess |
|---|---|---|---|---|---|---|
| Training and methodological support | 2 | 7 | 17 | 18 | 5 | 51 |
| Legal advice | 1 | 4 | 16 | 20 | 6 | 54 |
| Negotiations with the administration | 1 | 4 | 12 | 12 | 3 | 69 |
| Help in courts | 1 | 4 | 8 | 9 | 3 | 75 |
| Support of collective protests | 1 | 2 | 12 | 16 | 6 | 62 |
| All-Russian actions | 1 | 3 | 14 | 19 | 7 | 56 |
| Participation in local tripartite commission | 1 | 3 | 12 | 14 | 5 | 66 |
| Social support of the population | 2 | 6 | 13 | 12 | 3 | 64 |

Source: ISITO Survey

Although in interviews (and at trade union conferences) many primary group presidents are vociferous in their complaints about the inadequacy of the service they receive, particularly if their enterprise is not located in the regional capital, in the ISITO survey of trade union presidents they reported that they were pretty satisfied with the work of their regional trade union organisations, though the relatively large number who said they were not able to assess the performance of the obkom (Table 8.28) and the very large number who could not assess the performance of the regional federation (Table 8.29) suggests that they have little contact with their regional bodies (some respondents did not even know that the regional branch committee and the regional federation were distinct bodies – they are usually located in the same building). Those presidents who said that they had conflictual relations with their enterprise administration gave the obkom and the Federation a significantly lower rating under every heading, but especially regarding negotiations with the administration and help in the courts.

Trade union presidents had very little contact with one another outside regional trade union meetings. Only a quarter of presidents said that they had regular contact with their colleagues, while a further 17 per cent said that they made contact from time to time. This absence of independent interaction between primary group trade union presidents reduces the possibility of their learning from each other. It also makes it much easier for the apparatus to keep control of the regional trade union organisations since it is impossible for the primary group presidents to form a coherent opposition.

## Conflict

According to Russian labour legislation, conflicts over the terms and conditions of employment are defined as individual labour disputes unless they relate to the non-fulfilment of the collective agreement, and the appropriate formal channel for the resolution of such conflicts is the Labour Disputes Commission (KTS), with the right of appeal to the courts. Recourse to a strike in the pursuit of an individual labour dispute is illegal.

The vast majority of conflicts that arise are individual disputes relating to such issues as the miscalculation of wages and bonuses, holiday entitlements and pension rights, which can usually be resolved by informal negotiation with the relevant managers, or illegal transfer or dismissal, which may require the use of more formal channels. However, many issues which affect the labour force as a whole, most particularly delays in the payment of wages or the failure to pay the legally prescribed rates for overtime working, stoppages or administrative leave, are also defined as individual labour disputes if they are not included in the collective agreement. Table 8.30 shows the assessment of trade union leaders of the main reasons for individual and collective labour conflicts in the 1999 CLMS survey. The assessment of employers more or less corresponded to that of trade union leaders, but employees were less likely to refer to low wages as a source of conflict and much more likely to refer to an increased intensity of work without any wage increase. Compared to the 1995 CLMS survey, when respondents were offered fewer options, trade union leaders were much more likely to cite wage arrears as the main source of conflict in 1999 and employees less likely to cite lower wages. Dismissal and redundancy had been a significant cause of conflict in 1995, but had almost ceased to be an issue for employees and the trade union in 1999, although 12 per cent of employers still cited it as a cause of conflict.

Table 8.30: Trade union leaders' assessment of the main reasons for collective and individual labour conflicts

|  | Collective conflicts | Individual conflicts |
| --- | --- | --- |
| Low wages | 33.3 | 28.6 |
| Wage arrears | 39.6 | 21.4 |
| Poor work conditions | 0.0 | 1.8 |
| Change in work schedule | 6.3 | 7.1 |
| Dismissal | 4.2 | 14.3 |
| Transfer to a lower-paid job | 0.0 | 7.2 |
| Increase in the volume of work without wage increase | 2.1 | 8.9 |

Source: Centre for Labour Market Studies Survey, 1999

Conflicts sometimes arise over issues beyond the terms and conditions of labour, particularly in relation to the corruption or incompetence of management, the restructuring of an enterprise or changes of ownership. These issues may have implications for the wages and working conditions of employees, but they often also involve conflicts within management or between management and outside bodies, particularly shareholders or the local authorities, in which the trade union may mobilise the labour force in support of one or another faction. This has been the basis of some of the most militant trade union actions of the late nineties, including armed factory occupations (Burnyshev and Clarke, 2000; Pulaeva and Clarke, 2000).

### Individual labour disputes

In the FTUI survey of employees of nine enterprises, respondents were asked what method was most acceptable in resolving social-labour problems. Just over half said that they would turn to their immediate manager, just over one-third to the trade union committee, one-fifth each to the Labour Disputes Commission and the courts and 11 per cent to influential friends or acquaintances.[1] Respondents were also asked who had helped them with specific problems that had arisen in the previous three years. The majority had appealed to the trade union for help with social welfare issues, only a minority seeking help with other problems. Of those who did seek help from the trade union, around half said that they had received help and half that they had not, with the trade union being rather more helpful with social welfare questions than in such matters as health and safety and working conditions. The majority had turned to the administration for help with all issues, except for the provision of subsidised vacation vouchers, and about half said that they had received help. Around

---

[1]   In an analysis of this data Petr Bizyukov and Sergei Alasheev have shown that people are most likely to turn to that channel of which they have already had a positive experience (Bizyukov and Alasheev, 2001).

20 per cent had turned to influential friends and acquaintances for help, again with a fairly even balance of success and failure.

More than a third of respondents did not know whether there was a Labour Disputes Commission (KTS) in their enterprise. Only four per cent of respondents had appealed to the KTS in the previous three years, three-quarters of them only once, and 87 per cent of the cases which had been completed had been resolved more or less in the respondent's favour. Forty-three per cent of respondents thought that the KTS could defend the labour rights of people like themselves, one-third did not and the remainder found it difficult to say.

Respondents were asked under what circumstances it was worth turning to the courts to defend their rights. Half the respondents thought that the courts could defend the labour rights of people like themselves, one-third did not and the remainder found it difficult to say. Just over half the respondents considered that it was worthwhile in relation to the violation of their rights when made redundant and 39 per cent in relation to delays in the payment of wages, 26 per cent in the event of outrageous managerial behaviour, while only around one in eight thought it worth appealing other violations of their rights to the courts and 18 per cent thought that it was never worth appealing to the courts. Eleven per cent of respondents had engaged in court action in the previous three years (most probably over the non-payment of wages), almost half of whom had been to court more than once. The worker had won the suit, in whole or in part, in 99 per cent of the cases which had been resolved. A quarter of respondents said that they had done this without any reference to the trade union, and a further 18 per cent said they had received no help from the union, but half those who turned to the court had union help in drawing up their suit, 22 per cent in the proceedings themselves, seven per cent in the preparation of an appeal and a quarter in securing the enforcement of a favourable judgement. Members of alternative unions had received a little more help than members of traditional unions.

In the ISITO survey of trade union presidents, the presidents were asked what was the most effective means of defending individual members, nominating up to three (Table 8.31). Negotiation with management was again overwhelmingly the preferred channel, followed by referral to the Labour Disputes Commission, failing which the presidents would look for the external support of higher trade union bodies, the courts or the state administration, with very few presidents thinking that collective action was an appropriate method of resolving an individual labour dispute. This pattern of preferences is reflected in overall statistical data. According to the data submitted by 59 regional trade union federations, in 1999 the trade union was involved in 618 474 cases which were referred to a Labour Disputes Commission, in 44 322 cases which were referred to the courts, but only in 2110 registered collective labour disputes and strikes (*Vesti FNPR*, 3–4, 2000, pp. 14–42).

Table 8.31: What action do you consider most effective if a worker turns to you concerning an individual labour conflict? (Up to three choices)

|  | Per cent |
|---|---|
| Negotiations with management | 90.2 |
| Apply to Labour Disputes Commission (KTS) | 53.4 |
| Appeal to a higher trade union body | 53.0 |
| Appeal to the courts or prosecutor | 18.6 |
| Appeal to state supervisory bodies | 4.6 |
| Appeal to the local authorities | 3.3 |
| Organise collective protest actions | 2.1 |
| Appeal to the public (mass media, deputies, political parties) | 1.5 |
| Difficult to say | 2.1 |

Source: ISITO Survey

In the CLMS 1999 survey, employers and employees were asked how conflicts had been resolved. The question did not distinguish between individual and collective conflicts, but it is likely that employees would be referring to individual conflicts (Table 8.32). The predominant response of both employers and employees was that conflicts were resolved through agreement with management, with little trade union involvement. Almost half the conflicts reported by employees were unresolved, but from the employers' responses it would appear that they regard many of these as having expired. The disparity of response with respect to dismissal is not surprising, since employees who had been dismissed would have fallen out of the sample. Employers were almost four times as likely to report that a conflict had been resolved through dismissal in non-union than in unionised enterprises. This supports the contention of those who argue that, although trade unions normally approve dismissals, the need to seek union approval is a significant factor restraining management that will be removed with the revision of the Labour Code.

Table 8.32: Means of resolving labour conflicts reported by employers and employees

|  | Employer | Employee |
|---|---|---|
| Reaching agreement with employer | 18.6 | 35.8 |
| Labour Disputes Commission | 3.9 | 2.7 |
| Trade union committee | 4.9 | 7.0 |
| Court | 9.8 | 3.7 |
| Conflict expired | 22.5 | 4.8 |
| Dismissal | 17.6 | 0.5 |
| Conflict is not resolved yet | 15.7 | 44.3 |

Source: Centre for Labour Market Studies survey, 1999

### Collective labour conflicts

Trade union presidents were asked in the ISITO survey to define which were the most effective forms of action in the event of a collective labour conflict, again selecting up to three options (Table 8.33). Trade union presidents who said that their relations with the administration were conflictual were more likely to have a positive evaluation of collective actions but, overall, collective action was clearly seen to be much less effective than negotiation and judicial processes, with a heavy reliance on higher trade union bodies to secure agreement with the employer. The least popular option is the legally prescribed process of arbitration. In the 1999 CLMS survey a quarter of trade union presidents responded that they considered a strike to be an effective means of defending workers' interests (almost twice as many as in 1995), but the remaining three-quarters considered strikes either to be useless or as only creating economic difficulties for the enterprise.

Table 8.33: Which actions do you consider most effective in the event of a collective labour conflict in your enterprise?

| Form of action | Per cent |
| --- | --- |
| Negotiations with management | 80.6 |
| Appeal to a higher trade union body | 54.3 |
| Apply to Labour Disputes Commission (KTS) | 34.9 |
| Appeal to the courts or prosecutor | 15.1 |
| Appeal to the local authorities | 7.2 |
| Organise collective protest actions – strikes, work stoppages | 6.3 |
| Appeal to state supervisory bodies | 6.0 |
| Organise collective actions – meetings, pickets | 5.0 |
| Appeal to the public (mass media, deputies, political parties) | 3.9 |
| Appeal to an independent arbitrator | 2.7 |
| Difficult to say | 5.6 |

Source: ISITO Survey

The preferences of trade union presidents appear to coincide quite closely with those of their members. The FTUI survey showed a very similar distribution of responses when respondents were asked to identify the most acceptable forms of collective action to defend the labour rights of people like themselves. Two-thirds identified negotiation with the administration and one-third reference to the courts, 13 per cent identified an appeal to the local authorities, seven per cent an appeal to the mass media and six per cent an appeal to deputies or political parties. More militant forms of collective action were supported by nine per cent (work stoppages), 11 per cent (strikes), seven per cent (meetings, pickets), while only 0.7 per cent supported a factory occupation. In general, those who had experienced particular forms of action in their enterprise, particularly if they had participated in that action personally, were substantially more likely to select that form of action as appropriate. For example, three-quarters of those who had been to court and one-third of those who had participated in a strike identified it as an appropriate form of action.

The MFP survey of enterprises without a collective agreement found that the majority of directors and presidents tried to resolve all conflicts within the enterprise without bringing in any outside mediators. Thirty per cent of the employees surveyed thought that they could get full justice in their enterprise, 43 per cent did not think that they could always get justice, 15 per cent thought that it was completely unrealistic and 13 per cent found it difficult to say. But the trade union could not always resolve conflicts internally. Fifteen per cent of presidents had turned for help to the city committee of the union or to central trade union bodies, while five per cent had turned to the prosecutor and five per cent to the court.

Thirty-six per cent of directors and a quarter of trade union presidents thought that it was likely that the trade union committee could organise a strike or other protest action, 41 per cent of directors and 20 per cent of presidents were doubtful and 18 per cent of directors and 55 per cent of presidents said that their trade union committee absolutely could not do it. This lack of confidence of the trade union presidents was not just a matter of their inability to organise a strike, but more importantly of their unwillingness to do so, a reflection of the clientelism that dominated these enterprises, so many trade union presidents said it was pointless and absurd to undertake any such action (Tatarnikova, 1999).

On the basis of case studies we can identify the typical pattern of development of collective conflict in Russian enterprises and organisations. The most common cause of conflict during the 1990s was the non-payment of wages, which first arose in 1992 and which reached a peak in 1996, but once conflict arises it tends to become endemic and other issues are added to the initial cause of the dispute. Conflicts usually arise spontaneously and involve one shop or section, or just a small group of like-minded workers, who may simply walk out or may establish a strike committee and put forward demands backed up with threats of a strike or hunger-strike, the latter being more typical of small groups of workers. Where a whole shop or section is involved, it is most likely that the action has at least the tacit support of the shop or section chief and may involve the shop trade union president, although the trade union is often by-passed. The initiators may try to generalise the conflict to the enterprise as a whole through the trade union committee. If the trade union committee chooses or is compelled to take up the issue, it will seek to pursue the dispute through formal channels with the establishment of a conciliation commission, followed by reference to arbitration and the initiation of legal action, sometimes backed up with the threat of a strike, which can drag the dispute out for months or even years. During this period there may well be spontaneous strikes and work stoppages involving some or all of the labour collective. If the employer applies to the court to declare the strike illegal, he will usually eventually succeed (Table 8.34), but few strikes lead to such an application and they are usually resolved by promises from management and partial payment of the wage debt to those involved in the action.

Table 8.34: Involvement of courts and trade unions in strikes and collective labour disputes 1995-9

|  | 1995 | 1996 | 1997 | 1998 | 1999 |
|---|---|---|---|---|---|
| Number of enterprises in which strikes registered* | 8856 | 8278 | 18746 | 11162 | 7285 |
| Number of enterprises in which collective labour disputes registered | 15534 | 16095 | 6972 | 5062 | 4606 |
| Number of strikes and collective labour disputes involving or receiving help from the trade union |  |  | 1314 | 2453 | 2110 |
| Number of strikes whose legality was referred to courts | 114 | 151 | 214 | 154 | 68 |
| Number of cases resolved | 66 | 98 | 160 | 108 | 64 |
| Of which, number declared illegal | 60 | 90 | 133 | 71 | 50 |

* Up to 1997 includes warning strikes

Data on strikes and collective labour disputes is from the Ministry of Labour, data on court referrals from the Ministry of Justice. Data on trade union involvement is from trade union reporting. The data from different sources is not strictly comparable because it is collected on different bases: many strikes and disputes are not reported to the Ministry of Labour, while the coverage of trade union reporting is incomplete. There are enormous regional variations in the relationship between the different indicators. In Bryansk, 1381 strikes were registered in 1998, but only 63 disputes involving trade unions, while in Dagestan only seven strikes were registered but the trade unions reported that they were involved in 62 disputes. In Moscow City no strikes were recorded in 1998 or 1999, but five and four were declared illegal in the same years. Arkhangelsk alone accounted for more than a quarter of all strikes reported as involving trade unions in these two years.
Source: *Vesti FNPR*, 3–4, 2000, p. 42.

In the budget sectors of health and education, the non-payment of wages is primarily the result of the failure of local government to provide funds, in coal-mining it is often the result of the failure of the government to transfer the subsidies guaranteed by the tariff agreement, and in other branches it is often the direct or indirect result of the failure of government or state enterprises to pay their debts. In such cases the enterprise director might tacitly support the action of the workers and harness it to try to extract resources from the government. In other cases, the director might use the conflict to persuade the local or regional authorities to provide a subsidy or extend a loan to the enterprise, reproducing the traditional relationship between director and trade union in lobbying for resources in the soviet period. A typical example of management encouragement was a strike in a privatised textile enterprise in Ivanovo in 1994. Against a journalist's accusation that the (communist) director was himself the president of the strike committee, the president of the trade union committee replied:

No, purely formally Vladimir Il'ich [the director] is not a member of our strike committee. And because of his position he is not supposed to be. But he did get us together and organise us himself. And he said at once that he understood that we would have to strike the very first blow precisely against him. But he was ready for that and understood our problems. We immediately discussed together which demands the strike committee should put to our director, which to the regional administration and which to the government (Fedotov, 1995 p. 92).

The overwhelming majority of recorded strikes have been in the state or state-subsidised sectors of coal-mining, health and education, where they have been co-ordinated actions to extract funds from the state in response to the non-payment of wages, with the more or less active support of the employers. The substantial increase in the incidence of strikes in the mid-90s is explained by the increase in the number of such 'directors' strikes'. The sharp decline in the number of strikes at the end of the decade (Table 8.35) is partly explained by the decline in the non-payment of wages and growing fear of dismissal, but also by the increasing recourse of the authorities to the traditional soviet method of suppressing overt conflict by dismissing directors who were held responsible for the outbreak of a strike.

Table 8.35: Official statistics of strikes in Russia

| Year | Number of enterprises in which strikes occurred | Number of workers involved | | Number of working days lost to strikes | | Average number of working days lost per strike participant |
|---|---|---|---|---|---|---|
| | | Thousand | Average per enterprise | Thousand | Average per enterprise | |
| 1990 | 260 | 99.5 | 383 | 207.7 | 799 | 2.1 |
| 1991 | 1 755 | 237.7 | 135 | 2 314.2 | 1 319 | 9.7 |
| 1992 | 6 273 | 357.6 | 57 | 1 893.3 | 302 | 5.3 |
| 1993 | 264 | 120.2 | 455 | 236.8 | 897 | 2.0 |
| 1994 | 514 | 155.3 | 302 | 755.1 | 1 469 | 4.9 |
| 1995 | 8 856 | 489.4 | 55 | 1 367.0 | 154 | 2.8 |
| 1996 | 8 278 | 663.9 | 80 | 4 009.4 | 484 | 6.0 |
| 1997 | 17 007 | 887.3 | 52 | 6 000.5 | 353 | 6.8 |
| 1998 | 11 162 | 530.8 | 48 | 2 881.5 | 258 | 5.4 |
| 1999 | 7 285 | 238.4 | 33 | 1 827.2 | 251 | 7.7 |
| 2000 | 817 | 31.0 | 38 | 236.4 | 289 | 7.6 |

Source: Goskomstat, 2000b, p. 133; Goskomstat, 2001, p. 91.
Note: Many strikes are not reported to the state statistical agency so the incidence of strikes is substantially under-reported, but the trend is probably accurately reflected. The fall in the average number involved is a reflection of the growing relative weight of strikes in the education sector, which also dominated the 1992 figures.

The enterprise trade union committee will be much more likely to support militant action against the enterprise director over such issues as the non-payment of wages if there is already opposition to the director within management, such opposition often involving the discontent of shop chiefs at the failure of the director to provide them with adequate financial resources, which is usually attributed to the incompetence and/or corruption of the director, sometimes compounded by his or her subordination to the interests of outside shareholders. In such cases the conflict may well escalate into a struggle for control of the enterprise in which the trade union mobilises the labour force in support of the opposing faction. In other cases, the trade union might mobilise the support of the labour force for the existing director, in opposition to attempts by outside forces to take control of the enterprise. In this situation (most famously the Vyborg Cellulose Paper Combine and the Kuznetsk Metallurgical Complex – see Pulaeva and Clarke, 2000; Burnyshev and Clarke, 2000) the workers may even establish an armed militia to defend the enterprise, and the outside actors may try to seize the premises by force.

Where the management team is united, and the trade union committee has close relations with management, the trade union committee is more likely to oppose the initial conflict on the grounds that it is a sectional conflict involving only a small group of workers, disrupting the enterprise and pursuing their own interests at the expense of the labour collective as a whole, which the trade union claims to represent. In this case the workers in dispute might try to raise the issue at a meeting or conference of the labour collective and if they get the support of their colleagues they may be able to carry a vote of no confidence in the trade union and replace the trade union leadership with their own activists. This is likely to initiate a phase of more militant conflict between the trade union committee and enterprise management, which will often include the demand for the replacement of the enterprise director, typically with a former director or a respected shop chief. More often, however, the management and the trade union president have sufficient levers of influence over the labour collective to be able to isolate the workers involved in the conflict.

The workers engaged in the conflict will often appeal to outside bodies, particularly if they do not get the support of their own trade union committee. They most commonly turn to the regional trade union organisation or to an alternative trade union, and address their appeals to the mass media, the regional administration and even to the Russian President and government. In many cases, particularly if there is a threat of the intervention of an alternative trade union, the regional branch trade union committee plays a more or less active role in the dispute, even where the enterprise trade union president has failed to support the workers, putting pressure on the enterprise director and trade union president both directly and by mobilising connections in the regional administration and sometimes through the regional tripartite commission. Such pressure will sometimes be backed up by demonstrations and pickets organised by and on behalf of the workers engaged in the conflict. Where the regional administration becomes involved in the dispute it may facilitate a resolution through conciliation or through the courts or by providing financial assistance to the enterprise, and it may use its influence to secure the replacement of the director. If the director has the support of the regional administration, however, the latter may use its resources to pressure the workers to end their dispute.

Once conflict erupts in an enterprise it tends to become endemic. This is partly because of the failure of the trade union adequately to represent the interests of its members and of the absence of appropriate channels of conflict resolution, but it is also because the most common causes of conflict are structural and beyond the control of management and the trade union. Although the non-payment of wages was often the result of the incompetence or venality of the enterprise director, underlying the phenomenon was the growing degree of insolvency, compounded by the acute shortage of liquidity and the very high levels of non-payment of commercial and government debt in the Russian economy, which meant that many enterprises really did not have the money to pay their wages (Clarke, 1998). The partial remonetisation and recovery of the Russian economy after the August 1998 crisis reduced these constraints and led to a rapid reduction in the incidence of non-payment and in the backlog of wages due, with a corresponding decline in the levels of conflict over the non-payment of wages. From 1999, the non-payment of wages was increasingly a result of insolvency rather than illiquidity, and trade unions began to turn their attention to the bankruptcy procedure as a means of securing the payment of wages, the removal of an incompetent director and the introduction of new owners who, it was hoped, would restore the enterprise to prosperity.

## Militant trade union organisations

The enterprise trade union organisation nearly always retains its traditional role of being a branch of the enterprise administration, responsible for social welfare and personnel functions, and is perceived as such by most trade union members. More combative trade union organisations do exist, particularly in more profitable privatised branches, such as metallurgy, where management tends to be more assertive and the trade union has some bargaining power, but even in these cases the combativity of the trade union generally depends on the personality of the president and his or her personal relationship with the director, so that the replacement of the trade union president can immediately 'tame' the trade union organisation.

Militant trade union organisations usually develop out of spontaneous conflicts in which either the existing trade union leadership is replaced or a branch of an alternative trade union is set up. However, the dependence of the trade union on the enterprise administration and the limited expectations of trade union members make it very difficult to sustain a militant trade union organisation. In the first half of the nineties enterprise directors tended to end conflicts by paying-off militant workers, which provided a material incentive for militancy, but in the latter half of the decade they showed themselves increasingly willing to confront such militancy, to the extent of using force against strikers and hunger strikers (Borisov, 2001). Moreover, a militant union organisation usually has its roots in a small section of the labour force which has some bargaining power: typically a core production shop or key skilled workers, which makes it relatively easy for management, often supported by the enterprise trade union committee, to isolate the militant trade union organisation, claiming that it is trying 'to pull the blanket over itself' by, for example, securing the payment of unpaid wages at the expense of other workers. The isolation of the militant section of the labour force presents serious barriers to collective mobilisation, so militant trade union organisations generally rely heavily on court action and on symbolic protests, such as hunger strikes, picketing and demonstrations, occasionally resorting to acts of 'labour terrorism', including occupations and hostage-taking, in their desperation. The revisions to the Labour Code agreed between the government and FNPR will make it much more difficult for sectional opposition to the traditional trade union to develop or survive, since the new Labour Code provides representative rights to the trade union representing the majority of the labour force and requires a majority vote of the whole labour force or a representative conference of the whole establishment for a legal strike to take place.

If the militant faction manages to take control of the enterprise trade union the conflict tends to develop into a highly personalised struggle for control of the enterprise between the trade union president and the enterprise director, with each attempting to remove the other. Internally, the position of managers, particularly shop chiefs, plays a critical role in the development of the conflict, but the outcome is often determined by external forces, with the position of the local administration, which has a wide range of levers of influence, being critical. The regional trade union organisation is unlikely to compromise its relations with its counterparts in the regional administration by supporting a trade union president in conflict with a director who is supported by the regional administration. The outcome of this kind of conflict is usually the replacement of the enterprise director or the trade union president or both, although this may signal a new phase of conflict rather than its end.

For a militant trade union organisation to survive it has to keep the labour force in a constant state of mobilisation, which is exhausting for the leaders and generally unproductive for the members. If the organisation is not able to secure tangible benefits for its members, such as the regular payment of wages or pay increases, it has to fall back on the traditional activities of the trade union, the provision of material assistance and social and welfare benefits, if it is to retain the allegiance of its members. This forces it into an accommodation with management so that the typical fate of militant trade union organisations is either to fade away or to collaborate increasingly closely with management and adopt the traditional forms of trade union activity. This is why the alternative trade unions, which presented a militant alternative to the traditional unions at the beginning of the nineties, have gradually lost their distinctiveness and have come to collaborate more closely with the traditional trade unions from enterprise to federal levels. Nevertheless, there is a small number of enterprises in which an active and energetic trade union organisation has been able to capture the imagination and enthusiasm of the members to weld them into a strong collective force. These are generally organisations which do not depend on a demagogic trade union president but on an active trade union committee which engages with members in their workplaces. These organisations do not necessarily reject the traditional functions of the trade union, but use them as a basis on which to develop solidarity. It is these activists and their organisations who are the best hope and model for the future of Russian trade unionism.

## Do Russian workers need trade unions?

We have seen that the Russian trade unions have not been able to protect their members from the catastrophic decline in employment and living standards over the 1990s, but to what extent have trade unions been able at least to alleviate the worst impact of the crisis on their members? Are workers in unionised establishments better off than those in establishments which do not have a trade union?

Analysis of the data of the ISITO survey of the members of 4,000 households conducted in four cities in April and May 1998 shows that those working in enterprises with a trade union organisation were much less likely to be hired (illegally) on a verbal agreement, much more likely to have a formal definition of the responsibilities of their job and of their working hours, slightly less likely to have to take on work outside their normal responsibilities, less likely to work overtime and more likely to be paid for their overtime work and less liable to be punished or dismissed without formal procedures. All of this suggests that a trade union does provide some effective protection for its members. However, this impression may be misleading, since most of the difference is explained by sectoral differences in working conditions and union penetration: labour relations in small enterprises in the new private sector, where union penetration is minimal, tend to be much less formalised than in state and former state enterprises (Clarke, 1999b, Chapter 5). Once we control for the size and sector of the enterprise, the presence of a trade union ceases to be a significant factor. Thus, the differences do not seem to derive from the presence or absence of a trade union, but from the difference between more and less formalised labour relations. In smaller establishments, particularly in the new private sector, management has more discretion in determining wages and working conditions, whether or not there is a trade union.

The ISITO household survey data shows that wages are higher in non-union than in unionised workplaces, but again much of this difference is explained by sectoral differences in wages and in union penetration, so that union membership is not a significant variable in wage regressions which control for branch and enterprise size. The same is true of the enterprise data of the RLFS. Chetvernina's finding that enterprises without trade unions have lower managerial pay differentials is also likely to be because they are significantly smaller than those with unions.

The absence of a trade union does not imply the absence of conflict, and indeed it is not uncommon for directors of non-union enterprises to approach the regional trade union organisations to create a trade union in order to contain conflict (though they often decide against proceeding with the creation of a union when they realise that it may not be entirely under their control). One-third of the non-union enterprises in the 1995 CLMS survey and almost half in the 1999 survey reported conflict in the last three years, usually over wages and usually initiated by the collective as a whole, rather than individual groups of employees, but over two-thirds of the conflicts in 1995 were reportedly resolved in favour of employees or to the mutual satisfaction of both parties, which is presumably why 40 per cent of directors and one-quarter of employees in such enterprises thought a trade union was useless, and about a third saw the main role of the trade union as the distribution of benefits. The majority of employees, and two-thirds of directors, in these non-union enterprises saw management as the body to protect the interests of employees, a further 29 per cent of employees looked to nobody or themselves and only 12 per cent had any confidence in the support of the labour collective, figures which are in fact very similar to those for unionised enterprises, a finding reproduced in the 1999 CLMS survey (Table 8.26). Where the union had disappeared from enterprises it was because people had left the union and nobody had tried to reconstitute it. There was only a very small number of cases in which the union had been removed by the administration (Chetvernina, Smirnov and Dunaeva, 1995). Nevertheless, the liquidation of a trade union organisation is an indication of a lack of employer interest, if not of opposition, since the employer can always find somebody to run the union if a union organisation is required.

Overall, from the rather limited data available, it does not appear that the presence of a trade union organisation makes a significant difference to the wages and working conditions of employees. This does not mean that Russian workers do not need trade unions, but only that the trade unions have to be more effective in organising their members in the workplace and pressing their demands on management.

The economic and social results of unrestrained managerial power in a condition of unprecedented economic crisis were detailed earlier in this chapter: an excessively high degree of labour flexibility manifested in falling wages, increased wage dispersion, high labour mobility, deskilling, the cessation of training, declining conditions of health and safety and the absence of incentives to increase labour productivity or to invest in new plant and equipment. And this is in a situation in which substantial elements of the traditional managerial paternalism and most of the protective labour legislation remain in place! The social and political consequences of unrestrained managerial power may be judged to be as damaging. The systematic violation of law and collective agreements from the government down undermines respect for the rule of law and for the processes of negotiation and collective bargaining. Russian workers certainly need effective trade union organisations to provide some check on managerial power.

Creating effective workplace trade union organisations is easier said than done. The development of active workplace trade unionism in Russia is impeded by the fact that the majority of trade union presidents are unable or unwilling to enter into conflict with the employer. Many are unable to enter into conflict because, however strong the legal protection that trade unions may enjoy, they are intimidated. As one inexperienced trade union president in a hospital in Samara explained 'I will not get into conflict with the administration. I have got too much to lose by it'. Many more trade union leaders, on the other hand, are unwilling to enter into conflict because they identify with the employer.

The conclusion reached by Chetvernina and her colleagues is that collective agreements are ineffective because of the passivity of both trade unions and employees. We have argued above that this passivity is not just a subjective failing, nor merely an historical legacy, but is a structural characteristic of the role of the trade union in the Russian enterprise in transition. Studies of enterprises in which official or alternative trade union leaders try to assert their independence of management all reveal the structural constraints imposed on the union: an independent leader may secure an initial success at shop or enterprise level, but management controls the resources at the disposal of the union and can withhold those resources at any time, so undermining the authority of the militant leader and demonstrating to the workers that passivity pays.

This structural barrier is not inevitable, but the progressive union leader finds him or herself caught in a vicious circle in which independence depends on effective trade union organisation, but effective organisation depends on independence. In a situation in which laws and agreements are systematically violated with impunity by politicians, managers and administrators at all levels, workers can only effectively defend their rights through constant mobilisation. But, as is well-known from trade union experience elsewhere, it is extremely difficult and very wearing for a union organisation to maintain a high degree of worker mobilisation, to say nothing of the wider consequences of a permanent aggressive polarisation. Thus, mobilisation and collective organisation is not an alternative to the pursuit of trade union aims through the structures of social partnership but is its essential complement. The most fruitful channel of trade union renewal could be systematic campaigning to secure the enforcement of the law and collective agreements by collective mobilisation in support of judicial proceedings. This was the primary route chosen by the new alternative trade unions, but without a significant membership base it often proved self-defeating since it simply led to the victimisation of activists. Thus, the law on its own is an insufficient base on which to establish and defend the rights of workers and their representatives: recourse to the law has to be a support for the development of effective collective organisation. However, such a trade union strategy presumes that both trade unionists and workers see the union as an instrument for the defence of workers, rather than as a branch of management.

# 9

# The Future of Russian Trade Unionism

In this concluding chapter we will briefly review the limitations of the strategy of social partnership adopted by the Russian trade unions over the 1990s in order to identify the prospects for the development of more effective trade union practice. Rather than measure the achievements of the Russian trade unions against some unattainable ideal, we will locate the issues in comparative perspective.

## The limitations of social partnership

Soviet trade unions were an integral part of the Party-state and their functions were primarily Party-state functions: participating in the elaboration and implementation of the Party's social and labour policies and acting as the 'eyes and ears' of the Party in the workplace, managing the social and welfare infrastructure, administering the systems of social insurance and health and safety inspection and monitoring the performance of both management and workers. The collapse of the soviet system removed the prop that had sustained the authority of the trade union in the workplace and in society. If the trade unions were to survive they had to find a new basis for their authority and a new justification for their existence.

In the period of perestroika the trade unions declared their independence of state and Party and sought to find a new role as the protector of the workers, resisting liberal reforms under the pretext of seeking guarantees for the jobs and living standards of the mass of the population. The trade unions committed themselves to a strategy of 'social partnership', through which they sought recognition as representatives of the mass of the population (not only trade union members, but 'workers and their families') within tripartite structures in which government, trade unions and employers would have 'equal rights'. But the hope that the trade unions could establish a new authority as representative institutions was from the start a vain one. Workers in the great strike waves of 1989 and 1991 pressed for more rapid reform and did not look to the trade unions for leadership but formed their own strike committees, which they transformed into new independent trade unions. The attempt of FNPR to articulate popular opposition to Yeltsin's reforms foundered on its inability to mobilise its membership. This was highlighted during Yeltsin's confrontation with parliament in 1993, when Klochkov's appeal to trade unionists to support the 'defenders of the White House' not only evoked no response, but also split the trade union movement, leading to the replacement of Klochkov by Mikhail Shmakov.

The weakness of the trade unions lay not only in their inability to mobilise their own members, but also in their dependence for their institutional survival on the property and on the legal rights and privileges inherited from the soviet past. This made the trade unions particularly vulnerable to any attempt by the state to confiscate their property or to annul their legal rights and privileges and forced them into an accommodation with the existing structures of power at federal, regional and enterprise level. The ideology of social partnership provided a framework within which the trade unions could secure their institutional future not on the basis of their strength as representatives of organised labour, but by establishing their usefulness for those in power, seeking to adapt to new circumstances within the limits of their existing form. Having lost the support of the Party, and being unable to mobilise their membership, the trade unions sought to restore their authority within the framework of the institutions of social partnership and on the basis of the legal regulation of labour and social relations, collaborating with state institutions and lobbying legislatures to secure the passage of favourable legislation. Social partnership, therefore, provided the ideological and institutional framework within which the trade unions could retain or reconstitute their traditional functions.

Social partnership proved a very successful survival strategy for the traditional trade unions, which many commentators had written off at the beginning of the 1990s. The unions retained their property, consolidated their legal rights and privileges and retained or recovered most of their traditional functions. They lost about half their membership, but as a result of the decline of the traditional sectors of the economy rather than of a voluntary exodus from the trade unions. Moreover, in their commitment to pursuing their objectives strictly within the framework of the Constitution and the law, the trade unions made a very important, and much undervalued, contribution to the consolidation of democratic institutions and the establishment of the rule of law in Russia.

Simply to have survived has been a considerable achievement, so we have to be careful not to evaluate the achievements of the Russian trade unions against an impossible standard. Nevertheless, in the course of this book we have argued that the strategy of 'social partnership' adopted by the Russian trade unions from their foundation has proved double-edged. It has enabled them to find a place in the new Russia, and it has made a substantial contribution to the consolidation of Russian democracy, but it has provide few tangible benefits for the members of trade unions and their families, and it has set up barriers to the further development of trade unionism to become an effective means by which workers can defend their livelihoods and protect their interests.

The negotiation of the General, branch and regional agreements and participation in the Russian and regional Tripartite Commissions has become a bureaucratised process of government consultation with the trade unions on labour and social issues in which the employers' representatives play a very limited role. The agreements offer little of substance and their terms are unenforceable. Lobbying of the legislature has enabled the trade unions to retain their own legal rights and privileges and to preserve or even extend the legally enforceable guarantees of the social and labour rights of their members, but government and employers continue to evade or violate the law with impunity. Participation in the government bureaucracy at federal, branch and regional levels has allowed the trade unions to express their views but not to have any tangible influence on policy.

FNPR has increasingly come to recognise that the limitations of its strategy of social partnership stem from the weakness of its primary organisations. The implementation of the achievements of social partnership and the enforcement of the law depend on the activism of its primary organisations and on the willingness of its primary group presidents to confront management to enforce the rights embodied in legislation and to negotiate and enforce effective collective agreements. However, the vast majority of trade union primary organisations are not only dependent on management, but are integrated into management structures, performing social and welfare functions and providing material assistance to their members. FNPR has identified its regional organisations as the other weak link in the chain, regularly criticising them for failing to activate their primary organisations and failing to mobilise the membership in campaigns and national actions.

The analysis that we have presented in this book supports FNPR's diagnosis that the key to trade union renewal lies in the activation of workplace trade union organisation. On the one hand, FNPR needs to back up its lobbying and legislative achievements with the organised strength of its membership. On the other hand, the implementation and observance of legislation and regulation can only be achieved at the work place by an active trade union organisation which is able to realise the rights of its members embodied in the law. In general, the application of the terms of federal and regional agreements depends on their incorporation into enterprise collective agreements, but this is rarely done as the terms of the enterprise collective agreement are generally dictated by management. The enforcement of legislation and regulations depends on the effective monitoring of observance by the primary trade union organisation and on that organisation taking the appropriate steps in the case of violation of laws and regulations, but the primary trade union organisation generally lacks the strength, expertise, resources and will to confront management over its failures.

At the same time, the FNPR leadership does not appear to recognise that its commitment to social partnership has itself been a powerful factor in securing the reproduction of the inactivity of primary organisations. There are three aspects to this question. First, the conciliatory approach of FNPR and the branch unions not only reflects but also provides a model for conciliatory trade unionism at the enterprise level. Second, the hierarchical approach of FNPR to social partnership fosters divisions within the trade union movement and an alienation of branch and enterprise trade union organisations from the federative structures. Third, the bureaucratic, legalistic and individualistic approach to the representation of the membership and the resolution of conflicts undermines attempts to develop the collective organisation of members in the workplace.

## The vicious circle of conciliation

We have seen that the conciliatory approach of FNPR to social partnership has in large part been underpinned by the weakness of its primary trade union organisations. It was the inability of FNPR to mobilise its membership in defence of their jobs and living standards in 1991-3 that forced the FNPR leadership to look to the state and the law for support. It was the collaboration between unions and employers in the enterprise that underpinned the strategic collaboration between trade unions and employers at federal level, expressed in the alliance of FNPR with Vol'skii and Luzhkov and the orientation of the branch and regional trade union organisations to the interests of their branch and region. The President of Unity For Progress (ERP), the joint organisation of the Leningrad and Saint Petersburg trade unions and the regional employers' organisation, argued in an interview that even though the tactical aims of the trade unions and employers differed, their strategic aims, the regeneration of industry, coincided. Similarly, the leader of the Russian Association of Industrialists and Entrepreneurs, Arkadii Vol'skii, explained his alliance with FNPR in the 1995 Duma election by noting that 'disagreements with the trade unions can appear in the future, when there will be a question of the distribution of profit, but at the moment we have nothing to divide', while Andrei Isaev, Ideology Secretary of FNPR, explained that such an alliance was possible because the fundamental cleavage was between the government and industry, not between workers and employers. The President of the chemical workers' union declared in an interview in 2000:

> The trade union does not at the moment support any of the existing parties, it is in favour of the association of the efforts of industrialists and entrepreneurs to get the Russian economy out of crisis and is for a strong legal state.

This conciliatory approach to the employers at branch, regional and federal levels is reflected in FNPR's representation of the collective agreement as an instrument of social peace, which implies that the collective agreement will represent the formal acknowledgement of the power of the employer and the dependence of the trade union. It should hardly be surprising that the commitment to conciliatory social partnership at higher levels is reflected in a similar approach at the workplace. As one trade union president of a large foreign-owned paper mill explained to an interviewer, his priority tasks were:

> First, that the collective, the workers should trust management. Second, that not only the chiefs, but also ordinary workers should be drawn in to the life of the

collective, that everyone should feel themselves an owner in their own place and not passively observe what is being created around them.

The trade union president of a subsidiary of the same company likewise emphasised the importance of co-operation:

We need to press [the company] to increase wages. In general, I think that the administration and trade union should work together, on the same side. So the president of the trade union committee must know production very well.

Maybe the way things were in the past suits us better, from the point of view of trade union activity and its directions – together with the administration (though without the Party committee). By our combined efforts. I feel closer to that kind of conception… Basically I am glad that we have an understanding with the administration. That is a mutual aspiration.

In general I think that if a man goes into trade-union work with a mood for struggle, then he will certainly find himself a battlefield. But maybe one has simply got to work?! After all, in actual fact the director also thinks about the worker, cannot but think about him, otherwise with whom will he carry out his plan? And the trade-union leader should not clamber on to a platform or on the TV, but get on with his concrete daily work – with people. There are some trade unionists who at the slightest provocation will go immediately into opposition, conflict. But both parties are always guilty in a conflict! Therefore it is necessary to think not about opposition, but about cooperation.

Such ideas are very common. Indeed, one of the legacies of the soviet era is the idea that concord between trade unions and management is 'natural', conflict being seen as a pathological phenomenon resulting from bad management (for more details see Ashwin, 1999, pp. 175-179). This can be neatly illustrated by one of our case studies. Having managed to curb the arbitrary behaviour of the chief doctor at a St Petersburg clinic, the president of the recently-established trade union at the clinic asked her mentor, the president of the raikom, 'perhaps he's turned over a new leaf, and we already don't need a trade union?' After being warned that dissolution of the union would mean no more help from the raikom, the president decided against shutting up shop, but her question itself reveals the extent to which workplace harmony, rather than conflict, is perceived to be the norm.

Such co-operative orientations give trade unionism a good name with the employers, many of whom are very happy to work with trade unions such as that at the paper mill. The President of the Komi employers' association commended such trade unionism in his speech to the conference of the Republican Trade Union Federation in March 2001:

We have examples, when many trade unions understand the problems of the employer. For example, in Komienergo, where there was a difficult financial position for six months. But the trade unions ensured that there were no protest actions, because they went in to the situation and as a result it was corrected. It is a vivid example, that if you conduct yourself wisely, it is always possible to agree with the trade unions.

While trade unions see their role as being to collaborate with the employers at every level to press the government to modify the course of its reforms, it is not the government but the employers (including the government as employer) who are paying wages below the subsistence minimum or not paying wages at all; it is the employers who are making workers work unpaid overtime, in conditions which violate health and safety norms; it is employers who are forcing workers out of their jobs without even giving them their statutory redundancy compensation. As long as FNPR persists in trying to secure jobs and wages by lobbying on employers' behalf at regional, branch and federal levels, it can hardly be surprised that its primary trade union organisations similarly join forces with the employer to suppress conflict and deflect the blame for the appalling living and working conditions of their members away from the employer and onto the government.

## Hierarchy and trade union democracy

It was inevitable, given the weakness of trade union primary organisations, that the institutions of social partnership should have been constructed from the top down. However, despite the abandonment of democratic centralism, the trade unions still take a hierarchical approach to the fulfilment of their trade union functions, with FNPR setting the priorities and defining the tasks of the trade union movement as a whole, looking to the lower levels to give substance to the agreements, laws and regulations negotiated by FNPR at the federal level. The failure of the lower levels to perform their allotted tasks is not simply a matter of the abandonment of democratic centralism and the lack of 'trade union discipline', but is also a reflection of the fact that the paper achievements of social partnership at the federal level are irrelevant to a substantial portion of the membership.

For example, the priority commitment of FNPR to increasing the statutory minimum wage is commendable, but is at best irrelevant to better-paid workers in more prosperous enterprises and more dynamic branches of production and at worst is regarded as contrary to their interests in threatening to compress differentials. These differences of branch interest have underpinned divisions between branch trade unions and the alienation of many branch unions from FNPR at federal and regional levels. Such divisions within the trade union movement have simmered beneath the surface and been neutralised through informal wheeling and dealing between trade union leaders, without being addressed openly within the ruling bodies of FNPR.

Because they have not been addressed and resolved within a democratic framework, they have undermined the cohesion of FNPR and carried the constant threat of splits in the trade union movement. A split was averted in 1993 with the replacement of Klochkov by Shmakov as President of FNPR, but the formation of the Association of Trade Union Organisations of Workers of Pan-National and Transnational Enterprises in 2001 presented a serious renewed threat not only to Shmakov's position, but also to the integrity of FNPR.

## The demobilisation of the membership

While the conciliatory approach of FNPR reinforces the subordination of primary trade union organisations to management and the hierarchical approach of FNPR to social partnership impedes the unification of the trade union movement around a common programme, the bureaucratic, legalistic and individualistic means of pursuing the interests of the trade union members undermines the attempt to develop collective organisation based on an active membership.

The strategy of the trade unions has proved its worth to employers by ameliorating social tension. This has been achieved through the individualisation of conflict, through enterprise trade union committees interceding with management on behalf of individual workers or taking conflicts through the procedure for resolving individual labour disputes, sometimes going as far as court action, rather than through encouraging collective action or allowing a collective labour dispute to arise. The success of primary trade union organisations in ameliorating conflict is shown by the extraordinarily low and rapidly falling level of officially recorded collective labour disputes and strikes in Russia (Table 8.35). There has not been a single strike recorded in Moscow city since 1994, and even in 'hot Kuzbass', seat of the 1989 and 1991 miners' strikes, the first mass teachers' strike of 1992 and the 'rails wars' of 1996–8, there has not been a single recorded strike, or even a registered collective labour dispute, since 1999.

Despite the appearance of harmony between employers and employees that might be given by the strike statistics, conflict between employees and employers is endemic in Russian enterprises. Much of this conflict occurs over relatively minor individual issues, such as the miscalculation of wages or pension entitlement, but very often it arises over major issues which concern the labour force as a whole, most dramatically the non-payment of wages, but also such issues as the level of wages, bonus systems, compulsory overtime, holiday entitlements, compensation for working in harmful conditions, redundancy terms and so on. In all these cases, as we have seen, the overwhelming preference of trade union primary organisations is to address these issues through bureaucratic channels of informal negotiation with management behind closed doors. If such informal negotiation is not successful, the trade union organisation may drop the case or may refer it to the regional organisation in the hope that this body will exert further bureaucratic pressure. If the case is still unresolved, and the union wants to press the issue, it will usually take the issue up through the courts, as one or a series of individual cases, where the issue can be bogged down for months or, if it goes to appeal, for years. Throughout all such negotiation and litigation the trade union will only very rarely back up its claims with the threat of any kind of collective action. The individualistic, bureaucratic and legalistic approach to conflict resolution is implicitly and explicitly posited as an alternative rather than as a complement to collective action.

When collective action does take place, it is nearly always, at least in the first instance, a spontaneous eruption of a group of employees, which may then spread to a whole shop or department and even to the enterprise as a whole. When such a conflict takes place, again the priority of the trade union is to channel the conflict into the bureaucratic channels of conflict resolution laid down by the law. Although the law sets a strict timetable for the conciliation and arbitration procedures which are a necessary prelude to collective action, this timetable is rarely adhered to and the process can drag on for months or years, sometimes interspersed with further spontaneous expressions of anger by the workers involved, though only very rarely with any kind of collective action, other than symbolic pickets or demonstrations, organised by the trade union.

In bureaucratising conflict, turning it into a purely legal battle, trade union organisations shift the locus of action from the enterprise to the courts, and transfer responsibility for ensuring employers' fulfilment of the law or commitments made in agreements from themselves to the state. Even when such tactics are successful in redressing the grievance in question, an opportunity to engage workers in the life of the union and demonstrate its capacity to represent them is lost, along with the enthusiasm and hope which often emerge at moments of spontaneous mobilisation. Moreover, frequently such tactics are *not* particularly successful. Even when a court or arbitration body decides in the union's favour, compliance on the part of the employer is far from automatic and securing this often requires further legal action, perhaps backed up by political intervention from the authorities, particularly if the dispute is continuing to provoke outbursts of collective action. This highlights the problem with the unions' bureaucratic and legalistic methods. A strategy which relies so heavily on the courts, the conclusion of agreements, and lobbying for ever more detailed legal regulation is of questionable value in a context in which the rule of law is yet to be established. If unions do not develop the capacity to mobilise to secure their enforcement, laws and agreements will remain a dead letter: in the words of one distinguished British labour lawyer, 'It is a truism of labour relations law everywhere that workers' interests cannot be protected, let alone advanced, without legitimising and promoting collective action by them in autonomous organisations' (Wedderburn, 1995, p. 350). Developing mobilisational capacity is not a universal panacea – strikers, hunger strikers and those involved in other forms of direct action are also regularly fobbed off with agreements which are subsequently only partially fulfilled or ignored altogether. Nevertheless, when sustained, such action usually induces employers and local political leaders to take greater care in their dealings with workers. Conciliation and legal action have no such impact.

The other negative aspect of the unions' emphasis on perfecting the regulatory framework is that it reproduces their traditional dependence on the state. As we have seen, it is the authorities who ultimately decide which aspects of the law and agreements will be respected, while their concessions to the unions are rarely a result of union strength: rather, they are a form of political patronage which can be withdrawn at will. In the light of Putin's move to exert greater control over the union movement in the run up to the November 2001 congress, the dangers of this state-dependent strategy are readily apparent. At worst, the government's campaign against Shmakov's leadership of the FNPR could have culminated in a return of the trade unions to something akin to their familiar role as 'transmission belts'. The elaborate structures of social partnership which the FNPR has striven so hard to develop will be no defence against such stratagems. An active membership, on the other hand, would render Kremlin meddling in the union movement far more problematic.

Finally, the inactivity of primary trade union organisations cannot be blamed on the passivity of the membership. The apparent 'passivity' of Russian workers is a complex phenomenon (see Ashwin, 1999). Workers' instinctive reaction to difficulties, like that of trade union leaders, is to turn to managers or the political authorities for protection (Ashwin, 1999, 175-179). In this sense, FNPR can be said to 'represent' its members, but it cannot be said to lead them. Encouraging trade union officers at all levels to employ legal and bureaucratic forms of conflict resolution only reinforces the perception that conflict is a deviation from some natural equilibrium which must be restored by state intervention. More importantly, it inhibits the development of any collective mobilisation that does occur among workers. Thus, while it would be wrong to see FNPR as holding back the radical tendencies of a militant membership, it is fair to say that its policies serve to reproduce rather than challenge worker demobilisation. The failure to achieve results through bureaucratic channels leads to growing frustration among the workforce which is sometimes expressed in outbreaks of extreme militancy and even 'labour terrorism' which have no institutional channels within which to develop constructively. The result is the alternation of passivity and unrestrained spontaneous militancy which has been a feature of the workers' movement in Russia since 1987 and which underlies the dual fear that the bulk of the population will, in its passive moment, vote for the authoritarian leader who can make the most radical promises and, in its active moment, take to the streets in outbursts of mass civil unrest.


## Russian trade unionism in comparative perspective

The Russian trade unions are not alone in having struggled through a period of crisis. Trade unions are in deep crisis in most developed countries. If, for example, union density is taken as the measure of health, the Russian union movement looks in quite good shape: trade union density in Russia is still well over 50 per cent, while the French union movement has a density of approximately nine per cent and the US movement organises only 13.5 per cent of the workforce. The traditional Russian trade unions have also been more successful than most of their former communist counterparts in Central and Eastern Europe, most of which have been deprived of their property and legal privileges by hostile governments and which have in some cases lost a substantial part of their membership to alternative trade unions. Meanwhile, social partnership in Eastern Europe has been scarcely more successful than in Russia. As in Russia, tripartism at the national level has not served to facilitate genuine dialogue over the reform process (Kohl, Lecher and Platzer, 2000; Boda and Neumann, 2000), and now constitutes little more than an 'institutional shell' in most Central and East European countries (Martin and Cristescu-Martin, 2000, p. 359).

The failings of Russian trade unionism cannot be ascribed to social partnership, for social partnership merely provided the ideological and institutional framework which the trade unions exploited to seek an accommodation with the authorities at all levels. The term 'social partnership' covers a wide range of different practices in different countries, in different circumstances at different times, some of which have proved more productive for trade unions and their members than others.

Nor can the failings of Russian trade unionism be put down to the failure to realise social partnership in some ideal form, because such an ideal is achievable only under particular conditions.[1] The paradigmatic 'success stories' of concertation or neo-corporatism came from countries such as Sweden, Austria and Germany during the post-WW2 reconstruction boom. In this era neo-corporatism could be seen as a process of 'gain sharing' in which the products of sustained growth were divided up between capital and labour to mutual (though not necessarily equal) advantage.[2] In the 1980s and 1990s, however, neo-corporatism has assumed a very different shape. It can now be characterised as a 'pain sharing' rather than a 'gain sharing' exercise in which trade unions attempt to influence the form of 'flexibility' they are called upon to swallow.[3] Such flexibilisation through concertation has occurred in countries such as the Netherlands, Denmark, Spain and Italy during the 1980s and 1990s (Bordogna and Cella, 1999), with the Dutch unions exchanging wage restraint for reduced working hours (Visser, 1998) and the Italian unions negotiating the abolition of the *scala mobile* (a wage indexation mechanism) and the reform of the pension system (Regini, 1997). That is, neo-corporatist systems are no longer facilitating the forward

---

[1]   This, for example, is a mistake that David Ost (Ost, 2000) arguably makes when he compares the 'illusory corporatism' of contemporary Eastern Europe with the neo-corporatism of Scandinavia and Germany in the 1970s. He argues that 'genuine neo-corporatism entails social democratic outcomes' (p. 508), while neglecting the fact that the gains of 1970s social democracy are currently under attack throughout Europe regardless of the existence or otherwise of a neo-corporatist framework.

[2]   For a critique of corporatism of this era see Panitch, 1980.

[3]   For a comprehensive overview of these developments see Fagertag and Pochet, 1997.

march of labour, but have rather served to allow its controlled and orderly retreat.[1] This inauspicious global context (quite apart from the catastrophic local one) needs to be kept in mind when assessing the limited achievements of social partnership in Russia.

As has been argued in earlier chapters, however, these have not been great. Optimists in the Russian trade union movement stress the progress they have made, and highlight the improvements in the content and monitoring of social partnership agreements. As one of the department heads of the Ul'yanovsk regional federation put it:

> At first agreements were at the level of declaration, and then, of course, we already established monitoring…. Of course, it's not easy, not all measures are fulfilled…. They are not as good as they should be. All the same, we try to support partnerly relations with the administration and employers…. With the passage of time, concretisation is occurring, that is, on some questions we can either lay down a figure, or concretely cite someone as the executor.

As has been seen, there is some evidence for such claims. The increasing tendency to conclude regional agreements before rather than after the regional budgets are set is a good example of this. The question, however, is why this is occurring. Is it related to a development of union strength, or have the authorities merely found social partnership a useful administrative tool? The evidence presented in this book suggests the latter. Certainly, where social partnership is most concrete – in regions such as Moscow and Kemerovo – the authorities use it as a means of implementing a paternalist politics in which there is little room for opposition. The trade unions are granted a clear role in the administration of the social and welfare infrastructure, but effectively forfeit their independence in return for inclusion. Nevertheless, it is too early to write off social partnership altogether: its final form is yet to be determined.

Its future will be decided in the enterprise. This is the level where regulation can no longer be deferred or displaced; where commitments must either be met or not. The enterprise trade union committee is the main interface between the union and its members; the enterprise is the level at which mobilisation around the FNPR's key demands must occur – or not. But, as the analysis of this book shows, enterprise trade unions are in a difficult position. There are pressures on them from all sides to adopt a moderate, even collaborationist, stance, while management has innumerable means of neutralising and intimidating a more combative trade union leader. When viewed in comparative perspective, the prospects for the development of trade unionism at the enterprise look even bleaker. As Wolfgang Streeck has convincingly argued with regard to Germany, in periods of economic difficulty the tendency is for 'wildcat co-

---

[1]   As Andrew Martin puts it 'there is nothing much that social pacts can do in the current historical context except redistribute work' (1997, p. 41).

operation' between workers and managers to develop at enterprise level (Streeck, 1984, p. 297):

> Under crisis conditions the rule of the market asserts itself not just over the behaviour of firms but also over workers' definitions of their interests – with their interests in the economic survival of 'their' employer becoming so intense that they escape union control (Streeck, 1984, p. 297).

In Russia, for somewhat different reasons, workers' association with 'their' employers is also strong – and often, as the previous chapter shows, stronger than their bond with their trade unions. The relationship of Russian workers to their unions has a different history, form and nature to that of German workers to theirs; most importantly, the latter have a proven capacity for solidarity and mobilisation around union demands.[1] If hard times can erode this ability in Germany, it is not surprising that Russian trade unions have had problems developing such capacity from scratch in the context of the deepest and most sustained recession in history.

## The future of Russian trade unionism

The first priority of the Russian trade unions after the collapse of the soviet system was to secure their institutional survival and in that context they had little choice but to insert themselves into conciliatory structures of social partnership, even at the expense of their ability to develop their own structures of collective organisation. The FNPR leadership has shown a growing awareness of the need to stimulate the activism of primary trade union organisations in order to increase the weight of the trade unions within tripartite structures so that they can achieve their aspiration of a social partnership based on equal rights. However, in practice FNPR has continued to give priority to its own institutional interests, as was shown in the campaigns over the Unified Social Tax and the reform of the Labour Code (pp.62–68 above), and has repeatedly shied away, at federal, regional and enterprise levels, from attempting to mobilise its membership around concerted campaigns or even to give consistent support to members or trade union organisations engaged in conflict with the employer. Every level of the trade union organisation looks to the other levels to take the initiative. FNPR berates its regional organisations for their failure to activate enterprise trade union organisations. The regional organisations berate their primary organisations for withholding funds to spend on social welfare and material assistance and expect federal structures to advance their interests by lobbying government on

---

[1]  Indeed, as Lowell Turner points out, the German form of social partnership is very much bound up with conflict. Russian trade unionists would do well to note his assessment that 'intense conflict, followed by conflict resolution, is not only compatible with but may be necessary for the preservation, reinvigoration and appropriate reform of social partnership relations' (1998, p. 117).

their behalf. Primary trade union organisations similarly expect the regional, branch and federal trade union structures to fight their battles for them. Despite the abolition of democratic centralism and the adoption of a formally decentralised and fully democratic structure, FNPR continues to operate on a hierarchical basis, only to bemoan the failure of its regional organisations to implement its policies.

It is unlikely that significant changes in the structure and practices of the Russian trade unions will come from the top but, while there are undoubtedly a few active and effective primary trade union organisations, we have seen that there are also formidable barriers to the development of more active forms of trade unionism in the workplace. In present circumstances, the future does not look very bright. Wolfgang Streeck, concluding his gloomy assessment of the prospects of the German trade union movement quoted above, foresaw the development of what he called 'social partnership without corporatism', something which he saw as implying the 'Japanisation' of German industrial relations (Streeck, 1984, p. 309). If 'wildcat co-operation' at the enterprise level continued, then industry collective bargaining would be undermined, leaving only the structures of partnership intact.

Although the convergence is from a different direction, the Japanese model also looks like the most appropriate comparison with the emerging pattern of Russian industrial relations. Leaving aside the glaring gap in economic success, there are a number of similarities between the two systems: the collaborative relations between unions and management at enterprise level; the unions' lack of involvement in controlling the shopfloor;[1] the tradition of enterprise paternalism, and the confinement of protest to symbolic 'offensives'. Indeed, as noted above (p. 39), it was following a visit to Japan that Klochkov called FNPR's 'spring offensive' in 1992.

Development in the Japanese direction would not augur well for the union movement. For while this form of enterprise unionism can bring economic gains for those workers lucky enough to be employed in prosperous firms, it has little to offer workers at less successful enterprises. This, in short, is not a model for union growth and renewal, but for the stabilisation of unions in the strongest enterprises. It effectively implies an abandonment of the weak. In the Russian context this can only lead to a division of the trade union movement into one wing which adopts quasi-Japanese forms of industrial relations, while the other wing seeks to defend the living standards of the lowest paid and most vulnerable workers through political action. This is precisely the kind of division that is prefigured by the formation of the Association of Trade Union Organisations of Workers of Pan-National and Transnational Enterprises (above p. 70), which had the potential to provide the nucleus of a Japanese type of trade union federation, drawing the most prosperous enterprise and branch unions away from FNPR, which would be left as a federation dominated by the budget-sector trade unions.

---

[1]   On the union's lack of involvement in job control in Japan see Kumazawa, 1996.

Such a development would undermine what is the most distinctive feature of Russian in comparison to Japanese trade unions, which provides a potential basis for trade union renewal, that is the level of national integration of the Russian trade unions and their claim to represent not only their members, but all workers, their families, former workers and students, not only at work but also in their daily lives. The challenge presented to FNPR is to give substance to the formal unity of the trade union movement not by re-establishing the hierarchical relations of democratic centralism, but by transforming the trade unions into participatory democratic structures within which unity can be forged out of an honest reconciliation of differences. The challenge is similarly to give substance to FNPR's claim to represent the interests of the whole working population not by offering itself as the executor of the social and welfare policy of the state and employers, but by building effective solidarity between trade union members and member organisations in defence of what remains of Russia's social infrastructure. As a delegate from the Inta coalfield commented at the last conference of the Komi *oblsovprof* in 1990,

> The Miners' Congress recently took place in Moscow. At the Congress we met representatives, presidents of mining and energy trade unions, from Germany, England and Australia. I tell you that not one of their trade unions maintains planned cultural institutions. The trade unions must occupy themselves with the professional defence of the rights of workers. And to say that we must increase the allocation for culture is not professional. Culture must be managed by professionals, not by trade union committee presidents trained as miners and engineers. So we must give culture back to the soviet authorities.

The Russian trade unions still have enormous potential. They represent over half the labour force. We can estimate their total income from membership dues alone as over $300 million a year, even if the majority of this is returned to the members in the form of material assistance and social and welfare benefits. The unions still have a unified national structure, with FNPR even enjoying more or less collaborative relations with the main alternative trade union federations, VKT and KTR. The traditional trade unions have overcome the legacy of their past to establish their legitimacy in Russia and in the international trade union community as representative of the interests of the employed population (and their families).

There is no longer the justification for the caution and timidity that was understandable in the first half of the nineties. The threat from the government is no longer of the liquidation of the trade unions, but of their reversion to their historical role of 'transmission belt' between the state and the people. The caution of FNPR and its continued commitment to legalistic and bureaucratic forms of trade unionism only reinforces its dependence on the authorities at all levels and makes it more vulnerable to the kinds of intrigues by which the government was apparently seeking to subvert it in the run up to the November 2001 Congress. Caution also does nothing to strengthen the appeal of the unions in the eyes of workers, who have seen very few tangible results from the elaborate enterprise of social partnership. So far this 'safety-first' strategy has secured the institutional survival of the FNPR and its constituent parts. In the longer term, however, risk-avoidance may prove the most risky strategy of all.

# Bibliography


S. Alasheev, 'Informal Relations in the Process of Production' in S. Clarke (ed.) *Management and Industry in Russia: Formal and Informal Relations in the Russian Industrial Enterprise* (Cheltenham: Edward Elgar, 1995) 28–68.

T. Andrievskaya, 'Mer Moskvy – Nash professor. Eto Zdorovo!' in *Mer Moskvy Yurii Mikhailovich Luzhkov – pochetnyi professor Akademii truda i sotsial'nykh otnoshenii* (Moscow: Akademiya truda i sotsial'nykh otnoshenii, 1996).

S. Ashwin, 'The 1991 Miners' Strike: New Departures in the Independent Workers' Movement', *RFE/RL Report on the USSR* 3, 33 (1991) 1–7.

S. Ashwin, 'Trade Unions after the Fall of Communism in Eastern Europe and Russia', *Journal of Area Studies*, 5 (1994) 137–52.

S. Ashwin, 'Russia's Official Trade Unions: Renewal or Redundancy?', *Industrial Relations Journal* 26, 3 (1995) 192–203.

S. Ashwin, *Russian Workers: The Anatomy of Patience* (Manchester: Manchester University Press, 1999).

P. Bizyukov and S. Alasheev, *Rossiiskie profsoyuzy: kto oni?* (Kemerovo and Samara: ISITO, 2001; www.warwick.ac.uk/russia/docs/Koncept3_op.doc).

D. Boda and L. Neumann, 'Social Dialogue in Hungary and its Influence on EU Accession', *Transfer* 6, 3 (2000) 416–33.

L. Bordogna and J. Cella, 'Admission, Exclusion, Correction: the Changing Role of the State in Industrial Relations', *Transfer* 5, 1–2 (1999) 14–33.

V. Borisov and S. Clarke (eds) *Profsoyuznoe prostranstvo sovremennoi Rossii* (Moscow: ISITO, 2001a).

V. Borisov, *Zabastovki v ugolnoi promyshlennosti (analiz shakhterskogo dvizheniya za 1989–99gg.)* (Moscow: ISITO, 2001b).

V. Borisov and S. Clarke, 'Reform and Revolution in the Communist National Park', *Capital and Class*, 53 (1994) 9–14.

V. Borisov, P. Fairbrother and S. Clarke, 'Is There Room for an Independent Trade Unionism in Russia? The Case of the Federation of Air Traffic Controllers' Unions', *British Journal of Industrial Relations* 32, 3 (1994) 359–78.

K. Buketov, 'Osen' 1993: profsoyuzy v period krizisa', *Rabochaya politika* 4 (1995) 15–31.

K. Buketov and A. Nikul'nikov, 'Profsoyuzy Rossii v predvybornoi kampanii 1995 goda', *Rabochaya politika*, 1 (1996) 5–15.

M.G. Burlutskaya, 'Profsoyuznye kar'ery: organizatsionnye regulatory mobil'nosti' (ISITO Annual Conference, Alanya, Turkey, 2001; www.warwick.ac.uk/russia/docs/careers.doc).

M.O. Burnova, K.N. Gusov, M.L. Zakharov, I.O. Snigireva, L.A. Syrovatskaya, V.N. Tolkunova and Ye.G.Tuchkova (eds.) *Kommentarii k kodeksu zakonov o trude rossiiskoi federatsii* (Moscow: Prospekt, 1996).

K. Burnyshev and S. Clarke, *Factory Occupations in Kuzbass* (Novokuznetsk and Coventry: ISITO, www.warwick.ac.uk/russia/docs/KMK.doc, 2000).

W.E. Butler, *Soviet Law* (London: Butterworths, 1988).

E.H. Carr, *The Bolshevik Revolution, 1917 – 1923* (London: Macmillan, 1952).

T. Chetvernina et al., *Collective Agreements in Russia: Current Practice* (Moscow: IE RAN, TACIS, ICFTU, 1995).

T. Chetvernina, P. Smirnov and N. Dunaeva, 'Mesto profsoyuza na predpriyatii', *Voprosi Ekonomiki*, 6 (1995) 83–9.

S. Clarke, 'Privatisation and the Transition to Capitalism in Russia', *New Left Review* 196, November/December 1992 (1992a) 3–28.

S. Clarke, 'The Workers' Movement in Russia', *Capital and Class*, 49 (1992b) 7–17.

S. Clarke, 'Trade Unions, Industrial Relations and Politics in Russia', *Journal of Communist Studies* 9, 4 (1993) 133–60.

S. Clarke, 'The Politics of Labour and Capital' in S. White, A. Pravda and Z. Gitelman (eds.) *Developments in Russian and Post-Soviet Politics* (Harmondsworth: Macmillan, 1994) 162–86.

S. Clarke (ed.) *Management and Industry in Russia: Formal and Informal Relations in the Period of Transition* (Cheltenham: Edward Elgar, 1995).

S. Clarke, *Conflict and Change in the Russian Industrial Enterprise* (Cheltenham: Edward Elgar, 1996a).

S. Clarke (ed.) *Labour Relations in Transition* (Cheltenham: Edward Elgar, 1996b).

S. Clarke (ed.) *The Russian Enterprise in Transition* (Cheltenham: Edward Elgar, 1996c).

S. Clarke, 'Trade Unions and the Non-Payment of Wages in Russia', *International Journal of Manpower* 19, 1/2 (1998) 68–94.

S. Clarke, *The Formation of a Labour Market in Russia* (Cheltenham: Edward Elgar, 1999a).

S. Clarke, *New Forms of Employment and Household Survival Strategies in Russia* (Coventry: Centre for Comparative Labour Studies, 1999b).

S. Clarke, 'New Forms of Labour Contract and Labour Flexibility in Russia', *Economics of Transition* 7, 3 (1999c) 593–614.

S. Clarke, 'Russian Trade Unions in the 1999 Duma Election', *Journal of Communist Studies and Transition Politics* 17, 2 (2001) 43–69.

S. Clarke, 'Labour in Post-Soviet Russia' in J. Hughes and M. Light (eds.) *Russia: Ten Years After* (Oxford: Oxford University Press, 2002).

S. Clarke and V. Borisov, 'The Russian Miners' Strike of February 1996', *Capital and Class* 59 (1996) 23–30.

S. Clarke and I. Donova, 'Internal Mobility and Labour Market Flexibility in Russia', *Europe-Asia Studies* 51, 2 (1999) 213–43.

S. Clarke and P. Fairbrother, 'The Emergence of Industrial Relations in the Workplace' in R. Hyman and A. Ferner (eds.) *New Frontiers in European Industrial Relations* (Oxford: Blackwell, 1994) 368–97.

S. Clarke, P. Fairbrother and V. Borisov, 'Does Trade Unionism have a Future in Russia?', *Industrial Relations Journal* 25, 1 (1994) 15–25.

S. Clarke, P. Fairbrother and V. Borisov, *The Workers' Movement in Russia* (Cheltenham: Edward Elgar, 1995).

S. Clarke, P. Fairbrother, V. Borisov and P. Bizyukov, 'The Privatisation of Industrial Enterprises in Russia: Four Case Studies', *Europe-Asia Studies* 46, 2 (1994) 179–214.

S. Clarke, P. Fairbrother, M. Burawoy and P. Krotov, *What about the Workers? Workers and the Transition to Capitalism in Russia* (London: Verso, 1993).

S. Clarke and V. Kabalina, 'Privatisation and the Struggle for Control of the Enterprise in Russia' in D. Lane (ed.) *Russia in Transition* (London: Longman, 1995) 142–58.

S. Clarke and V. Kabalina, 'Employment in the New Private Sector in Russia', *Post-Communist Economies* 11, 4 (1999) 421–43.

W.D. Connor, *Tattered Banners: Labor, Conflict and Corporatism in Postcommunist Russia* (Boulder, Colorado, 1996).

R. Conquest (ed.) *Industrial Workers in the USSR* (London: Bodley Head, 1967).

L.J. Cook, *The Soviet Social Contract and Why It Failed: Welfare Policy and Workers' Politics from Brezhnev to Yeltsin* (Cambridge, Mass.: Harvard University Press, 1993).

L.J. Cook, *Labor and Liberalization: Trade Unions in the New Russia* (New York: The Twentieth Century Fund Press, 1997).

M. de Melo and G. Ofer, *Private Sector Firms in a Transitional Economy: Findings of a Survey in St Petersburg* (Washington DC: World Bank, 1993).

G. Fajertag and P. Pochet (eds.) *Social Pacts in Europe* (Brussels: ETUI and OSE, 1997).

V.P. Fedotov, 'Rabochee i profsoyuznoe dvizhenie v Ivanovskoi oblasti, leto-osen' 1994 g.', *Russko-Amerikanskii fond profsoyuznykh issledovanii i obucheniya. Soobshcheniya korrespondentov fonda* 1 (1995) 68–93.

FNPR, *Ot Vtorogo k Tretemu S'ezdu Profsoyuzov Rossii (FNPR)* (Moscow: FNPR, 1996).

FNPR, *Informatsiya o tarifno-dogovornoi kampanii 1999–2000 godov* (Moscow: FNPR, 2001a).

FNPR, *Ot Tretogo k Chetvortemu S'ezdu Profsoyuzov Rossii (FNPR)* (Moscow: FNPR, 2001b).

I.A. Germanov, *'Rol' regional'nykh trekhstoronnikh soglashenii v regulirovanii sotsial'no-trudovykh otnoshenii'* (ISITO Annual Conference, Alanya, Turkey, 2001; www.warwick.ac.uk/russia/docs/Germanov01.doc).

J. Godson, 'The Role of the Trade Unions' in L. Schapiro and J. Godson (eds.) *The Soviet Worker. Illusions and Realities* (London and Basingstoke: Macmillan, 1981) 106–29.

R. Godson, *The Kremlin and Labor: A Study in National Security* (New York: Crane, Russak, 1977).

Goskomstat, *Obsledovanie naseleniya po problemam zanyatosti, mai 2000 goda* (Moscow: Goskomstat Rossii, 2000a).

Goskomstat, *Rossiiskii Statisticheskii Ezhegodnik* (Moscow: Goskomstat Rossii, 2000b).

Goskomstat, *Sotsialnoe polozhenie i uroven' zhizni naseleniya Rossii 2000* (Moscow: Goskomstat Rossii, 2000c).

Goskomstat, *Rossiya v Tsifrakh* (Moscow: Goskomstat Rossii, 2001).

N.N. Gritsenko, V.A. Kadeikina and E.V. Makukhina, *Istoriya profsoyuzov Rossii* (Moscow: Akademiya truda i sotsial'nykh otnoshenii, 1999).

P. Hauslohner, 'Gorbachev's Social Contract', *Soviet Economy* 3, 1 (1987) 54–89.

K. Hendley, 'Does Law Matter in the Soviet Economic Reform Process? A Case Study of the Law Governing Internal Transfers', *Review of Central and East European Law*, 2 (1992) 101–34.

K. Hendley, *Trying to Make Law Matter: Legal Reform and Labor Law in the Soviet Union* (Ann Arbor, MI: University of Michigan Press, 1996).

F. Hoffer, *Traditional Trade Unions during Transition and Economic Reform in Russia* (Bremen, 1997).

R. Hyman, *Social Dialogue in Western Europe: The 'State of the Art'* (Geneva: International Labour Office, 2000).

R. Hyman, *Understanding European Trade Unionism: Between Market, Class and Society* (London, Thousand Oaks, New Delhi: Sage, 2001).

ICFTU, *Annual Survey of Violations of Trade Union Rights* (Brussels: ICFTU, 1996).

IEPPP, *Ekonomiko-politicheskaya situatsiya v Rossii* (Moscow: IEPPP, 1995).

V. Ilyin, 'Russian Trade Unions and the Management Apparatus in the Transition Period' in S. Clarke (ed.) *Conflict and Change in the Russian Industrial Enterprise* (Cheltenham: Edward Elgar, 1996) 32–64.

V. Ilyin, *'Chlenskie vznosy v profsoyuznom prostranstve'* (ISITO Annual Conference, Alanya, Turkey, 2001; www.warwick.ac.uk/russia/docs/Paper_Ilyin.doc).

A. Isaev, 'Novyi KZoT pisalsya pod diktovku MVF', *Vesti FNPR*, 1–2 (1999) 62–5.

ISITO, St Petersburg branch, *OOO Neste SPB* (St Petersburg: ISITO, www.warwick.ac.uk/russia/docs/Neste.doc, 2000).

V. Kabalina and G. Monousova, 'Kollektivnye dogovory i deyatel'nost' profsoyuzov na predpriyatiyakh' in L. Gordon, V. Gimpel'son, E. Klopov and V. Komarovski (eds.) *Profsoyuznoe dvizhenie: tendentsii i problemy perekhodnogo perioda* (Moscow: IMEMO, RAN, 1995) 22–33.

V.N. Kiselev, ''Rossiiskaya model' sotsial'nogo partnerstva (sushchnost', problemy, factory stanovleniya)', *Trud i sotsial'nye otnosheniya* 2, 8 (2000) 4–18.

E. Klopov, 'Sostoyanie rabochego dvizheniya', *Sotsiologicheskii Zhurnal* 1 (1995).

H. Kohl, W. Lecher and H.-W. Platzer, 'Transformation, EU Membership, and Labour Relations in Central and Eastern Europe: Poland – Czech Republic – Hungary – Slovenia', *Transfer* 6, 3 (2000) 399–415.

I. Kozina and V. Borisov, 'The Changing Status of Workers in the Enterprise' in S. Clarke (ed.) *Conflict and Change in the Russian Industrial Enterprise* (Cheltenham: Edward Elgar, 1996) 136–61.

A. Krest'yaninov, *Rabochee dvizhenie v sovremennoi Rossii i profsoyuzy* (Moscow: Proftsentr 'Soyuzmetall', 1995).

P. Krotov, *'Realisation of social functions of the organs of self-management of the labour collective'* (Candidate's Dissertation, Institute of Sociology, Russian Academy of Sciences, 1990).

M. Kumazawa, *Portraits of the Japanese Workplace: Labour Movements, Workers and Managers* (Boulder, Colo.: Westview Press, 1996).

V.I. Lenin, [1919] 'Report at the Second All-Russia Trade Union Congress, 20 January, 1919' in *On Trade Unions* (Moscow: Progress Publishers, 1970).

V.I. Lenin, [1921] 'Preliminary Draft Resolution of the Tenth Congress of the Russian Communist Party on the Syndicalist and Anarchist Deviation' in *The Essentials of Lenin* (London: Lawrence and Wishart, 1947) 683–6.

V.I. Lenin, [1922] 'Draft Theses on the Role and Functions of the Trade Unions Under the New Economic Policy' in *The Essentials of Lenin* (London: Lawrence and Wishart, 1947) 760–9.

B.Q. Madison, 'Trade Unions and Social Welfare' in A. Kahan and B. Ruble (eds.) *Industrial Labour in the USSR* (New York and Oxford: Pergamon Press, 1979) 85–115.

T.M. Maleva, P.M. Kudyukin, S.G. Misikhina and S.V. Surikov, *Skol'ko Stoit Trudovoi Kodeks?* (Moscow: Moscow Carnegie Center, 2001).

D. Mandel, *The Russian Working Class and Labour Movement in the Fourth Year of 'Shock Therapy'* (Montreal, Mimeo, 1995).

A. Martin, 'Social pacts: a means of distributing unemployment or achieving full employment' in G. Fajertag and P. Pochet (eds.) *Social Pacts in Europe* (Brussels: ETUI and OSE, 1997).

R. Martin and A. Cristescu-Martin, 'Industrial Relations in Central and Eastern Europe in 1999: Patterns of Protest', *Industrial Relations Journal* 31, 4 (2000) 345-62.

M. McAulay, *Labour Disputes in Soviet Russia 1957-65* (Oxford: Clarendon Press, 1969).

Y.N. Milovidov, *Profsoyuznaya sobstvennost' dolzhna sluzhit' vsem chlenam profsoyuzov* (Moscow: Komitet obshchestvennogo kontrolya imushchestvennoi deyatel'nosti profsoyuzov, Mimeo, 2001).

J.C. Moses, 'Worker Self-Management and the Reformist Alternative in Soviet Labour Policy, 1979–85', *Soviet Studies* 39, 2 (1987) 205–28.

V. Naboishchikov, 'O zakonotvorcheskoi deyatel'nosti i pravozashchitnoi rabote' (mimeo. Moscow: FNPR, 2001).

OECD, *Labour Restructuring in Four Russian Enterprises: A Case Study* (Paris: OECD, 1996).

D. Ost, 'Illusory Corporatism in Eastern Europe: Neoliberal Tripartism and Postcommunist Class Identities', *Politics and Society* 28, 4 (2000) 503–30.

L. Panitch, 'Recent Theorisations of Corporatism: Reflections on a Growth Industry', *British Journal of Sociology* 31 (1980) 159–87.

S. Perfilev, *'Rossiiskie profsoyuzy: taktiki vklyucheniya v regional'nye politicheskie rezhimi'* (ISITO Annual Conference, Albena, Bulgaria, 2000; www.warwick.ac.uk/russia/docs/TU_pol8.doc).

L.E. Petrova, *Sozdanie i likvidatsiya profsoyuznoi organisatsii v OOO 'Coca-Cola Bottlers Yekaterinburg'* (Yekaterinburg: ISITO, www.warwick.ac.uk/russia/docs/Coca_Cola_case.doc, 2000).

O. Pulaeva and S. Clarke, *Vyborg Cellulose Paper Combine* (St Petersburg and Coventry: ISITO, www.warwick.ac.uk/russia/docs/VBK.doc, 2000).

M. Regini, 'Still Engaging in Corporatism? Recent Italian Experiences in Comparative Perspective', *European Journal of Industrial Relations* 3, 3 (1997) 259–78.

R. Rose, *Getting Things Done with Social Capital: New Russia Barometer VII* (Glasgow: Centre for the Study of Public Policy, University of Strathclyde, 1998).

B. Ruble, *Soviet Trade Unions: Their Development in the 1970s* (Cambridge: Cambridge University Press, 1981).

L. Schapiro and J. Godson, *The Soviet Worker. Illusions and Realities* (London and Basingstoke: Macmillan, 1981).

S.A. Shalaev, N.N. Gritsenko and I.O. Snigireva (eds.) *Federalnyi Zakon 'O Professional'nykh Soyuzakh'* (Moscow: Scientific Centre of the Trade Unions in collaboration with the Academy of Labour, 1996).

L. Shelley, 'Law in the Soviet Workplace: The Lawyer's Perspective', *Law and Society Review* 16, 3 (1981) 429–54.

L. Shelley, *Lawyers in Soviet Work Life* (New Brunswick, NJ: Rutgers University Press, 1984).

A. Shershukov, 'Posle pobedy – boi' *Solidarnost'*, 27 (2001).

M. Shmakov, 'Nasha sotrudnichestvo – v interesakh cheloveka i vsego obshchestva' in *Mer Moskvy Yurii Mikhailovich Luzhkov – pochetnyi professor Akademii truda i sotsial'nykh otnoshenii* (Moscow: Akademiya truda i sotsial'nykh otnoshenii, 1996) 12–16.

R. Simon, *Labour and Political Transformation in Russia and Ukraine* (Aldershot: Ashgate, 2000).

D. Slider, 'Reforming the Workplace: the 1983 Soviet Law on Labour Collectives', *Soviet Studies* 37, 2 (1985) 173–83.

I.O. Snigireva (ed.) *Federalnyi Zakon 'O Poryadke razresheniya kollektivnykh trudovykh sporov* (Moscow: Scientific Centre of the Trade Unions in collaboration with the Academy of Labour, 1996).

A.L. Sokova (ed.) *Prakticheskoe rukovodstvo profsoyuznogo rabotnika* (Moscow: Rosugleprof, 1996).

J.B. Sorenson, *The Life and Death of Soviet Trade Unionism 1917–1928* (New York: Atherton Press, 1969).

G. Standing, *Russian Unemployment and Enterprise Restructuring: Reviving Dead Souls* (Basingstoke: Macmillan, 1996).

W. Streeck, 'Neo-corporatism, Industrial Relations and the Economic Crisis in West Germany' in J. Goldthorpe (ed.) *Order and Conflict in Contemporary Capitalism* (Oxford: Clarendon Press, 1984) 291– 394.

S.N. Tatarnikova, 'Sotsialnoe partnerstvo na predpriyatii', *Solidarnost'* 2 (1995).

S.N. Tatarnikova, *Soderzhanie kollektivnogo dogovora* (Moscow: Uchebno-issledovatel'skii Tsentr Moskovskoi Federatsii Profsoyuzov, 1999).

E. Teague, *Solidarity and the Soviet Worker* (London: Croom Helm, 1986).

E. Teague, 'Russian Government Seeks 'Social Partnership'', *RFE/RL Research Report* 125, 19 June (1992) 16–22.

E. Teague, 'Pluralism Versus Corporatism: Government, Labor and Business in the Russian Federation' in C.R. Saivetz and A. Jones (eds.) *In Search of Pluralism: Soviet and Post-Soviet Politics* (Boulder: Westview Press, 1994).

F. Traxler, 'Two Logics of Collective Action in Industrial Relations?' in C. Crouch and F. Traxler (eds.) *Organised Industrial Relations in Europe: What Future?* (Aldershot and Vermont: Avebury, 1995) 23–44.

Tsentr issledovannii rynka truda, *Mekhanizmy adaptatsii vnutrennego rynka truda predpriyatii k novym ekonomicheskim usloviyam,* (Moscow: IE, RAN, 1995).

Tsentr issledovannii rynka truda, *Ekonomika promyshlennykh predpriyatii, zanyatost', dokhody i l'goty dlya rabotnikov* (Moscow: IE, RAN, 2001).

L. Turner, *Fighting for Partnership: Labor and Politics in Unified Germany* (Ithaca, NY: ILR Press, 1998).

I. Tyurina, '*Politika FNPR v otnoshenii sotsial'no znachimykh problem: KZoT – popytka revansha za proigrysh s edinym sotsial'nym nalogom*' (ISITO Annual Conference, Alanya, Turkey, 2001; www.warwick.ac.uk/russia/docs/Tyurina.doc).

V. Vedeneeva, 'Payment Systems and the Restructuring of Production Relations in Russia' in S. Clarke (ed.) *Management and Industry in Russia: Formal and Informal Relations in the Period of Transition* (Cheltenham: Edward Elgar, 1995) 224–39.

J. Visser, 'Two Cheers for Corporatism, One for the Market: Industrial Relations, Wage Moderation and Job Growth in the Netherlands', *British Journal of Industrial Relations* 36, 2 (1998) 269–92.

B. Wedderburn, 'Labour Law and the Individual: Convergence or Diversity?' in B. Wedderburn (ed.) *Labour Law and Freedom* (London: Lawrence and Wishart, 1995) 286 – 349.

# Index